A·N·N·U·A·L E·D·I·T·I·O·N·S

Marketing

Twenty-Fifth Edition

03/04

EDITOR

John E. Richardson

Pepperdine University

Dr. John E. Richardson is professor of marketing in The George L. Graziadio School of Business and Management at Pepperdine University. He is president of his own consulting firm and has consulted with organizations such as Bell and Howell, Dayton-Hudson, Epson, and the U.S. Navy as well as with various service, nonprofit, and franchise organizations. Dr. Richardson is a member of the American Marketing Association, the American Management Association, the Society for Business Ethics, and Beta Gamma Sigma honorary business fraternity.

McGraw-Hill/Dushkin

530 Old Whitfield Street, Guilford, Connecticut 06437

Visit us on the Internet
http://www.dushkin.com

Credits

1. **Marketing in the 2000s and Beyond**
   Unit photo—© 2003 by Sweet By & By/Cindy Brown.
2. **Research Markets and Consumer Behavior**
   Unit photo—© 2003 by Sweet By & By/Cindy Brown.
3. **Developing and Implementing Marketing Strategies**
   Unit photo—© 2003 by PhotoDisc, Inc.
4. **Global Marketing**
   Unit photo—TRW Inc. photo.

Copyright

Cataloging in Publication Data
Main entry under title: Annual Editions: Marketing. 2003/2004.
1. Marketing—Periodicals. I. Richardson, John E., *comp.* II. Title: Marketing.
ISBN 0–07–283821–3   658'.05   ISSN 0730–2606

Twenty-Fifth Edition

Cover image © 2003 PhotoDisc, Inc.
Printed in the United States of America   1234567890BAHBAH543   Printed on Recycled Paper

Editors/Advisory Board

Members of the Advisory Board are instrumental in the final selection of articles for each edition of ANNUAL EDITIONS. Their review of articles for content, level, currentness, and appropriateness provides critical direction to the editor and staff. We think that you will find their careful consideration well reflected in this volume.

To the Reader

In publishing ANNUAL EDITIONS we recognize the enormous role played by the magazines, newspapers, and journals of the public press in providing current, first-rate educational information in a broad spectrum of interest areas. Many of these articles are appropriate for students, researchers, and professionals seeking accurate, current material to help bridge the gap between principles and theories and the real world. These articles, however, become more useful for study when those of lasting value are carefully collected, organized, indexed, and reproduced in a low-cost format, which provides easy and permanent access when the material is needed. That is the role played by ANNUAL EDITIONS.

The new millennium should prove to be an exciting and challenging time for the American business community. Recent dramatic social, economic, and technological changes have become an important part of the present marketplace. These changes—accompanied by increasing domestic and foreign competition—are leading a wide array of companies and industries toward the realization that better marketing must become a top priority now to ensure their future success.

How does the marketing manager respond to this growing challenge? How does the marketing student apply marketing theory to the real world practice? Many reach for the *Wall Street Journal, Business Week, Fortune,* and other well-known sources of business information. There, specific industry and company strategies are discussed and analyzed, marketing principles are often reaffirmed by real occurrences, and textbook theories are supported or challenged by current events.

The articles reprinted in this edition of *Annual Editions: Marketing 03/04* have been carefully chosen from numerous different public press sources to provide current information on marketing in the world today. Within these pages you will find articles that address marketing theory and application in a wide range of industries. In addition, the selections reveal how several firms interpret and utilize marketing principles in their daily operations and corporate planning.

The volume contains a number of features designed to make it useful for marketing students, researchers, and professionals. These include the *Industry/Company Guide,* which is particularly helpful when seeking information about specific corporations; a *topic guide* to locate articles on specific marketing subjects; *World Wide Web* pages; the *table of contents* abstracts, which summarize each article and highlights key concepts; a *glossary* of key marketing terms; and a comprehensive *index.*

The articles are organized into four units. Selections that focus on similar issues are concentrated into subsections within the broader units. Each unit is preceded by a list of unit selections, as well as a list of key points to consider that focus on major themes running throughout the selections, Web links that provide extra support for the unit's data, and an overview that provides background for informed reading of the articles and emphasizes critical issues.

This is the twenty-fifth edition of *Annual Editions: Marketing.* Since its first edition in the mid-1970s, the efforts of many individuals have contributed toward its success. We think this is by far the most useful collection of material available for the marketing student. We are anxious to know what you think. What are your opinions? What are your recommendations? Please take a moment to complete and return the *article rating form* on the last page of this volume. Any book can be improved and this one will continue to be, annually.

John E. Richardson
Editor

Contents

UNIT 1
Marketing in the 2000s and Beyond

Thirteen selections examine the current and future status of marketing, the marketing concept, service marketing, and marketing ethics.

Unit Overview   xvi

The concepts in bold italics are developed in the article. For further expansion, please refer to the Topic Guide and the Index.

UNIT 2
Research Markets and Consumer Behavior

Nine selections provide an analysis of consumer demographics and lifestyles, the growth and maturation of markets, and the need for market research and planning.

The concepts in bold italics are developed in the article. For further expansion, please refer to the Topic Guide and the Index.

UNIT 3
Developing and Implementing Marketing Strategies

Twelve selections analyze factors that affect the development and implementation of marketing strategies.

The concepts in bold italics are developed in the article. For further expansion, please refer to the Topic Guide and the Index.

UNIT 4
Global Marketing

Six selections discuss the increasing globalization of markets, trends in world trade, and increasing foreign competition.

Unit Overview   **178**

The concepts in bold italics are developed in the article. For further expansion, please refer to the Topic Guide and the Index.

The concepts in bold italics are developed in the article. For further expansion, please refer to the Topic Guide and the Index.

Topic Guide

This topic guide suggests how the selections in this book relate to the subjects covered in your course. You may want to use the topics listed on these pages to search the Web more easily.

On the following pages a number of Web sites have been gathered specifically for this book. They are arranged to reflect the units of this *Annual Edition*. You can link to these sites by going to the DUSHKIN ONLINE support site at *http://www.dushkin.com/online/*.

ALL THE ARTICLES THAT RELATE TO EACH TOPIC ARE LISTED BELOW THE BOLD-FACED TERM.

World Wide Web Sites

The following World Wide Web sites have been carefully researched and selected to support the articles found in this reader. The easiest way to access these selected sites is to go to our DUSHKIN ONLINE support site at *http://www.dushkin.com/online/*.

AE: Marketing 03/04

The following sites were available at the time of publication. Visit our Web site—we update DUSHKIN ONLINE regularly to reflect any changes.

General Sources

Krislyn's Favorite Advertising & Marketing Sites
http://www.krislyn.com/sites/adv.htm

This is a complete list of sites that include information on marketing research, marketing on the Internet, demographic sources, and organizations and associations. The site also features current books on the subject of marketing.

Retail Learning Initiative
http://www.retailsmarts.ryerson.ca

This series of small business and retail marketing links from Canada connects to many more business links in the United States and to workshops and dialogue forums.

STAT-USA/Internet Site Economic, Trade, Business Information
http://www.stat-usa.gov

This site, from the U.S. Department of Commerce, contains Daily Economic News, Frequently Requested Statistical Releases, Information on Export and International Trade, Domestic Economic News and Statistical Series, and Databases.

UNIT 1: Marketing in the 2000s and Beyond

American Marketing Association Code of Ethics
http://www.tri-media.com/ama.html

At this American Marketing Association's site, use the search mechanism to access the Code of Ethics for Marketing.

Futures Research Quarterly
http://www.wfs.org/frq.htm

Published by the World Future Society, this publication describes futures research that encompasses both an evolving philosophy and a range of techniques, with the aim of assisting decision-makers in all fields to understand better the potential consequences of decisions by developing images of alternative futures. From this page explore the current and back issues and What's Coming Up!

Center for Innovation in Product Development (CIPD)
http://web.mit.edu/cipd/research/prdctdevelop.htm

CIPD is one of the National Science Foundation's engineering research centers. It shares the goal of future product development with academia, industry, and government.

Marketing in the Service Sector
http://www.ext.colostate.edu/pubs/ttb/tb010424.html

At this site, Frank Leibrock discusses and recommends two books by Harry Beckwith that target marketing in the service sector. Read his reasons for thinking they make sense to owners of small businesses and then read the books themselves.

Professor Takes Business Ethics to Global Level
http://www.miami.com/mld/miamiherald/4426429.htm

This is a discussion by Professor Robert W. McGee of the challenges that the new century brings to business and its relation to ethical issues at a global level. The article by Mike Seemuth provides interesting reading about the important part that government plays in business decisions. Tariffs and protectionism are highlighted.

Remarks by Chairman Alan Greenspan
http://www.federalreserve.gov/boarddocs/speeches/2000/20000322.htm

These remarks were made by chairman Alan Greenspan on March 22, 2000, and concern the challenges that face American businesses, workers, and consumers as the U.S. economy embarked on the new century.

UNIT 2: Research Markets and Consumer Behavior

Canadian Innovation Centre
http://www.innovationcentre.ca/company/Default.htm

The Canadian Innovation Centre has developed a unique mix of innovation services that can help a company from idea to market launch. Their services are based on the review of 12,000 new product ideas through their technology and market assessment programs over the past 20 years.

CBA.org: Research and Develop
http://www.cba.org/CBA/National/Marketing/research.asp

This interesting article, written by Elizabeth Cordeau, president of a Calgary-based management consulting firm to law firms and legal associations(featured on the Web by CBA, the information service of the Canadian Bar Association), claims that good marketing begins with excellent market research.

CyberAtlas Demographics
http://cyberatlas.internet.com/big_picture/demographics/

The Baruch College–Harris poll commissioned by *Business Week* is used at this site to show interested businesses who is on the Net in the United States. Statistics for other countries can be found by clicking on Geographics.

General Social Survey
http://www.icpsr.umich.edu/GSS99/

The GSS (see DPLS Archive: *http://DPLS.DACC.WISC.EDU/SAF/*) is an almost annual personal interview survey of U.S. households that began in 1972. More than 35,000 respondents have answered 2,500 questions. It covers a broad range of variables, many of which relate to microeconomic issues.

Industry Analysis and Trends
http://www.bizminer.com/market_research.asp

The importance of using market research databases and pinpointing local and national trends, including details of industry and small business startups, is emphasized by this site of the Brandow Company which offers samples of market research profiles.

www.dushkin.com/online/

Market Intelligence Advisor
http://www.zweigwhite.com/home/mi/mia011700.htm

This article discusses five market intelligence blunders that include stressing numbers over people, doing research in a vacuum, and letting results speak for themselves.

Marketing Tools Directory
http://www.maritzresearch.com

Maritz Marketing Research Inc. (MMRI) specializes in custom-designed research studies that link the consumer to the marketer through information. At this spot on their Web site they offer a Marketing Tools Directory, which is a comprehensive guide to resources for finding, reaching, and keeping customers. Sections include Demographics, Direct Marketing, Ethnic Marketing, Market Research, and more.

U.S. Census Bureau Home Page
http://www.census.gov

This is a major source of social, demographic, and economic information, such as income/employment data and the latest indicators, income distribution, and poverty data.

USADATA
http://www.usadata.com

This leading provider of marketing, company, advertising, and consumer behavior data offers national and local data covering the top 60 U.S. markets.

WWW Virtual Library: Demography & Population Studies
http://demography.anu.edu.au/VirtualLibrary/

Over 150 links can be found at this major resource to keep track of information of value to researchers in the fields of demography and population studies.

UNIT 3: Developing and Implementing Marketing Strategies

American Marketing Association Homepage
http://www.marketingpower.com

This site of the American Marketing Association is geared to managers, educators, researchers, students, and global electronic members. It contains a search mechanism, definitions of marketing and market research, and links.

Consumer Buying Behavior
http://www.courses.psu.edu/mktg/mktg220_rso3/sls_cons.htm

The Center for Academic Computing at Penn State posts this course data that includes a review of consumer buying behaviors; group, environment, and internal influences; problem-solving; and post-purchasing behavior.

Product Branding, Packaging, and Pricing
http://www.fooddude.com/branding.html

Put forward by fooddude.com, the information at this site is presented in a lively manner. It discusses positioning, branding, pricing, and packaging in the specialty food market, but applies to many other retail products as well.

UNIT 4: Global Marketing

CIBERWeb
http://ciber.centers.purdue.edu

The Centers for International Business Education and Research were created by the U.S. Omnibus Trade and Competitiveness Act of 1988. Together, the 26 resulting CIBER sites in the United States are a powerful network focused on helping U.S. business succeed in global markets. Many marketing links can be found at this site.

Emerging Markets Resources
http://www.usatrade.gov/website/ccg.nsf

Information on the business and economic situation of foreign countries and the political climate as it affects U.S. business is presented by the U.S. Department of Commerce's International Trade Administration.

International Business Resources on the WWW
http://globaledge.msu.edu/ibrd/ibrd.asp

This Web site includes a large index of international business resources. Through *http://ciber.bus.msu.edu/ginlist/* you can also access the Global Interact Network Mailing LIST (GINLIST), which brings together, electronically, business educators and practitioners with international business interests.

International Trade Administration
http://www.ita.doc.gov

The U.S. Department of Commerce is dedicated to helping U.S. businesses compete in the global marketplace, and at this site it offers assistance through many Web links under such headings as Trade Statistics, Cross-Cutting Programs, Regions and Countries, and Import Administration.

World Chambers Network
http://www.worldchambers.net

International trade at work is viewable at this site. For example, click on Global Business eXchange (GBX) for a list of active business opportunities worldwide or to submit your new business opportunity for validation.

World Trade Center Association On Line
http://iserve.wtca.org

Data on world trade is available at this site that features information, services, a virtual trade fair, an exporter's encyclopedia, trade opportunities, and a resource center.

We highly recommend that you review our Web site for expanded information and our other product lines. We are continually updating and adding links to our Web site in order to offer you the most usable and useful information that will support and expand the value of your Annual Editions. You can reach us at: *http://www.dushkin.com/annualeditions/*.

UNIT 1

Marketing in the 2000s and Beyond

Unit Selections

1. **Future Markets**, Philip Kotler
2. **High Performance Marketing**, Jagdish N. Sheth and Rajendra S. Sisodia
3. **Marketing High Technology: Preparation, Targeting, Positioning, Execution**, Chris Easingwood and Anthony Koustelos
4. **The Internet as Integrator: Fast Brand Building in Slow-Growth Markets**, David A. Aaker
5. **Marketing Myopia (With Retrospective Commentary)**, Theodore Levitt
6. **Why Customer Satisfaction Starts With HR**, Patrick J. Kiger
7. **Stairs of Loyalty**, Tony Alessandra
8. **What Drives Customer Equity**, Katherine N. Lemon, Roland T. Rust, and Valarie A. Zeithaml
9. **A Primer on Quality Service: Quality Service Makes Happy Customers and Greater Profits**, Gene Milbourn Jr. and G. Timothy Haight
10. **Why Service Stinks**, Diane Brady
11. **Lighting the Way**, Dana James
12. **Trust in the Marketplace**, John E. Richardson and Linnea Bernard McCord
13. **To Tell the Truth**, Erin Strout

Key Points to Consider

- Dramatic changes are occurring in the marketing of products and services. What social and economic trends do you believe are most significant today, and how do you think these will affect marketing in the future?

- Theodore Levitt suggests that as times change the marketing concept must be reinterpreted. Given the varied perspectives of the other articles in this unit, what do you think this reinterpretation will entail?

- In the present competitive business arena, is it possible for marketers to behave ethically in this environment and both survive and prosper? What suggestions can you give that could be incorporated into the marketing strategy for firms that want to be both ethical and successful?

 **Links: www.dushkin.com/online/**
These sites are annotated in the World Wide Web pages.

American Marketing Association Code of Ethics
http://www.tri-media.com/ama.html

Futures Research Quarterly
http://www.wfs.org/frq.htm

Center for Innovation in Product Development (CIPD)
http://web.mit.edu/cipd/research/prdctdevelop.htm

Marketing in the Service Sector
http://www.ext.colostate.edu/pubs/ttb/tb010424.html

Professor Takes Business Ethics to Global Level
http://www.miami.com/mld/miamiherald/4426429.htm

Remarks by Chairman Alan Greenspan
http://www.federalreserve.gov/boarddocs/speeches/2000/20000322.htm

"If we want to know what a business is we must start with its purpose.... There is only one valid definition of business purpose: to create a customer. What business thinks it produces is not of first importance—especially not to the future of the business or to its success. What the customer thinks he is buying, what he considers 'value' is decisive— it determines what a business is, what it produces, and whether it will prosper."

—Peter Drucker, The Practice of Management

When Peter Drucker penned these words in 1954, American industry was just awakening to the realization that marketing would play an important role in the future success of businesses. The ensuing years have seen an increasing number of firms in highly competitive areas—particularly in the consumer goods industry—adopt a more sophisticated customer orientation and an integrated marketing focus.

The dramatic economic and social changes of the last decade have stirred companies in an even broader range of industries—from banking and air travel to communications—to the realization that marketing will provide them with their cutting edge. Demographic and lifestyle changes have splintered mass, homogeneous markets into many markets, each with different needs and interests. Deregulation has made once-protected industries vulnerable to the vagaries of competition. Vast and rapid technological changes are making an increasing number of products and services obsolete. Intense international competition, rapid expansion of the Internet-based economy, and the growth of truly global markets have many firms looking well beyond their national boundaries.

Indeed, it appears that during the new millennium marketing will take on a unique significance—and not just within the industrial sector. Social institutions of all kinds, which had thought themselves exempt from the pressures of the marketplace, are also beginning to recognize the need for marketing in the management of their affairs. Colleges and universities, charities, museums, symphony orchestras, and even hospitals are beginning to give attention the marketing concept—to provide what the consumer wants to buy.

The selections in this unit are grouped into four areas. Their purposes are to provide current perspectives on marketing, discuss differing views of the marketing concept, analyze the use of marketing by social institutions and nonprofit organizations, and examine the ethical and social responsibilities of marketing.

The four articles in the first subsection provide significant clues about salient approaches and issues that marketers need to address in the future in order to create, promote, and sell their products and services in ways that meet theexpectation of consumers. Some of them reflect the positioning of the Internet as a significant part of their marketing focus.

The four selections that address the marketing concept include Levitt's now classic "Marketing Myopia," which first appeared in the *Harvard Business Review* in 1960. This version includes the author's retrospective commentary, written in 1975, in which he discusses how shortsightedness can make management unable to recognize that there is no such thing as a growth

industry. The second article shows convincing evidence that HR drives customer satisfaction. The next article reflects the importance of the "stairs of loyalty" in developing optimal customer relationships. The last article in this subsection, "What Drives Customer Equity," discloses the significance of customer equity as a significant determinant of the long-term value of a company.

In the *Services and Social Marketing* subsection, the first article describes how quality products and appropriate and exemplary cyberservice may be critical benchmarks and determinants for future marketing success. The second article reveals how sometimes service is focused on elite consumers—while putting other consumers in a secondary position. The final article in this subsection shares stories of legendary service that customers have recently received.

In the final subsection, a careful look is taken at the strategic process and practice of incorporating ethics and social responsibility into the marketplace. "Trust in the Marketplace" discusses the importance of gaining and maintaining customers' trust. "To Tell the Truth" reveals that some salespeople are willing to lie or mislead their clients in order to close a deal.

Future Markets

In the future, marketers will target niches. In niches there are riches.
By serving a niche well, we can earn a high margin.

Philip Kotler

OUR ONLY CERTAINTY is that things will change. Back in the 1950s, who would have anticipated Internet home shopping, home banking, satisfaction guarantees on new automobiles, customized bicycles, and factory-outlet shopping malls? We will see the marketplace go through more radical changes. Specifically, we can anticipate the following eight developments.

1. Shifting demographics. More consumer marketing will focus on mature consumers—the 55-year-olds and older. The focus will shift toward health products, retirement homes, and forms of recreation and entertainment.

Mature consumers will want to be healthy forever. We'll see healthcare facilities where mature consumers pay to have regular diagnostic checks. Medical people will present a complete recommendation on exercise, nutrition, and stress management.

We will also witness a growing demand for light foods, low-calorie beverages, home exercise equipment, vitamins, beauty care and skin-care cosmetics—anything that will make you look and feel younger and healthier. Mature consumers will pay for luxuries like cosmetic surgery, personal exercise coaches, exotic travel, and continuing education.

They will have youthful attitudes and outlooks.

At the other end of the age spectrum, children and teenagers will be more grown-up. These "mini-adults" will master computers and have access to information over the Internet that was never before available. They will be smart consumers who shop electronically.

2. Entertainment explosion. I expect an explosion in entertainment. People will want to be entertained whatever they are doing, whether they're working, shopping, or consuming. Recently, I saw a cyclist on an expensive bike, peddling at a furious speed while listening to music on his Walkman. These multiprocessing consumers will do two or three things at the same time, primarily because their time is short and there is so much they still want to do. Smart retailers, restaurants, hotels, museums, and orchestras will build special atmospheres and surprises into their offerings.

3. High-income consumers. We'll see the buying market segmented into high-income consumers and low-income consumers, while the middle class will diminish in size. Many companies will still target the middle class. But more companies will clearly target their products and services at either the high-income or low-income class. High-income con-

sumers will demand high-quality products and personalized services. At the opposite end will be people who just want basic, no-frills products and services at the lowest possible price. Each class can be further segmented by education, occupation, and lifestyle variables. High-income consumers will be high-achieving people with technical knowledge. They will work to live, not live to work. They will want more quality time apart from work to enjoy other pursuits.

4. Convenience. Time-starved, high-income people want products and services made available to them in a hassle-free way. Their resistance to buying something may not be the price—it's the time, risk, and the psychic costs involved. There will be a great increase in home-based shopping and banking. More people will order clothes, appliances, and other products and services from catalogues.

5. New media. The key is response measurement. Direct marketing is about sending messages to specific addressable consumers and learning which ones placed an order. It started with direct mail and moved to telemarketing. Today, we have added infomercials, audio and videotape, CD-ROMs, computer disks, fax-mail, e-mail, and voice-mail. Companies are rapidly building customer databases from which they can draw the best prospects for an offer. Products, too, will increasingly be customized. Companies will work with you to design your own bicycle, bathing suit, computer, and car. The buying process will become far more interactive, with consumers co-designing the product.

6. *The importance of brands*. Brands will always be important, although the importance of national brands is diminishing. Consumers are comparing the brands on price, and if one is on sale they will buy that brand, regardless of preference. No wonder more money is pouring into sales promotion and price incentives, and less into advertising. And with less advertising, perceived brand differences are eroding. Also giant retailers are introducing private brands that cost less. If your brand is not No. 1 or 2, you may be kicked out of the market.

7. *Quality, pricing, and service*. If your company doesn't produce high quality, you must either sell to low-income groups or go out of business. High product quality will become a ticket into the marketplace. But to win, companies offer high quality for a lower price. The key to good pricing is to figure out to whom you want to sell the product and what they think the product is worth—and then to design the product and its service bundle so it can be priced that way. You will need to justify your prices, using arguments with substance rather than relying on image alone. Service will grow as a competitive tool, especially as products become more similar. Companies must enhance the use-value, or service-value, which goes beyond purchase-value.

8. *Cause-related marketing*. Many companies will differentiate themselves by seriously sponsoring high-consensus social causes, such as environmental protection, helping the homeless, and saving the whales. Building a civic character, not just a business character, can build interest, respect, and loyalty.

Philip Kotler is the SC Johnson & Son Distinguished Professor of Intl. Marketing at the Kellogg Graduate School of Management and author of Philip Kotler on Marketing *(Free Press). This article was adapted with permission from* Rethinking the Future *(Nicholas Brealey), edited by Rowan Gibson; 800-462-6420.*

High Performance Marketing

Marketing must become a leader for change across the corporation

By Jagdish N. Sheth and Rajendra A. Sisodia

EXECUTIVE briefing

Marketing productivity as we define it includes both efficiency and effectiveness to generate loyal and satisfied customers at low cost. However, many companies either create loyal customers at an unacceptably high cost or alienate customers—and employees—in their search for marketing efficiencies. We believe marketing needs to change in order to reestablish itself as a fundamental driver of business success and that the solution lies in "high performance marketing."

Two major changes have emerged in marketing practice over the past five years. The first is the use of the Internet in marketing. An era of intense experimentation with this technology has taught us several lessons. For example, applicability for business-to-consumer e-commerce turned out to be much narrower than most marketers expected. E-mail marketing appeared to be an efficient marketing channel at first, but its abuse and overuse may soon dilute its effectiveness just as direct mail became synonymous with junk mail and telemarketing degenerated from a cost-effective two-way interactive channel into sometimes intrusive customer harassment.

The Internet has empowered customers—usually to the disadvantage of marketers. Now customers can readily search for the best "deal" on every transaction and can communicate with each other to spread word—both positive and negative—about their product purchase experiences. Marketers have been at least moderately successful in the use of "mass personalization" technologies such as collaborative filtering to tailor recommendations to customers and generate some incremental sales.

The second major development has been the popularization of customer relationship management (CRM) software and the rise of 1-to-1 marketing. The CRM industry has exploded in the last few years, growing at 40% per year as more than 2,000 vendors have emerged, promising to achieve the seamless integration of sales, marketing, and customer service around the needs of individual customers. The CRM software market is expected [to] reach $10 billion in 2001 (according to AMR Research), while the worldwide CRM services business reached $34 billion in revenues in 1999, growing

at an annual 20% rate with a projected reach of $125 billion by 2004, according to IDC.

These developments, though momentous, have not brought marketing appreciably closer to our stated ideal of "effective efficiency." In many ways, the marketing function remains as troubled as ever. Major new problems have arisen, such as the ability of customers to readily organize themselves into powerful groups speaking with a unified voice, while others have subsided somewhat. For example, as media continue to get fragmented and more addressable, marketing noise levels have decreased somewhat.

The Trouble With Marketing

Marketing is still not truly customer-centric. For all the lip service that has been paid, marketers are still attempting to control and drive customers to behave in ways they want, rather than organizing their own activities around customer needs. The Internet has not altered this in any significant way.

Most CRM implementations have been expensive failures. CRM, fundamentally, is really just fine-tuned target marketing, albeit with better coordination between sales, marketing, and customer service than we have had in the past. Many companies rushed to embrace CRM as a cure-all that would make them more customer-focused and successful, ignoring the reality that no software can overcome the lack of a customer-centric culture and mindset. Even for companies already possessing a strong customer-centric orientation, there is no guarantee that grafting a CRM system on top will lead to major improvements; it can even lead to deteriorated performance if it takes away from employees' flexibility and responsiveness in dealing with customers.

Most CRM systems do little to improve the customer experience; they just enable marketers to better deploy their resources. Overall, companies have probably lost more money than they have gained through these implementations. In fact, it is estimated that 60% to 80% of CRM projects do not achieve their goals, and 30% to 50% fail outright. CRM implementations in most companies have been initiated by CEOs and led by CIOs; the marketing function has rarely taken the lead or even been actively involved in the decision making. CEOs have embraced CRM technology as a way to finally get some precision and accountability in their marketing efforts. However, the treatment has rarely matched the disease, with the unsurprising result that the marketing function remains as malaise-ridden as ever.

Marketing spending continues to yield poor returns, especially on advertising and branding. For example, many dot-coms spent the bulk of their venture funding on outrageously expensive advertising campaigns, under the delusion that having a recognizable brand would solve all of their other business problems.

The promise of radically efficient business models that leverage the uniqueness of the Internet has given way to widespread disillusionment and a seeming return to "business as usual." However, the root cause of the dot-com debacle was not poor technology or lack of capital, but companies' failure to understand customer behavior. They were left dumbfounded when the anticipated huge changes in behavior required for success didn't happen. Companies especially failed to understand the psychology of consumer resistance to innovation and failed to develop strategies to overcome such resistance.

We believe marketers have not yet fully examined how their function needs to change in order to reestablish itself as a primary driver of business success. High performance marketing (HPM) may be the solution to their problems.

High Performance Organizations

Jordan defines high performance organizations as "groups of employees who produce desired goods or services at higher quality with the same or fewer resources. Their productivity and quality improve continuously, from day to day, week to week, and year to year, leading to the achievement of their mission." (See Additional Reading)

High performance organizations share many characteristics. In addition to identifying and eliminating non-value-added activities, leveraging technology in the service of their mission, and having a strong, organization-wide customer orientation, they also have inspirational and transformational leadership that focuses their resources and energies on achieving a clearly defined mission.

Organizations that perform well empower employees to act autonomously to achieve the corporate mission and provide incentives to individual employees to align their behaviors with the achievement of better outcomes for customers. They also have organizational cultures that embody a high degree of trust—what Carnevale calls "an expression of faith and confidence that a person or an institution will be fair, reliable, ethical, competent, and non-threatening."

High performance organizations tend to use systems thinking, so all employees have a dynamic understanding of how the "living" organization functions and the interdependencies between components and subsystems. They are flexible and adaptable to changing circumstances, emphasizing continuous improvement, reinvention, and innovation.

High Performance Marketing

The operations and manufacturing functions at many leading companies today can be described as "high performance" because they have demonstrated continuous quality improvements and cost reductions. More than anything else, marketers will have to start thinking in new and creative ways about everything in their domain—markets, customers, budgets, organizational structures, information, and incentives. We propose the marketing function needs to adopt the following tenets in order to move toward true high performance.

Customer centricity. Customer-centric marketing will lead to non-intuitive consequences. First, whereas traditional marketing has been concerned with demand management, customercentric marketing will lead the marketing function toward "supply management"—the ability to rapidly respond to customer requirements rather than focusing on controlling them. Second, traditional marketing practices emphasize the acquisition of customers, while customer-centric marketing emphasizes the retention of the "right" customers along with the "outsourcing" of the rest. Third, whereas traditional firms and customers are institutionally separate with little interaction, customer-centric marketing will lead to customers and firms co-creating products, pricing, and distribution. Fourth, customer-centric marketing will be characterized by more "fixed costs" and fewer variable costs; companies will make infrastructure investments that greatly reduce transaction costs. Finally, the vocabulary, metrics, and organizations will evolve toward a customer focus rather than product focus or segment focus. For example, Procter & Gamble renamed its channel sales organization "customer business development" in early 1999.

Investment orientation. In most companies, sales and marketing expenditures are several times greater than capital expenditures. Yet capital expenditures are subject to a far greater amount of analysis and evaluation than marketing expenditures. Most marketing activities involve a substantial lag between action and effect. When marketing is treated as an expense, the causality often becomes reversed, as marketing budgets tend to be determined by sales forecasts. Treating marketing as an investment forces companies to come to grips with the temporal relationship between current marketing actions and future marketplace reactions.

Well-spent marketing resources applied to a brand in its early years can build a stock of value that can be sustained or even enhanced with very small amounts of spending. Marketing investments can pay off if they are well-timed and targeted. Investments made at the right stage of the product life cycle and directed at the most profitable customers deliver superior returns.

Systems thinking. Systems modeling is an integrative approach that combines systems thinking and the principles of cybernetics. It incorporates causal-loop diagramming to show sequences of cause-and-effect relationships as well as stock-and-flow diagrams to represent systemic effects of feedback on the accumulations and rates of flow in the system. These two system representations are coupled in order to simulate the behavior of the system. Modeling and simulating the system helps managers recognize and understand the dynamic patterns of system behavior. Systems dynamics offers a great deal of potential to marketers, but is hardly used. For example, it is a useful approach to model the customer acquisition and retention process.

Incentive alignment. The incentives provided to marketing employees are haphazard and often at odds. Most advertising agencies are still paid a commission proportional to the volume of advertising run, creating a disincentive for higher impact advertising that needs fewer exposures. Many salespeople are still compensated on short-term customer acquisition measures, with little regard for customer profitability or longevity.

The guiding principle in creating incentive systems is to use market mechanisms wherever possible. In their book, *Free to Choose* (1990, Harcourt Brace), Milton and Rose Friedman present a framework for evaluating the relative productivity of spending in different circumstances. The "Friedman Matrix" categorizes business spending along two dimensions: whose money is spent and for whose benefit the money is spent. The way to align employee and company interests is to organize every spending decision in such a manner that employees act as though they are spending their own money for their own benefit. This will ensure that they are both effective and efficient in their resource allocation.

The framework suggests that resources are spent most optimally when they are "owned" by an individual and spent by that individual for his or her own purposes. In buying a family car, for example, individuals are likely to spend what they know they can afford and get a car that satisfies their needs. On the other hand, individuals able to spend someone else's money on themselves (e.g., buying an expense account meal) are likely to get what they want (effective), but will probably spend more than if they were paying their own money (inefficient). A third situation exists when an individual spends his or her own money (staying within a budget) to purchase a gift for someone else; while efficient, this is unlikely to optimally satisfy the recipient (ineffective). Finally, when individuals (e.g., bureaucrats) are charged with spending other people's money (e.g., taxpayers) on things that do not affect them directly (e.g., welfare), spending is neither effective nor efficient.

Incentive alignment is a guiding principle for moving toward high performance marketing. Examples include creating sales force compensation schemes to reward customer retention and profitability (as the insurance industry has done in recent years) and incentivizing new product development teams to create high quality new products in a short time without consuming inordinate resources.

Avoid incremental thinking. When it comes to changes in how the marketing function is defined, organized, and compensated, incremental thinking will not suffice. Given product parity and near-perfect information availability and matching, the quality of a firm's marketing strategy and execution will be prime drivers of market capitalization.

For too long, the marketing function has been content to focus on relatively trivial tactics and has been lackadaisical about taking a prominent role in shaping the overall fortunes of the corporation. In other words, marketing has not aspired to a higher level and has demonstrated no zeal or passion to elevate its respect and relevance within the corporation. Other functional areas have rallied around ambitious and organization-transforming initiatives, such as TQM and Six Sigma (driven by operations), Economic Value Added (driven by CFOs), and the Balanced Scorecard (driven by accounting).

Marketing needs to break out of its "doer rather than leader" role and its preoccupation with the mundane. We believe marketing needs to become a leader for change and transformation across the corporation. Marketing must take hold of the leadership levers for the corporation. The best way for it to do so is to leverage its fundamental identity as the voice of the customer within the corporation. Marketing needs to go outside the box and break many of the self-imposed rules that have relegated it to a constricted role.

Understand market growth. One of the biggest gaps remaining in marketing know-how is an understanding of what determines market growth. Marketers must attempt to grow the total market, not just try to protect and grow their market share. Several factors can contribute to market growth, such as an emphasis on emerging markets and the creative "dematuring" or revitalization of mature markets through the fusion of non-traditional technologies (as Yamaha did by incorporating digital electronics into pianos) or injecting elements of fashion and personalization (as some European manufacturers have done with small appliances). Commodity markets in developing markets such as India and China are ripe for dematuring, through the introduction of packaging, processing, and other value-adding functions.

View customers differently. Just as we have gone through significant changes in how we think about employees and shareholders, we will need to engage in some fresh thinking about customers. Customers should be viewed and managed as assets of the organization to be invested in, depreciated, and replaced. In addition to the outsourcing of customers (e.g., using business partners to serve certain customer groups), companies also need to think about trading, sharing, firing, and outright selling customers.

Harness marketing information. In *2020 Vision* (1992, Simon & Schuster), Stan Davis and Bill Davidson described the "information exhaust" that companies generate through their ongoing transactions and relationships with customers. In the past, most of this exhaust was discharged into the atmosphere and disappeared. Smart companies, however, have developed ways to "turbocharge" the core business by harnessing this information flow. Through feedback mechanisms, this allows the marketing "engine" to operate at a higher level of efficiency. Information exhaust also can generate highly profitable sidelines that in some cases may become more profitable than the core business. For example, by focusing on the lifetime value of customers, General Motors' U.S. operation sees the potential for substantial synergies across its automotive, consumer credit, mortgage, and even its communications businesses.

Firms can use this thinking to guide strategic decisions on entering new businesses. For example, entry into the credit card business is often dictated not by the economics of that business per se, but by the usable information used to improve the core business. Similar examples can be found in the magazine and software industries, as the recent merger of AOL and Time Warner demonstrates. Given their potential value, it is imperative that firms develop sound mechanisms for sharing information and managing marketing knowledge. Marketing employees need to receive incentives to share information that could be of broader value to the corporation.

Prepare for a new role. Senior management needs to reconsider how to control and integrate the marketing function for best results—to determine the proper role of the marketing function in a corporation where virtually all functions have become market-oriented. To start with, the sales-marketing-customer service separation must end, and marketers must take on the responsibility for attracting as well as retaining and growing profitable customers. Additionally, marketing has to be accorded greater say over key decision areas such as procurement, pricing,

product development, and logistics, all of which have been gradually taken away from marketing departments.

In the future marketing will get wider but shallower; it will encompass a wider range of activities but will perform fewer of them in house. Many activities will be outsourced to best-in-class external suppliers, while others will be performed in various parts of the corporation. The marketing manager's job will evolve from a "doer" to a coordinator of internal and external resources pertinent to customer retention and profitable growth.

The marketing function will also, in a more deliberate way, formally incorporate upstream linkages that were once the domain of the purchasing department. Key suppliers will become an integral part of the marketing team and will be involved in strategic planning and new product development. For example, this is already happening in the automotive industry.

Employ dynamic budgeting. The budgeting process is probably one of the biggest contributors to marketing's problems. Budgeting is static, forecast-driven (based on notoriously inaccurate forecasts subject to intense and deliberate distortions and game playing), counterintuitive (e.g., mixing cause and effect in advertising), and subject to the "use it or lose it" rule. Budgets escalate year after year in prosperous times, with little consideration for changes in actual needs over time.

Static budgeting needs to be replaced with dynamic budgeting, where resources are requested and allocated based on an "as needed and justified" basis. Rather than budget by scale or in some proportion to the top line, budgeting should be driven by the size of the opportunity, the anticipated ROI, and increase in shareholder value. This requires decoupling the marketing budgeting for a brand from the current brand's revenue level and instead coupling it to the opportunity for revenue and profit growth that the brand presents. In situations where more traditional budgeting procedures persist, managers need to receive direct incentives not to fully use their budgets, just as U.S. farmers are often given incentives not to plant crops.

Consider how marketing budgets and customer-related responsibilities are typically allocated in companies. The marketing budget usually covers advertising, sales promotions, market research, and some portion of distribution costs. It may include the cost of the sales force, though in many companies it does not. It almost never includes the cost of customer service, and usually does not include product development.

It is not unusual to find situations where sales, customer service, and new product development are funded out of budgets that are not under marketing's control. Clearly, we need to create transparent incentive schemes to focus all marketing personnel on the essentials: the profitability of what they do and the maintenance of high levels of customer satisfaction and retention.

Change marketing metrics. Marketing employees for too long have been measured on market share, with little or no consideration to the profitability of that market share. Of late, there has been some movement toward thinking more about the bottom-line impact or measuring marketing based on its profit impact.

Ultimately, the measure that matters most for a business is shareholder value or market capitalization. It is a summary descriptor of all the value the business has created and is expected to create in the future. The question for the marketing function is: How can it affect the company's market capitalization? The measure of marketing's success must move from "share of market" to "share of market capitalization" within the industry. Operationalizing this will be one of the key challenges for marketing in the years to come.

Filling the Void

Reflecting the greater emphasis on shareholder value in recent years, the CFO today drives most companies. However, a preoccupation with finances can be dangerous because it can lead companies to lose sight of the true driver of business success—the long-term satisfaction and retention of profitable customers.

In our view, marketing has a great opportunity to create excitement around becoming customer-centric and in the process can satisfy both the CEO and the CFO. If, on the other hand, it continues to take a back seat within the corporation, it will be abdicating its fiscal responsibilities. High performance marketing is really "inspirational marketing" that can rally the corporation to set and achieve much higher goals than ever before. While it has a number of tenets as discussed earlier, its defining characteristic is that it is customer-centric. In order to operationalize customer-centric marketing fully, it is essential that companies create a new senior executive role that takes an outside-in perspective rather than the inside-out perspective adopted by others. This role is that of a "chief customer officer" (CCO).

The CCO position, while currently seen mostly in small high-tech companies, is expected to become commonplace. The Meta Group projects that 25% of Global 2000 businesses will have a CCO by 2003, while Gartner expects 15% of U.S. companies to have such a position by 2003. Cisco Systems has been a pioneer in this regard; it established the position of senior vice president of customer advocacy in 1991, with Cisco's customer service, product design, and IT groups reporting to it.

There is a void at the top of most major corporations, and marketing must move quickly to fill it. If it does not, marketing will continue to become more marginalized, and all stakeholders—customers, employees, and shareholders—will suffer as a result.

Additional Reading

Carnevale, David G. (1995), *Trustworthy Government: Leadership and Management Strategies for Building Trust and High Performance*. New York: Jossey-Bass.

Jordan, Sephena A. (1999), "Innovative Cultures + Empowered Employees = High Performance Organizations," *Public Productivity & Management Review*, (23:1),109–113.

Sheth, Jagdish N., Rajendra S. Sisodia, and Arun Sharma (2000), "The Antecedents and Consequences of Customer-Centric Marketing," *Journal of the Academy of Marketing Science*, (28:1), 55–66.

About the Authors

Jagdish N. Sheth is the Charles H. Kellstadt professor of marketing at the Goizueta Business School at Emory University in Atlanta.

Rajendra S. Sisodia is trustee professor of marketing at Bentley College in Waltham, Mass. He may be reached at rsisodia@bentley.edu.

Marketing High Technology: Preparation, Targeting, Positioning, Execution

A range of strategies are available to the high-tech marketing manager taking a shot at launching the latest technology.

Chris Easingwood and Anthony Koustelos

Commercialization of new high-tech products is often the costliest stage of the entire product development process. Yet even when the process is well managed, the risk of failure remains high. New high-tech products usually have just one shot at the market. Get it wrong and the consequences are invariably fatal. And although the launch strategy is critical, this stage is largely neglected in the business press and academic literature on high-tech marketing, innovation, and new product development.

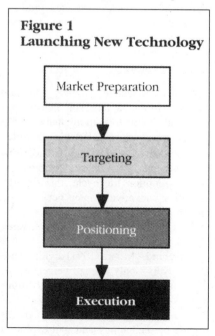

**Figure 1
Launching New Technology**

Market Preparation → Targeting → Positioning → Execution

Persuading a market to adopt a new technology is generally comprised of four stages, shown in Figure 1. The first step, market preparation, involves readying customers and other companies for the change. Typically this stage takes place while the product is still in development, though not necessarily so. The second stage in planning the marketing of the product is targeting, followed by positioning based on the expected competitive situation. The final stage involves execution and consists of the strategies that are often the most visible part of the mix, used to achieve specific results. Each of the four stages will be described in turn.

MARKET PREPARATION

Market preparation is intended to get the market ready for the new technology by building awareness and, most important, forming relationships. Figure 2 shows some examples.

Cooperation/Licensing/Alliances

In many cases, the way a marketer chooses to set up the market is crucial. Some form of cooperation is increasingly seen not as an option but as a necessity. Few companies can go it alone, at least not when the launch of major technology is concerned.

Alliances and licensing arrangements encourage the adoption of technological standards for at least two good reasons.

One is because of the expected boost to sales. Customers are reluctant to adopt when faced with competing and incompatible technologies (recall the days of the VHS and Betamax videocassette formats). They realize that markets rarely allow two competing technologies to thrive, and eventually coalesce around the preferred one, condemning the other(s) to decline.

The other reason is that companies sometimes seek to establish their own technology as the standard, to preempt those of rivals and avoid having a competing standard imposed. This was very much the reason for Psion, Motorola, Ericsson, and Nokia forming a consortium called Symbian. The four agreed to adopt Psion's computer operating system, called EPOC, in the hope that this would become the industry standard for the next generation of wireless communication devices, such as mobile phones and palm-top computers. The mobile phone is expected to become "smart," sending and receiving data, downloading from the Internet, and storing large amounts of information. The alliance is also an attempt to prevent Microsoft's Windows CE operating system in consumer electronics from becoming the standard. Ericsson, Motorola, and Nokia each had to abandon its own operating system in adopting Psion's—a sacrifice that may prove worthwhile, given *Fortune's* claim that David Potter, Psion's CEO, is the man Microsoft's Bill Gates fears the most (Wallace 1998).

Figure 2
Market Preparation: Some Examples

Form alliances	Psion, Motorola, Ericsson, and Nokia adopting Psion's computer operating system to thwart Microsoft's Windows CE operating system
Supply to OEMs	IBM licensing its hard disk drives
Provide pre-launch information	Apple providing information on the Macintosh NC

Sometimes the alliances formed can be informal or "loose," arising through mutual advantage. This is because, more and more, technological products rarely stand alone. They depend on the existence of other products and technologies. A good example is the World Wide Web, with its groupings of businesses that include browsers, on-line news, e-mail, network retailing, and financial services. Arthur (1996) calls these networks of products and services that support and enhance each other "mini-ecologies." They are increasingly the basic frameworks of knowledge-based industries, and companies have to secure themselves a place in these loose alliances built around a mini-ecology.

Supply to OEMs

Market preparation can also be tackled by sharing the new technology with original equipment manufacturers (OEMs). This increases the awareness of the product and the technology, and boosts sales via expansion to new markets. IBM developed two powerful hard disk drives, Travel-Star 8GS and 3GN, for its own ThinkPad notebooks, but decided to license them to Acer, Gateway 2000, Dell, and other OEMs as well, which plan to use the drives in their portable PCs. This market preparation tactic enables the producer to retain full ownership of its technology while at the same time expanding market potential beyond its own marketing capacity, albeit at a lower margin.

Provide Pre-Launch Information

The type of information released before launch, and the manner in which it is delivered, can be a key tactical decision in the product launch. The publicly visible demonstration of this strategy is the article in the press, detailing the time the product

will reach the market, the basis of the technology, and other information. Intel has been releasing details of its new MMX technology-based Pentium-II chip. Articles have also appeared on the Macintosh NC, Apple's forthcoming network computer, based on the company's powerful new chip, PowerPC 750. Those who typically need to be informed before the launch are the distribution network, service suppliers (such as software houses), and the media, who in turn inform potential customers.

The information to be released has to be planned carefully so as to arouse sufficient interest in the new product without losing a competitive edge in a market where imitation can materialize with lightning speed. A careful balance must be drawn that allows for the need to have influential components of the market's infrastructure informed without giving a technological lead away to competitors.

Educate the Market

A special form of providing pre-release information is an education program. This is very ambitious and more long-term than merely releasing information, and thus it is less common. It is exactly what Intel did in the early days of the microchip. Rather than marketing the product directly—there were just too many markets with too many applications for that—it set about educating the various markets on the potential of the technology, leaving them with much greater in-depth knowledge to work out how the product might be used in their particular markets.

However, education has to be managed and timed carefully. Otherwise, the company sells the vision before it has the product to deliver that vision. Not surprisingly, smaller companies shy away from trying to educate markets, leaving it to larger corpo-

rations with their greater resources and longer planning horizons.

Create Special Distribution Arrangements

Finally, technology may be launched into new markets as well as currently served markets, which would entail establishing new channels of distribution. Distribution rights may be given to competitors in these new markets. New distribution can also be gained through joint ventures, possibly involving collaborative development of the technology.

TARGETING

Adoption of a new technology is likely to be faster if the marketing strategy is compatible with the segment targeted. Easingwood and Lunn (1992) examined the diffusion of telecommunications products and found that clearly targeted products diffused more rapidly than non-targeted ones (see Figure 3 for examples).

Target Innovative Adopters

Targeting innovative adopters can take two main forms: (a) targeting both companies and innovative individuals within those companies, or (b) targeting sectors.

Innovative Companies and Individuals. Based on the familiar model, the technology adoption life cycle, this strategy identifies innovative adopters because they are prepared to buy without seeing the product up and running elsewhere. They do not insist that the technology have a "track record." Moore (1991) divides these early buyers—only a small percentage of the total potential market, but hugely influential—into technological enthusiasts, or "techies," and visionaries. Techies are intrigued by technology and will explore a

Figure 3
Targeting: Some Examples

Target innovative adopters	NTT taking its global photo transmission system to sectors, such as the insurance industry, that are likely to be early adopters
Target pragmatists	Amgen using a large sales force to promote its hepatitis C drug to *all* hospital specialists
Target conservatives	Microsoft aiming its integrated software product Works at the PC conservative market
Target current customers	IBM Software Group working with many of the Global 5000
Target competitors' customers	Xerox targeting its digital copiers at Hewlett-Packard customers

product's potential for themselves. Their endorsement is vital because it means the product does, in fact, work. Visionaries are the managers with clout, often very senior, who can see a product's potential for over-turning existing ways of operating, deliv-ering significant value and competitive advantage to those organizations prepared to grasp the new technology.

Technological enthusiasts and visionar-ies, although placed together in this inno-vative group, are very different in some regards. Techies are excited by the tech-nology itself, whereas the visionaries try to find its greater worth—some single, com-pelling application that uses the full range of the new technology. A visionary is mo-tivated by a potentially significant leap forward, not by the newness of the tech-nology.

Visionaries are a rare breed. They not only have the ability to see the potential when no one else can, they also have the management drive and charisma to per-suade the rest of an organization to back the vision. They anticipate a radical dis-continuity between the old ways and the new, realizing that this rarely happens smoothly, and so they will tolerate the glitches and setbacks that inevitably occur before this is achieved.

The only way to work with visionaries, says Moore, is to use a small, high-level sales force. Constantly looking to leverage technology, visionaries typically maintain good relationships with techies, so this segment should not be neglected. And techies can be reached fairly easily through the technical and business press. It is their job to stay alert to all developments, wher-ever their sources, not just to focus on their own industry.

Early Adopting Sectors. Innovators can sometimes be hard to identify, but they are worth searching out. They start the ball rolling. However, an alternative to identi-fying individuals with these special attrac-tive characteristics is to target whole sectors that are likely to be early buyers.

USDC developed an active-matrix flat panel display screen—in effect, the first "paper-quality" screen, with each pixel linked to its own transistor—and targeted the product at some of the world's leading air forces, a sector with a pressing need for the latest technology.

In the telecommunications sector, NTT has developed Digital Photo System, a means of transmitting a photo by a digital camera over the airways via cellular phones to a laptop computer and from there to a printer. The whole process takes about 10 seconds and can be done globally. The service was aimed initially at the newspaper and insurance sectors, both of which would particularly benefit from an acceleration in the speed of the internal processing of photographs.

Target the Pragmatists

Sometimes called the "early majority," pragmatists (as Moore calls them) are the large group of adopters following behind the techies and visionaries, though Moore argues that the gap between the two groups is so large it deserves to be called a chasm. Pragmatists typically comprise large orga-nizations with a clear need to adopt new technologies to retain or improve competi-tiveness, but with a reluctance to do so. The dislocation would be so extensive and the size of the investment required to switch the whole firm over to the new tech-nology so large that they are risk-averse. People in this group are reasonably com-fortable about taking on new technology, but only when some well-established ref-erences exist. Their preference is for evo-lution, not revolution. They are looking for something that can be slotted into existing ways of doing things. "If the goal of vi-sionaries is to take a quantum leap for-ward," explains Moore, "the goal of pragmatists is to make a percentage im-provement—incremental, measurable, predict-able progress."

Marketing to pragmatists is a matter of:

- attending the industry conferences and trade shows;
- getting frequent mentions in the indus-try magazines;
- being installed in other companies in the same industry;
- developing industry-specific applica-tions;
- having alliances with other key suppli-ers to the industry.

As Moore observes, pragmatists like to hear companies talk about their new prod-ucts as "industry standards." What they hate to hear is products described as "state-of-the-art." This makes them extremely edgy. Pharmaceutical companies are well known for targeting their new drugs at hos-pital specialists working in the leading teaching hospitals. However, they do not neglect the pragmatists either. Amgen has assembled a sales team of about 50 people to promote its new hepatitis C drug to all the hematologists and gastroenterologists working in hospitals who may have to treat patients with the ailment.

Target Conservatives

The "conservatives," or "late adopters," really are not that keen on new technology. By and large, they would really rather not adopt any if they could get away with it, but competitive pressures may force them to do so. They are not that confident in their ability to adapt to new technology, so they like to see evidence of support. By the time the technology gets to them, there will probably be an established standard. Conservatives like to buy pre-assembled packages, with everything bundled. "They want high-tech products to be like refrigerators," says Moore. "You open the door, the light comes on automatically, your food stays cold, and you don't have to think about it."

However, it can he a big mistake to neglect this section of the market. For one thing, it is large—probably around a third of the whole market. It is often not developed as systematically as it should be, possibly because high-tech companies do not generally find it easy to empathize with this group. The product development costs are apt to be fully amortized at this stage, so extending the product's life should be highly profitable.

Because of conservatives' reluctance to come to grips with a new technology and its implications, a product has to be made increasingly easy to adopt if a high-tech company is to succeed with this group. The DOS PC operating system stalled when it reached the late adopter segment—the home market, the home office, the small business. This segment does not have the support offered in large companies and was disinclined to teach itself DOS. It took the greater simplicity of Windows 3.0 to bring it into the market. Microsoft has aimed its product Works, an integrated, all-in-one word processor, spreadsheet, and database (none of which are state-of-the-art), at the PC conservative market.

Target Current Customers

Existing customers can be an obvious target group for well-established companies. So it makes sense for IBM Software Group, the world's second largest software firm—which has very strong customer relationships with the Global 5000, the world's largest companies—to think first of its current customers. Although current customers ought to be the most secure market, this is not necessarily the case. They can he hard to satisfy and quite costly to retain. Such is Intel's experience. It is having to cut the prices of some of its computer chips in an attempt to retain big corporate customers such as Compaq and Packard Bell. The latter are threatening to switch to Cyrix, the rival microprocessor producer, as they do everything possible to reduce the costs of their lowest-priced PCs.

Targeting existing customers is a strategy particularly appropriate to rapidly changing, advanced technologies. It can be particularly relevant for complex technologies when the decision to adopt often relies on a high degree of technical expertise and mutual trust between buyer and supplier.

Target Competitors' Customers

Finally, competitors' customers can present a prime opportunity, especially when the company's own product is competitive and the competitor has a large market share. Xerox would claim that this is the case for the new digital copiers designed by its Office Document Product Group. The copiers, which have faxing, scanning, and printing capabilities when connected to the personal computers of Hewlett-Packard's customers, are targeted toward HP and its dominance in the printer market.

Such a practice is commonplace in the pharmaceutical industry. Amgen has pitched its new hepatitis C treatment drug, Infeger, at those customers for whom the existing treatments, such as Schering-Plough's Intron A or Roche Holdings' Roferon A, have not been successful.

Of course, this strategy is very aggressive. For brand new technologies, it may be counterproductive. Aggressive competitive tactics may be seen as undermining the credibility of the entire technology, rather than just the competitor's product, as may have been intended.

POSITIONING

Some new technologies are so specialized that targeting and positioning strategies are too unambiguous and virtually redundant. Other new technologies are so wide-ranging in their potential applications that the market needs some strong clues as to targeting and positioning before it will respond. Many products fall between these two extremes.

Positioning can be based on tangible (technological) or intangible characteristics (such as image), with technologically intensive industrial markets favoring the former. Where the market is not so technologically informed, or the benefits of the new technology are not so easily differentiated from competitors, positioning characteristics are likely to be more intangible. Positioning possibilities can be numerous, but some of those used most often are described here (see Figure 4 for examples).

Emphasize Exclusivity

A way to differentiate the product offer is by emphasizing how exclusive it is. In other words, can the product be placed in the upper segment of the market, where the margins are usually higher? For example, by focusing on quality, engineering, and adjustability, Recaro is offering a top-of-the-range child's safety seat—the Recaro-Start—that appeals to wealthier parents who place high priority on their children's safety. The company is playing heavily on its reputation for producing high-tech safety seats for Porsche and Aston-Martin.

Emphasize a Low Price

It used to be that low prices were considered an inappropriate lever for high-tech products and services. The market's reluctance to purchase was due to the misgivings it held about the new product's performance, which was largely unproven. The best strategy, marketers believed, was to address this reluctance directly by lowering the perceived risk that the product would not come up to expectations, or by reducing the perceived likelihood that it might be made redundant by a superior technology. In any case, high margins were needed to recoup the high costs of development.

Well, not necessarily anymore. Low price is used more and more in high-tech markets. For instance, phone companies will have to pay just $5 per device to use EPOC from Symbian, versus a reported $25 for Microsoft's Windows CE.

Emphasize Technological Superiority

Focusing on the technological superiority of a new high-tech product is common. When technology is changing rapidly and perhaps radically, it would seem that positioning a product on the basis of the latest technology built into it should reflect the product's true *raison d'etre*.

```
┌─────────────────────────────────────────────────────────────────┐
│ Figure 4                                                          │
│ Positioning: Some Examples                                       │
│                                                                   │
│  ┌──────────────────────┬────────────────────────────────────┐  │
│  │ Emphasize            │ Recaro (supplier to Porsche and    │  │
│  │ exclusivity          │ Aston Martin) with its top-of-the- │  │
│  │                      │ range child's safety seat          │  │
│  ├──────────────────────┼────────────────────────────────────┤  │
│  │ Emphasize            │ Just $5 per mobile phone for the   │  │
│  │ a low price          │ operating system from Symbian      │  │
│  │                      │ ($25 quoted for the alternative)   │  │
│  ├──────────────────────┼────────────────────────────────────┤  │
│  │ Emphasize techno-    │ Xerox focusing on the superiority  │  │
│  │ logical superiority  │ of digital copiers over the old    │  │
│  │                      │ technology                         │  │
│  ├──────────────────────┼────────────────────────────────────┤  │
│  │ Emphasize            │ Lucent Technologies designing its  │  │
│  │ a "safe bet"         │ digital phones to be compatible    │  │
│  │                      │ with international standards        │  │
│  └──────────────────────┴────────────────────────────────────┘  │
└─────────────────────────────────────────────────────────────────┘
```

Xerox's new digital copiers are priced about 10 percent higher than old-style copiers because of the greater quality and reliability they offer compared to the old "light lens" technology copiers. This practice is also observed in the computer component manufacturing industry, where such new products as "bonded modems," storing units, and processor chips justify their premium pricing through their advanced technological features.

However, emphasizing such superiority does have its drawbacks. First, by stressing technological features, the marketer is assuming a certain level of knowledge that may not be present in at least part of the target market. Second, the preoccupation with technological specifications may obscure the genuine benefits customers could realize from the technology. Given the buying center nature of many high-tech adoption decisions involving technical specialists and nonspecialists, not all of whom are capable of translating technical specifications into everyday benefits, it may be more successful to come up with a more benefit-specific positioning tactic.

Emphasize a 'Safe Bet'

Stressing customer protection in the product is important because it enhances the product's credibility element and reduces the associated risk of moving to a new technology. Lucent Technologies focused on the fact that the specifications of both of its two newly introduced digital phones fall under established standards. One of the phones operates on the Code Division Multiple Access (CDMA) technology standard of the United States. The other, which is a "dual mode/dual band" handset, operates on the Time Division Multiple Access (TDMA) standard introduced by

AT&T to serve the entire European market, where the existence of different networks can otherwise hinder compatibility.

EXECUTION

As the final stage and therefore the one that completes the product's projection into the marketplace, execution is designed to trigger a positive purchase decision. The strategies used depend on the objectives of the launch itself, which in turn depend on the state of technology and the awareness the market has of it. For a very new technology, of which the market is unaware, execution tends to focus on conveying the generic benefits. At the other extreme, where the technology is well known to the market, the launch objectives focus more on establishing a brand name and competitive advantage. Figure 5 provides examples.

Use Opinion Leaders

It makes good sense to obtain the support of opinion leaders. As Moore states, "No company can afford to pay for every marketing contact made. Every programme must rely on some on-going chain-reaction effects, what is usually called 'word of mouth.'" Word-of-mouth is invaluable, of course, but the support of opinion leaders, who are industrial rather than public celebrities, can also be taken on board more formally, such as in advertising or through appearances at company seminars.

Compaq and NEC Technologies have managed to secure the endorsement of a number of well-known technical journalists for their FPDS screen. Pharmaceutical companies try to communicate the views of prominent doctors on their new drugs to influence the views of general practitioners and other doctors.

Reduce the Risk of Adoption

It is sometimes possible to reduce adoption risks. Can the product be offered on an introductory trial? Can it be leased? Luz Engineering, a producer of industrial solar heaters costing between $2–4 million, came up with a novel variation on this approach. Now Luz is prepared to sell its systems. However, it is also prepared to install and operate the solar heaters itself, in which case the client merely contracts to buy steam at 350°F for 20 years at a discount from the prevailing local power company rate. This is a "no-lose deal" from the client's perspective. The client pays for none of the installation and operating costs, but enjoys most of the expected benefits of the technology, without the associated risks.

Cultivate a Winner Image

Individuals and organizations can easily be confused by too much choice. Their first reaction, when faced with a confusing purchasing decision, is to postpone it. But when this is no longer possible, they vote for the safe choice: the market leader. There is safety in numbers. And this position can be reinforcing in technology markets. Other companies will recognize the leadership position and design supporting products and services around the market leader, which will thus become even more the preferred choice. The number one product becomes easier to use, cheaper to use, and better supported. There is a "winner take most" tendency, as Arthur states—the phenomenon of increasing returns. The bigger you get, the more apt you are to get bigger still. Conversely, the smaller you get, the more apt you are to shrink even more. Success breeds success, failure breeds failure. You have to become

Figure 5
Execution: Some Examples

Use opinion leaders	Compaq and NEC Technologies securing endorsements from technical journalists
Reduce the risk of adoption	Luz Engineering installing and running its industrial solar heaters that supply clients with energy at guaranteed prices
Cultivate a winner image	IBM advertising its position as recipient of the most U.S. patents for the fifth year running
Concentrate on a particular application	Lotus Notes focusing on worldwide accounting and consulting firms

a "gorilla," because if you do not, you'll be a "chimpanzee" or, more likely, a "monkey."

Thus, companies should try to cultivate a winner image for themselves and their products. However, this often involves allocating considerable resources to a big media splash aimed at communicating the (preordained) success of the new product. So this strategy is most popular with large companies. When Microsoft launched Windows 95, it did not pull its punches or spare its expenses. In the U.S., the Empire State Building was bathed in Windows colors. In the U.K., the *Times*, sponsored by Microsoft, doubled its print run and was given away free. In Australia, the Sydney Opera House was commandeered. The worldwide event, accompanied by the Rolling Stones' hit "Start Me Up," was said to have cost $200 million, but was hugely successful: one million copies sold in the U.S. in the first four days, compared to the 60 days it took the upgrade to MS-DOS to reach that level.

Of course, the approach to this position can be more subtle. In the last year, IBM received more U.S. patents than any other company, taking the top spot for the fifth consecutive year in a list that used to be dominated primarily by Japanese firms. This achievement has been stressed by IBM through articles in the technology sections of top-rated journals. It has also been the theme of an advertising campaign that aims to build a leader image for the company.

Sometimes the leadership position cannot be established across the entire market, in which case it should be established in a market segment. It is important to be the biggest fish in the pond, even if it means searching out a very small pond.

A market leader position is particularly important for pragmatists. These are the people who are contemplating committing their organizations to the new product—a much less risky gamble if the new product is the market leader.

A company that can establish a lead in a segment is in a very strong position. All the major customers have committed themselves to the product and so want it to remain the standard. The company can only lose such a position by shooting itself in the foot. Moore believes that segments conspire, unconsciously, "to install some company or product as the market leader and then do everything in their power to keep [it] there." This, of course, puts up huge barriers to entry for other competitors. If the leader plays its cards right, it can end up "owning" the segment.

Concentrate on a Particular Application

Concentrating on a particular application is all about crossing the chasm, the huge gulf that separates the techies and visionaries, few in number, from the much larger mainstream market dominated by pragmatists. The way across the chasm is to target the company's resources to one or two very specific niche markets where it can dominate rapidly and force out competitors. It can then use the dominance of the first niche to attack the surrounding niches.

Moore uses the analogy of the Allies' D-Day invasion strategy in World War II: assembling a huge invasion force and focusing it on one narrowly defined target, the beaches of Normandy, routing the enemy, then moving out to dominate surrounding areas of Normandy. In other words, establish a beachhead, then broaden the basis of operations.

Serving the needs of a particular segment is all about focusing the company's resources on customizing the product to the needs of that segment. The segment wants a customized solution. It wants the "whole product" with all relevant services, not 80 percent of the whole product with the responsibility of supplying the missing 20 percent itself. Sales in several segments would soon stretch the company's development resources to the breaking point as it tried to customize the product to each segment's needs. Lotus Notes managed to escape the chasm when it focused on the global account management sector; particularly on worldwide accounting and consulting firms.

In addition, niche sales are driven by references and word-of-mouth within that niche. Failure to build up a core level of business in a particular segment means that momentum in any one single segment is never established. Pragmatists and conservatives talk to people in their own industry and look for solutions that have been proven to work there.

Tactical Alliances. Companies sometimes have the opportunity to form tactical alliances with smaller firms to help put a "complete product" in place. Market niches will coalesce behind a product much more readily—elevating it effectively to the position of a standard—if that product is supported by a number of products that fill in the gaps the market values but that the main product could not possibly supply. Producers of software packages often welcome the entry of smaller firms with their add-on programs to help provide the fully rounded complete product. It is a matter of gathering the appropriate partners and allies to jointly deliver a more complete product.

This is, however, very different from the cooperation/licensing/alliance approach discussed earlier, which is more formal and strategic. Tactical alliances tend to occur spontaneously at a later stage in a technology's development as smaller companies, realizing that a product has the potential to become a standard, desire to become associated with that standard.

Introducing a new technology offers a marketplace the first opportunity to experience the brand new product. So the manner in which the introduction is handled is critical. Everything has to come together in what is usually a narrow window of opportunity. Get it wrong, and there may be little time to put things right. By this stage, the investment in the new technology may be considerable, yet the chances of rejection or indifference are quite high.

The strategies proposed here are all designed to reduce the risks of failure. Of course, a complete and consistent strategy will assemble one or more components from each of the preparation, targeting, positioning, and execution stages.

Technology-intensive products and companies are at the leading edge of many Western countries' economies. By examining the range of illustrations included here, it is hoped that managers can help the new technology take its intended role in these economies.

References

W. Brian Arthur, "Increasing Returns and the New World of Business," *Harvard Business Review*, July–August 1996, pp. 100–109.

Christopher Easingwood and Simon O. Lunn, "Diffusion Paths in a High-Tech Environment: Clusters and Commonalities," *R&D Management,* 22, 1 (1992): 69–80.

Geoffrey A. Moore, *Crossing the Chasm: Marketing and Selling High-Technology Products to Mainstream Customers* (New York: HarperBusiness, 1991).

Geoffrey A. Moore, *Inside the Tornado: Marketing Strategies from Silicon Valley's Cutting Edge* (New York: HarperBusiness, 1995).

Charles P. Wallace, "The Man Bill Gates Fears Most," *Fortune*, November 23, 1998, pp. 257–260.

Chris Easingwood is the Caudwell Professor of Marketing and Head of Marketing and Strategy at Manchester Business School, Manchester, England, where **Anthony Koustelos** was an MBA student before becoming a market analyst with the Competitive Intelligence Unit, Business Development Group, DHL Worldwide Network NV/SA Brussels, Belgium.

The Internet as Integrator:
Fast Brand Building in Slow-Growth Markets

To link and augment marketing communications programs, spin the Web around them.

by David A. Aaker

Today, as most industries confront overcapacity and weakening demand in the face of an uncertain economic environment, the need for cost-effective brand building has never been greater. There are two ways to improve the ROI of brand marketing: Create more brand-building programs that are so differentiated and efficient that they boost awareness, purchase intent, and ultimately sales and market share; or increase the synergies and impact among the firm's individual brand-building programs so that the whole is greater than the sum of the parts.

Each path is strewn with obstacles, however. Achieving home runs in brand building has always been difficult; the increasingly cluttered and complex media environment makes it even more so. The era of mass media, when the challenge was merely to have memorable advertising, is itself a memory. The modern explosion of television channels and magazine titles, combined with many new brand-building options, means that it is much harder for on-brand executions to break out of the clutter and gain notice. Equally problematic, with so many channels and vehicles involved, brand-building efforts are increasingly diffuse, inconsistent, and ad hoc—not the coherent, consistent, and integrated programs they should be.

Similar forces conspire to inhibit the effectiveness of individual and integrated brand-building programs, taxing even the best marketing organizations. Brand implementation in a fragmented media environment needs to involve sets of disparate communications companies or autonomous parts of companies; victory for a particular brand-building effort is just as hard to attain as are powerful, integrative, synergistic programs. Creating alliances or virtual firms to deliver integrated brand building has had, at best, limited and ephemeral success.

Brand building is an area in which the Internet could change everything. Indeed, the real transforming power of the Internet derives from its ability to serve as the central organizing platform for integrated marketing communications programs—the glue that holds disparate channels and executions together, making them a cohesive force. Turning the Internet into the medium that rationalizes a firm's multiplicity of brand-building programs has the potential to change both perception and (the resulting) reality for the brand marketer.

But the Internet can address today's communications challenges only if its role in the brand-building process and its place in the organization are reimagined and reshaped. Too often, companies perceive the Internet simply as another channel. That view positions the Net as a minor player in the media mix—a direct-marketing vehicle for some, an ancillary brand-communications venue for others, analogous to the painted VW Beetles some companies deploy as traveling billboards.

If a business wants the Internet to add leverage to a brand and its communications program, the business must start with a holistic view of brand building. An organizational structure and culture that encourages and supports synergies between brand-building programs in general, and between the Internet and other programs in particular, must exist. The all-too-typical treatment of the interactive channel as a specialized silo, separated from other communications support, makes it very hard to generate the synergies that are usually possible.

Companies must mesh Internet capabilities into the entire brand-building effort, with the whole driven by a common brand vision. They need to think creatively and more broadly about brand-building programs, recognizing the Internet as one of the components. Can employing the Internet leverage existing or conventional brand-building programs? Are there new programs that simply would not work without the Internet? Can the product offering itself be enhanced by adding an Internet component? Just considering these questions will create opportunities.

The Power of Involvement

Three concepts, already in use by a few advanced marketers, illustrate how the Internet can be turned into a mechanism to integrate multichannel marketing programs effectively.

• **Amplification**. The Internet can add continuity and depth to single-channel marketing programs; the goal is to increase the engagement of existing and potential customers. The Internet can also provide a critical market-sensing test, providing marketers with metrics that help them decide whether to scale up or cut back programs in other media.

• **Differentiation**. The Internet can support a feature or service that will differentiate the brand, by augmenting a firm's services or products with information, entertainment, or other added values.

• **Integration**. The Internet can help integrate multiple brand-building approaches by being a common component and a forum where they can appear together, thus demonstrating synergy and consistency.

Behind all three concepts lies a single force: *involvement*. Absent its consideration, it is easy to dismiss the Internet as an insignificant brand-building tool. With click-through rates averaging around 0.2 percent, it's clear that most banner advertising doesn't work. The meltdown of so many e-commerce and e-content concepts (recall Pets.com and Eve.com) has shown that early assumptions about the Internet, such as that first-time visitors not only return again and again, but also respond to banner ads, were simply wrong.

Looking at the smoldering ruin that was digital mania, it is tempting to conclude that the Internet was overrated and oversold, and that its appropriate place is at the margins of a company's brand building, tucked somewhere between the catalog division and point-of-purchase display design.

But the medium's growth alone indicates that something powerful—and powerfully different—is at work in the online world. There are more than 75 million active users each month in the United States and 260 million worldwide, according to Nielsen//NetRatings Inc., which projects growth for at least five more years. Yahoo and AOL each get more than 100 million visitors a month worldwide.

Moreover, the time consumers spend on the medium continues to grow. The average at-home user in the U.S. now spends more than 10 hours per week on the Web, a figure that has increased markedly for at least the last three years. For AOL members, the number is much higher, as it is for workplace users. This involvement in the medium—for consumption of the Internet is, by definition, active, requiring a continuing series of decisions and actions, which distinguishes it from the more passive consumption of conventional media—adds a dimension

to communications between the brand and consumer that is potentially even greater than the engagement difference of radio over newspapers, or television over radio.

The involvement power of a medium is of central importance to marketers. The strength of a brand depends on customer–brand relationships. Such relationships are defined by the quality, intensity, and quantity of the experiences that link the brand with its customers or potential customers. Relationships can translate into loyalty, which, even if weak, can help drive crucial incremental sales and share gains. The Internet provides the opportunity to create additional experiences, experiences that are potentially positive and meaningful, even when they are not intense.

Leverage and Amplify

Brand-building programs can be rendered more effective when the online presence is used to amplify such offline programs as customer promotions, sponsorships, guerrilla marketing, retail experience, and even advertising. Offline programs can do the same for online branding.

Sometimes online support can mean the difference between failure and success for a *customer promotion*. For example, from August to December 2000, PepsiCo Inc. ran a joint promotion with Yahoo Inc. in which 1.5 billion bottles of Pepsi and Mountain Dew branded soft drinks had caps containing codes that could be converted to "Pepsi-stuff points" on the www.pepsistuff.com or www.dew-stuff.com sites. Consumers could accumulate points they could then use to obtain prizes or as currency for shopping and auctions on Yahoo. The promotion attracted 3.5 million participants and boosted sales of both beverages by a total of 5 percent, especially impressive in the context of an industry experiencing almost no growth. Pepsi had held a similar version of that promotion offline three years earlier, with results so disappointing it abandoned the project. The Web support, however, turned it into a significant success.

Measurement tools, some unique to the Internet, help to make promotions more effective. By quantifying results and tracking user behavior, marketers can learn not only how many users visited a site, but also how many forwarded news of a given promotion to friends, how many product purchases were involved, and often from which sites visitors came. Such information can contribute to a marketing ROI analysis. In the Pepsi–Yahoo alliance, Pepsi could send e-mails to support the promotion, drawing its target audience from Yahoo's database of more than 200 million users. Responses by segment can lead to program refinement.

Sponsorships, too, can be leveraged via the Internet for greater effectiveness. For a sponsorship to realize its potential as a brand builder, the brand needs to be strongly associated and intimately involved with the event. Most sponsorship linkages to events suffer because they lack continuity and depth. The Internet can be a vehicle to create or support the association and involvement of the core audience.

Take the Valvoline auto racing program. The Valvoline Web site (http://www.valvoline.com/) extends and enriches the sponsorship experience. Valvoline.com has become a destination site for those involved with racing—the core customer base for Valvoline, a maker of motor oil and other automobile products. Visitors can access the schedule for NASCAR and other racing circuits and obtain results of recent races, complete with driver photos and interviews. The "Behind Closed Garage Doors" section provides commentary and analyses from a well-connected member of the motorsports community. Site visitors can "adopt" the Valvoline NASCAR team and learn about its finishes and the activities of the team members. In addition, it is possible to send Valvoline racing greeting cards, buy official Valvoline racing gear, download a Valvoline racing screensaver, and sign up for a weekly newsletter, *Track Talk*, which provides updates on the racing circuits. For customers, Valvoline thus becomes closely associated with the racing experience—it is far more involving than a mere logo on a car, and it has greater reach than any hospitality tent could ever hope to have.

For all the talk of virtuality, the Internet clearly can support the physical, in-store *retail experience*. At the Internet site of electronics retailer CompUSA Inc. (http://www.compusa.com/), for instance, visitors can check whether an item is in stock at a nearby store and get a map to find the store's location. Using in-store computers, customers can order out-of-stock or even never-stocked items from the company's Web site. The retail shopping experience becomes richer (and less frustrating) when the Web site is viewed as a complement to, rather than a competitor of, the retail presence.

Guerrilla marketing programs can also be leveraged using the Web. Guerrilla marketing covers offbeat—but on-brand—programs that use unconventional communications vehicles to create conversation and awareness, breaking through the clutter that diminishes the effectiveness of measured media. By now, most brand marketers are aware of the guerrilla campaign that helped create buzz around the independently produced film *The Blair Witch Project* a few years ago.

Mainstream consumer products companies have also begun to employ the Internet to undergird offline guerrilla efforts. The venerable Oscar Mayer Wienermobile qualifies. Eight frankfurter-shaped vehicles tour the U.S.—each tagged with an appropriate license plate, such as "Hot Dog"—turning up at special sports events, parades, fairs, and the like. As engaging as these ambassadors for Oscar Mayer are, the Wienermobiles have limited reach; for most consumers, encountering one is a one-time experience. But, through its Web site, http://www.oscar-mayer.com/, Oscar Mayer allows children (or adults, for that matter) to experience the Wienermobile in multiple ways, over an extended time period. Consumers can take a virtual tour of the interior of a Wienermobile, and they can visit Oscartown, checking out such places as the Oscar Museum, the Oscar Mart, and Town Hall. At the online Family Fun Park, they can choose to play a game of "Weiner Pong," which uses hot dogs as paddles, or drive the animated Wiener Patrol, gaining points by picking up schoolchildren and Oscar Mayer products while avoiding mustard slicks. Wienermobilia such as T-shirts, Hot Wheels toy Weinermobiles, and Wienerwhistles can be purchased. There is a postcard pit stop from which an e-card featuring the Wienermobile can be sent. This "World Wide Wiener Web" leverages the Wienermobile program against the core target, giving the program much more power than it otherwise would have had.

Finally, even that most respectable of marketing communications tools, *measured media advertising*, can be amplified through the loudspeaker of the Internet. Too often, buying an ad represents the purchase of reach and frequency for a message that does not stick. An integrative Web program can multiply not only the exposure of the advertising, but, more important, its impact. Anheuser-Busch's Budweiser site (http://www.budweiser.com/) shows how. When the delightful Lizard and "Whassup" TV ads were attracting attention, customers could go to the Web site and play the spots. Fans could also purchase T-shirts and pool toys depicting Frank and Louis, the star lizards from the campaign. Further, e-cards were available to send to friends and family—an inexpensive but powerful way to leverage advertising symbols because they add personal endorsement to brand imagery. The potential of extending the life of the media message in a meaningful way, especially among the core target audience, can change the economics of the advertising.

Augmenting the Product

Differentiation, being perceived as uniquely and positively unlike competing offerings, is the key to strong brands. Without differentiation, there is no basis for selection or loyalty except price, which turns a brand into a commodity. Analyses by the global advertising agency Young & Rubicam Inc. (through its Brand Asset Evaluator database, which tracked thousands of brands over a nearly 10-year period) found that new brands enjoyed success when differentiation was high even if relevance, esteem, and recognition had not yet developed. Conversely, brands that saw their differentiation fade lost position even though their relevance, esteem, and recognition remained high.

As product classes mature—whether computers or retailing or packaged goods or pharmaceuticals or financial services—there is a tendency to see sameness in the product and service offerings. It is more difficult to create differentiation. Product refinements often get lost in a cluttered environment, and technical advances are copied quickly.

A classic way to achieve differentiation in mature categories is to augment the product, thereby redefining what is being purchased. For example, an industrial firm making expendable supplies may differentiate on the basis of logistical services, or even by supplying advice on managing operations rather than on the core product. The augmented product is differentiated, and it becomes the basis for a deeper customer relationship. When the augmented product defines a new product class, and the firm brands and actively manages it to create a lasting point of differentiation, it's a home run. Charles Schwab & Company hit just such a home run with its mutual fund One-Source branded service, which is now integrated into its Web site and represents a new and distinct category of Schwab brokerage services.

In contrast to offline avenues, which have been nearly exhausted through the years, the Internet still provides wide-open territory for product and service augmentation, and will be more likely to result in first-mover or fast-follower advantages. Again, though, the key is to think of the Internet not as a stand-alone media vehicle, but, rather, as a way to leverage the products and services of the business.

Consider the FedEx Corporation's Internet-based tracking system, which allows customers to find out exactly where their package is at any given point in the delivery process. FedEx has extended tracking to the handheld world of PDAs. The company has even moved beyond tracking to offer other online services, such as the FedEx Ship Manager, which allows registered users to track shipments, prepare labels online, maintain an online address book, get rate quotes, arrange pickups and dropoffs, and request delivery announcements and confirmations via e-mail. Such services augment FedEx's offerings, actually changing the customer's perception of what is being purchased, and transforming the nature of that customer's relationship with FedEx.

Financial and delivery services are both information-rich categories. But even the most conventional and mature product categories are open to Web-based differentiation.

Procter & Gamble Company's Pampers is a consumer good that struggles to create and maintain points of differentiation from other disposable-diaper brands. With the Pampers Web site (http://www.pampers.com/), it has created online programs to augment the basic product in a variety of ways. During last year's Pampers Perks loyalty program, consumers collected Pampers Points from diaper and wipes purchases and exchanged them for Fisher-Price and Sesame Street toys. The recent Pampers Vantastic Sweepstakes gave customers a chance to win a Chrysler minivan filled with diapers. The Pampers Gift Packs provide a convenient way to send a supply of Pampers—along with a Fisher-Price toy—to a friend. There is a playing center, learning center, and sharing center, where visitors can explore a variety of practical topics posted by other parents. The Pampers Parenting Institute offers advice from experts in child care, health, and development, as well as a parenting newsletter, *Parent Pages*, delivered by e-mail and customized to each stage of life from the third trimester through age 4. The Pampers Parenting Institute is also the visible driver of such programs as a public service campaign to reduce the risk of sudden infant death syndrome.

In part because of the Pampers Parenting Institute, Pampers is the second most popular baby-care site on the Web, with about 1 million unique visitors per month, many times more than are attracted to the site of the Kimberly-Clark Corporation's Huggies, Pampers's arch-competitor. And the financial impact is real; consumers visiting the Pampers site are 30 percent more likely to purchase Pampers, according to *Advertising Age*.

Another Procter & Gamble brand, Tide, has an online Tide Stain Detective (http://www.clothesline.com/) to stimulate traffic (and bookmarking) from those who realize that at some point in life, they will need advice on stain removal. The Stain Detective provides credibility and differentiation for a brand in a functional category.

Kraft boasts the Kraft Interactive Kitchen (http://www.kraftfoods.com/), one of the leading food sites, which features Kraft Kids Corner, Just for You, and Wisdom of Moms. Such branded features provide points of differentiation, which enhance brands that have a difficult time breaking out from the clutter of low-involvement activities and brands. It is no coincidence that, in early 2002, Kraftfoods.com and Tide.com were the No. 2 and No. 3 packaged-goods sites (after http://www.pg.com/), according to ComScore Networks.

Television, too, has historically been a commodity product, with networks—in the pre-cable age, certainly—all trafficking promiscuously in news, talk shows, situation comedies, dramas, and other conventional programming forms. Although the explosion of cable and satellite television channels has allowed producers more opportunity to create targeted programming, it has also made differentiation a necessity if a network is to attract and hold an audience and embed itself as the brand of choice.

In the competitive children's television category, Nickelodeon has maintained its leadership among the 8- to 12-year-old set in part via the Nick.com Web site, which gets 1.5 million visitors a week. This site gives the brand much more depth and a qualitatively stronger relationship with its target audience than would be possible with the television network alone.

Nickelodeon's favored position on the Web expands and deepens the parent brand's "have fun" brand experience, in large part by allowing kids to engage actively with the content (something that a passive medium like television cannot provide on its own). Kids can vote all day for their favorite music video, then see the winner played the same evening. Real-time multiplayer trivia tournaments can be played on the site, and winners can see their name on national television. Jimmy Neutron, a science-loving nerd, was introduced with several 30-second TV vignettes whose endings were available only on the Web site. The character has become one of Nickelodeon's strongest. Nick.com also started an e-Collectibles program that allows viewers to "buy" (with points earned by Web activi-

Internet Brand Building's Five Success Factors

Five success factors must be addressed if the Internet is to play an effective role in amplifying, differentiating, and integrating a brand and its communications.

1. The firm needs a clear brand identity and vision that drives all the brand-building programs. The key is to know your brand and what associations you want it to have—what user profiles, brand personality, organizational associations, emotional and self-expressive benefits, and functional benefits.

2. Companies must create an organization that allows the Internet to be integrated into the total brand-building effort of the firm. Indeed, the Internet must be integrated into the actual product and service offerings of the firm. For some companies, this will require a fundamental change in structure, people, and culture. No longer can the Internet be perceived as another communications medium to be managed by silo organizations of specialists.

3. Design matters. The Web site and other Internet components need to support the brand with a look, feel, and personality that is on-brand and consistent with the brand presence elsewhere. A good example is Pottery Barn's site (http://www.potterybarn.com/), where visitors can shop by viewing completely furnished rooms accompanied by lists of the products that decorate them. Consider also Harley-Davidson Inc. (http://www.harley-davidson.com/), whose site opens with a picture of an open road hugging a rugged shoreline and provides links to the Harley experience—all with the Harley feel and colors.

When the brand is represented by on-brand visuals and content, it becomes easier to detect programs that have not achieved on-brand focus. Achieving that focus is surprisingly difficult; even a casual surfer knows that few Web sites consistently represent what the brand stands for. This rather sad state of affairs is due in part to the functional need to be comprehensive, easy to navigate, and uncluttered, and in part to the lack of a clear vision.

4. Customers need to be motivated to come to the site and return regularly. Motivation usually involves information, entertainment, or interactive communication. The "if we build it, they will come" philosophy, heavy on "brochureware," has long been obsolete. There are a variety of ways to motivate return visits. ESPN.com, with more than 5 million visitors per day, attracts people regularly with its news from current sporting events. Sony's game site (www2.station.sony.com), which includes several versions of the popular Jeopardy game, was one of the most visited gaming sites in late 2001, with more than 6 million unique visitors per month. Nabiscoworld.com's games and sweepstakes have helped it become one of the top 10 packaged-goods sites in terms of the number of visitors, ahead of Coke and Pepsi. People come to the Pampers site to compare notes on the progress their babies have made and the challenges at each stage.

The restaurateur located on a busy corner will thrive. Similarly, the easiest way to get Internet traffic is to become part of a site that already has it. For example, Bolt, a leading site for teens and young adults, features sponsored contests from the likes of Hawaiian Punch, Ford, Kodak, Nike, Verizon, and Maybelline. Such an approach will have legs and long-term equity if a branded subsection of a well-traveled site such as Bolt, or ESPN or Disney or Yahoo, can be established. If not, much of the brand benefit will be transient. But the affiliated site must be on-brand as well as heavily trafficked because its associations will affect the brand in question.

5. The brand Web site needs to be linked to other brand-building programs or to the product or service itself. When the offline and online efforts are truly linked, traffic will be driven to the Web site. People are motivated to go to the Harley-Davidson site to relive "H.O.G. Rallys" and to plan new ones, for example. By comparison, using banner advertising or offline media spending to attract people to particular sites is usually expensive and ineffective.

The big payoff occurs when visiting the Web site is not a discrete action, but rather part of a large brand experience. Having the Nickelodeon television experience amplified with the interactive online component deepens the audience experience and thereby the audience's relationship with the brand.

—**D.A.A**.

ties) or trade cards to accumulate complete sets. When a Jimmy Neutron set of cards became available, 50,000 kids got involved during the first week.

To make Web-enabled product or service augmentation a sustainable point of differentiation, it is critical to brand it. Amazon.com was a pioneer in developing one of its most powerful features: the ability to recommend books and other products based on a customer's interests, as reflected by the individual's purchase and search history and the purchase history of others who bought similar offerings. But, regrettably, it never branded this service, and the feature quickly became a commodity—an expected offering of many e-commerce sites. If Amazon had branded the service and then actively managed it as part of the brand, improving the feature over time, it would have had a lasting point of differentiation that would have created an invaluable—perhaps insurmountable—barrier to entry. The Seattle retailer did not make the same mistake with 1-Click, a branded checkout service that plays a key role in defining Amazon in the messy e-tail marketplace.

The point is, you need to brand it! Pampers Perks, Tide Stain Detective, and Jimmy Neutron are all brands that are actively controlled and managed by their firms. As a result, each has the potential to gain the authenticity and energy that accompany a strong brand.

Building's Strongest Link

Perhaps the most powerful role the Internet can play in brand-building programs is that of integrator. It has the potential to provide a unifying link among the totality of communications efforts that surround a brand. Moreover, the medium can do this both internally and externally, helping the company improve its brand marketing and sales efforts while galvanizing support in the consumer marketplace.

Internally, the Web provides a single place in which all the firm's brand-building programs can appear. When one or more of these programs is off strategy in presentation or in content, the departure can be observed and understood by senior executives. The medium becomes a version of the big wall on which companies and their ad agencies used to attach and view the entirety of a brand's visual representations (i.e., ads, packaging, product designs, and brochures) in order to observe inconsistencies.

Externally, the Internet site has the potential to play an integrating role similar to that of an "event store," the way Niketown does for Nike. Niketown provides a total brand experience, with the full scope of the brand portrayed in a controlled context. Such a use of retail stores (the outdoor equipment retailers REI and L.L. Bean also employ them) portrays a brand in all its richness to an important segment of consumers, who get to see the brand as a whole, in an on-brand context, rather than in bits and pieces.

A well-designed Web site performs a comparable function, integrating disparate business units and communications programs into a coherent and cohesive narrative. The Martha Stewart site (http://www.marthastewart.com/), for example, brings together a wide spectrum of business units on a single site that effectively communicates the core identity of the brand—improve the quality of living in the home, elevate homemaking, and encourage do-it-yourself ingenuity. The Martha Stewart Signature section of the site details collections of coordinated decorator fabrics (sold through fabric retailers) and

paints (sold exclusively through Sherwin-Williams stores). Visitors clicking on Martha Stewart Everyday are linked to Kmart's site (http://www.bluelight.com/), where the housewares line is presented with a design characteristic of Martha Stewart, despite being on a different site. Martha Stewart Shop, the online version of the Martha by Mail catalog, sells a variety of cookware and gardening tools Ms. Stewart uses on her TV shows, as well as such on-brand products as craft kits and holiday-themed decorations. Visitors can preview the content of *Martha Stewart Living* magazine, check out the TV program lineup, and order transcripts of radio spots. Registered members of the site can share tips and ideas in the Bulletin Boards section.

The total impact of Marthastewart.com thus does more than support individual businesses and programs; it reflects the Martha Stewart brand in its entirety. Like many integrative sites, Marthastewart.com is primarily aimed at the loyal user: Its greatest value is in maximizing retention and increased purchases from "brand friends," and it has only a marginal effect on fringe buyers. Successful Internet brand builders have a core target group on which to focus. They don't try to service a broad audience.

The Internet has the power to revolutionize brand building, to create new forms of differentiation, to make brand-building programs more effective, and to help companies move toward the elusive goal of providing integrated, consistent, and synergistic brand building. Businesses need to get out of the silo mentality both conceptually and organizationally. The Internet can make that happen because it can link to all the other brand-building efforts.

Resources

David A. Aaker, "Tactical Blunders in Internet Advertising," *s+b*, Second Quarter 2000.
Horacio D. Rozanski, Gerry Bollman, and Martin Lipman, "Seize the Occasion! The Seven-Segment System for Online Marketing," *s+b*, Third Quarter 2001.
David A. Aaker, *Building Strong Brands* (Simon & Schuster Inc., Free Press, 1995)
David A. Aaker and Erich Joachimsthaler, *Brand Leadership: Building Assets in an Information Economy* (Simon & Schuster Inc., Free Press, 2000)

David A. Aaker, aaker@haas.berkeley.edu is the vice chairman of Prophet Brand Strategy, a brand marketing consulting group, and professor emeritus of marketing strategy at the Haas School of Business, University of California, Berkeley. He is the author of 11 books, most recently *Brand Leadership: Building Assets in an Information Economy* (Simon & Schuster Inc., Free Press, 2000), written with Erich Joachimsthaler

From *strategy+business*, Third Quarter 2002, Issue 28, pp. 48-57. © 2002 by strategy+business.

Marketing myopia
(With Retrospective Commentary)

Shortsighted managements often fail to recognize that in fact there is no such thing as a growth industry

Theodore Levitt

How can a company ensure its continued growth? In 1960 "Marketing Myopia" answered that question in a new and challenging way by urging organizations to define their industries broadly to take advantage of growth opportunities. Using the archetype of the railroads, Mr. Levitt showed how they declined inevitably as technology advanced because they defined themselves too narrowly. To continue growing, companies must ascertain and act on their customers' needs and desires, not bank on the presumptive longevity of their products. The success of the article testifies to the validity of its message. It has been widely quoted and anthologized, and HBR has sold more than 265,000 reprints of it. The author of 14 subsequent articles in HBR, Mr. Levitt is one of the magazine's most prolific contributors. In a retrospective commentary, he considers the use and misuse that have been made of "Marketing Myopia," describing its many interpretations and hypothesizing about its success.

Every major industry was once a growth industry. But some that are now riding a wave of growth enthusiasm are very much in the shadow of decline. Others which are thought of as seasoned growth industries have actually stopped growing. In every case the reason growth is threatened, slowed, or stopped is *not* be- cause the market is saturated. It is because there has been a failure of management.

Fateful purposes: The failure is at the top. The executives responsible for it, in the last analysis, are those who deal with broad aims and policies. Thus:

• The railroads did not stop growing because the need for passenger and freight transportation declined. That grew. The railroads are in trouble today not because the need was filled by others (cars, trucks, airplanes, even telephones), but because it was *not* filled by the railroads themselves. They let others take customers away from them because they assumed themselves to be in the railroad business rather than in the transportation business. The reason they defined their industry wrong was because they were railroad-oriented instead of transportation-oriented; they were product-oriented instead of customer-oriented.

• Hollywood barely escaped being totally ravished by television. Actually, all the established film companies went through drastic reorganizations. Some simply disappeared. All of them got into trouble not because of TV's inroads but because of their own myopia. As with the railroads, Hollywood defined its business incorrectly. It thought it was in the movie business when it was actually in the entertainment business. "Movies" implied a specific, limited product. This produced a fatuous contentment which from the beginning led producers to view TV as a threat. Hollywood scorned and rejected TV when it should have welcomed it as an opportunity—an opportunity to expand the entertainment business.

Today TV is a bigger business than the old narrowly defined movie business ever was. Had Hollywood been customer-oriented (providing entertainment), rather then product-oriented (making movies), would it have gone through the fiscal purgatory that it did? I doubt it. What ultimately saved Hollywood and accounted for its recent resurgence was the wave of new young writers, producers, and directors whose previous successes in television had decimated the old movie companies and toppled the big movie moguls.

There are other less obvious examples of industries that have been and are now endangering their futures by improperly defining their purposes. I shall discuss some in detail later and analyze the kind of policies that lead to trouble. Right now it may help to show what a thoroughly customer-oriented management can do to keep a growth industry growing, even after the obvious opportunities have been exhausted; and here there are two examples that have been around for a long time. They are nylon and glass—specifically,

E. I. duPont de Nemours & Company and Corning Glass Works.

Both companies have great technical competence. Their product orientation is unquestioned. But this alone does not explain their success. After all, who was more pridefully product-oriented and product-conscious than the erstwhile New England textile companies that have been so thoroughly massacred? The DuPonts and the Cornings have succeeded not primarily because of their product or research orientation but because they have been thoroughly customer-oriented also. It is constant watchfulness for opportunities to apply their technical knowhow to the creation of customer-satisfying uses which accounts for their prodigious output of successful new products. Without a very sophisticated eye on the customer, most of their new products might have been wrong, their sales methods useless.

Aluminum has also continued to be a growth industry, thanks to the efforts of two wartime-created companies which deliberately set about creating new customer-satisfying uses. Without Kaiser Aluminum & Chemical Corporation and Reynolds Metals Company, the total demand for aluminum today would be vastly less.

Error of analysis: Some may argue that it is foolish to set the railroads off against aluminum or the movies off against glass. Are not aluminum and glass naturally so versatile that the industries are bound to have more growth opportunities than the railroads and movies? This view commits precisely the error I have been talking about. It defines an industry, or a product, or a cluster of know-how so narrowly as to guarantee its premature senescence. When we mention "railroads," we should make sure we mean "transportation." As transporters, the railroads still have a good chance for very considerable growth. They are not limited to the railroad business as such (though in my opinion rail transportation is potentially a much stronger transportation medium than is generally believed).

What the railroads lack is not opportunity, but some of the same managerial imaginativeness and audacity that made them great. Even an amateur like Jacques Barzun can see what is lacking when he says:

"I grieve to see the most advanced physical and social organization of the last century go down in shabby disgrace for lack of the same comprehensive imagination that built it up. [What is lacking is] the will of the companies to survive and to sat-

isfy the public by inventiveness and skill."[1]

Shadow of obsolescence

It is impossible to mention a single major industry that did not at one time qualify for the magic appellation of "growth industry." In each case its assumed strength lay in the apparently unchallenged superiority of its product. There appeared to be no effective substitute for it. It was itself a runaway substitute for the product it so triumphantly replaced. Yet one after another of these celebrated industries has come under a shadow. Let us look briefly at a few more of them, this time taking examples that have so far received a little less attention:

• *Dry cleaning*—This was once a growth industry with lavish prospects. In an age of wool garments, imagine being finally able to get them safely and easily clean. The boom was on.

Yet here we are 30 years after the boom started and the industry is in trouble. Where has the competition come from? From a better way of cleaning? No. It has come from synthetic fibers and chemical additives that have cut the need for dry cleaning. But this is only the beginning. Lurking in the wings and ready to make chemical dry cleaning totally obsolescent is that powerful magician, ultrasonics.

• *Electric utilities*—This is another one of those supposedly "no-substitute" products that has been enthroned on a pedestal of invincible growth. When the incandescent lamp came along, kerosene lights were finished. Later the water wheel and the steam engine were cut to ribbons by the flexibility, reliability, simplicity, and just plain easy availability of electric motors. The prosperity of electric utilities continues to wax extravagant as the home is converted into a museum of electric gadgetry. How can anybody miss by investing in utilities, with no competition, nothing but growth ahead?

But a second look is not quite so comforting. A score of nonutility companies are well advanced toward developing a powerful chemical fuel cell which could sit in some hidden closet of every home silently ticking off electric power. The electric lines that vulgarize so many neighborhoods will be eliminated. So will the endless demolition of streets and service interruptions during storms. Also on

the horizon is solar energy, again pioneered by nonutility companies.

Who says that the utilities have no competition? They may be natural monopolies now, but tomorrow they may be natural deaths. To avoid this prospect, they too will have to develop fuel cells, solar energy, and other power sources. To survive, they themselves will have to plot the obsolescence of what now produces their livelihood.

• *Grocery stores*—Many people find it hard to realize that there ever was a thriving establishment known as the "corner grocery store." The supermarket has taken over with a powerful effectiveness. Yet the big food chains of the 1930s narrowly escaped being completely wiped out by the aggressive expansion of independent supermarkets. The first genuine supermarket was opened in 1930, in Jamaica, Long Island. By 1933 supermarkets were thriving in California, Ohio, Pennsylvania, and elsewhere. Yet the established chains pompously ignored them. When they chose to notice them, it was with such derisive descriptions as "cheapy," "horse-and-buggy," "cracker-barrel storekeeping," and "unethical opportunists."

The executive of one big chain announced at the time that he found it "hard to believe that people will drive for miles to shop for foods and sacrifice the personal service chains have perfected and to which Mrs. Consumer is accustomed."[2] As late as 1936, the National Wholesale Grocers convention and the New Jersey Retail Grocers Association said there was nothing to fear. They said that the supers' narrow appeal to the price buyer limited the size of their market. They had to draw from miles around. When imitators came, there would be wholesale liquidations as volume fell. The current high sales of the supers was said to be partly due to their novelty. Basically people wanted convenient neighborhood grocers. If the neighborhood stores "cooperate with their suppliers, pay attention to their costs, and improve their service," they would be able to weather the competition until it blew over.[3]

It never blew over. The chains discovered that survival required going into the supermarket business. This meant the wholesale destruction of their huge investments in corner store sites and in established distribution and merchandising methods. The companies with "the courage of their convictions" resolutely stuck to the corner store philosophy. They kept their pride but lost their shirts.

Self-deceiving cycle: But memories are short. For example, it is hard for people who today confidently hail the twin messiahs of electronics and chemicals to see how things could possibly go wrong with these galloping industries. They probably also cannot see how a reasonably sensible businessman could have been as myopic as the famous Boston millionaire who 50 years ago unintentionally sentenced his heirs to poverty by stipulating that his entire estate be forever invested exclusively in electric streetcar securities. His posthumous declaration, "There will always be a big demand for efficient urban transportation," is no consolation to his heirs who sustain life by pumping gasoline at automobile filling stations.

Yet, in a casual survey I recently took among a group of intelligent business executives, nearly half agreed that it would be hard to hurt their heirs by tying their estates forever to the electronics industry. When I then confronted them with the Boston streetcar example, they chorused unanimously, "That's different!" But is it? Is not the basic situation identical?

In truth, *there is no such thing* as a growth industry, I believe. There are only companies organized and operated to create and capitalize on growth opportunities. Industries that assume themselves to be riding some automatic growth escalator invariably descend into stagnation. The history of every dead and dying "growth" industry shows a self-deceiving cycle of bountiful expansion and undetected decay. There are four conditions which usually guarantee this cycle:

1. The belief that growth is assured by an expanding and more affluent population.
2. The belief that there is no competitive substitute for the industry's major product.
3. Too much faith in mass production and in the advantages of rapidly declining unit costs as output rises.
4. Preoccupation with a product that lends itself to carefully controlled scientific experimentation, improvement, and manufacturing cost reduction.

I should like now to begin examining each of these conditions in some detail. To build my case as boldly as possible, I shall illustrate the points with reference to three industries—petroleum, automobiles, and electronics—particularly petroleum, because it spans more years and more vicissitudes. Not only do these three have excellent reputations with the general public and also enjoy the confidence of sophisticated investors, but their managements have become known for progressive thinking in areas like financial control, product research, and management training. If obsolescence can cripple even these industries, it can happen anywhere.

Population myth

The belief that profits are assured by an expanding and more affluent population is dear to the heart of every industry. It takes the edge off the apprehensions everybody understandably feels about the future. If consumers are multiplying and also buying more of your product or service, you can face the future with considerably more comfort than if the market is shrinking. An expanding market keeps the manufacturer from having to think very hard or imaginatively. If thinking is an intellectual response to a problem, then the absence of a problem leads to the absence of thinking. If your product has an automatically expanding market, then you will not give much thought to how to expand it.

One of the most interesting examples of this is provided by the petroleum industry. Probably our oldest growth industry, it has an enviable record. While there are some current apprehensions about its growth rate, the industry itself tends to be optimistic.

But I believe it can be demonstrated that it is undergoing a fundamental yet typical change. It is not only ceasing to be a growth industry, but may actually be a declining one, relative to other business. Although there is widespread unawareness of it, I believe that within 25 years the oil industry may find itself in much the same position of retrospective glory that the railroads are now in. Despite its pioneering work in developing and applying the present-value method of investment evaluation, in employee relations, and in working with backward countries, the petroleum business is a distressing example of how complacency and wrongheadedness can stubbornly convert opportunity into near disaster.

One of the characteristics of this and other industries that have believed very strongly in the beneficial consequences of an expanding population, while at the same time being industries with a generic product for which there has appeared to be no competitive substitute, is that the individual companies have sought to outdo their competitors by improving on what they are already doing. This makes sense, of course, if one assumes that sales are tied to the country's population strings, because the customer can compare products only on a feature-by-feature basis. I believe it is significant, for example, that not since John D. Rockefeller sent free kerosene lamps to China has the oil industry done anything really outstanding to create a demand for its product. Not even in product improvement has it showered itself with eminence. The greatest single improvement—namely, the development of tetraethyl lead—came from outside the industry, specifically from General Motors and DuPont. The big contributions made by the industry itself are confined to the technology of oil exploration, production, and refining.

Asking for trouble: In other words, the industry's efforts have focused on improving the *efficiency* of getting and making its product, not really on improving the generic product or its marketing. Moreover, its chief product has continuously been defined in the narrowest possible terms, namely, gasoline, not energy, fuel, or transportation. This attitude has helped assure that:

• Major improvements in gasoline quality tend not to originate in the oil industry. Also, the development of superior alternative fuels comes from outside the oil industry, as will be shown later.

• Major innovations in automobile fuel marketing are originated by small new oil companies that are not primarily preoccupied with production or refining. These are the companies that have been responsible for the rapidly expanding multipump gasoline stations, with their successful emphasis on large and clean layouts, rapid and efficient driveway service, and quality gasoline at low prices.

Thus, the oil industry is asking for trouble from outsiders. Sooner or later, in this land of hungry inventors and entrepreneurs, a threat is sure to come. The possibilities of this will become more apparent when we turn to the next dangerous belief of many managements. For the sake of continuity, because this second belief is tied closely to the first, I shall continue with the same example.

Idea of indispensability: The petroleum industry is pretty much persuaded that there is no competitive substitute for its major product, gasoline—or if there is, that it will continue to be a derivative of crude oil, such as diesel fuel or kerosene jet fuel.

There is a lot of automatic wishful thinking in this assumption. The trouble is that most refining companies own huge amounts of crude oil reserves. These have value only if there is a market for products into which oil can be converted—hence the tenacious belief in the continuing competitive superiority of automobile fuels made from crude oil.

This idea persists despite all historic evidence against it. The evidence not only shows that oil has never been a superior product for any purpose for very long, but it also shows that the oil industry has never really been a growth industry. It has been a succession of different businesses that have gone through the usual historic cycles of growth, maturity, and decay. Its overall survival is owed to a series of miraculous escapes from total obsolescence, of last-minute and unexpected reprieves from total disaster reminiscent of the Perils of Pauline.

Perils of petroleum: I shall sketch in only the main episodes.

First, crude oil was largely a patent medicine. But even before that fad ran out, demand was greatly expanded by the use of oil in kerosene lamps. The prospect of lighting the world's lamps gave rise to an extravagant promise of growth. The prospects were similar to those the industry now holds for gasoline in other parts of the world. It can hardly wait for the underdeveloped nations to get a car in every garage.

In the days of the kerosene lamp, the oil companies competed with each other and against gaslight by trying to improve the illuminating characteristics of kerosene. Then suddenly the impossible happened. Edison invented a light which was totally nondependent on crude oil. Had it not been for the growing use of kerosene in space heaters, the incandescent lamp would have completely finished oil as a growth industry at that time. Oil would have been good for little else than axle grease.

Then disaster and reprieve struck again. Two great innovations occurred, neither originating in the oil industry. The successful development of coal-burning domestic central-heating systems made the space heater obsolescent. While the industry reeled, along came its most magnificent boost yet—the internal combustion engine, also invented by outsiders. Then when the prodigious expansion for gasoline finally began to level off in the 1920s, along came the miraculous escape of a central oil heater. Once again, the escape was provided by an outsider's invention and development. And when that market weakened, wartime demand for aviation fuel came to the rescue. After the war the expansion of civilian aviation, the dieselization of railroads, and the explosive demand for cars and trucks kept the industry's growth in high gear.

Meanwhile, centralized oil heating—whose boom potential had only recently been proclaimed—ran into severe competition from natural gas. While the oil companies themselves owned the gas that now competed with their oil, the industry did not originate the natural gas revolution, nor has it to this day greatly profited from its gas ownership. The gas revolution was made by newly formed transmission companies that marketed the product with an aggressive ardor. They started a magnificent new industry, first against the advice and then against the resistance of the oil companies.

By all the logic of the situation, the oil companies themselves should have made the gas revolution. They not only owned the gas; they also were the only people experienced in handling, scrubbing, and using it, the only people experienced in pipeline technology and transmission, and they understood heating problems. But, partly because they knew that natural gas would compete with their own sale of heating oil, the oil companies pooh-poohed the potentials of gas.

The revolution was finally started by oil pipeline executives who, unable to persuade their own companies to go into gas, quit and organized the spectacularly successful gas transmission companies. Even after their success became painfully evident to the oil companies, the latter did not go into gas transmission. The multibillion dollar business which should have been theirs went to others. As in the past, the industry was blinded by its narrow preoccupation with a specific product and the value of its reserves. It paid little or no attention to its customers' basic needs and preferences.

The postwar years have not witnessed any change. Immediately after World War II the oil industry was greatly encouraged about its future by the rapid expansion of demand for its traditional line of products. In 1950 most companies projected annual rates of domestic expansion of around 6% through at least 1975. Though the ratio of crude oil reserves to demand in the Free World was about 20 to 1, with 10 to 1 being usually considered a reasonable working ratio in the United States, booming demand sent oil men searching for more without sufficient regard to what the future really promised. In 1952 they "hit" in the Middle East; the ratio skyrocketed to 42 to 1. If gross additions to reserves continue at the average rate of the past five years (37 billion barrels annually), then by 1970 the reserve ratio will be up to 45 to 1. This abundance of oil has weakened crude and product prices all over the world.

Uncertain future: Management cannot find much consolation today in the rapidly expanding petrochemical industry, another oil-using idea that did not originate in the leading firms. The total United States production of petrochemicals is equivalent to about 2% (by volume) of the demand for all petroleum products. Although the petrochemical industry is now expected to grow by about 10% per year, this will not offset other drains on the growth of crude oil consumption. Furthermore, while petrochemical products are many and growing, it is well to remember that there are nonpetroleum sources of the basic raw material, such as coal. Besides, a lot of plastics can be produced with relatively little oil. A 5,000-barrel-per-day oil refinery is now considered the absolute minimum size for efficiency. But a 5,000-barrel-per-day chemical plant is a giant operation.

Oil has never been a continuously strong growth industry. It has grown by fits and starts, always miraculously saved by innovations and developments not of its own making. The reason it has not grown in a smooth progression is that each time it thought it had a superior product safe from the possibility of competitive substitutes, the product turned out to be inferior and notoriously subject to obsolescence. Until now, gasoline (for motor fuel, anyhow) has escaped this fate. But, as we shall see later, it too may be on its last legs.

The point of all this is that there is no guarantee against product obsolescence. If a company's own research does not make it obsolete, another's will. Unless an industry is especially lucky, as oil has been until now, it can easily go down in a sea of red figures—just as the railroads have, as the buggy whip manufacturers have, as the corner grocery chains have, as most of the big movie companies have, and indeed as many other industries have.

The best way for a firm to be lucky is to make its own luck. That requires knowing what makes a business successful. One of the greatest enemies of this knowledge is mass production.

Production pressures

Mass-production industries are impelled by a great drive to produce all they can. The prospect of steeply declining unit costs as output rises is more than most companies can usually resist. The profit possibilities look spectacular. All effort focuses on production. The result is that marketing gets neglected.

John Kenneth Galbraith contends that just the opposite occurs.[4] Output is so prodigious that all effort concentrates on trying to get rid of it. He says this accounts for singing commercials, desecration of the countryside with advertising signs, and other wasteful and vulgar practices. Galbraith has a finger on something real, but he misses the strategic point. Mass production does indeed generate great pressure to "move" the product. But what usually gets emphasized is selling, not marketing. Marketing, being a more sophisticated and complex process, gets ignored.

The difference between marketing and selling is more than semantic. Selling focuses on the needs of the seller, marketing on the needs of the buyer. Selling is preoccupied with the seller's need to convert his product into cash, marketing with the idea of satisfying the needs of the customer by means of the product and the whole cluster of things associated with creating, delivering, and finally consuming it.

In some industries the enticements of full mass production have been so powerful that for many years top management in effect has told the sales departments, "You get rid of it; we'll worry about profits." By contrast, a truly marketing-minded firm tries to create value-satisfying goods and services that consumers will want to buy. What it offers for sale includes not only the generic product or service, but also how it is made available to the customer, in what form, when, under what conditions, and at what terms of trade. Most important, what it offers for sale is determined not by the seller but by the buyer. The seller takes his cues from the buyer in such a way that the product becomes a consequence of the marketing effort, not vice versa.

Lag in Detroit: This may sound like an elementary rule of business, but that does not keep it from being violated wholesale. It is certainly more violated than honored. Take the automobile industry.

Here mass production is most famous, most honored, and has the greatest impact on the entire society. The industry has hitched its fortune to the relentless requirements of the annual model change, a policy that makes customer orientation an especially urgent necessity. Consequently the auto companies annually spend millions of dollars on consumer research. But the fact that the new compact cars are selling so well in their first year indicates that Detroit's vast researches have for a long time failed to reveal what the customer really wanted. Detroit was not persuaded that he wanted anything different from what he had been getting until it lost millions of customers to other small car manufacturers.

How could this unbelievable lag behind consumer wants have been perpetuated so long? Why did not research reveal consumer preferences before consumers' buying decisions themselves revealed the facts? Is that not what consumer research is for—to find out before the fact what is going to happen? The answer is that Detroit never really researched the customer's wants. It only researched his preferences between the kinds of things which it had already decided to offer him. For Detroit is mainly product-oriented, not customer-oriented. To the extent that the customer is recognized as having needs that the manufacturer should try to satisfy, Detroit usually acts as if the job can be done entirely by product changes. Occasionally attention gets paid to financing, too, but that is done more in order to sell than to enable the customer to buy.

As for taking care of other customer needs, there is not enough being done to write about. The areas of the greatest unsatisfied needs are ignored, or at best get stepchild attention. These are at the point of sale and on the matter of automotive repair and maintenance. Detroit views these problem areas as being of secondary importance. That is underscored by the fact that the retailing and servicing ends of this industry are neither owned and operated nor controlled by the manufacturers. Once the car is produced, things are pretty much in the dealer's inadequate hands. Illustrative of Detroit's arm's-length attitude is the fact that, while servicing holds enormous sales-stimulating, profit-building opportunities, only 57 of Chevrolet's 7,000 dealers provide night maintenance service.

Motorists repeatedly express their dissatisfaction with servicing and their apprehensions about buying cars under the present selling setup. The anxieties and problems they encounter during the auto buying and maintenance processes are probably more intense and widespread today than 30 years ago. Yet the automobile companies do not *seem* to listen to or take their cues from the anguished consumer. If they do listen, it must be through the filter of their own preoccupation with production. The marketing effort is still viewed as a necessary consequence of the product, not vice versa, as it should be. That is the legacy of mass production, with its parochial view that profit resides essentially in low-cost full production.

What Ford put first: The profit lure of mass production obviously has a place in the plans and strategy of business management, but it must always *follow* hard thinking about the customer. This is one of the most important lessons that we can learn from the contradictory behavior of Henry Ford. In a sense Ford was both the most brilliant and the most senseless marketer in American history. He was senseless because he refused to give the customer anything but a black car. He was brilliant because he fashioned a production system designed to fit market needs. We habitually celebrate him for the wrong reason, his production genius. His real genius was marketing. We think he was able to cut his selling price and therefore sell millions of $500 cars because his invention of the assembly line had reduced the costs. Actually he invented the assembly line because he had concluded that at $500 he could sell millions of cars. Mass production was the *result* not the cause of his low prices.

Ford repeatedly emphasized this point, but a nation of production-oriented business managers refuses to hear the great lesson he taught. Here is his operating philosophy as he expressed it succinctly:

"Our policy is to reduce the price, extend the operations, and improve the article. You will notice that the reduction of price comes first. We have never considered any costs as fixed. Therefore we first reduce the price to the point where we believe more sales will result. Then we go ahead and try to make the prices. We do not bother about the costs. The new price forces the costs down. The more usual way is to take the costs and then determine the price; and although that method may be scientific in the narrow sense, it is not scientific in the broad sense, because what earthly use is it to know the cost if it tells you that you cannot manufacture at a price at which the article can be sold? But more to the point is the fact that, although one may calculate what a cost is, and of course all of our costs are carefully calculated, no one knows what a cost ought to be. One of the ways of discovering ... is to name a price so low as to force everybody in the place to the highest point of efficiency.

The low price makes everybody dig for profits. We make more discoveries concerning manufacturing and selling under this forced method than by any method of leisurely investigation."[5]

Product provincialism: The tantalizing profit possibilities of low unit production costs may be the most seriously self-deceiving attitude that can afflict a company, particularly a "growth" company where an apparently assured expansion of demand already tends to undermine a proper concern for the importance of marketing and the customer.

The usual result of this narrow preoccupation with so-called concrete matters is that instead of growing, the industry declines. It usually means that the product fails to adapt to the constantly changing patterns of consumer needs and tastes, to new and modified marketing institutions and practices, or to product developments in competing or complementary industries. The industry has its eyes so firmly on its own specific product that it does not see how it is being made obsolete.

The classical example of this is the buggy whip industry. No amount of product improvement could stave off its death sentence. But had the industry defined itself as being in the transportation business rather than the buggy whip business, it might have survived. It would have done what survival always entails, that is, changing. Even if it had only defined its business as providing a stimulant or catalyst to an energy source, it might have survived by becoming a manufacturer of, say, fanbelts or air cleaners.

What may some day be a still more classical example is, again, the oil industry. Having let others steal marvelous opportunities from it (e.g., natural gas, as already mentioned, missile fuels, and jet engine lubricants), one would expect it to have taken steps never to let that happen again. But this is not the case. We are now getting extraordinary new developments in fuel systems specifically designed to power automobiles. Not only are these developments concentrated in firms outside the petroleum industry, but petroleum is almost systematically ignoring them, securely content in its wedded bliss to oil. It is the story of the kerosene lamp versus the incandescent lamp all over again. Oil is trying to improve hydrocarbon fuels rather than develop *any* fuels best suited to the needs of their users, whether or not made in different ways and with different raw materials from oil.

Here are some things which nonpetroleum companies are working on:

• Over a dozen such firms now have advanced working models of energy systems which, when perfected, will replace the internal combustion engine and eliminate the demand for gasoline. The superior merit of each of these systems is their elimination of frequent, time-consuming, and irritating refueling stops. Most of these systems are fuel cells designed to create electrical energy directly from chemicals without combustion. Most of them use chemicals that are not derived from oil, generally hydrogen and oxygen.

• Several other companies have advanced models of electric storage batteries designed to power automobiles. One of these is an aircraft producer that is working jointly with several electric utility companies. The latter hope to use off-peak generating capacity to supply overnight plug-in battery regeneration. Another company, also using the battery approach, is a medium-size electronics firm with extensive small-battery experience that it developed in connection with its work on hearing aids. It is collaborating with an automobile manufacturer. Recent improvements arising from the need for high-powered miniature power storage plants in rockets have put us within reach of a relatively small battery capable of withstanding great overloads or surges of power. Germanium diode applications and batteries using sintered-plate and nickel-cadmium techniques promise to make a revolution in our energy sources.

• Solar energy conversion systems are also getting increasing attention. One usually cautious Detroit auto executive recently ventured that solar-powered cars might be common by 1980.

As for the oil companies, they are more or less "watching developments," as one research director put it to me. A few are doing a bit of research on fuel cells, but almost always confined to developing cells powered by hydrocarbon chemicals. None of them are enthusiastically researching fuel cells, batteries, or solar power plants. None of them are spending a fraction as much on research in these profoundly important areas as they are on the usual run-of-the-mill things like reducing combustion chamber deposit in gasoline engines. One major integrated petroleum company recently took a tentative look at the fuel cell and concluded that although "the companies actively working on it indicate a belief in ultimate success … the

timing and magnitude of its impact are too remote to warrant recognition in our forecasts."

One might, of course, ask: Why should the oil companies do anything different? Would not chemical fuel cells, batteries, or solar energy kill the present product lines? The answer is that they would indeed, and that is precisely the reason for the oil firms having to develop these power units before their competitors, so they will not be companies without an industry.

Management might be more likely to do what is needed for its own preservation if it thought of itself as being in the energy business. But even that would not be enough if it persists in imprisoning itself in the narrow grip of its tight product orientation. It has to think of itself as taking care of customer needs, not finding, refining, or even selling oil. Once it genuinely thinks of its business as taking care of people's transportation needs, nothing can stop it from creating its own extravagantly profitable growth.

'Creative destruction': Since words are cheap and deeds are dear, it may be appropriate to indicate what this kind of thinking involves and leads to. Let us start at the beginning—the customer. It can be shown that motorists strongly dislike the bother, delay, and experience of buying gasoline. People actually do not buy gasoline. They cannot see it, taste it, feel it, appreciate it, or really test it. What they buy is the right to continue driving their cars. The gas station is like a tax collector to whom people are compelled to pay a periodic toll as the price of using their cars. This makes the gas station a basically unpopular institution. It can never be made popular or pleasant, only less unpopular, less unpleasant.

To reduce its unpopularity completely means eliminating it. Nobody likes a tax collector, not even a pleasantly cheerful one. Nobody likes to interrupt a trip to buy a phantom product, not even from a handsome Adonis or a seductive Venus. Hence, companies that are working on exotic fuel substitutes which will eliminate the need for frequent refueling are heading directly into the outstretched arms of the irritated motorist. They are riding a wave of inevitability, not because they are creating something which is technologically superior or more sophisticated, but because they are satisfying a powerful customer need. They are also eliminating noxious odors and air pollution.

Once the petroleum companies recognize the customer-satisfying logic of what another power system can do they will see that they have no more choice about working on an efficient, long-lasting fuel (or some way of delivering present fuels without bothering the motorist) than the big food chains had a choice about going into the supermarket business, or the vacuum tube companies had a choice about making semiconductors. For their own good the oil firms will have to destroy their own highly profitable assets. No amount of wishful thinking can save them from the necessity of engaging in this form of "creative destruction."

I phrase the need as strongly as this because I think management must make quite an effort to break itself loose from conventional ways. It is all too easy in this day and age for a company or industry to let its sense of purpose become dominated by the economies of full production and to develop a dangerously lopsided product orientation. In short, if management lets itself drift, it invariably drifts in the direction of thinking of itself as producing goods and services, not customer satisfactions. While it probably will not descend to the depths of telling its salesmen, "You get rid of it; we'll worry about profits," it can, without knowing it, be practicing precisely that formula for withering decay. The historic fate of one growth industry after another has been its suicidal product provincialism.

Dangers of R&D

Another big danger to a firm's continued growth arises when top management is wholly transfixed by the profit possibilities of technical research and development. To illustrate I shall turn first to a new industry—electronics—and then return once more to the oil companies. By comparing a fresh example with a familiar one, I hope to emphasize the prevalence and insidiousness of a hazardous way of thinking.

Marketing shortchanged: In the case of electronics, the greatest danger which faces the glamorous new companies in this field is not that they do not pay enough attention to research and development, but that they pay *too much* attention to it. And the fact that the fastest growing electronics firms owe their eminence to their heavy emphasis on technical research is completely beside the point. They have vaulted to affluence on a sudden crest of unusually strong general receptiveness to new technical ideas. Also, their success has been shaped in the virtually guaranteed market of military subsidies and by military orders that in many cases actually preceded the existence of facilities to make the products.

Their expansion has, in other words, been almost totally devoid of marketing effort.

Thus, they are growing up under conditions that come dangerously close to creating the illusion that a superior product will sell itself. Having created a successful company by making a superior product, it is not surprising that management continues to be oriented toward the product rather than the people who consume it. It develops the philosophy that continued growth is a matter of continued product innovation and improvement.

A number of other factors tend to strengthen and sustain this belief:

1. Because electronic products are highly complex and sophisticated, managements become top-heavy with engineers and scientists. This creates a selective bias in favor of research and production at the expense of marketing. The organization tends to view itself as making things rather than satisfying customer needs. Marketing gets treated as a residual activity, "something else" that must be done once the vital job of product creation and production is completed.

2. To this bias in favor of product research, development, and production is added the bias in favor of dealing with controllable variables. Engineers and scientists are at home in the world of concrete things like machines, test tubes, production lines, and even balance sheets. The abstractions to which they feel kindly are those which are testable or manipulatable in the laboratory, or, if not testable, then functional, such as Euclid's axioms. In short, the managements of the new glamour-growth companies tend to favor those business activities which lend themselves to careful study, experimentation, and control—the hard, practical realities of the lab, the shop, the books.

What gets shortchanged are the realities of the *market*. Consumers are unpredictable, varied, fickle, stupid, shortsighted, stubborn, and generally bothersome. This is not what the engineer-managers say, but deep down in their consciousness it is what they believe. And this accounts for their concentrating on what they know and what they can control, namely, product research, engineering, and production. The emphasis on production becomes particularly attractive when the product can be made at declining unit costs. There is no more in-

viting way of making money than by running the plant full blast.

Today the top-heavy science-engineering-production orientation of so many electronics companies works reasonably well because they are pushing into new frontiers in which the armed services have pioneered virtually assured markets. The companies are in the felicitous position of having to fill, not find markets; of not having to discover what the customer needs and wants, but of having the customer voluntarily come forward with specific new product demands. If a team of consultants had been assigned specifically to design a business situation calculated to prevent the emergence and development of a customer-oriented marketing viewpoint, it could not have produced anything better than the conditions just described.

Stepchild treatment: The oil industry is a stunning example of how science, technology, and mass production can divert an entire group of companies from their main task. To the extent the consumer is studied at all (which is not much), the focus is forever on getting information which is designed to help the oil companies improve what they are now doing. They try to discover more convincing advertising themes, more effective sales promotional drives, what the market shares of the various companies are, what people like or dislike about service station dealers and oil companies, and so forth. Nobody seems as interested in probing deeply into the basic human needs that the industry might be trying to satisfy as in probing into the basic properties of the raw material that the companies work with in trying to deliver customer satisfactions.

Basic questions about customers and markets seldom get asked. The latter occupy a stepchild status. They are recognized as existing, as having to be taken care of, but not worth very much real thought or dedicated attention. Nobody gets as excited about the customers in his own backyard as about the oil in the Sahara Desert. Nothing illustrates better the neglect of marketing than its treatment in the industry press.

The centennial issue of the *American Petroleum Institute Quarterly*, published in 1959 to celebrate the discovery of oil in Titusville, Pennsylvania, contained 21 feature articles proclaiming the industry's greatness. Only one of these talked about its achievements in marketing, and that was only a pictorial record of how service station architecture has changed. The issue also contained a special section on "New

Horizons," which was devoted to showing the magnificent role oil would play in America's future. Every reference was ebulliently optimistic, never implying once that oil might have some hard competition. Even the reference to atomic energy was a cheerful catalogue of how oil would help make atomic energy a success. There was not a single apprehension that the oil industry's affluence might be threatened or a suggestion that one "new horizon" might include new and better ways of serving oil's present customers.

But the most revealing example of the stepchild treatment that marketing gets was still another special series of short articles on "The Revolutionary Potential of Electronics." Under that heading this list of articles appeared in the table of contents:

- "In the Search for Oil"
- "In Production Operations"
- "In Refinery Processes"
- "In Pipeline Operations"

Significantly, every one of the industry's major functional areas is listed, *except* marketing. Why? Either it is believed that electronics holds no revolutionary potential for petroleum marketing (which is palpably wrong), or the editors forgot to discuss marketing (which is more likely, and illustrates its stepchild status).

The order in which the four functional areas are listed also betrays the alienation of the oil industry from the consumer. The industry is implicitly defined as beginning with the search for oil and ending with its distribution from the refinery. But the truth is, it seems to me, that the industry begins with the needs of the customer for its products. From that primal position its definition moves steadily back-stream to areas of progressively lesser importance, until it finally comes to rest at the "search for oil."

Beginning & end: The view that an industry is a customer-satisfying process, not a goods-producing process, is vital for all businessmen to understand. An industry begins with the customer and his needs, not with a patent, a raw material, or a selling skill. Given the customer's needs, the industry develops backwards, first concerning itself with the physical *delivery* of customer satisfactions. Then it moves back further to *creating* the things by which these satisfactions are in part achieved. How these materials are created is a matter of indifference to the customer, hence the particular form of manufacturing, processing, or what-have-you cannot be considered as a vital aspect of the industry.

Finally, the industry moves back still further to *finding* the raw materials necessary for making its products.

The irony of some industries oriented toward technical research and development is that the scientists who occupy the high executive positions are totally unscientific when it comes to defining their companies' overall needs and purposes. They violate the first two rules of the scientific method—being aware of and defining their companies' problems, and then developing testable hypotheses about solving them. They are scientific only about the convenient things, such as laboratory and product experiments.

The reason that the customer (and the satisfaction of his deepest needs) is not considered as being "the problem" is not because there is any certain belief that no such problem exists, but because an organizational lifetime has conditioned management to look in the opposite direction. Marketing is a stepchild.

I do not mean that selling is ignored. Far from it. But selling, again, is not marketing. As already pointed out, selling concerns itself with the tricks and techniques of getting people to exchange their cash for your product. It is not concerned with the values that the exchange is all about. And it does not, as marketing invariably does, view the entire business process as consisting of a tightly integrated effort to discover, create, arouse, and satisfy customer needs. The customer is somebody "out there" who, with proper cunning, can be separated from his loose change.

Actually, not even selling gets much attention in some technologically minded firms. Because there is a virtually guaranteed market for the abundant flow of their new products, they do not actually know what a real market is. It is as if they lived in a planned economy, moving their products routinely from factory to retail outlet. Their successful concentration on products tends to convince them of the soundness of what they have been doing, and they fail to see the gathering clouds over the market.

Conclusion

Less than 75 years ago American railroads enjoyed a fierce loyalty among astute Wall Streeters. European monarchs invested in them heavily. Eternal wealth was thought to be the benediction for anybody who could scrape a few thousand dollars together to put into rail stocks. No other form of transportation could compete with the

railroads in speed, flexibility, durability, economy, and growth potentials.

As Jacques Barzun put it, "By the turn of the century it was an institution, an image of man, a tradition, a code of honor, a source of poetry, a nursery of boyhood desires, a sublimest of toys, and the most solemn machine—next to the funeral hearse—that marks the epochs in man's life."[6]

Even after the advent of automobiles, trucks, and airplanes, the railroad tycoons remained imperturbably self-confident. If you had told them 30 years ago that in 30 years they would be flat on their backs, broke, and pleading for government subsidies, they would have thought you totally demented. Such a future was simply not considered possible. It was not even a discussable subject, or an askable question, or a matter which any sane person would consider worth speculating about. The very thought was insane. Yet a lot of insane notions now have matter-of-fact acceptance—for example, the idea of 100-ton tubes of metal moving smoothly through the air 20,000 feet above the earth, loaded with 100 sane and solid citizens casually drinking martinis—and they have dealt cruel blows to the railroads.

What specifically must other companies do to avoid this fate? What does customer orientation involve? These questions have in part been answered by the preceding examples and analysis. It would take another article to show in detail what is required for specific industries. In any case, it should be obvious that building an effective customer-oriented company involves far more than good intentions or promotional tricks; it involves profound matters of human organization and leadership. For the present, let me merely suggest what appear to be some general requirements.

Visceral feel of greatness: Obviously the company has to do what survival demands. It has to adapt to the requirements of the market, and it has to do it sooner rather than later. But mere survival is a so-so aspiration. Anybody can survive in some way or other, even the skid-row bum. The trick is to survive gallantly, to feel the surging impulse of commercial mastery; not just to experience the sweet smell of success, but to have the visceral feel of entrepreneurial greatness.

No organization can achieve greatness without a vigorous leader who is driven onward by his own pulsating *will to succeed*. He has to have a vision of grandeur, a vision that can produce eager followers in vast numbers. In business, the followers are the customers.

In order to produce these customers, the entire corporation must be viewed as a customer-creating and customer-satisfying organism. Management must think of itself not as producing products but as providing customer-creating value satisfactions. It must push this idea (and everything it means and requires) into every nook and cranny of the organization. It has to do this continuously and with the kind of flair that excites and stimulates the people in it. Otherwise, the company will be merely a series of pigeonholed parts, with no consolidating sense of purpose or direction.

In short, the organization must learn to think of itself not as producing goods or services but as *buying customers*, as doing the things that will make people *want* to do business with it. And the chief executive himself has the inescapable responsibility for creating this environment, this viewpoint, this attitude, this aspiration. He himself must set the company's style, its direction, and its goals. This means he has to know precisely where he himself wants to go, and to make sure the whole organization is enthusiastically aware of where that is. This is a first requisite of leadership, for *unless he knows where he is going, any road will take him there.*

If any road is okay, the chief executive might as well pack his attaché case and go fishing. If an organization does not know or care where it is going, it does not need to advertise that fact with a ceremonial figurehead. Everybody will notice it soon enough.

Retrospective commentary

Amazed, finally, by his literary success, Isaac Bashevis Singer reconciled an attendant problem: "I think the moment you have published a book, it's not any more your private property.... If it has value, everybody can find in it what he finds, and I cannot tell the man I did not intend it to be so." Over the past 15 years, "Marketing Myopia" has become a case in point. Remarkably, the article spawned a legion of loyal partisans—not to mention a host of unlikely bedfellows.

Its most common and, I believe, most influential consequence is the way certain companies for the first time gave serious thought to the question of what businesses they are really in.

The strategic consequences of this have in many cases been dramatic. The best-known case, of course, is the shift in think-

ing of oneself as being in the "oil business" to being in the "energy business." In some instances the payoff has been spectacular (getting into coal, for example) and in others dreadful (in terms of the time and money spent so far on fuel cell research). Another successful example is a company with a large chain of retail shoe stores that redefined itself as a retailer of moderately priced, frequently purchased, widely assorted consumer specialty products. The result was a dramatic growth in volume, earnings, and return on assets.

Some companies, again for the first time, asked themselves whether they wished to be masters of certain technologies for which they would seek markets, or be masters of markets for which they would seek customer-satisfying products and services.

Choosing the former, one company has declared, in effect, "We are experts in glass technology. We intend to improve and expand that expertise with the object of creating products that will attract customers." This decision has forced the company into a much more systematic and customer-sensitive look at possible markets and users, even though its stated strategic object has been to capitalize on glass technology.

Deciding to concentrate on markets, another company has determined that "we want to help people (primarily women) enhance their beauty and sense of youthfulness." This company has expanded its line of cosmetic products, but has also entered the fields of proprietary drugs and vitamin supplements.

All these examples illustrate the "policy" results of "Marketing Myopia." On the operating level, there has been, I think, an extraordinary heightening of sensitivity to customers and consumers. R&D departments have cultivated a greater "external" orientation toward uses, users, and markets—balancing thereby the previously one-sided "internal" focus on materials and methods; upper management has realized that marketing and sales departments should be somewhat more willingly accommodated than before, finance departments have become more receptive to the legitimacy of budgets for market research and experimentation in marketing, and salesmen have been better trained to listen to and understand customer needs and problems, rather than merely to "push" the product.

A mirror, not a window

My impression is that the article has had more impact in industrial-products compa-

nies than in consumer-products companies—perhaps because the former had lagged most in customer orientation. There are at least two reasons for this lag: (1) industrial-products companies tend to be more capital intensive, and (2) in the past, at least, they have had to rely heavily on communicating face-to-face the technical character of what they made and sold. These points are worth explaining.

Capital-intensive businesses are understandably preoccupied with magnitudes, especially where the capital, once invested, cannot be easily moved, manipulated, or modified for the production of a variety of products—e.g., chemical plants, steel mills, airlines, and railroads. Understandably, they seek big volumes and operating efficiencies to pay off the equipment and meet the carrying costs.

At least one problem results: corporate power becomes disproportionately lodged with operating or financial executives. If you read the charter of one of the nation's largest companies, you will see that the chairman of the finance committee, not the chief executive officer, is the "chief." Executives with such backgrounds have an almost trained incapacity to see that getting "volume" may require understanding and serving many discrete and sometimes small market segments, rather than going after a perhaps mythical batch of big or homogeneous customers.

These executives also often fail to appreciate the competitive changes going on around them. They observe the changes, all right, but devalue their significance or underestimate their ability to nibble away at the company's markets.

Once dramatically alerted to the concept of segments, sectors, and customers, though, managers of capital-intensive businesses have become more responsive to the necessity of balancing their inescapable preoccupation with "paying the bills" or breaking even with the fact that the best way to accomplish this may be to pay more attention to segments, sectors, and customers.

The second reason industrial products companies have probably been more influenced by the article is that, in the case of the more technical industrial products or services, the necessity of clearly communicating product and service characteristics to prospects results in a lot of face-to-face "selling" effort. But precisely because the product is so complex, the situation produces salesmen who know the product more than they know the customer, who are more adept at explaining what they have and what it can do than learning what the customer's needs and problems are. The result has been a narrow product orientation rather than a liberating customer orientation, and "service" often suffered. To be sure, sellers said, "We have to provide service," but they tended to define service by looking into the mirror rather than out the window. They *thought* they were looking out the window at the customer, but it was actually a mirror—a reflection of their own product-oriented biases rather than a reflection of their customers' situations.

A manifesto, not a prescription

Not everything has been rosy. A lot of bizarre things have happened as a result of the article:

- Some companies have developed what I call "marketing mania"—they've become obsessively responsive to every fleeting whim of the customer. Mass production operations have been converted to approximations of job shops, with cost and price consequences far exceeding the willingness of customers to buy the product.
- Management has expanded product lines and added new lines of business without first establishing adequate control systems to run more complex operations.
- Marketing staffs have suddenly and rapidly expanded themselves and their research budgets without either getting sufficient prior organizational support or, thereafter, producing sufficient results.
- Companies that are functionally organized have converted to product, brand, or market-based organizations with the expectation of instant and miraculous results. The outcome has been ambiguity, frustration, confusion, corporate infighting, losses, and finally a reversion to functional arrangements that only worsened the situation.

- Companies have attempted to "serve" customers by creating complex and beautifully efficient products or services that buyers are either too risk-averse to adopt or incapable of learning how to employ—in effect, there are now steam shovels for people who haven't yet learned to use spades. This problem has happened repeatedly in the so-called service industries (financial services, insurance, computer-based services) and with American companies selling in less-developed economies.

"Marketing Myopia" was not intended as analysis or even prescription; it was intended as manifesto. It did not pretend to take a balanced position. Nor was it a new idea—Peter F. Drucker, J. B. McKitterick, Wroe Alderson, John Howard, and Neil Borden had each done more original and balanced work on "the marketing concept." My scheme, however, tied marketing more closely to the inner orbit of business policy. Drucker—especially in *The Concept of the Corporation* and *The Practice of Management*—originally provided me with a great deal of insight.

My contribution, therefore, appears merely to have been a simple, brief, and useful way of communicating an existing way of thinking. I tried to do it in a very direct, but responsible fashion, knowing that few readers (customers), especially managers and leaders, could stand much equivocation or hesitation. I also knew that the colorful and lightly documented affirmation works better than the tortuously reasoned explanation.

But why the enormous popularity of what was actually such a simple preexisting idea? Why its appeal throughout the world to resolutely restrained scholars, implacably temperate managers, and high government officials, all accustomed to balanced and thoughtful calculation? Is it that concrete examples, joined to illustrate a simple idea and presented with some attention to literacy, communicate better

than massive analytical reasoning that reads as though it were translated from the German? Is it that provocative assertions are more memorable and persuasive than restrained and balanced explanations, no matter who the audience? Is it that the character of the message is as much the message as its content? Or was mine not simply a different tune, but a new symphony? I don't know.

Of course, I'd do it again and in the same way, given my purposes, even with what more I now know—the good and the bad, the power of facts and the limits of rhetoric. If your mission is the moon, you don't use a car. Don Marquis's cockroach, Archy, provides some final consolation: "an idea is not responsible for who believes in it."

Notes

1. Jacques Barzun, "Trains and the Mind of Man," *Holiday*, February 1960, p. 21.

2. For more details see M. M. Zimmerman, *The Super Market: A Revolution in Distribution* (New York, McGraw-Hill Book Company, Inc., 1955), p. 48.

3. Ibid., pp. 45–47.

4. *The Affluent Society* (Boston, Houghton Mifflin Company, 1958), pp. 152–160.

5. Henry Ford, *My Life and* Work (New York, Doubleday, Page & Company, 1923), pp. 146–147.

6. Jacques Barzun, "Trains and the Mind of Man," *Holiday*, February 1960, p. 20.

At the time of the article's publication, Theodore Levitt was lecturer in business administration at the Harvard Business School. He is the author of several books, including The Third Sector: New Tactics for a Responsive Society *(1973) and* Marketing for Business Growth *(1974).*

Why Customer Satisfaction
Starts with HR

There's convincing evidence that HR drives customer satisfaction—and corporate revenues—by careful attention to who is hired, how they are trained, how they are coached, and how they are treated on the job.

By Patrick J. Kiger

In a conference room at Philadelphia-based Rosenbluth International, one of the country's most successful travel agencies, a dozen new employees are participating in a customer-service training exercise. What's astonishing is that the new company associates are practicing how to provide *bad* customer service.

One group is asked to dream up the rudest ways a motor-vehicle bureau staff member could treat a hapless customer who comes in to apply for a driver's license. After a few minutes of preparation, the associates perform a skit for an audience of other new employees. The trainee who plays the customer arrives at the ersatz office and stands in line. Just as he reaches the counter, the trainee portraying the clerk posts a sign proclaiming that he'll be back in 15 minutes. Other trainees make the hands move on a fake clock to simulate the wait stretching to 20 minutes, then 30, then 40. As the customer pleads for service, the clerk—who is sitting behind the counter, reading a magazine and loudly cracking gum—berates him for his impatience. The ultimate indignity comes when the customer proceeds to the license-photo area and learns that the camera is broken.

Rosenbluth's HR team uses the exercise because it's fun, but mainly to focus trainees on a serious lesson: Customer service arguably is the most critical factor in an organization's long-term success and even survival.

There was a time when customer service was seen as the responsibility of sales managers and tech-support team leaders. Today that attitude is as dated as rotary telephones at corporate call centers. Increasingly, companies are recognizing that HR plays a seminal role in building a customer-friendly culture. Throughout the business world, HR departments are focusing their efforts on improving customer satisfaction. They're using HR activities—hiring, training, coaching, and evaluation pro-

grams—to give employees the tools and support they need to develop and nurture positive, lasting relationships with clients.

The evidence is compelling that HR practices can promote customer satisfaction—and, in the process, improve corporate revenues. A landmark 1999 analysis of 800 Sears Roebuck stores, for example, demonstrated that for every 5 percent improvement in employee attitudes, customer satisfaction increased 1.3 percent and corporate revenue rose a half-percentage point.

Most service-quality gurus say that hiring is not only the first, but the most critical step in building a customer-friendly company.

Moreover, subtle changes in hiring or training sometimes can produce major improvements in customer happiness. One of this year's *Workforce* Optimas Award winners, NCCI Holdings Inc., discovered in a survey last year that its customers wanted more help in using the company's insurance-data software products. As a result, NCCI created a training initiative to give its customer-service reps more technical expertise. By the fourth quarter, the surveys were showing that customers were much more favorably impressed with the reps' technical abilities. Apparently as a result, the overall customer-satisfaction rating rose 33 percent during that period, from 6 to 8 on a 10-point scale.

A company with strong customer satisfaction and loyalty can survive and prosper even when faced with a tough economy or an unforeseen disaster. The salient example: Southwest Airlines, which consistently ranks first among airlines in customer satisfaction. Following the September 11 terrorist attacks, which pushed many airline companies to the brink of demise, Southwest actually managed to post a profit in the fourth quarter of 2001, and was confident enough about the future to add new routes.

Conversely, a company that provides lousy service may have trouble hanging on to its customers over time, and thus may be forced to continually replace lost accounts that have fled in frustration. The cost of acquiring new customers is five times higher than the expense of servicing existing ones, says Michael DeSanto, a consultant for Walker Information, an Indianapolis-based business research firm. At that rate, chronically dysfunctional customer service becomes a monster that can devour whatever gains a company is making in other areas. If that company runs into a stalled economy or an aggressive competitor, its bad customer karma can prove fatal.

For proof, you only have to look at Kmart, the once-mighty discount retailer that went bankrupt in January, at least in part because it couldn't compete with the famously courteous folks at Wal-Mart. (A recent study by MOHR Learning, a New Jersey-based consulting firm, found that 20 percent of customers will immediately walk out of a store when confronted by bad service, and 26 percent will warn their friends and neighbors not to shop there.) Last year, the Dow Jones News Service reported that customer dissatisfaction was costing the McDonald's chain a breathtaking $750 million in lost business annually.

Identifying employees with customer-satisfaction potential

Most service-quality gurus say that hiring is the first and most critical step in building a customer-friendly company. "You need to be selective," says Ron Zemke, president of the consulting firm Performance Research Associates, located in Minneapolis. "It's a lot easier to start with people who've got the right personality qualities to work with customers than it is to struggle to teach those skills to whoever walks in the door."

> ## "We don't want people who are mavericks or into self-aggrandizement. We're looking for a person who plays nicely with others."

Zemke says the key indicator of customer-service potential is a high level of what mental-health professionals call "psychological hardiness"—qualities such as optimism, flexibility, and the ability to handle stressful situations or criticism without feeling emotionally threatened. Those are, of course, good qualities for many jobs. But experts note that the personality of a customer-service maven may be markedly different from those of achievers in other business venues. Verbal eloquence and

persuasiveness, for example, aren't as important as the ability to listen.

"The great customer-relationship person has a very even-handed view of things, a strong sense of fairness," says Dianne Durkin, who teaches customer-satisfaction techniques at Loyalty Factor, an HR consulting firm in New Castle, New Hampshire. "This is a person who tends to balance his or her own interests and the company's interests with the customer's interests."

Ruth Cohen, Rosenbluth's director of HR/learning and development, says her company doesn't want "people who are mavericks or into self-aggrandizement. We're looking for a person who plays nicely with others."

Five HR Tips for Improving the Customer Relationship
tools

- **Look for customer-pleasing personalities**. The ability to empathize with others, flexibility, and emotional resilience under pressure are qualities that aren't easy to teach. Design a structured, situational interviewing process to find those special people.

- **Don't be afraid to emphasize the negative**. Good service isn't always noticed, but bad service invariably is. Use role-playing exercises and encourage trainees to discuss their own experiences as mistreated customers to help them understand the impact on the company's fortunes when they don't make a good impression.

- **Give employees tools for understanding their customers**. Your training program should include training in techniques such as "active listening" and advice on how to interpret customers' verbal cues.

- **Don't neglect "hard" skills**. A nice smile and polite telephone manners aren't enough when a customer needs advice on which hardware to pick or help with a product that isn't working. Make sure your customer-service people have a good working knowledge of whatever you're selling.

- **Promote a service-oriented culture from the top**. A company's customer relationships are heavily influenced by the tone of the management/employee relationship. Sell your top leaders on the importance of company rituals that emphasize service as a core value—for example, an employee tea or luncheon where executives do the serving.

—PJK

What's the best way to distinguish those who are the most likely to please customers from a raft of applicants? Some companies have tried standardized psychological tests. But many consultants and HR professionals say that it's more effective to observe an applicant at work. At Rosenbluth, the scrutiny begins the moment that a job-seeker walks in the door for an interview. "We're looking for a person who shows the same courtesy to everyone he or she encounters," says Cecily Carel, company vice president for HR. "Our receptionist, who's been with the company 20 years, is a pretty good judge of character.

One time she called me from her desk to say, 'This person is not polite.' That applicant wasn't hired."

Patrick Wright, director of the Center for Advanced HR Studies at Cornell University, recommends a carefully structured, situational interview process like the one he helped develop for Whirlpool. "You want to present an applicant with a series of potential scenarios that he might face on the job, and ask him what he would do," Wright says. "Just because a person gives a good answer, of course, doesn't ensure that he's going to actually do that when he becomes an employee. But you want to make sure you've got a person who at least has the right instincts, which you can reinforce through training."

Talent+, Inc., an HR consulting firm in Lincoln, Nebraska, has designed a system for evaluating job applicants that compares their answers in an open-ended interview to analyses of the traits of top performers in that particular field. The company's managing director, Lisa French, says the process can predict a candidate's job performance 80 to 85 percent of the time. In the case of customer service, she says, one of the key determinants is a strong sense of values. A good customer-service performer will work hard on a customer's behalf, not with the hope of getting a raise or a promotion, but because it's the right thing to do. "This is the sort of person who will go down fighting for his or her customers," she says.

Talent+ started working with Ritz-Carlton in 1992, when the rate of "customer defects"—people who complained about the service—had reached a disturbing 27 percent. The consultants helped Ritz-Carlton overhaul its interview and hiring practices, with a focus on identifying applicants with the best customer-service potential. With the new system in place, complaints dropped steadily. By 2000, they had dropped to 1 percent. At the same time, annual job turnover at Ritz-Carlton also decreased from 75 percent to 25 percent.

Turning the knack for niceness into skilled service

Service-quality consultants and HR professionals from service-conscious companies say that even an employee with the right personality traits needs guidance on how to channel positive qualities into developing good customer relationships. At a time of economic uncertainty, when many companies may try to cut costs by scrimping on customer-service training, it's all the more crucial for HR to make a strong case for its vital importance.

One of the most basic steps in teaching good customer-service skills is fostering employees' self-awareness, Durkin says. "You're not going to be good at customer relations unless you first understand yourself. You have to know how you come across to other people, how you react under stress, what your communication style is."

To help an employee become more self-aware, a company may want to use an assessment tool. The Myers-Briggs Type Indicator, for example, helps an employee see her own personality style, such as whether she is a "thinker," a methodical person; a "sensor," one who learns through observation; an "intuitor,"

who is enthusiastic and excitable; or a "feeler," who tends to avoid conflict. With training, a customer-service employee also can learn more about identifying customers' personality types.

Another crucial area of customer-service training is communication skills. "Research shows that only 7 percent of the impact of your communication with another person is in the words you use," Durkin says. "Thirty-eight percent is in the tone of voice. The remaining 55 percent of the message comes from physical appearance, mannerisms, eye contact, and so on." Because so much of communication is nonverbal, customer-service employees who have to deal with customers primarily over the phone find themselves at a major disadvantage in getting across their message—or, conversely, in understanding the customer's need.

One way to compensate for the lack of human contact is by teaching customer-service employees the technique of "active listening"—restating and summarizing what the customer tells them. This not only helps understanding but also conveys a message of attentiveness and concern. Employees also can be taught to notice and respond to subtle cues in a customer's speech.

A big part of achieving great customer service turns out to be keeping customer-service employees happy.

Rosenbluth takes a slightly different approach. The travel agency focuses on educating its customer-service associates to use what it calls "elegant language"—words and phrases intended to create a tone of courtesy, respect, and attentiveness to detail. A company associate uses the word "certainly" instead of "yeah" or "sure," and after helping a customer with a problem, reflexively responds, "It has been my pleasure." And they always, always ask for permission—and wait for the response—before putting a customer on hold. "We think this gives customers a message about how much attention we pay to little details," Cecily Carel says. "It's subtle, but important."

But good customer service requires more than just "soft," or non-technical, skills. Customer-service consultant Zemke notes that organizations frequently neglect to give their customer-service employees adequate product training. "If I order something and it doesn't work, I want somebody who knows the product and can help me, not somebody who's been trained to smile at the right times." Companies such as NCCI have successfully used surveys to find out what kind of technical knowledge and assistance customers most need, and incorporate the information into customer-service training.

Supervising to build a customer-friendly environment

In order for carefully selected, well-trained employees to build great relationships with customers, a company must develop its own good internal relationships, HR professionals say.

Discovering and Fixing Customer-Service Ills

business results

When Don Frye joined Process Software as a manager of technical support and management information systems in August 2001, he quickly found himself in the midst of a customer-service crisis. The company's meal ticket is a narrow technological niche: Internet-related software for business and university computer servers running the VMS platform.

"Basically, we compete against a product that Compaq gives away for free," Frye says. "That's why for us, customer service is really crucial. We need to demonstrate on a daily basis that we treat people well, so that they'll be motivated not only to purchase our product but also to purchase tech support services from us."

But when Frye received the results of an annual customer-satisfaction survey, he was disheartened to see a number of clients who rated their experience with Process as below their expectations. "I contacted every one of those people, to see what was the matter with us," he says. "It wasn't the quality of the product. Basically, the problem was account management. Those customers told me that they felt forgotten, out of the loop. They were frustrated about having to call repeatedly to get updates on their cases."

Hiring new people with better customer skills wasn't an option for Frye, because the company's veteran tech-support staff had accumulated crucial knowledge that wasn't easily replaceable. Instead, he brought in an outside consultant, Loyalty Factor, to analyze the staff's customer woes and develop an individualized prescription for fixing them.

In addition to using the Myers-Briggs test to give employees insight about their own personalities and style of relating to customers, the consultant helped Frye make subtle but important adjustments to the team's communication with customers. A third of contact with customers was through e-mail, a mode that, because it strips away facial expressions, tone of voice, and other nonverbal cues, conveys only about 7 percent of the intended message.

To reduce the number of misunderstandings, employees were coached to choose their words more carefully and to utilize emotions. To lessen customer frustration, the staff studies "active listening" techniques, learning to repeat and summarize what customers told them. "One of the big benefits is that it shows people that you're paying attention to their problems," Frye says. Follow-up and continuity were other problems that emerged in the analysis, so the staff learned to take more thorough and systematic case notes on calls. "That way, when the customer called back, whoever answered the phone could immediately pick up their service without missing a beat."

The fix worked, even better than Frye had hoped. Within a month of tech-support completing its training, complaints were down by more than 50 percent. More important, one of the company's most critical indicators, the renewal rate for customers, actually rose 2 percent over the previous year.

—PJK

Walker Information's Michael DeSanto says that he's noticed an intriguing phenomenon: customers' and employees' relationships with companies tend to have striking parallels.

Research at Cornell University's Center for Advanced HR Studies and at other institutions indicates that there's a strong link between customer and employee satisfaction. "The really crucial issues are retention and, more important, loyalty," DeSanto says. "Both of them tend to operate in a three- to five-year cycle. Brand-new employees tend to love you, because they're still learning new skills and have the potential to move up in the company. New customers love you because you'll do anything to keep them happy." Three years down the road, both the employee and customer relationships with the company suddenly are different, he notes. "The employee may feel like he's buried in the organization. Chances are, he's already got whatever training you're going to give him. He's hearing from headhunters. And the customer is in a similar rut. He's being taken for granted, and he's already learned about the business from you, so maybe he doesn't need you as much."

Strong relationships between employees and customers may actually keep both from fleeing the company. "Good customer relationships may actually be a factor in employee retention," DeSanto says.

A large part of achieving great customer service is keeping the employees happy. Service-quality experts say that customer-service employees tend to model externally the treatment they receive from management. An intensely top-driven, autocratic corporate culture with spotty internal communication leads to tense, confused customer relations. A company with a collegial atmosphere and good channels of communication will be a lot better at keeping its customers happy.

There are many things HR can do to help create an environment that nurtures good service and customer relationships. Rosenbluth International has developed a culture that encourages associates to seek one another's help in solving customer problems, and emphasizes its concern for the customer with "elegant language." CEO Hal Rosenbluth often personally serves tea and cookies to new associates at the completion of their training. "It's a little corporate ritual that sets the mood," Carel says. At the same time, it helps Rosenbluth talk with new employees about what they can do to serve customers.

Rosenbluth's HR team has discovered an important truth. Just as subtle qualities such as a facial expression, choice of words, or a nuance of etiquette can help make a good impression on a customer, any comprehensive HR strategy for customer satisfaction depends on attention to detail. In designing hiring, training, evaluation, and other programs, nothing should be left to chance.

Patrick J. Kiger is a freelance writer in Washington, D.C. E-mail editors@workforce.com to comment.

Stairs of Loyalty

*The stairs of customer loyalty
show you how to shape a plan
for developing your customer relationships.*

Tony Alessandra

MANY COMPANIES FOLLOW OLD formulas for bringing them closer to what they think their customers really want.

To set yourself apart from the competition and to be a leader in your market, you have to move beyond "customer focus" and "customer satisfaction" and practice things like "customer intimacy," "customer interaction," "customer loyalty," and "customer partnership." Partnership is a single-thread relationship. It is being "one." Such a relationship is built upon a plan that reflects the nature and needs of all parties involved. This is not a re-defining of the same, tired concepts of sales and service. Instead, it is a paradigm shift, moving away from transactional customer satisfaction and toward permanent customer loyalty.

To achieve sales success, your company must develop long-term relationships with your best customers. Too often, the constant push to increase sales and market share leads companies away from their current customers toward finding new ones. Such a strategy is a terrible waste of time and money. The most effective way to assure the growth in profitability is to turn your existing customers into champions.

For many companies, the overriding focus of their growth strategy is on increasing sales and market share. Many companies today dedicate far more of their resources to expanding sales at the expense of their existing clientele.

I have learned that converting new sales into champions is the best path toward stable, long term growth.

The stairs of customer loyalty show you how to convert your prospects into sales, and then to customers, and then into raving fans who will "preach your message" and "sing your praises" to the marketplace.

Finding the Right Prospects

Possessing the right marketing skills is crucial to identifying the right prospects for a company. Smart companies profile the top 20 percent of their current customers who typically provide 80 percent of their profits. Criteria like profitability, frequency of purchase, after-sales service required, revenues, and loyalty potential are quantified and used as measures in determining the characteristics of a company's best, most loyal customers.

Since winning new business is very expensive, companies need to avoid the wrong prospects by outlining the characteristics that make-up the bottom 20 percent of their customer base. The complainers, price-grinders, and transaction-oriented clients cost more to handle than they're worth. These customers give more grief, chew up more time with requests and complaints, and, generally, cause the most stress for a company. By understanding the bad traits of those bottom 20 percent, companies can more easily avoid the wrong prospects and focus their resources on the upper 20 percent instead.

Steps to Successful Sales

When a company is ready to contact the right prospect, three face-to-face steps are used to make the sale:

1. Exploring needs. This gives you the chance to get deeply involved with your prospects to determine exactly how your product or service can help them. It's where the partnering process begins. The purpose of exploring is to get enough information from the client to enable you to recommend appropriate options.

2. Collaborating solutions. After you've worked with your prospects to identify needs and concerns, next determine whether your product or service will solve a problem or seize an opportunity for them. Usually there are several ways you can package your product or service to meet the needs of your prospects. Involve your prospects in deciding which option makes the most sense for them.

3. Confirming the sale. Your customer should now be asking to buy from you. The commitment becomes a *how* and *when*, not an *if*. Signing the agreement is merely a formality. However, before confirming the sale, make sure your prospect has all the information they need to increase their perceived value of your product or service.

Building Long-Term Customers

To nurture long-term customers, practice these three principles:

• *Be customer-driven, not operations-driven*. Assure that customer expectations are consistently identified, managed, and monitored. Then, exceeding customer expectations becomes the compelling focus.

• *Create moments of magic, not moments of misery or mediocrity*. Any time a customer comes into contact with any aspect of your company is a moment of truth. When the customer encounters a member of your staff, a piece of advertising, or anything else that can be tied to your company, they formulate opinions, beliefs, impressions, and ideas about who you are and what you're about. Customers who consistently have their expectations exceeded receive moments of magic and become apostles for your organization.

• *Convert customers into apostles*. Strong intimacy with the customer characterizes this stair of loyalty. Creating apostles should be the highest goal, as apostles will do more for your organization through their good will and word of mouth than any other form of marketing or sales. Try to double the number of apostles each year by moving prospects and customers up the stairs of customer loyalty.

Companies that become "apostle-driven" do not constantly have to dedicate limited resources of time and money to always finding new customers. Their apostles accomplish this task for them. Such companies will dominate their industries.

Tony Alessandra is a speaker and has authored 13 books, including Customer-Driven Service, *1-800-222-4383 or www.alessandra.com.*

From *Executive Excellence,* November 2001, p. 19. © 2001 by Executive Excellence.

What **Drives** Customer **Equity**

A company's current customers provide the most
reliable source of future revenues and profits.

By Katherine N. Lemon, Roland T. Rust, and Valarie A. Zeithaml

Consider the **issues** facing a typical brand
manager, product manager, or marketing-oriented CEO:
How do I manage the brand? How will my customers
react to changes in the product or service offering?
Should I raise price? What is the best way to enhance the
relationships with my current customers? Where should
I focus my efforts?

Business executives can answer such questions by
focusing on customer equity—the total of the discounted
lifetime values of all the firm's customers. A strategy
based on customer equity allows firms to trade off
between customer value, brand equity, and customer
relationship management. We have developed a new
strategic framework, the Customer Equity Diagnostic,
that reveals the key drivers increasing the firm's customer
equity. This new framework will enable managers to
determine what is most important to the customer and to
begin to identify the firm's critical strengths and hidden
vulnerabilities. Customer equity is a new approach to
marketing and corporate strategy that finally puts the
customer and, more important, strategies that grow the
value of the customer, at the heart of the organization.

For most firms, customer equity is certain to be the
most important determinant of the long-term value of the
firm. While customer equity will not be responsible for
the entire value of the firm (eg., physical assets, intellectual property, and research and development competencies), its current customers provide the most reliable
source of future revenues and profits. This then should be
a focal point for marketing strategy.

Although it may seem obvious that customer equity
is key to long-term success, understanding how to grow
and manage customer equity is more complex. How to
grow it is of utmost importance, and doing it well can
create a significant competitive advantage. There are
three drivers of customer equity—value equity, brand
equity, and relationship equity (also known as retention
equity). These drivers work independently and together.
Within each of these drivers are specific, incisive actions,

or levers, the firm can take to enhance its overall customer
equity.

Value Equity

Value is the keystone of the customer's relationship
with the firm. If the firm's products and services do not
meet the customer's needs and expectations, the best
brand strategy and the strongest retention and
relationship marketing strategies will be insufficient.
Value equity is defined as the customer's objective
assessment of the utility of a brand, based on perceptions
of what is given up for what is received. Three key levers
influence value equity: quality, price, and convenience.

EXECUTIVE
briefing

Customer equity is critical to a firm's long-term success. We developed a strategic marketing framework
that puts the customer and growth in the value of the
customer at the heart of the organization. Using a
new approach based on customer equity—the total of
the discounted lifetime values of all the firm's customers—we describe the key drivers of firm growth:
value equity, brand equity, and relationship equity.
Understanding these drivers will help increase customer equity and, ultimately, the value of the firm.

Quality can be thought of as encompassing the
objective physical and nonphysical aspects of the product
and service offering under the firm's control. Think of the
power FedEx holds in the marketplace, thanks, in no
small part, to its maintenance of high quality standards.
Price represents the aspects of "what is given up by the
customer" that the firm can influence. New e-world
entrants that enable customers to find the best price (e.g.,
www.mysimon.com) have revolutionized the power of

price as a marketing tool. Convenience relates to actions that help reduce the customer's time costs, search costs, and efforts to do business with the firm. Consider Fidelity Investments' new strategy of providing Palm devices to its best customers to enable anytime, anywhere trading and updates—clearly capitalizing on the importance of convenience to busy consumers.

Brand Equity

Where value equity is driven by perceptions of objective aspects of a firm's offerings, brand equity is built through image and meaning. The brand serves three vital roles. First, it acts as a magnet to attract new customers to the firm. Second, it can serve as a reminder to customers about the firm's products and services. Finally, it can become the customer's emotional tie to the firm. Brand equity has often been defined very broadly to include an extensive set of attributes that influence consumer choice. However, in our effort to separate the specific drivers of customer equity, we define brand equity more narrowly as the customer's subjective and intangible assessment of the brand, above and beyond its objectively perceived value.

The key actionable levers of brand equity are brand awareness, attitude toward the brand, and corporate ethics. The first, brand awareness, encompasses the tools under the firm's control that can influence and enhance brand awareness, particularly marketing communications. The new focus on media advertising by pharmaceutical companies (e.g., Zyban, Viagra, Claritin) is designed to build brand awareness and encourage patients to ask for these drugs by name.

Second, attitude toward the brand encompasses the extent to which the firm is able to create close connections or emotional ties with the consumer. This is most often influenced through the specific nature of the media campaigns and may be more directly influenced by direct marketing. Kraft's strength in consumer food products exemplifies the importance of brand attitude—developing strong consumer attitudes toward key brands such as Kraft Macaroni and Cheese or Philadelphia Cream Cheese. The third lever, corporate ethics, includes specific actions that can influence customer perceptions of the organization (e.g., community sponsorships or donations, firm privacy policy, and employee relations). Home Depot enhanced its brand equity by becoming a strong supporter of community events and by encouraging its employees to get involved.

Relationship Equity

Consider a firm with a great brand and a great product. The company may be able to attract new customers to its product with its strong brand and keep customers by meeting their expectations consistently. But is this enough? Given the significant shifts in the new economy—from goods to services, from transactions to relationships—the answer is no. Great brand equity and value equity may not be enough to hold the customer. What's needed is a way to glue the customers to the firm, enhancing the stickiness of the relationship. Relationship equity represents this glue. Specifically, relationship equity is defined as the tendency of the customer to stick with the brand, above and beyond the customer's objective and subjective assessments of the brand.

The key levers, under the firm's control, that may enhance relationship equity are loyalty programs, special recognition and treatment, affinity programs, community-building programs, and knowledge-building programs. Loyalty programs include actions that reward customers for specific behaviors with tangible benefits. From airlines to liquor stores, from Citigroup to Diet Coke, the loyalty program has become a staple of many firms' marketing strategy. Special recognition and treatment refers to actions that recognize customers for specific behavior with intangible benefits. For example, US Airways' "Chairman Preferred" status customers receive complimentary membership in the US Airways' Club.

Affinity programs seek to create strong emotional connections with customers, linking the customer's relationship with the firm to other important aspects of the customer's life. Consider the wide array of affinity Visa and MasterCard choices offered by First USA to encourage increased use and higher retention. Community-building programs seek to cement the customer-firm relationship by linking the customer to a larger community of like customers. In the United Kingdom, for example, soft drink manufacturer Tango has created a Web site that has built a virtual community with its key segment, the nation's youth.

Finally, knowledge-building programs increase relationship equity by creating structural bonds between the customer and the firm, making the customer less willing to recreate a relationship with an alternative provider. The most often cited example of this is amazon.com, but learning relationships are not limited to cyberspace. Firms such as British Airways have developed programs to track customer food and drink preferences, thereby creating bonds with the customer while simultaneously reducing costs.

Determining the Key Drivers

Think back to the set of questions posed earlier. How should a marketing executive decide where to focus his or her efforts: Building the brand? Improving the product or service? Deepening the relationships with current customers? Determining what is the most important driver of customer equity will often depend on characteristics of the industry and the market, such as market maturity or consumer decision processes. But determining the critical driver for your firm is the first step in building the truly customer-focused marketing organization.

When Value Equity Matters Most

Value equity matters to most customers most of the time, but it will be most important under specific circumstances. First, value equity will be most critical when discernible differences exist between competing products. In commodity markets, where products and competitors are often fungible, value equity is difficult to build. However, when there are differences between competing products, a firm can grow value equity by influencing customer perceptions of value. Consider IBM's ThinkPad brand of notebook computers. Long recognized for innovation and advanced design, IBM has been able to build an advantage in the area of value equity by building faster, thinner, lighter computers with advanced capabilities.

Second, value equity will be central for purchases with complex decision processes. Here customers carefully weigh their decisions and often examine the trade-offs of costs and benefits associated with various alternatives. Therefore, any company that either increases the customer benefits or reduces costs for its customers will be able to increase its value equity. Consider consumers contemplating the conversion to DSL technology for Internet access. This is often a complex, time-consuming decision. DSL companies that can reduce the time and effort involved in this conversion will have the value equity advantage.

Third, value equity will be important for most business-to-business purchases. In addition to being complex decisions, B2B purchases often involve a long-term commitment or partnership between the two parties (and large sums of money). Therefore, customers in these purchase situations often consider their decisions more carefully than individual consumers do.

Fourth, a firm has the opportunity to grow value equity when it offers innovative products and services. When considering the purchase of a "really new" product or service, customers must carefully examine the components of the product because the key attributes often may be difficult to discern. In many cases, consumers make one-to-one comparisons across products, trying to decide whether the new product offers sufficient benefits to risk the purchase. New MP3-type devices that provide consumers with online access to music are examples of such innovative products and services. Consumers will seek out substantial information (e.g., from the Web, friends, and advertisements) to determine the costs and benefits of new products. Firms that can signal quality and low risk can grow value equity in such new markets.

Finally, value equity will be key for firms attempting to revitalize mature products. In the maturity stage of the product life cycle, most customers observe product parity, sales level off, and, to avoid commoditization, firms often focus on the role of the brand. But value equity also may grow customer equity. By introducing new benefits for a current product or service, or by adding new features to the current offering, firms can recycle their products and services and grow value equity in the process. Consider the new Colgate "bendable" toothbrush. It seeks to revitalize the mature toothbrush market with a new answer to an age-old problem. The success of this new innovation increases Colgate's value equity.

Clearly then, the importance of value equity will depend on the industry, the maturity of the firm, and the customer decisionmaking process. To understand the role of value equity within your organization, ask several key customers and key executives to assess your company using the set of questions provided in the Customer Equity Diagnostic on the following page.

When Brand Equity Matters Most

While brand equity is generally a concern, it is critical in certain situations. First, brand equity will be most important for low-involvement purchases with simple decision processes. For many products, including frequently purchased consumer packaged goods, purchase decisions are often routinized and require little customer attention or involvement. In this case, the role of the brand and the customer's emotional connection to the brand will be crucial. In contrast, when product and service purchase decisions require high levels of customer involvement, brand equity may be less critical than value or relationship equity. Coca-Cola, for example, has been extremely successful making purchases a routine aspect of consumer's shopping trips by developing extremely strong connections between the consumer and the brand.

Second, brand equity is essential when the customer's use of the product is highly visible to others. Consider Abercrombie & Fitch, the home of in-style gear for the "Net Generation." For A&F aficionados, the brand becomes an extension of the individual, a "badge" or statement the individual can make to the world about himself or herself. These high-visibility brands have a special opportunity to build brand equity by strengthening the brand image and brand meanings that consumers associate with the brand.

Third, brand equity will be vital when experiences associated with the product can be passed from one individual or generation to another. To the extent that a firm's products or services lend themselves to communal or joint experiences (e.g., a father teaching his son to shave, shared experiences of a special wine), the firm can build brand equity. The Vail ski resort knows the value of this intergenerational brand value well. The resort encourages family experiences by promoting multigenerational visits.

Fourth, the role of the brand will be critical for credence goods, when it is difficult to evaluate quality prior to consumption. For many products and services, it is possible to "try before you buy" or to easily evaluate the quality of specific attributes prior to purchase. However, for others, consumers must use different cues for quality. This aspect of brand equity is especially key for law firms, investment banking firms, and advertising agencies, which are beginning to recognize the value of strong brand identities as a key tool for attracting new clients.

Customer Equity Diagnostic

How much do your customers care about value equity?

❑ Do customers perceive discernible differences between brands? Do they focus on the objective aspects of the brand?

❑ Do you primarily market in a B2B environment?

❑ Is the purchase decision process complex in your industry?

❑ Is innovation a key to continued success in your industry?

❑ Do you revitalize mature products with new features and benefits?

How are you doing?

❑ Are you the industry leader in overall quality? Do you have initiatives in place to continuously improve quality?

❑ Do your customers perceive that the quality they receive is worth the price they paid?

❑ Do you consistently have the lowest prices in your industry?

❑ Do you lead the industry in distribution of your products and services?

❑ Do you make it most convenient for your customers to do business with you?

How important is brand equity?

❑ Are the emotional and experiential aspects of the purchase important? Is consumption of your product highly visible to others?

❑ Are most of your products frequently purchased consumer goods?

❑ Is the purchase decision process relatively simple?

❑ Is it difficult to evaluate the quality of your products or services prior to consumption or use?

❑ Is advertising the primary form of communication to your customers?

How are you doing?

❑ Are you the industry leader in brand awareness?

❑ Do customers pay attention to and remember your advertising and the information you send them?

❑ Are you known as a good corporate citizen? Active in community events?

❑ Do you lead your industry in the development and maintenance of ethical standards?

❑ Do customers feel a strong emotional connection to the brand?

How does relationship equity weigh in?

❑ Are loyalty programs a necessity in your industry?

❑ Do customers feel like "members" in your community?

❑ Do your customers talk about their commitment to your brand?

❑ Is it possible to learn about your customers over time and customize your interactions with them? Do your customers perceive high switching costs?

❑ Are continuing relationships with customers important?

How are you doing?

❑ Do customers perceive that you have the best loyalty program in your industry?

❑ Do you lead the industry in programs to provide special benefits and services for your best customers?

❑ To what extent do your customers know and understand how to do business with you?

❑ Do customers perceive you as the leader in providing a sense of community?

❑ Do you encourage dialogue with your customers?

Therefore, brand equity will be more important in some industries and companies than others. The role of brand equity will depend on the level of customer involvement, the nature of the customer experience, and the ease with which customers can evaluate the quality of the product or service before buying it. Answering the questions in the Customer Equity Diagnostic will help determine how important brand equity is for your organization.

When Relationship Equity Matters Most

In certain situations, relationship equity will be the most important influence on customer equity. First, relationship equity will be critical when the benefits the customer associates with the firm's loyalty program are significantly greater than the actual "cash value" of the benefits received. This "aspirational value" of a loyalty program presents a solid opportunity for firms to strengthen relationship equity by creating a strong incentive for the customer to return to the firm for future purchases. The success of the world's frequent flyer programs lies, to some extent, in the difference between the "true" value of a frequent flyer mile (about three cents) and the aspirational value—the customer's perception of the value of a frequent flyer mile ("I'm that much closer to my free trip to Hawaii!").

Second, relationship equity will be key when the community associated with the product or service is as important as the product or service itself. Certain products and services have the added benefit of building a strong community of enthusiasts. Customers will often continue to purchase from the firm to maintain "membership" in the community. Just ask an active member of a HOG (Harley-Davidson Owners Group) to switch to a Honda Gold Wing; or ask a committed health club member to switch to an alternate health club. Individuals who have become committed to brand communities tend to be fiercely loyal.

Third, relationship equity will be vital when firms have the opportunity to create learning relationships with customers. Often, the relationship created between the firm and the customer, in which the firm comes to appreciate the customer's preferences and buying habits, can become as important to the customer as the provision of the product or service. Database technology has made such "learning" possible for any company or organization willing to invest the time and resources in collecting, tracking, and utilizing the information customers reveal. For example, Dell has created learning relationships with its key business customers through Dell's Premier Pages—customized Web sites that allow customers to manage their firm's purchases of Dell computers. The benefit: It becomes more difficult for customers to receive the same personal attention from an alternative provider without "training" that new provider.

Finally, relationship equity becomes crucial in situations where customer action is required to discontinue the service. For many services (and some product continuity programs), customers must actively decide to stop consuming or receiving the product or service (e.g., book clubs, insurance, Internet service providers, negative-option services). For such products and services, inertia helps solidify the relationship. Firms providing these types of products and services have a unique opportunity to grow relationship equity by strengthening the bond with the customer.

As with value and brand equity, the importance of relationship equity will vary across industries. The extent to which relationship equity will drive your business will depend on the importance of loyalty programs to your customers, the role of the customer community, the ability of your organization to establish learning relationships with your customers, and your customer's perceived switching costs. Answer the questions in the Customer Equity Diagnostic framework to see how important relationship equity is to your customers.

A New Strategic Approach

We have now seen how it is possible to gain insight into the key drivers of customer equity for an individual industry or for an individual firm within an industry. Once a firm understands the critical drivers of customer equity for its industry and for its key customers, the firm can respond to its customers and the marketplace with strategies that maximize its performance on elements that matter.

Taken down to its most fundamental level, customers choose to do business with a firm because (a) it offers better value, (b) it has a stronger brand, or (c) switching away from it is too costly. Customer equity provides the diagnostic tools to enable the marketing executive to understand which of these three motivators is most critical to the firm's customers and will be most effective in getting the customer to stay with the firm, and to buy more. Based on this understanding, the firm can identify key opportunities for growth and illuminate unforeseen vulnerabilities. In short, customer equity offers a powerful new approach to marketing strategy, replacing product-based strategy with a competitive strategy approach based on growing the long-term value of the firm.

Additional Reading

Aaker, David A. (1995), *Managing Brand Equity*. NY: The Free Press.

Dowling, Grahame R. and Mark Uncles (1997), "Do Customer Loyalty Programs Really Work?" *Sloan Management Review*, 38 (Summer), 71–82.

Keller, Kevin L. (1998), *Strategic Brand Management: Building, Measuring and Managing Brand Equity*. NJ: Prentice-Hall.

Newell, Frederick (2000), *Loyalty.com: Customer Relationship Management in the New Era of Internet Marketing*. NY: McGraw-Hill.

Rust, Roland T., Katherine N. Lemon, and Valarie A. Zeithaml (2000), *Driving Customer Equity: How Customer Lifetime Value Is Reshaping Corporate Strategy*. NY: The Free Press.

Zeithaml, Valarie A. (1988), "Consumer Perceptions of Price, Quality and Value: A Means-End Model and Synthesis of Evidence," *Journal of Marketing*, 52 (July), 2-22.

About the Authors

Katherine N. Lemon is an assistant professor at Wallace E. Carroll School of Business, Boston College. She may be reached at katherine.lemon@bc.edu.

Roland T. Rust holds the David Bruce Smith Chair in Marketing at the Robert H. Smith School of Business at the University of Maryland, where he is director of the Center for E-Service. He may be reached at rrust@rhsmith.umd.edu.

Valarie A. Zeithaml is professor and area chair at the Kenan-Flagler Business School of the University of North Carolina, Chapel Hill. She may be reached at valariez@unc.edu.

From *Marketing Management*, Spring 2001, Vol. 10, No. 1, pp. 20-25. © 2001 by the American Marketing Association. Reprinted by permission.

A Primer on Quality Service

Quality Service Makes Happy Customers and Greater Profits

Gene Milbourn, Jr.
G. Timothy Haight

"Pul-eeze! Will Someone Help Me?" screamed a headline in *Time* magazine in the late 1980s. The cover story focused on the deterioration of customer service and blamed it on general economic upheavals such as high inflation, labor shortage, and low-cost business strategies.[1] Prices for consumer goods had increased 87 percent during the 1970s and, to keep prices from further skyrocketing, customer-service training was slashed and computers and self-service schemes were introduced in wholesale fashion. Businesses developed the same habits and inattention to quality service that had plagued American manufacturers in previous years.

In the new millennium, a new force is pressuring the bricks-and-mortar businesses to upgrade their customer focus to be competitive—e-commerce. A recent article about a customer service survey in *Marketing Week* asserted, "... in a competitive world driven by new technology and the Internet, what was an acceptable level of service five or ten years ago may no longer be good enough today."[2]

There is ample evidence that the economic success of companies fluctuates with the quality of service that is offered. Among the most recent scholarship is a study published in the *Journal of Business Research* that validated an earlier much-discussed work that linked market orientation with business performance.[3]

The Strategic Planning Institute studied confidential data provided by thousands of business units—the PIMS database—and found that quality service leads to financial and strategic success.[4] Grouping businesses into those offering low and those offering high quality service revealed that, in addition to maintaining a price differential of 11 percent, return on sales was 11 percent higher, and annual sales growth was 9 percent higher in the group providing high quality service. In addition, the high service quality group experienced a 4 percent increase in market share while the low quality service group registered a –2 percent change.

An earlier report concluded that many companies "overinvest in cost reduction and capacity-expansion projects because they believe they can 'run the numbers' to 'justify' a project. They underinvest in quality service improvement because they have not learned how to calibrate its strategic or financial payoff."[5]

Research Is Consistent

Research on the behavior of dissatisfied customers is consistent and expected.[6] Typically, a dissatisfied customer does not complain and simply purchases from another store. Research across eight industries revealed that 25 percent of dissatisfied customers do not return to the offending store; 41 percent of customers experience a problem in shopping; 94 percent of customers do not complain about a problem; 63 percent of customers are not pleased with a business' responses to their complaints; and, customers are five times more likely to switch stores because of service problems than for price or product quality issues. However, when customers *do* complain and when their problems are *quickly* resolved, an impressive 82 percent would buy again from the business.[7]

> *"There is ample evidence that the economic success of companies fluctuates with the quality of service that is offered."*

Research contained in a *Harvard Business Review* article found that high quality service is a dominant cause of repeat customers across industries.[8] More noteworthy, however, is that a customer generates an increasing amount of profit each year that the "customer is a customer." A business becomes skilled in dealing with the customer and the customer buys more and refers others to the business.

Quality Service Model

A 22-item survey tool called the ServQual is used to collect information from customers on five factors of quality service:

- **reliability**—the ability to provide what was promised, dependably and accurately
- **assurance**—the knowledge and courtesy of employees, and their ability to convey trust and confidence
- **tangibles**—the physical facilities, equipment, and the appearance of personnel
- **empathy**—the degree of caring and individual attention provided to customers

- **responsiveness**—the willingness to help customers and provide prompt service.

These five factors account for much of the variation of customer's perception of quality service across industries (see the *Journal of Retailing*, Spring, 1990, Volume 66, No. 1 for a copy of the ServQual or Report No. 86–108, Marketing Science Institute, Cambridge, Mass.).

The Quality Service Model is shown in Figure One. The model shows that five general factors of quality service influences three customer behaviors that are desired by businesses—repurchasing, providing positive word-of-mouth advertising, and cross buying.

> *"We have found that disenchanted rank- and-file employees are an excellent source for ideas to improve service."*

The model also identified ten specific factors such as the guarantee, repair and maintenance, and technical support that are components of the general factors. For instance, a business can be *reliable* in repair and maintenance but *unreliable* in technical support and ordering and billing. A below average restaurant may serve unevenly prepared food (poor reliability), on oily trays (poor tangibles), slowly (poor responsiveness), to customers in an impersonal manner (low empathy). Customers would likely not return to this business or provide positive word-of-mouth advertising. Conversely, customers would likely return and tell others about the experience if they rated the

business highly according to the five dimensions of service quality.

Improvement Strategies

The Forum Corporation, a research company that specializes in this topic, says the reliability dimension is the most important followed by responsiveness, assurance, empathy, and the tangible elements. However, some research shows that companies do best in dealing with the dimensions in almost the reverse order. In other words, they do very well in taking care of what customers view as relatively unimportant.[9]

The organizational themes that differentiate the best customer-focused companies include these actions:

- Setting customer-focused performance goals and standards
- Taking personal action to help solve customers' problems
- Seeking innovative ways to serve customers better
- Helping employees learn how to serve customers better

Some of the improvement strategies underlying this customer-focus that the Forum Corporation has found helpful include:
- Companies must address all dimensions of service quality

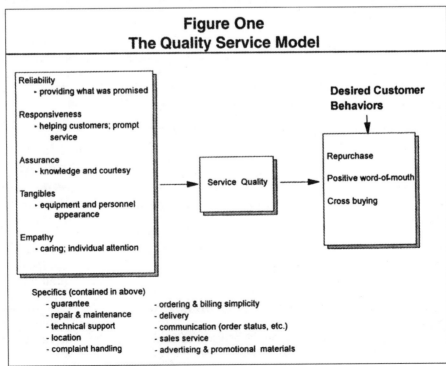

**Figure One
The Quality Service Model**

Reliability
- providing what was promised

Responsiveness
- helping customers; prompt service

Assurance
- knowledge and courtesy

Tangibles
- equipment and personnel appearance

Empathy
- caring; individual attention

Service Quality

Desired Customer Behaviors

Repurchase

Positive word-of-mouth

Cross buying

Specifics (contained in above)
- guarantee
- repair & maintenance
- technical support
- location
- complaint handling
- ordering & billing simplicity
- delivery
- communication (order status, etc.)
- sales service
- advertising & promotional materials

Figure Two
The Quality Service Questionnaire

DIRECTIONS: This survey asks you about how well a business serves customers. Show your opinion by circling one of the five (5) numbers next to each statement. If you think the company does **much worse** than expected **select 1.** If the company does **much better** than expected **select 5.** If your feelings are not strong, circle one of the numbers in the **middle.**

1 Much worse than expected	2 Somewhat worse than expected	3 About what I expected	4 Better than expected	5 Much better than expected
1. The quality of our equipment	1	2	3	4	5
2. The appearance of our physical facilities	1	2	3	4	5
3. The appearance of our employees	1	2	3	4	5
4. The appearance of our materials (pamphlets, statements, etc.)	1	2	3	4	5
5. Delivering on promises to do something by a certain time	1	2	3	4	5
6. The sincerity of our interest in solving your problems	1	2	3	4	5
7. Performing service right the first time	1	2	3	4	5
8. Providing services at the time we promise to do so	1	2	3	4	5
9. The accuracy of records	1	2	3	4	5
10. Telling you exactly when services will be performed	1	2	3	4	5
11. Receiving prompt service from our employees	1	2	3	4	5
12. The willingness of our employees to help you	1	2	3	4	5
13. Never being too busy to respond to your requests	1	2	3	4	5
14. Employee actions that instill confidence in you	1	2	3	4	5
15. The safety you feel in transactions with our employees	1	2	3	4	5
16. The courteousness of our employees	1	2	3	4	5
17. The ability of our employees to answer your questions	1	2	3	4	5
18. The individual attention you received from us	1	2	3	4	5
19. The convenience of our operating hours	1	2	3	4	5
20. The personal attention you received from our employees	1	2	3	4	5
21. Having your best interests at heart	1	2	3	4	5
22. The ability of our employees to understand your specific needs	1	2	3	4	5

Overall Quality

23. How would you rate the overall service you received?	1	2	3	4	5
24. Considering the time, effort and money you spent with us, how would you rate the overall value provided?	1	2	3	4	5

Source: Parasuraman, A., et al., "Servqual: A Multiple-item Scale for Measuring Customer Perceptions of Service Quality," Report No. 86-108, Marketing Science Institute, Cambridge, Mass.

- Companies must be accurate and specific about what employees must do to improve service quality
- Companies seeking a simple way to look at how their customers judge service should evaluate the general viewpoint of employees, because employees are good estimators of service
- Companies must seek ways to reduce, avoid, and speedily solve problems with customers
- Companies should work to retain customers who report that they are satisfied, but rate the company as having only fair or poor service
- Companies must examine and correct anything that impedes employee performance to maximize customer focus

The Survey Questionnaire

A popular research tool that was developed to collect attitudes about quality service is called the ServQual scale.[10] A copy of the most recent version is shown in Figure Two.

Once the 22-item survey is customized, it is given to a sample of customers to complete. Scores are tabulated and average scores are calculated for each of the five factors of quality service. Some of the 22 categories in the survey may not be appropriate. A task force should review each item, re-write statements if necessary, and construct a final professional-looking instrument. Some norms that can be used for comparison are: overall average 3.89; overall service 4.05; overall value 4.13; and each service quality factor 3.50.

While the survey process is underway, other types of measurement can also be employed (see a good organizational development book on the topic of survey feedback). Some forms include focus groups of 'sophisticated' customers and a group of internal managers who brainstorm the factors that are rated below average by customers. We have found that disenchanted rank-and-file employees are an excellent source for ideas to improve service.

"Quality service need not be your businesses Achilles' heel."

What are needed are specific statements such as: "We need to improve the *reliability* of our repair and maintenance process," "We need to improve our *responsiveness* in deliveries and complaint handling," and "We need to improve our *empathy* in addressing complaints." An improvement plan can then be developed that places the ideas for change into "fix first," "fix second," and "fix last" categories. The task force leader must identify the cost, time frame, labor intensity, and review process needed for each recommendation.

Quality service need not be your businesses Achilles' heel. Employing a quality service model such as that which we've presented in this article will decidedly result in greater business—and profits.

References

1. *Time*, "Pul-eeze! Will Someone Help Me?" *Economics and Business,* cover story, February 2, 1987.

2. Hemsley, Steve, "Keeping Customers," *Marketing Week*, March 16, 2000, 39.

3. Slater, Stanley F., John C. Narver, "The Positive Effect of a Market Orientation on Business Profitability; A Balanced Replication, *Journal of Business Research*, Vol. 48, No. 1, April, 2000.

4. Gale, B. T., *Managing Customer Value*, The Free Press, NY, 1994, Chapter 6.

5. Strategic Planning Institute, "Strategic Management of Service Quality," No. 33, 1985, Cambridge, MA.

6. TARP: Technical Assistance Research Program, *"Tarp's Approach to Customer Driven Quality: Moving From Measuring to Managing Customer Satisfaction*, TARP Corporation, Arlington, VA, 1995.

7. Gale, B. T., op. cit., 17.

8. Reichheld, F. F. and W. Earl Sasser, "Zero Defections: Quality Comes to Service," *Harvard Business Review*, 69, September–October, 1990, 7.

9. Forum Corporation, *"Customer Focus Research: Executive Briefing,"* Boston, MA, 1988.

10. Parasuraman, A., V. A. Zeithaml and L. L. Berry, *"Servqual: A Multiple-item Scale for Measuring Customer Perceptions of Service Quality,"* Report No. 86–108, August, 1986, Marketing Science Institute, Cambridge, MA.

GENE MILBOURN, JR., Ph.D., is a professor of management at the University of Baltimore. He teaches undergraduate and graduate business policy and strategy as well as organizational behavior. He is a noted consultant to business and industry on issues that include quality service, leadership, and motivation. He is the author of the organizational behavior textbook, Human Behavior in the Work Environment: A Managerial Perspective.

G. TIMOTHY HAIGHT, D.B.A. is dean of the School of Business and Economics at California State University, Los Angeles. He is an expert in the field of financial management, investment and securities analysis. He is the general editor of Insurer's Guide to Enterprise-Wide Management *and* Derivatives Risk Management Service. *In addition to many articles published in magazines and journals, he is the author of* The Analysis of Portfolio Management Performance: An Institute Guide to Assessing and Analyzing Pension Fund, Endowment, Foundation, and Trust Investment Performance *(McGraw-Hill, 1998).*

From *Business Forum*, Vol. 23, Nos. 3-4, pp. 15-18. © 1998 by Business Forum. Reprinted by permission.

WHY SERVICE STINKS

Companies know just how good a customer you are—and unless you're a high roller, they would rather lose you than take the time to fix your problem

BY DIANE BRADY

When Tom Unger of New Haven started banking at First Union Corp. several years ago, he knew he wasn't top of the heap. But Unger didn't realize just how dispensable he was until mysterious service charges started showing up on his account. He called the bank's toll-free number, only to reach a bored service representative who brushed him off. Then he wrote two letters, neither of which received a response. A First Union spokeswoman, Mary Eshet, says the bank doesn't discuss individual accounts but notes that customer service has been steadily improving. Not for Unger. He left. "They wouldn't even give me the courtesy of listening to my complaint," he says.

And Unger ought to know bad service when he sees it. He works as a customer-service representative at an electric utility where the top 350 business clients are served by six people. The next tier of 700 are handled by six more, and 30,000 others get Unger and one other rep to serve their needs. Meanwhile, the 300,000 residential customers at the lowest end are left with an 800 number. As Unger explains: "We don't ignore anyone, but our biggest customers certainly get more attention than the rest."

As time goes on, that service gap is only growing wider. Studies by groups ranging from the Council of Better Business Bureaus Inc. to the University of Michigan vividly detail what consumers already know: Good service is increasingly rare (charts). From passengers languishing in airport queues to bank clients caught in voice-mail hell, most consumers feel they're getting squeezed by Corporate America's push for profits and productivity. The result is more efficiencies for companies—and more frustration for their less valuable customers. "Time

saved for them is not time saved for us," says Claes Fornell, a University of Michigan professor who created the school's consumer satisfaction index, which shows broad declines across an array of industries. Fornell points to slight improvements in areas like autos and computers.

FLYING

Canceled flight? No problem. With top status, you're whisked past the queue, handed a ticket for the next flight, and driven to the first-class lounge. The rest can cross their fingers and come back tomorrow

Andrew Chan's experience with Ikea is typical. The Manhattan artist recently hauled a table home from an Ikea store in New Jersey only to discover that all the screws and brackets were missing. When he called to complain, the giant furniture retailer refused to send out the missing items and insisted he come back to pick them up himself, even though he doesn't own a car. Maybe he just reached the wrong guy, says Tom Cox, customer-service manager for Ikea North America, noting that the usual procedure is to mail small items out within a couple of days.

NO ELEPHANT? Life isn't so tough for everyone, though. Roy Sharda, a Chicago Internet executive and road warrior is a "platinum" customer of Starwood Hotels & Resorts World-

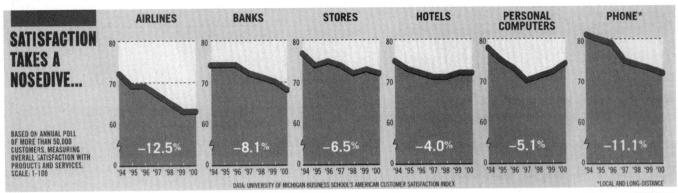

SATISFACTION TAKES A NOSEDIVE...

BASED ON ANNUAL POLL OF MORE THAN 50,000 CUSTOMERS, MEASURING OVERALL SATISFACTION WITH PRODUCTS AND SERVICES. SCALE: 1-100

AIRLINES −12.5%
BANKS −8.1%
STORES −6.5%
HOTELS −4.0%
PERSONAL COMPUTERS −5.1%
PHONE* −11.1%

DATA: UNIVERSITY OF MICHIGAN BUSINESS SCHOOL'S AMERICAN CUSTOMER SATISFACTION INDEX

*LOCAL AND LONG-DISTANCE

CHARTS BY RAY VELLA/BW

wide. When he wanted to propose to his girlfriend, Starwood's Sheraton Agra in India arranged entry to the Taj Mahal after hours so he could pop the question in private. Starwood also threw in a horse-drawn carriage, flowers, a personalized meal, upgrades to the presidential suite, and a cheering reception line led by the general manager. It's no wonder Sharda feels he was "treated like true royalty."

Welcome to the new consumer apartheid. Those long lines and frustrating telephone trees aren't always the result of companies simply not caring about pleasing the customer anymore. Increasingly, companies have made a deliberate decision to give some people skimpy service because that's all their business is worth. Call it the dark side of the technology boom, where marketers can amass a mountain of data that gives them an almost Orwellian view of each buyer. Consumers have become commodities to pamper, squeeze, or toss away, according to Leonard L. Berry, marketing professor at Texas A&M University. He sees "a decline in the level of respect given to customers and their experiences."

More important, technology is creating a radical new business model that alters the whole dynamic of customer service. For the first time, companies can truly measure exactly what such service costs on an individual level and assess the return on each dollar. They know exactly how much business someone generates, what he is likely to buy, and how much it costs to answer the phone. That allows them to deliver a level of service based on each person's potential to produce a profit—and not a single phone call more.

BILLING

Big spenders can expect special discounts, promotional offers, and other goodies when they open their bills. The rest might get higher fees, stripped-down service, and a machine to answer their questions

The result could be a whole new stratification of consumer society. The top tier may enjoy an unprecedented level of personal attention. But those who fall below a certain level of profitability for too long may find themselves bounced from the

customer rolls altogether or facing fees that all but usher them out the door. A few years ago, GE Capital decided to charge $25 a year to GE Rewards MasterCard holders who didn't rack up at least that much in annual interest charges. The message was clear: Those who pay their bills in full each month don't boost the bottom line. GE has since sold its credit-card business to First USA. Others are charging extra for things like deliveries and repairs or reducing service staff in stores and call centers.

Instead of providing premium service across the board, companies may offer to move people to the front of the line for a fee. "There has been a fundamental shift in how companies assess customer value and apply their resources," says Cincinnati marketing consultant Richard G. Barlow. He argues that managers increasingly treat top clients with kid gloves and cast the masses "into a labyrinth of low-cost customer service where, if they complain, you just live with it."

Companies have always known that some people don't pay their way. Ravi Dhar, an associate professor at Yale University, cites the old rule that 80% of profits come from 20% of customers. "The rest nag you, call you, and don't add much revenue," he says. But technology changed everything. To start, it has become much easier to track and measure individual transactions across businesses. Second, the Web has also opened up options. People can now serve themselves at their convenience at a negligible cost, but they have to accept little or no human contact in return. Such huge savings in service costs have proven irresistible to marketers, who are doing everything possible to push their customers—especially low-margin ones—toward self-service.

FRONT-LOADING ELITE. That's a far cry from the days when the customer was king. In the data-rich new millennium, sales staff no longer let you return goods without question while rushing to shake your hand. And they don't particularly want to hear from you again unless you're worth the effort. How they define that top tier can vary a lot by industry. Airlines and hotels love those who buy premier offerings again and again. Financial institutions, on the other hand, salivate over day traders and the plastic-addicted who pay heavy interest charges because they cover only the minimum on their monthly credit-card bills.

Almost everyone is doing it. Charles Schwab Corp.'s top-rated Signature clients—who start with at least $100,000 in assets or trade 12 times a year—never wait longer than 15 seconds

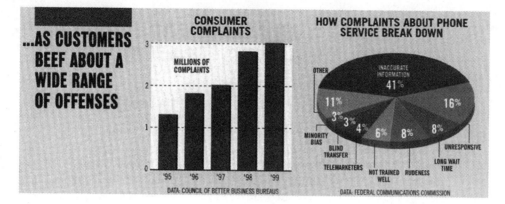

...AS CUSTOMERS BEEF ABOUT A WIDE RANGE OF OFFENSES

CONSUMER COMPLAINTS

MILLIONS OF COMPLAINTS

'95 '96 '97 '98 '99

DATA: COUNCIL OF BETTER BUSINESS BUREAUS

HOW COMPLAINTS ABOUT PHONE SERVICE BREAK DOWN

OTHER
INACCURATE INFORMATION 41%
11%
16%
3% 3% 4% 6% 8% 8%
MINORITY BIAS
BLIND TRANSFER
TELEMARKETERS
NOT TRAINED WELL
RUDENESS
UNRESPONSIVE
LONG WAIT TIME

DATA: FEDERAL COMMUNICATIONS COMMISSION

to get a call answered, while other customers can wait 10 minutes or more. At Sears, Roebuck & Co., big spenders on the company's credit card get to choose a preferred two-hour time slot for repair calls while regular patrons are given a four-hour slot. Maytag Corp. provides premium service to people who buy pricey products such as its front-loading Neptune washing machines, which sell for about $1,000, twice the cost of a top-loading washer. This group gets a dedicated staff of "product experts," an exclusive toll-free number, and speedy service on repairs. When people are paying this much, "they not only want more service; they deserve it," says Dale Reeder, Maytag's general manager of customer service.

BANKING

There's nothing like a big bank account to get those complaints answered and service charges waived every time. Get pegged as a money-loser, and your negotiating clout vanishes

Of course, while some companies gloat about the growing attention to their top tier, most hate to admit that the bottom rungs are getting less. GE Capital would not talk. Sprint Corp. and WorldCom Inc. declined repeated requests to speak about service divisions. Off the record, one company official explains that customers don't like to know they're being treated differently.

Obviously, taking service away from the low spenders doesn't generate much positive press for companies. Look at AT&T, which recently agreed to remove its minimum usage charges on the 28 million residential customers in its lowest-level basic plan, many of whom don't make enough calls to turn a profit. "To a lot of people, it's not important that a company make money," says AT&T Senior Vice-President Howard E. McNally, who argues that AT&T is still treated by regulators and the public as a carrier of last resort. Now, it's trying to push up profits by giving top callers everything from better rates to free premium cable channels.

SERIAL CALLERS. Is this service divide fair? That depends on your perspective. In an era when labor costs are rising while prices have come under pressure, U.S. companies insist they simply can't afford to spend big bucks giving every customer the hands-on service of yesteryear. Adrian J. Slywotzky, a

partner with Mercer Management Consulting Inc., estimates that gross margins in many industries have shrunk an average of 5 to 10 percentage points over the past decade because of competition. "Customers used to be more profitable 10 years ago, and they're becoming more different than similar" in how they want to be served, he says.

The new ability to segment customers into ever finer categories doesn't have to be bad news for consumers. In many cases, the trade-off in service means lower prices. Susanne D. Lyons, chief marketing officer at Charles Schwab, points out that the commission charged on Schwab stock trades has dropped by two-thirds over the past five years. Costs to Schwab, meanwhile, vary from a few cents for Web deals to several dollars per live interaction. And companies note that they're delivering a much wider range of products and services than ever before—as well as more ways to handle transactions. Thanks to the Internet, for example, consumers have far better tools to conveniently serve themselves.

Look at a company like Fidelity Investments, which not only has a mind-boggling menu of fund options but now lets people do research and manipulate their accounts without an intermediary. Ten years ago, the company got 97,000 calls a day, of which half were automated. It now gets about 550,000 Web site visits a day and more than 700,000 daily calls, about three-quarters of which go to automated systems that cost the company less than a buck each, including development and research costs. The rest are handled by human beings, which costs about $13 per call. No wonder Fidelity last year contacted 25,000 high-cost "serial" callers and told them they must use the Web or automated calls for simple account and price information. Each name was flagged and routed to a special representative who would direct callers back to automated services—and tell them how to use it. "If all our customers chose to go through live reps, it would be cost-prohibitive," says a Fidelity spokeswoman.

ENTITLED? Segmenting is one way to manage those costs efficiently. Bass Hotels & Resorts, owners of such brands as Holiday Inn and Inter-Continental Hotels, know so much about individual response rates to its promotions that it no longer bothers sending deals to those who did not bite in the past. The result: 50% slashed off mailing costs but a 20% jump in response rates. "As information becomes more sophisticated, the whole area of customer service is becoming much more complex," says Chief Marketing Officer Ravi Saligram.

'WE'RE SORRY, ALL OF OUR AGENTS ARE BUSY WITH MORE VALUABLE CUSTOMERS'

Companies have become sophisticated about figuring out if you're worth pampering—or whether to just let the phone keep ringing. Here are some of their techniques:

CODING

Some companies grade customers based on how profitable their business is. They give each account a code with instructions to service staff on how to handle each category.

ROUTING

Based on the customer's code, call centers route customers to different queues. Big spenders are whisked to high-level problem solvers. Others may never speak to a live person at all.

TARGETING

Choice customers have fees waived and get other hidden discounts based on the value of their business. Less valuable customers may never even know the promotions exist.

SHARING

Companies sell data about your transaction history to outsiders. You can be slotted before you even walk in the door, since your buying potential has already been measured.

Consumers themselves have cast a vote against high-quality service by increasingly choosing price, choice, and convenience over all else. Not that convenience always takes the sting out of rotten service—witness priceline.com Inc., the ultimate self-service site that lets customers name their own price for plane tickets, hotels, and other goods. Many consumers didn't fully understand the trade-offs, such as being forced to stop over on flights, take whatever brand was handed to them, and forgo the right to any refund. And when things went wrong, critics say, no one was around to help. The results: a slew of complaints that has prompted at least one state investigation. Priceline.com responds that its revamping the Web site and intensifying efforts to improve customer service. While many consumers refuse to pay more for service, they're clearly dismayed when service is taken away. "People have higher expectations now than two or three years ago because we have all this information at our fingertips," says Jupiter Communications Inc. analyst David Daniels.

Indeed, marketers point to what they call a growing culture of entitlement, where consumers are much more demanding about getting what they want. One reason is the explosion of choices, with everything from hundreds of cable channels to new players emerging from deregulated industries like airlines and telecom companies. Meanwhile, years of rewards programs such as frequent-flier miles have contributed to the new mindset. Those who know their worth expect special privileges that reflect it. Says Bonnie S. Reitz, senior vice-president for marketing, sales, and distribution at Continental Airlines Inc.: "We've got a hugely educated, informed, and more experienced consumer out there now."

For top-dollar clients, all this technology allows corporations to feign an almost small-town intimacy. Marketers can know your name, your spending habits, and even details of your personal life. Centura Banks Inc. of Raleigh, N.C., now rates its 2 million customers on a profitability scale from 1 to 5. The real moneymakers get calls from service reps several times a year for what Controller Terry Earley calls "a friendly chat" and even an annual call from the CEO to wish them happy holidays.

No wonder attrition in this group is down by 50% since 1996, while the percentage of unprofitable customers has slipped to 21% from 27%.

LODGING

Another day, another upgrade for frequent guests. Sip champagne before the chef prepares your meal. First-time guest? So sorry. Your room is up three flights and to the left

Even for the lower tier, companies insist that this intense focus on data is leading to service that's better than ever. To start with, it's more customized. And while executives admit to pushing self-help instead of staff, they contend that such service is often preferable. After all, many banking customers prefer using automated teller machines to standing in line at their local branch. American Airlines Inc., the pioneer of customer segmentation with its two-decade-old loyalty program, says it's not ignoring those in the cheap seats, pointing to the airline's recent move to add more legroom in economy class. Says Elizabeth S. Crandall, managing director of personalized marketing: "We're just putting more of our energies into rewarding our best customers."

MARKED MAN. This segmentation of sales, marketing, and service, based on a wealth of personal information, raises some troubling questions about privacy. It threatens to become an intensely personal form of "redlining"—the controversial practice of identifying and avoiding unprofitable neighborhoods or types of people. Unlike traditional loyalty programs, the new tiers are not only highly individualized but they are often invisible. You don't know when you're being directed to a different telephone queue or sales promotion. You don't hear about the benefits you're missing. You don't realize your power to negotiate with everyone from gate agents to bank employees is predetermined by the code that pops up next to your name on a computer screen.

HOW TO IMPROVE YOUR PROFILE

Even if you're not a big spender, there are ways to improve your standing with companies in order to command better service. The key is to recognize that your spending habits, payment history, and any information you volunteer can be used for or against you. What's more, if you do think you're being pegged at a low tier, there are ways to get the recognition you feel you deserve.

The first step in fighting segmentation is to be stingy with the information you give out—especially if it's unlikely to help your status. Don't fill our surveys, sweepstakes forms, or applications if you're not comfortable with how the information might be used. Be wary when a company asks if it can alert you to other products and services. A yes may permit them to sell data that you don't want distributed.

PIGEONHOLING. The Consumers Union points out that it's unnecessary to fill out surveys with warranty cards. Just send in a proof of purchase with your name and address. "Protecting your privacy is a significant tool to prevent yourself from being pigeonholed as undesirable," says Gene Kimmelman, Washington co-director for the CU. It's equally important to recognize what kind of information companies are looking for. If you don't live in an upmarket Zip Code, consider using your work address for correspondence. Be optimistic when estimating your income or spending: The better the numbers look, the better you'll be treated.

Still, it's tough to keep personal information to yourself, especially when companies are compiling data on the business they do with you. A critical concern for all consumers is their actual payment record. Donna Fluss, a vice-president at the technology consultants Gartner Group Inc., advises pulling your credit history at least once a year to check if there are any liens or mistakes. "You may discover that you're listed as having missed a payment that you thought you made on time," she says. The three main reporting bureaus—Experian, Trans Union, and Equifax—charge a small fee for a copy of your credit history. If, however you have recently been denied credit, employment, or insurance, such a report is free from all three companies. The largest bureau is Equifax, which has data on 190 million Americans, but all three may have slightly different records based on who reports to them.

Multiple credit cards can be a mistake, especially if they're the no-frills variety that are frequently offered to less desirable

MAKING THE GRADE
How to get better service

CONSOLIDATE YOUR ACTIVITIES Few things elevate status and trim costs like spending big in one place. Be on the lookout for packages or programs that reward loyal behavior.

PROTECT YOUR PRIVACY Avoid surveys and be frugal with releasing credit-card or Social Security information. The less companies know, the less they can slot you.

JUMP THE PHONE QUEUE If you want to reach a live human, don't admit to having a touch-tone phone at the prompt. Or listen for options that are less likely to be handled automatically.

FIGHT BACK If you feel badly treated, complain. Make sure management knows just how much business you represent and that you're willing to take it elsewhere.

candidates. Not only can they drain the credit you might need for other activities, but they're also unlikely to propel you into a higher category. Using a spouse's card or account is also to be avoided, because it robs you of a chance to build your own credit history. If a mistake is made on your account, fight it.

Pros disagree on tactics for bypassing the service maze. One customer representative argues that when calling a service center it's better to punch in no account number if you're a low-value customer. The reason? Without proper identification, he says, a live person has to get on the line. "Pretend you're calling from a rotary phone," he advises. But another tactic may be to punch zero or choose an option that's likely to get immediate attention.

In the end, resistance may be futile, and the best strategy for beating the system may be to join it. Shop around for the best company, and try to consolidate your business there. These days, the best way to ensure good service is to make yourself look like a high-value, free-spending customer.

By Diane Brady in New York

When the curtain is pulled back on such sophisticated tiering, it can reveal some uses of customer information that are downright disturbing. Steve Reed, a West Coast sales executive, was shocked when a United Airlines Inc. ticketing agent told him: "Wow, somebody doesn't like you." Not only did she have access to his Premier Executive account information but there was a nasty note about an argument he had had with a gate agent in San Francisco several months earlier. In retrospect, he feels that explained why staff seemed less accommodating following the incident. Now, Reed refuses to give more than his name for fear "of being coded and marked for repercussions." United

spokesman Joe Hopkins says such notes give agents a more complete picture of passengers. "It's not always negative information," says Hopkins, adding that the practice is common throughout the industry.

Those who don't make the top tier have no idea how good things can be for the free-spending few. American Express Co. has a new Centurion concierge service that promises to get members almost anything from anywhere in the world. The program, with an annual fee of $1,000, is open by invitation only. "We're seeing a lot of people who value service more than price," says Alfred F. Kelly Jr., AmEx group president for consumer and small-business services. Dean Burri, a Rock Hill (S.C.) insurance executive, found out how the other half lives when he joined their ranks. Once he became a platinum customer of Starwood Hotels, it seemed there was nothing the hotel operator wouldn't do for him. When the Four Points Hotel in Lubbock, Tex., was completely booked for Texas Tech freshman orientation in August, it bumped a lower-status guest to get Burri a last-minute room. Starwood says that's part of the platinum policy, noting that ejected customers are put elsewhere and compensated for inconvenience. With the right status, says Burri, "you get completely different treatment."

RETAILING

Welcome to an after-hours preview for key customers where great sales abound and staff await your every need. Out in the aisles, it's back to self-service

The distinctions in customer status are getting sliced ever finer. Continental Airlines Inc. has started rolling out a Customer Information System where every one of its 43,000 gate, reservation, and service agents will immediately know the history and value of each customer. A so-called intelligent engine not only mines data on status but also suggests remedies and perks, from automatic coupons for service delays to priority for upgrades, giving the carrier more consistency in staff behavior and service delivery. The technology will even allow Continental staff to note details about the preferences of top customers so the airline can offer them extra services. As Vice-President Reitz puts it: "We even know if they put their eyeshades on and go to sleep." Such tiering pays off. Thanks to its heavy emphasis on top-tier clients, about 47% of Continental's customers now pay higher-cost, unrestricted fares, up from 38% in 1995.

Elsewhere, the selectivity is more subtle. At All First Bank in Baltimore, only those slotted as top customers get the option to click on a Web icon that directs them to a live service agent for a phone conversation. The rest never see it. First Union, meanwhile, codes its credit-card customers with tiny colored squares that flash when service reps call up an account on their computer screens. Green means the person is a profitable customer and should be granted waivers or otherwise given white-glove treatment. Reds are the money losers who have almost no negotiating power, and yellow is a more discretionary category in between. "The information helps our people make decisions on fees and rates," explains First Union spokeswoman Mary Eshet.

Banks are especially motivated to take such steps because they have one of the widest gaps in profitability. Market Line Associates, an Atlanta financial consultancy, estimates that the top 20% of customers at a typical commercial bank generate up to six times as much revenue as they cost, while the bottom fifth cost three to four times more than they make for the company. Gartner Group Inc. recently found that, among banks with deposits of more than $4 billion, 68% are segmenting customers into profitability tranches while many more have plans to do so.

Tiering, however, poses some drawbacks for marketers. For one thing, most programs fail to measure the potential value of a customer. Most companies can still measure only past transactions—and some find it tough to combine information from different business units. The problem, of course, is that what someone spends today is not always a good predictor of what they'll spend tomorrow. Life situations and spending habits can change. In some cases, low activity may be a direct result of the consumer's dissatisfaction with current offerings. "We have to be careful not to make judgments based on a person's interaction with us," cautions Steven P. Young, vice-president for worldwide customer care at Compaq Computer Corp.s' consumer-products group. "It may not reflect their intentions or future behavior."

PAY NOT TO WAIT? Already, innovative players are striving to use their treasure trove of information to move customers up the value chain instead of letting them walk out the door. Capital One Financial Corp. of Falls Church, Va., is an acknowledged master of tiering, offering more than 6,000 credit cards and up to 20,000 permutations of other products, from phone cards to insurance. That range lets the company match clients with someone who has appropriate expertise. "We look at every single customer contact as an opportunity to make an unprofitable customer profitable or make a profitable customer more profitable," says Marge Connelly, senior vice-president for domestic card operations.

In the future, therefore, the service divide may become much more transparent. The trade-off between price and service could be explicit, and customers will be able to choose where they want to fall on that continuum. In essence, customer service will become just another product for sale. Walker Digital, the research lab run by priceline.com founder Jay S. Walker, has patented a "value-based queuing" of phone calls that allows companies to prioritize calls according to what each person will pay. As Walker Digital CEO Vikas Kapoor argues, customers can say: "I don't want to wait in line—I'll pay to reduce my wait time."

For consumers, though, the reality is that service as we've known it has changed forever. As Roger S. Siboni, chief executive of customer-service software provider E.piphany Inc., points out, not all customers are the same. "Some you want to absolutely retain and throw rose petals at their feet," Siboni says. "Others will never be profitable." Armed with detailed data on who's who, companies are learning that it makes financial sense to serve people based on what they're worth. The rest can serve themselves or simply go away.

With bureau reports

Lighting the way

Four tales of exceptional service from the best source—customers

By DANA JAMES

Contributing Editor

Service. At any dinner party, ask the guests for their stories of customer service, the bad and the good. There will be more of the former than of the latter, but everybody will have a story, or four or five.

While word of mouth by definition can't be quantified, marketers know intuitively that it's the most potent form of communication, to be harnessed in service to the corporation whenever possible, and addressed quickly when it runs counter to the firm's marketing goals. Good word of mouth is one of consumer marketing's most desirable, and most elusive, goals. That is, ensuring dependable customer service is one of a brand strategy's most important elements, but launching those extra-mile tales of employee effort—the ones that are passed like a good virus to hundreds of potential customers—seems to depend more on kismet than coaching.

In an effort to codify those corporate policies that seem to set the stage for such events, *Marketing News* invited consumers to tell us their stories of legendary service they received sometime in the last year or two. (Tellingly, some who received our invitation felt compelled to write us about unforgettably *bad* experiences.) Then we followed up with the company, or in some cases the employee who was praised, to pinpoint the common factors.

Our subjects range from a pharmacy chain to a lighter manufacturer, but share some characteristics, such as customer-focused mission statements, as well as formal programs that train employees to provide great care and recognize and reward those efforts. From their stores, we've pulled a lesson or two that help make out-of-the-ordinary service possible.

Zippo: A 70-year-old promise

John Hall's engraved Zippo lighter—a Christmas gift from his brother 15 years ago—had fallen into disrepair. It was dirty, scratched and the cover hinge was bent. So last October, Hall, a marketing manager for Premier Inc., a health care purchasing conglomerate in Oak Brook, Ill., sent the lighter to Zippo, with a note describing the problems. He'd found the mailing information and instructions on the company's Web site.

Two weeks later, the lighter was returned to Hall's mailbox in mint condition: Not only was the lid repaired, but his lighter fluid and flints had been replenished. Included in the package was a shiny penny encased in a silver emblem, the back of which reads: "The cent never spent to repair a Zippo product."

"This astounded me," Hall says. "Very few companies, much less American-owned companies like Zippo, stand behind their products and make such an incredible customer service statement like this."

"It's a whatever-it-takes attitude here," says Shirley Evers, consumer relations manager for Zippo Manufacturing Co., based in Bradford, Pa. The lifetime guarantee on Zippo products—as old as the 70-year-old company and first promised by its founder, George G. Blaisdell—remains the driving force behind its customer service.

In fact, when Evers hires representatives for her six-person department, her training regimen includes showing them a photo of Blaisdell and talking about his motto, "Build your product with integrity... stand behind it 100% and success will follow."

"I wouldn't want to do consumer relations for a lot of companies because of their poor attitude toward the consumer or because they don't stand behind their product. This makes my job so much easier," Evers says.

Zippo's lifetime guarantee has no disclaimers. A common customer inquiry is whether Zippo will repair an item that broke for reasons other than simple wear and tear, such as being run over by a car. Not only can Zippo consumer relations say, "yes," they are able to send a prepared repair packet, which includes a fiber-reinforced envelope with Zippo's address and a letter that begins, "We will not only repair your Zippo Lighter without charge, we would consider it a privilege."

Evers says her department receives from 15 to 20 thank-you letters a week from customers, most of which she keeps on file so she can recognize her employees during their annual reviews.

Evers is quick to point out that the commitment to the product's integrity is not confined to the consumer relations department. In Zippo's in-house repair clinic, which handles more than 131,000 lighters a year, 14 full-time employees not only repair what's broken, but look for other parts that may need attention soon, and will replace or fix those as well.

"That way, the customer won't have to go through the frustration of sending it in again," Evers says.

Enterprise: Seek entrepreneurs

When Randy Ross, a Boston-based executive editor of *PC World Magazine*, arrived early one Friday morning in January at an Enterprise Rent-A-Car office in Cambridge, Mass., to pick up an SUV to drive on a ski vacation to the Sugarbush resort in Vermont (a three-hour-plus drive away), there was no vehicle and no record of his reservation. Cambridge's customer service representative, Wilson Lowery, apologized profusely and called nearby branches until he found the car Ross wanted, a Chevy Trailblazer at a location several miles away.

So far, so good. But then Lowery drove Ross back to his house to pick up his ski gear, and to the other branch to retrieve the Trailblazer. He knocked 20% off the rental price, provided Ross the $2 toll he would have to pay to get on the highway (which he wouldn't have had to pay leaving from Cambridge) and gave him a half-tank of gas.

Within a month, Ross had rented twice more from Enterprise and "will probably rent more," he says.

St. Louis-based Enterprise Rent-A-Car closely ties customer service to employee success. With a tracking system called the Enterprise Service Quality index (ESQi), the company routinely follows up with customers by phone to determine their level of satisfaction with the company; only "completely satisfied" customers count toward a branch's ESQi score. At the employee level, the ranking is one factor in measuring potential for promotion.

"We are very serious about customer service and have done everything we can to link the needs and interests of our customers with those of our employees," says Sarah Bustamante, an Enterprise spokeswoman.

Like other companies lauded for exemplary service, corporate policy frees Enterprise employees to take steps that will make a customer happy, without having to get bureaucratic and time-consuming approvals from upper levels. In fact, Enterprise looks for and hires people who want to run their own business someday, and builds on that sense of initiative with an extensive employee training program.

"We try to instill in every employee a sense of ownership—that this is their business," says Todd Cody, area manager for the Cambridge branch.

Rite Aid: For the health of it

Last July, a day after his 51st birthday, Marty Pay, a Farmers Insurance agent in Tehachapi, Calif., developed what he thought was a bad case of heartburn during a bike ride. Before taking antacid, he called his pharmacy to ask whether it would interact with his diabetes medication. The Rite Aid pharmacist, Ronde Snell, asked about the nature of the pain and whether he had had heartburn before, and about his medical history.

Based on their 10-minute conversation, Snell told Pay that she thought he could be experiencing heart pains (which could be a precursor to a heart attack)—not heartburn—and that he should go to the emergency room. She said, "Even if it's not (heart pains), they will be glad you came in, so they can rule it out."

A couple hours later, Snell called the local hospital and learned that Pay hadn't been in yet. Then, she tracked him down at his office and told him again to go—immediately. The doctors confirmed Snell's suspicions: Pay had 95% blockage of one artery, and within days he underwent an angioplasty.

"Literally, if it wasn't for her…," Pay says, letting the sentence trail off. "A month later, I was back on my bike."

The pharmacist-customer relationship became a core focus of Camp Hill, Pa.-based Rite Aid two years ago, when the drugstore chain, looking for ways to stand out in a crowded market, learned through marketing research that customers wanted superior and personal customer service in their pharmacy, says John Learish, Rite Aid's vice president of marketing.

"Even though it's a chain of 3,600 stores, customers view each store as *their* pharmacy," Learish says.

Rite Aid execs visited pharmacies and interviewed and observed their pharmacists at work nationwide, and then took the important step of streamlining processes and procedures in Rite Aid pharmacies. For example, the company implemented a so-called basket system in which, once the pharmacy takes a prescription, that form and all related documents and components stay together in the same basket until the filled prescription reaches the customer.

"That way, the pharmacist doesn't have to go back and pick up components along the way—it's simple but efficient," Learish says. Also, it freed pharmacists of certain administrative tasks so they could spend more time with the customers.

Those moves have paid off. Says Snell of her customer care experience with Pay: "The biggest thing was that I had a lot of ancillary help. The technicians were able to cover the ins and outs of daily activities so I could talk to this person in-depth—and that made the difference."

Snell also credits other Rite Aid policies, such as its system of e-mail alerts about drug recalls or other changes, for improving her customer service.

"When Bayer Baycol (a cholesterol drug) was taken off the market, we had lots of customers calling in with questions—and Rite Aid made sure we had information for them that day," she says.

Such marketing successes often beget their own marketing campaigns: Last summer, Rite Aid launched a six-month national TV ad campaign showcasing pharmacist customer service stories like Snell's. In addition to reinforcing Rite Aid's customer focus, Learish says, "It also sets the expectation of what our deliverable is" among pharmacists, and challenges Rite Aid employees to live up to those expectations.

Bamix: Reps are owners, believers

Linda Travis' hand-held wand mixer was on the blink, and she figured since her father had bought it off a TV commercial and because it was made in Switzerland, she faced an uphill battle getting it repaired. As expected, her local repairman said he didn't have a source for the parts, and Travis, a Decatur, Ga.-based brand strategist, turned to the Internet to see if she could learn anything about the company, Bamix of Switzerland.

From the Mettlen-based company's site—which was available in English, German, French and Spanish—she sent an e-mail asking how and where to send her broken mixer. She also found an 800-number and left a message with the same question.

Two hours later, Bamix responded with an e-mail offering a mailing address and instructions. But then the customer service representative who sent the e-mail, Patti Pitcher, also called Travis to ask questions about her problem. Over the phone, she walked Travis step-by-step through an overhaul and repair ef-

fort, dismantling, cleaning and putting the mixer back together—which worked, saving Travis the cost and time of shipping it for repairs.

Pitcher *is* the customer service department for Bamix's North American distributor, 12-employee Ocean Sales Ltd., based in Olympia, Wash. Among the company's customer-friendly policies: Whenever a Bamix mixer is sold in North America, one copy of the 10-year warranty, along with the date and location of purchase, is automatically sent to Pitcher, who keeps it on file. ("Ten years is a long time to ask a customer to hold on to a warranty," she says.)

Meanwhile, for the past 14 years, Pitcher has owned a Bamix mixer. While it's not a Bamix company policy that she have her own, it's a move that other businesses may want to consider, or at least encourage, by giving customer sales reps deep discounts on the products or services they sell, for instance. Pitcher admits that the fact that she uses her mixer all the time often makes a difference in the level of service she is able to provide. Many people, she says, receive the $200 Bamix mixer as a wedding or birthday gift and don't know the first thing about using it.

"I'm able to give them some tips and answer their questions," she says. At the same time, she is a sincere spokeswoman for the product: "It's the queen of mixers," she says with pride. "You can whip non-fat milk into cream."

From *Marketing News*, April 1, 2002, pp. 1, 11. © 2002 by the American Marketing Association. Reprinted by permission.

TRUST
IN THE
MARKETPLACE

John E. Richardson and
Linnea Bernard McCord

Traditionally, ethics is defined as a set of moral values or principles or a code of conduct.

> ... Ethics, as an expression of reality, is predicated upon the assumption that there are right and wrong motives, attitudes, traits of character, and actions that are exhibited in interpersonal relationships. Respectful social interaction is considered a norm by almost everyone.
> ... the overwhelming majority of people perceive others to be ethical when they observe what is considered to be their genuine kindness, consideration, politeness, empathy, and fairness in their interpersonal relationships. When these are absent, and unkindness, inconsideration, rudeness, hardness, and injustice are present, the people exhibiting such conduct are considered unethical. A genuine consideration of others is essential to an ethical life. (Chewning, pp. 175–176).

An essential concomitant of ethics is of trust. Webster's Dictionary defines trust as "assured reliance on the character, ability, strength or truth of someone or something." Businesses are built on a foundation of trust in our free-enterprise system. When there are violations of this trust between competitors, between employer and employees, or between businesses and

consumers, our economic system ceases to run smoothly. From a moral viewpoint, ethical behavior should not exist because of economic pragmatism, governmental edict, or contemporary fashionability—it should exist because it is morally appropriate and right. From an economic point of view, ethical behavior should exist because it just makes good business sense to be ethical and operate in a manner that demonstrates trustworthiness.

Robert Bruce Shaw, in *Trust in the Balance*, makes some thoughtful observations about trust within an organization. Paraphrasing his observations and applying his ideas to the marketplace as a whole:

1. Trust requires consumers have confidence in organizational promises or claims made to them. This means that a consumer should be able to believe that a commitment made will be met.

2. Trust requires integrity and consistency in following a known set of values, beliefs, and practices.

3. Trust requires concern for the well-being of others. This does not mean that organizational needs are not given appropriate emphasis—but it suggests the importance of understanding the impact of decisions and actions on others—i.e. consumers. (Shaw, pp. 39–40)

Companies can lose the trust of their customers by portraying their products in a deceptive or inaccurate manner. In one recent example, a Nike advertisement exhorted golfers to buy the same golf balls used by Tiger Woods. However, since Tiger Woods was using custom-made Nike golf balls not yet available to the general golfing public, the ad was, in fact, deceptive. In one of its ads, Volvo represented that Volvo cars could withstand a physical impact that, in fact, was not possible. Once a company is "caught" giving inaccurate information, even if done innocently, trust in that company is eroded.

Companies can also lose the trust of their customers when they fail to act promptly and notify their customers of problems that the company has discovered, especially where deaths may be involved. This occurred when Chrysler dragged its feet in replacing a safety latch on its Minivan (Geyelin, pp. A1, A10). More recently, Firestone and Ford had been publicly brought to task for failing to expeditiously notify American consumers of tire defects in SUVs even though the problem had occurred years earlier in other countries. In cases like these, trust might not just be eroded, it might be destroyed. It could take years of painstaking effort to rebuild trust under these circumstances, and some companies might not have the economic ability to withstand such a rebuilding process with their consumers.

A *20/20* and *New York Times* investigation on a recent *ABC 20/20* program, entitled "The Car Dealer's Secret" revealed a sad example of the violation of trust in the marketplace. The investigation divulged that many unsuspecting consumers have had hidden charges tacked on by some car dealers when purchasing a new car. According to consumer attorney Gary Klein, "It's a dirty little secret that the auto lending industry has not owned up to." (*ABC News 20/20*)

The scheme worked in the following manner. Car dealers would send a prospective buyer's application to a number of lenders, who would report to the car dealer what interest rate the lender would give to the buyer for his or her car loan. This interest rate is referred to as the "buy rate." Legally a car dealer is not required to tell the buyer what the "buy rate" is or how much the dealer is marking up the loan. If dealers did most of the loans at the buy rate, they only get a small fee. However, if they were able to convince the buyer to pay a higher rate, they made considerably more money. Lenders encouraged car dealers to charge the buyer a higher rate than the "buy rate" by agreeing to split the extra income with the dealer.

David Robertson, head of the Association of Finance and Insurance Professionals—a trade group representing finance managers—defended the practice, reflecting that it was akin to a retail markup on loans. "The dealership provides a valuable service on behalf of the customer in negotiating these loans," he said. "Because of that, the dealership should be compensated for that work." (*ABC News 20/20*)

Careful examination of the entire report, however, makes one seriously question this apologetic. Even if this practice is deemed to be legal, the critical issue is what happens to trust when the buyers discover that they have been charged an additional 1–3% of the loan without their knowledge? In some cases, consumers were led to believe that they were getting the dealer's bank rate, and in other cases, they were told that the dealer had shopped around at several banks to secure the best loan rate they could get for the buyer. While this practice may be questionable from a legal standpoint, it is clearly in ethical breach of trust with the consumer. Once discovered, the companies doing this will have the same credibility and trustworthiness problems as the other examples mentioned above.

The untrustworthiness problems of the car companies was compounded by the fact that the investigation appeared to reveal statistics showing that black customers were twice as likely as whites to have their rate marked up—and at a higher level. That evidence—included in thousands of pages of confidential documents which *20/20* and *The New York Times* obtained from a Tennessee court—revealed that some Nissan and GM dealers in Tennessee routinely marked up rates for blacks, forcing them to pay between $300 and $400 more than whites. (*ABC News 20/20*)

This is a tragic example for everyone who was affected by this markup and was the victim of this secret policy. Not only is trust destroyed, there is a huge economic cost to the general public. It is estimated that in the last four years or so, Texas car dealers have received approximately $9 billion of kickbacks from lenders, affecting 5.2 million consumers. (*ABC News 20/20*)

Let's compare these unfortunate examples of untrustworthy corporate behavior with the landmark example of Johnson & Johnson which ultimately increased its trustworthiness with consumers by the way it handled the Tylenol incident. After seven individuals, who had consumed Tylenol capsules contaminated by a third party died, Johnson & Johnson instituted a total product recall within a week costing an estimated $50 million after taxes. The company did this, not because it was responsible for causing the problem, but because it was the right thing to do. In addition, Johnson & Johnson spearheaded the development of more effective tamper-proof containers for their industry. Because of the company's swift response, consumers once again were able to trust in the Johnson & Johnson name. Although Johnson & Johnson suffered a decrease in market share at the time because of the scare, over the long term it has maintained its profitability in a highly competitive market. Certainly part of this profit success is attributable to consumers believing that Johnson & Johnson is a trustworthy company. (Robin and Reidenbach)

The e-commerce arena presents another example of the importance of marketers building a mutually valuable relationship with customers through a trust-based collaboration process. Recent research with 50 e-businesses reflects that companies which create and nurture trust find customers return to their sites repeatedly. (Dayal.… p. 64)

In the e-commerce world, six components of trust were found to be critical in developing trusting, satisfied customers:

- State-of-art reliable security measures on one's site
- Merchant legitimacy (e.g., ally one's product or service with an established brand)
- Order fulfillment (i.e. placing orders and getting merchandise efficiently and with minimal hassles)
- Tone and ambiance—handling consumers' personal information with sensitivity and iron-clad confidentiality
- Customers feeling that they are in control of the buying process
- Consumer collaboration—e.g., having chat groups to let consumers query each other about their purchases and experiences (Dayal…, pp. 64–67)

Additionally, one author noted recently that in the e-commerce world we've moved beyond brands and trademarks to "trustmarks." This author defined a trustmark as a

… (D)istinctive name or symbol that emotionally binds a company with the desires and aspirations of its customers. It's an emotional connection—and it's much bigger and more powerful than the uses that we traditionally associate with a trademark.… (Webber, p. 214)

Certainly if this is the case, trust—being an emotional link—is of supreme importance for a company that wants to succeed in doing business on the Internet.

It's unfortunate that while a plethora of examples of violation of trust easily come to mind, a paucity of examples "pop up" as noteworthy paradigms of organizational courage and trust in their relationship with consumers.

In conclusion, some key areas for companies to scrutinize and practice with regard to decisions that may affect trustworthiness in the marketplace might include:

- Does a company practice the Golden Rule with its customers? As a company insider, knowing what you know about the product, how willing would you be to purchase it for yourself or for a family member?
- How proud would you be if your marketing practices were made public.… shared with your friends.…

or family? (Blanchard and Peale, p. 27)

- Are bottom-line concerns the sole component of your organizational decision-making process? What about human rights, the ecological/environmental impact, and other areas of social responsibility?
- Can a firm which engages in unethical business practices with customers be trusted to deal with its employees any differently? Unfortunately, frequently a willingness to violate standards of ethics is not an isolated phenomenon but permeates the culture. The result is erosion of integrity throughout a company. In such cases, trust is elusive at best. (Shaw, p. 75)
- Is your organization not only market driven, but also value-oriented? (Peters and Levering, Moskowitz, and Katz)
- Is there a strong commitment to a positive corporate culture and a clearly defined mission which is frequently and unambiguously voiced by upper-management?
- Does your organization exemplify trust by practicing a genuine relationship partnership with your customers—*before, during, and after* the initial purchase? (Strout, p. 69)

Companies which exemplify treating customers ethically are founded on a covenant of trust. There is a shared belief, confidence, and faith that the company and its people will be fair, reliable, and ethical in all its dealings. ***Total trust is the belief that a company and its people will never take opportunistic advantage of customer vulnerabilities***. (Hart and Johnson, pp. 11–13)

References

ABC News 20/20, "The Car Dealer's Secret," October 27, 2000.

Blanchard, Kenneth, and Norman Vincent Peale, *The Power of Ethical Management*, New York: William Morrow and Company, Inc., 1988.

Chewning, Richard C., *Business Ethics in a Changing Culture* (Reston, Virginia: Reston Publishing, 1984).

Dayal, Sandeep, Landesberg, Helen, and Michael Zeissner, "How to Build Trust Online," *Marketing Management*, Fall 1999, pp. 64–69.

Geyelin, Milo, "Why One Jury Dealt a Big Blow to Chrysler in Minivan-Latch Case," *Wall Street Journal*, November 19, 1997, pp. A1, A10.

Hart, Christopher W. and Michael D. Johnson, "Growing the Trust Relationship," *Marketing Management*, Spring 1999, pp. 9–19.

Hosmer, La Rue Tone, *The Ethics of Management*, second edition (Homewood, Illinois: Irwin, 1991).

Kaydo, Chad, "A Position of Power," *Sales & Marketing Management*, June 2000, pp. 104–106, 108ff.

Levering, Robert; Moskowitz, Milton; and Michael Katz, *The 100 Best Companies to Work for in America* (Reading, Mass.: Addison-Wesley, 1984).

Magnet, Myron, "Meet the New Revolutionaries," *Fortune*, February 24, 1992, pp. 94–101.

Muoio, Anna, "The Experienced Customer," *Net Company*, Fall 1999, pp. 025–027.

Peters, Thomas J. and Robert H. Waterman Jr., *In Search of Excellence* (New York: Harper & Row, 1982).

Richardson, John (ed.), *Annual Editions: Business Ethics 00/01* (Guilford, CT: McGraw-Hill/Dushkin, 2000).

_____, *Annual Editions: Marketing 00/01* (Guilford, CT: McGraw-Hill/Dushkin, 2000).

Robin, Donald P., and Erich Reidenbach, "Social Responsibility, Ethics, and Marketing Strategy: Closing the Gap Between Concept and Application," *Journal of Marketing*, Vol. 51 (January 1987), pp. 44–58.

Shaw, Robert Bruce, *Trust in the Balance*, (San Francisco: Jossey-Bass Publishers, 1997).

Strout, Erin, "Tough Customers," *Sales Marketing Management*, January 2000, pp. 63–69.

Webber, Alan M., "Trust in the Future," *Fast Company*, September 2000, pp. 209–212ff.

Dr. John E. Richardson *is Professor of Marketing in the Graziadio School of Business and Management at Pepperdine University, Malibu, California*

Dr. Linnea Bernard McCord *is Associate Professor of Business Law in the Graziadio School of Business and Management at Pepperdine University, Malibu, California*

To Tell the Truth

Call it what you like: a fib, an untruth, a fabrication.
A new *SMM* survey reveals that nearly half of all salespeople may
lie to clients. Are you creating a culture that promotes deception?

By **Erin Strout**

Every fat commission check has a price tag. For Matt Cooper* the cost of earning up to $150,000 per sale was spending every day lying to his customers. It was the promise of huge bonus checks—not his $40,000 base salary—that lured him to join the sales force of a large, well-known Internet company two years ago. In his early twenties, hungry, and aggressive, Cooper fit the dot-com's sales culture mold, but what he didn't realize was that dishonesty was the price of admission.

The New York–based start-up formed a big-deals team, a group that sold multimillion-dollar advertising campaigns to some of the world's largest companies. The sales force's key strategy? Do whatever it took to close those deals. Almost 100 percent of the time that meant lying to the client. "If you didn't lie you were fired," Cooper says. "It always came down to careful wording and fudging numbers."

Among various other deceptive tactics, the Internet company's salespeople would book $2 million deals, promising a certain amount of impressions on the client's banner ads for the first million and guaranteeing a certain amount of sales for the second million dollars. "We'd almost always be able to deliver the impressions, but you really can never guarantee somebody sales," Cooper says. "Back then you could base deals on the industry standard by taking the impression rate, comparing it to the industry standard, and using the conversion rate to determine a sales projection."

Renewals were, of course, out of the question, which might explain the eventual demise of this and thousands of other dot-coms. The boiler-room culture began to take its toll on Cooper, especially after he had to begin screening his calls to avoid irate customers. "Some of them had just spent two million dollars on an online campaign and got completely screwed," he says.

One particularly incensed client who had spent more than $1 million on a campaign that failed to produce the results Cooper had promised began pelting him with voice-mail messages that became increasingly hostile. Then came the death threats. "He left a message saying, 'I know you're there. I'm going to find out where you live and blow up your house.' I never spoke to the customer again—I just told the company about it so that it was out of my hands," Cooper says. "This kind of thing actually happened a few times."

Finally Cooper couldn't take it anymore. "I started selling only what I knew worked, because I couldn't lie anymore—so my managers told me to either close more deals or find another job," he says. "It was the kind of culture where they broke you down and rebuilt you to be an animal."

A reformed liar, Cooper quit and now works at another start-up in New York, but one that holds him to a higher ethical standard. Though this dot-com is still struggling through more rounds of funding, Cooper is finding that building relationships with clients is a better long-term sales strategy—not only for his own financial well-being, but for the long-term financial health of the company. Unfortunately, not all salespeople learn that lesson so early in their careers. A new *SMM*/Equation Research survey of 316 sales and marketing executives reveals that 47 percent of managers suspect that their salespeople have lied on sales calls—only 16.5 percent have never heard one of their reps make an unrealistic promise to a customer.

> **"Most people want to do the right thing, but when bad situations arise it's usually when the leadership has created an environment that tolerates it."**

But don't be too quick to blame your salespeople for their deceptive behavior. What drives sales and market-

FIVE SIGNS YOUR REPS ARE LYING

It's not often that sales executives are caught off guard when they discover salespeople are being dishonest. Experts say that typically, the behavior is ingrained in the corporate culture, starting at the top and permeating throughout the sales organization as accepted—and even expected. But even the most vigilant manager may hire a bad egg now and then. Here's what to look for if you suspect a salesperson is being untruthful:

YOU'RE GETTING CALLS FROM CUSTOMERS It's no surprise that usually the first person to recognize they're being duped is the customer. Clients are managers' best resource when it comes to checking up on salespeople, and if they've experienced bad service they won't hesitate to speak up. That's how Brett Villeneuve, operations manager at Go Daddy Software, discovered one of his salespeople was up to no good: A client called when he discovered activity on his account that he didn't authorize. "I rarely get customer calls, but one day I received a number of complaints," he says.

REPEAT BUSINESS IS DOWN You can only lie to a person once—after that trust is gone. If loyalty is something salespeople struggle to attain, it probably means that they don't do much to deserve it. "You only buy from people that you like," says Andy Zoltners, a marketing professor at the Kellogg School of Management. "In relationship selling you can't lie—if you mess up you'll never hear from the client again."

YOUR SALESPEOPLE ARE MOTIVATED BY FEAR It's not uncommon for sales organizations to have a do-or-die mentality. If executives subscribe to Darwinist philosophies, it's quite likely their salespeople are doing absolutely anything to close deals in order to earn their compensation and keep their jobs. "There are a few big U.S. companies that tell their salespeople that if they don't make quota they'll be fired," Zoltners says. "That doesn't encourage salespeople to focus on customer service, because they're too worried about survival."

RECOGNITION AND REWARDS ARE BASED SOLELY ON NUMBERS If the people heralded as sales superstars on your team are the reps closing the most sales, they probably aren't the ones giving the best service. Recognizing financial gain over how it's achieved isn't a sound strategy for producing an ethical sales team.

YOU LIE, TOO Salespeople are a product of their environment. If executives and managers practice unethical business strategies, it stands to reason that the sales force will too. "Executives have to make it clear to employees that the company is ethical and honest in everything it does," says Bill Blades, a sales consultant in Scottsdale, Arizona. "If it's an enforced part of the mission, salespeople will adhere to it."

—E.S.

ing professionals to lie is often a combination of factors—not the least of which can be the way they are managed.

"Greed is a U.S. phenomenon."

Back in the dot-com heyday one of the most commonly used tactics in the industry included selling advertising space that didn't exist. Telling clients that they had about a one-in-300,000 chance of actually seeing their banner ad appear on a page of the site, salespeople would sell a $500,000 ad, cut and paste it onto a page using Photoshop software, print it, and fax it to the customer to "prove" that the banner appeared as promised.

"We might have sold all of our telecommunications inventory, but then another company would call to say they wanted to spend $50,000 on a campaign," one rep at a New York dot-com says. "What would we do? Book it, even though all the space had already been sold. When the numbers didn't come back as high as the customer expected, we'd just chalk it up to a bad campaign. We'd take anybody who was willing to spend a dime."

Internet advertising isn't the only industry that has sold fictitious products. As California is painfully aware, Enron and other energy companies allegedly made a fortune by selling electricity that didn't exist, rewarding traders for coming up with new schemes and lying about how much energy the company had in its supply. As more details emerge about Enron, regulators are requiring traders to disclose full details of all energy sales starting this month. "Examples like Enron show that greed is really a U.S. phenomenon," says Andy Zoltners, a marketing professor at Northwestern University's Kellogg School of Management. "Some companies do whatever it takes to make money."

Such deception may be more common than we think. In the *SMM* survey, 36 percent of respondents said salespeople now conduct business in a less ethical manner than they did five years ago, and 36 percent believe there's been no change at all. What kind of fabrications do salespeople resort to? The survey shows that 45 percent of managers have heard their reps lying about promised delivery times, 20 percent have overheard their team members give false information about the company's service,

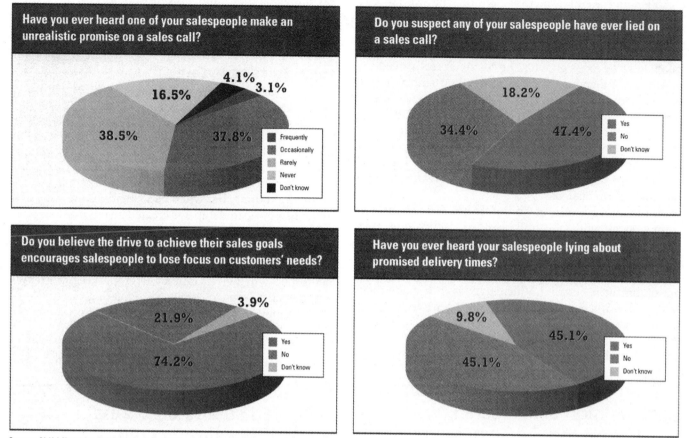

Have you ever heard one of your salespeople make an unrealistic promise on a sales call?

4.1% 3.1%
16.5%
38.5%
37.8%

- Frequently
- Occasionally
- Rarely
- Never
- Don't know

Do you suspect any of your salespeople have ever lied on a sales call?

18.2%
34.4%
47.4%

- Yes
- No
- Don't know

Do you believe the drive to achieve their sales goals encourages salespeople to lose focus on customers' needs?

3.9%
21.9%
74.2%

- Yes
- No
- Don't know

Have you ever heard your salespeople lying about promised delivery times?

9.8%
45.1%
45.1%

- Yes
- No
- Don't know

Source: **SMM**/*Equation Research survey of 316 sales and marketing executives*

and nearly 78 percent of managers have caught a competitor lying about their company's products or services. "It appears that misrepresentation of products or services is prevalent among salespeople," Zoltners says. "This is a losing strategy, and this kind of behavior is not what the best salespeople do."

In the short term unethical sales tactics may prove lucrative, but in the long term every executive should worry about resorting to such strategies. Dishonesty, experts say, eventually ensures a company will have zero customer loyalty. Unfortunately lying is what some of the most profitable salespeople resort to—and experts don't necessarily blame the behavior on the individual. "There are probably three participants in this—the customer, the salesperson, and the company," Zoltners says. "They are all a part of the pressure to make money and the combination can make a rep succumb to it."

"Making a three-percent commission off of a multimillion-dollar deal makes you willing to lie."

For top salespeople the pressure, especially in this rocky economy, is almost palpable. More than a quarter of the respondents in the *SMM* survey said that the recession is causing their salespeople to become more dishonest. In

tough economic times the quotas are as high as the stakes, and sometimes it's enough to make even the most reputable salesperson resort to unethical strategies.

"Where I worked, all of the reps were in this big room, standing up, pitching to clients over the phone," Cooper says. "People might hold their phones out so everybody could hear them closing a big deal. Making a three-percent commission off of a multimillion-dollar deal makes you willing to lie."

In fact, the majority of U.S. salespeople are dependent on commission-based pay plans. Experts say this is part of the problem. "If salespeople have to eat what they hunt, it puts stress on them and motivates them toward bad behavior," Zoltners says. "If you look at some of the companies that are in big trouble, you see that they give negative incentives, such as demanding that reps make quota or be fired. That does not create the best sales forces. You have to create fair rewards for people."

Brett Villeneuve, operations manager at Go Daddy Software, in Scottsdale, Arizona, says he purposely hires reps who are less money-driven and more relationship-oriented. "Quotas, in general, are usually set too high," he says. "We increase base pay and make realistic sales quotas that are challenging, but attainable. We don't want our people to run around scared of losing their jobs—that makes them lose focus on what needs to be done."

Villeneuve might be on to something. The *SMM* report indicates that quotas may inhibit salespeople more than motivate them. Seventy-four percent of respondents admitted the drive to achieve sales targets encourages salespeople to lose focus on what the customer really needs.

Though Villeneuve tries to run a tight ship when it comes to business ethics, he has experienced a few situations where salespeople have crossed the line. "I just had to fire one of our better sellers after I received a complaint from a customer," he says. "In two days I got four calls that a rep had put charges on clients' accounts that he wasn't supposed to. It made his sales look great, but that's not how we do business."

Another team leader at Go Daddy decided to boost his team's sales with an underhanded tactic—one that caused him to get fired. "A client would call in with a problem and his team would refund the order that the client had placed with another sales team, then put the reorder on his team's credit," Villeneuve says. "It made their sales look really good. Even though he wasn't really lying to the customer, that kind of behavior isn't tolerated. When you fire somebody because of it, the message you send internally is really strong."

"When the numbers didn't come back as high as expected, we'd chalk it up to a bad campaign. We'd take anybody willing to spend a dime."

That message is key to instilling an ethical standard in the corporate culture. Some managers do this by giving employees a means of questioning behavior they may observe. According to the *SMM* survey 56 percent of respondents have a process in place that enables salespeople to alert managers to ethical breaches. Executives at Go Daddy use the company's intranet to help employees bring up any questions or concerns. An anonymous section allows for executives to read and respond to e-mails written by coworkers who observe others lying, cheating, stealing, or otherwise behaving badly. "Initially we were scared that it might turn into minor bickering and tattling but so far it's helped keep us aware of legitimate concerns," Villeneuve says.

Though the intranet tool is still new to Go Daddy, executives say the most common type of anonymous notifications relate to customer treatment by individual salespeople. Other examples include reporting a coworker's uncontrollable attitude or anger with a client, and the failure of another salesperson to follow procedures in place to assure proper customer care. "We have zero tolerance for this kind of behavior here and our salespeople know it," says Bonnie Leedy, public relations director at Go Daddy. "Everybody is trained to understand that customers come to us with all levels of techni-

cal understanding, and no one should ever be treated with disrespect."

"Where I came from, sales drove everything."

The key driver of a sound sales strategy is that the leaders of the organization exhibit the values that they want employees to follow, says Steve Walker, president of Walker Communications, a stakeholder research and measurement firm in Indianapolis. "Most people want to do the right thing, but when bad situations arise it's usually when the leadership has created an environment that tolerates it," he says. "Until boards of directors want to sniff it out, the scheming will stay in the hallways."

Walker Communications offers clients products that determine whether a company's employees are telling lies, abusing drugs, or otherwise violating the rules. It's been a tough sell. "Offering these kinds of products in a litigious society is difficult," he says. "Executives actually don't want information that may indicate that there's a problem. They don't want to officially know that their sales force is lying."

"I started selling only what I knew worked because I couldn't lie anymore, so my managers told me to either close more deals or find another job."

Sometimes it's the executives themselves who promote deception. Take VeriSign Inc., a domain registration and Internet security provider. The marketing team sent out domain expiration notices to their competitors' customers, designed to look like the notices were coming from the company they currently used for their Internet domain registration. The hope was that the notices, which stated that owners would lose control of their domain name if they did not return the form and $29 by May 15, 2002, would get people to transfer or renew their domain names with VeriSign, in some cases at three-times the price they were paying.

A U.S. court ordered the company to cease the direct-mail campaign in May, saying it was misleading to consumers. VeriSign would not comment on the litigation, but a spokesperson said the company is complying with the court order. "The industry is plagued with unethical marketing and sales tactics," Leedy says (Go Daddy is a VeriSign competitor).

Some executives have their priorities focused solely on profits, thereby placing rewards on the wrong behavior. "I came from a sales organization where the culture was bottom-line focused," Leedy says. "The top performer was the roughest salesperson I'd ever seen. Customers complained about him, but there was never a response, because he was bringing in money."

Top salespeople with poor ethics are the trickiest creatures for managers to deal with, experts say. Bill Blades, a sales consultant in Scottsdale, Arizona, has walked away from projects that involved dishonest salespeople because CEOs hesitated to get rid of them. On one occasion Blades asked the president of a company to let one top salesperson go, because he consistently cheated on his expense reports—it was a well-known fact that the company was footing the bill for his "dates" with call girls. "The president agreed he should be fired, but in the end wouldn't do it. He was afraid of losing clients," Blades says. "I'd say that ninety-nine percent of all of my clients are ethical, but a bad banana shows up once in a while."

In May Blades and executives he was working with on a project sent a rep home for two weeks when they discovered he released false information about an acquisition to a customer. "He's not allowed to make any client calls while we figure out what value he brings to us," Blades says. "He's missing the national sales meeting, which is embarrassing for him."

Such discipline isn't necessarily the norm among sales organizations. The *SMM* survey shows that although 87 percent of respondents believe salespeople who are caught lying should be disciplined, 51 percent have never actually punished anybody. Maybe it's because they've never caught them, but likely a percentage of managers don't know how to deal with superstars fibbing to clients. Blades has suggestions. "If you have a top guy with a lying problem, get the vice president of sales to cover that territory to retain clients," he says. "If you don't, people will get hurt down the road. The only reason execs don't deal with this is cowardice."

Making an example of unethical salespeople is one way of letting the rest of the team know that lying won't be tolerated by the company. When somebody is allowed to sell by whatever means necessary, it sends a message that the behavior is acceptable. Where Go Daddy's Leedy used to work—a call center sales environment—the signals were clear to everybody. "You could hear the top sales guy making false comments to his customers, but no disciplinary actions were ever taken," she says. "To the people who were lower in the company it was an example of what they needed to do to be recognized."

Another way to safeguard your team against dishonesty is by making smarter hiring decisions. "I always talk to a potential hire's former employers because I find they will say more about a person's personality than anybody else," Blades says. "The best predictor of future behavior is looking at past behavior."

Keeping a sales organization honest means keeping close tabs on its performance. "I find that conducting monthly evaluations is more productive than annual evaluations," Blades says. "Get salespeople to tell you how they achieved something or what they think went wrong. You have to be strong and let reps know from the beginning that you're a straight shooter."

*Salesperson's name has been changed.

Senior Editor Erin Strout can be reached at estrout@salesandmarketing.com

UNIT 2

Research Markets and Consumer Behavior

Unit Selections

Key Points to Consider

- As marketing research become more advanced, and as psychographic analysis leads to more sophisticated models of consumer behavior, do you believe marketing will become more capable of predicting consumer behavior? Explain.

- Where the target population lives, its age, and its ethnicity are demographic factors of importance to marketers. What other demographic factors must be taken into account in long-range market planning?

- In what areas or ways do you feel that Generation Y significantly differs from prior generations?

DUSHKIN ONLINE   **Links: www.dushkin.com/online/**
These sites are annotated in the World Wide Web pages.

Canadian Innovation Centre
   http://www.innovationcentre.ca/company/Default.htm
CBA.org: Research and Develop
   http://www.cba.org/CBA/National/Marketing/research.asp
CyberAtlas Demographics
   http://cyberatlas.internet.com/big_picture/demographics/
General Social Survey
   http://www.icpsr.umich.edu/GSS99/
Industry Analysis and Trends
   http://www.bizminer.com/market_research.asp
Market Intelligence Advisor
   http://www.zweigwhite.com/home/mi/mia011700.htm
Marketing Tools Directory
   http://www.maritzresearch.com
U.S. Census Bureau Home Page
   http://www.census.gov
USADATA
   http://www.usadata.com
WWW Virtual Library: Demography & Population Studies
   http://demography.anu.edu.au/VirtualLibrary/

If marketing activities were all we knew about an individual, we would know a great deal. By tracing these daily activities over only a short period of time, we could probably guess rather accurately that person's tastes, understand much of his or her system of personal values, and learn quite a bit about how he or she deals with the world.

In a sense, this is a key to successful marketing management: tracing a market's activities and understanding its behavior. However, in spite of the increasing sophistication of market research techniques, this task is not easy. Today a new society is evolving out of the changing lifestyles of Americans, and these divergent lifestyles have put great pressure on the marketer who hopes to identify and profitably reach a target market. At the same time, however, each change in consumer behavior leads to new marketing opportunities.

The writings in this unit were selected to provide information and insight into the effects that lifestyle changes and demographic trends are having on American industry.

The first unit article in the *Marketing Research* subsection provides some guidelines on what types of marketing research are most valuable. The next article describes how a popular research technique helps marketers and consumers get what they really want.

The four articles in the *Markets and Demographics* subsection examine the importance of demographic data, geographic settings, economic forces, and age considerations in making marketing decisions. In the first article, "A Beginner's Guide to Demographics," Berna Miller provides a helpful background on understanding demographics. The remaining three articles scrutinize some unique demographic and psychographic considerations to be reckoned with for various generational and multicultural groupings.

The three articles in the final subsection examine how consumer behavior, social attitudes, cues, and quality considerations will have an impact on the evaluation and purchase of various products and services for different consumers.

Marketing Research

Are we doomed forever to suffer the pangs of our self-delusional, speculative bubbles and misguided ventures?

JERRY W. THOMAS

So WHAT HAVE WE LEARNED FROM THE $500 billion to $1 trillion dot.com meltdown? Not to mention the billions squandered on speculative telecommunications ventures, and the billions wasted on other technologies in search of a market, any market.

Okay, we've learned once again that we cannot trust Wall Street—they will sell us anything we are stupid enough to buy. We've learned not to trust the financial media—they'll fan the speculative flames to sell magazines and airtime. We've learned that you should not give millions of dollars and free rein to college students. We've learned that diversification is a good investment strategy. We've learned that arrogance is a prescription for disaster, and we've learned that ignorance is frequently arrogance's faithful companion.

But, what else did we learn? How many of the dot.com business ventures were based on solid marketing research? Virtually none. How many of the high-profile telecommunications ventures were based on sound marketing research? Very few. How many of the other high-tech ventures did their homework and conducted the basic marketing research necessary to accurately evaluate the market potential for their ventures? Very few. How many of these companies used marketing research to refine their business concepts and tweak their processes after the new ventures were launched? Very few.

Would good research have prevented all losses and saved these ventures? No, of course not. But, it would have stopped the launches of many of these ventures, and

dramatically reduced the number of failures among those that did go to market.

Marketing research, the application of the scientific method to help solve business problems, includes experiments, surveys, product tests, advertising tests, promotion tests, motivational research, strategy research, customer satisfaction monitoring, and other techniques.

Rules of Market Research

What types of research are most valuable, and when should you research? Here are some general rules:

1. Strategy research is critical. What's the grand scheme? Where are you going? What's the optimal target market for your business concept? What is the optimum strategic positioning for your concept? How will you differentiate your concept from competitive businesses? What's the best product line for your concept? What's the best set of product features or capabilities? What is your pricing strategy? How will you mute competitive counterattack? Answers to these questions are essential to the success of any business.

2. Product testing is the single most important research you'll ever do. Everyone tends to think their own inventions and products are wonderful, much better than those of competitors. Rarely is this self-delusional assumption true. If you are not regularly testing your products and services among your users, you don't know if your products are any good or not.

Most of the time your customers will not tell you your products are inferior—people are too polite, too concerned about hurting your feelings. When you develop new products, test them among potential users to make sure they are good. You can even use product testing to test the quality of your products over time, and monitor the threat posed by competitive products. Product testing among your target audience is a never-ending quest for improvement.

3. Advertising pretesting is extremely important. Much media advertising is wasted because the advertising is simply not effective. Advertising directors and marketing directors and advertising agencies tend to fall in love with their creative "offspring," and are very resistant to subjecting their "delicate art" to the crucible of consumer opinion. This is one of the greatest mistakes companies make: the failure to test their advertising.

Advertising is simply too important to trust creative decisions to one's advertising agency or to the penchants of a few executives. The only reliable jury is the consumers who make up the target audience for your product. Operations research evaluates and improves service levels and service processes, as perceived by your customers. What are key elements of perceived "service"? How can perceived service be improved? How can you recruit better employees? How should your employees treat your customers? These questions can all be answered by "marketing" research methods. A great product accompanied by poor support, delivered by surly employees, does not build a brand franchise.

4. Sales analysis. What is per capita consumption of your product by state or by country? What are your sales by channel or distribution, by state? What are the trends in your sales over the past three years, by channel of distribution? Who is buying your product, and who is not? What economic indices tend to correlate to your sales data? Can you identify "leading indicators" among the published economic indices that might help you anticipate conditions in your industry? Sales research is extremely valuable.

5. Other types of research might be valuable, depending upon your company's needs, such as awareness and attitude surveys, brand image surveys, advertising tracking, promotion testing, media-mix evaluation, new products research, marketing optimization research, and customer loyalty evaluation. Your marketing research should have a purpose. Do research when you can't afford to be wrong on a decision, when the risks are great, when the opportunities are big, or when you must convince your management. Do research, however, only when benefits exceed the costs of research.

You might start the process by calling companies in your area or industry that do a lot of marketing research. Then, talk to the candidate companies to determine "chemistry" and fit to your needs.

6. Magic techniques. Exotic approaches. Revolutionary technology. Let them experiment on your competitors. Rule one: If you don't understand it, don't buy it.

7. Guaranteed solutions. They know they can solve your problem. They are certain they are right. They are in possession of the Holy Grail. Let them bring salvation and ultimate truth to your competitors. Rule two: Don't do business with prophets or other guru consultants.

8. Price variance. If the prices quoted for research are extremely high, you should be wary. Make sure you are getting extra value for the extra price. Also be wary of the companies that quote very low prices. Never choose a research company just because its prices are the lowest, and risk making wrong decisions.

Return on Research

How do you get the most from the research company you choose?

1. Build a relationship. Involve the research company in your business. The more you work with one company, the better the job that company will do.

2. Set forth clear objectives. Tell the research company what decisions you wish to make. Be sure the research firm understands your objectives.

3. Look in on the research while it is in process. Listen to some of the telephone interviews. Observe the focus groups or depth interviews.

4. Once a study is completed, ask the research company to present the results to all of your key people in one room, at one time. This is essential for two reasons: first, many people don't read research reports; second, even if they do read them, many people don't understand them. A live presentation with all the key decision-makers in one room allows the researcher to explain the results, answer all questions, and clear up any confusion.

If used wisely, research can help your business avoid the next speculative meltdown. The future belongs to those who make informed decisions based on objective, research-based realities.

Jerry W. Thomas is president and CEO of Decision Analyst, providers of marketing research services and a world leader in on-line marketing research. 817-640-6166 or www.decisionanalyst.com.

From *Executive Excellence*, November 2001, pp. 11-12. © 2001 by Executive Excellence.

Product by Design

An increasingly popular research technique helps marketers and consumers get what they really want.

BY DAVID J. LIPKE

This past November, the Lands' End Web site launched "My Personal Shopper," a recommendation engine for customers who want help sorting through the retailer's vast selection of sweaters, skirts, and button-downs. Big whoop, you say—Amazon's been doing this for years. But unlike companies that use past purchases to proffer suggestions to cyber-browsers, Lands' End is the first apparel retailer to use a technique called conjoint analysis. In a brief survey, six pairs of outfits are shown to the shopper, who chooses a preferred outfit among each pair. Through analysis of these six simple choices, and the answers to a few other questions, the site sorts through 80,000 apparel options and presents the most suitable ones to the busy shopper.

While the use of conjoint analysis by Lands' End is unique, the methodology itself is not. It's a research technique that has been around for three decades, but which is increasing in popularity as software developments and the Internet make it easier to use, as well as more powerful and flexible. Understanding how conjoint analysis works, and the innovative ways it's now being used, provides a good opportunity

for any company to increase its chances of giving consumers more of what they want, and less of what they don't. "Use of this method will increase as more marketers realize what it can do, and how well it can work," says John Seal, senior analytical consultant at Burke, Inc., a Cincinnati-based research firm.

So what is conjoint analysis? The rationale underlying the technique is that consumers weigh all the many elements of a product or service—such as price, ingredients, packaging, technical specifications, and on and on—when choosing, say, a sweater, airline ticket, or stereo system. While this may seem obvious to anyone who's faced a wall of DVD players at Circuit City, figuring out how to leverage this concept in the marketing arena can be difficult. Conjoint analysis does this by breaking products down into their many elements, uncovering which ones drive consumer decisions and which combination will be most successful. But rather than directly asking survey respondents to state the importance of a certain component *à la* traditional surveys, participants judge hypothetical product profiles, consisting of a range of defining characteristics called "el-

ements." Their responses are run through an analytical process that indirectly identifies the importance and appeal of each element, based upon their pattern of preferences for the element groups.

If this process sounds more complicated than a traditional survey, it is. And it tends to be more expensive as well. But, as the saying goes, you get what you pay for. While traditional surveys can gauge interest in product features, the results can be misleading. This is because it can be difficult for respondents to directly relate how valuable a particular product feature will be to them. "If you ask respondents how much they are willing to pay for a certain feature, they often can't or won't answer truthfully," says Tom Pilon, a Carrollton, Texas-based consultant who specializes in conjoint research projects. "They'll tend to say they're interested in all the new features." They wouldn't be lying, but they might not actually pay for those features when the product comes to the market. Similarly, focus groups are a good way to draw out consumer opinion on new products, but it's difficult to accurately quantify how a product will perform in the marketplace from this data.

A BRIEF HISTORY OF CONJOINT

1964
The fundamental theories for conjoint analysis are laid out in a paper by R. D. Luce and J. W. Tukey, "Simultaneous Conjoint Measurement: A New Type of Fundamental Measurement," in the *Journal of Mathematical Psychology*.

1971
Conjoint is introduced to market research firm by Professors Paul Green and V. R. Rao, in the guide "Conjoint Measurement for Quantifying Judgemental Data," in the *Journal of Marketing Research*. First commercial use of conjoint analysis is conducted.

1980
Approximately 160 conjoint research projects are completed by market research firms, according to a survey of 17 firms known to conduct this type of research by Professors Philippe Cattin and Richard Wittink. In total, 700 projects are completed from 1971 through 1980.

1983
Choice-based conjoint is introduced to the market research industry by J. J. Louviere and G. G. Woodworth, in an article in the *Journal of Marketing Research*.

1985
Bretton-Clark introduces the first commercial, full-profile conjoint system, called Conjoint Designer.
Sawtooth Software introduces ACA, a software package for adaptive conjoint analysis. It is now the most widely used software for this type of research.

1989
Professors Cattin and Wittink find that 1,062 conjoint research projects have been completed since 1984, and estimate that close to 2,000 conjoint research projects will be conducted that year.

1990
SPSS introduces a full-profile conjoint analysis software package for the computer.

1993
Sawtooth Software introduces the first commercial choice-based conjoint software for the computer.

Source: Sawtooth Software: The Journal of Marketing, Summer 1982: The Journal of Marketing, July 1989; The Journal of Marketing Research, Fall 1995.

"Conjoint mimics the way that consumers actually think," says Joel Greene, director of database marketing at Akron, Ohio-based Sterling Jewelers. Greene first used conjoint research last spring, and is impressed with the results. Fed up with consumers tossing his mailings into the trash, Greene hired White Plains, New York-based market research firm Moscowitz Jacobs Inc. (MJI) to figure out a way to make them more appealing. Using a proprietary research tool called IdeaMap, MJI worked with Greene to systematically break down the brand image and communication efforts of Shaw's (a division of Sterling Jewelers) into bite-size elements. These factors were culled through focus groups and brainstorming sessions that examined previous marketing efforts and possible new approaches. Well over a hundred elements were part of the tested pool, which included different ways to convey messages about Shaw's stores, merchandise, brand differentiation, and emotional appeals. "We wanted to cast a wide net, because we didn't know what would work," says Greene.

MJI recruited a group of more than a hundred survey respondents to its testing facilities in Chicago and White Plains. Seated at computers, they were systematically exposed to the different elements, grouped as words, phrases, and pictures. For each random grouping of elements, the respondent would rate the appeal of the group as a whole. From an analysis of the pattern of ratings, MJI was able to give a utility score to each element. Using these scores, Shaw's could then create marketing messages from this universe of elements appealing to the widest group of customers, or to specific segments. The words, phrases, and pictures (i.e. elements) that scored highest for each segment were then used to create new mailings. And the glittering result? The creative geared toward each segment resulted in significantly higher rates of response, as well as increased dollar sales per response.

> Understanding how conjoint analysis works **is a good way for any company** to increase its chances of **giving consumers more of what they want,** and less of what they don't.

The effectiveness with which conjoint can be used to understand precisely which aspects and features of a product are driving sales is especially crucial in an industry such as consumer electronics. With an increase in digital convergence, and with hybrid electronic products coming to the market—think refrigerators connected to the Internet, and cameras as MP3 players—the question arises: Will consumers actually pay for these products, and how much? "We really have to avoid the 'if you build it, they will come' pitfall," says Maria Townsend-Metz, a marketing manager at Motorola.

Heeding this warning, Townsend-Metz used conjoint analysis while working on enhancing Motorola's popular TalkAbout two-way radios. "We couldn't put all the different options we were thinking about on the radio, so we needed to know which ones were going to be of most value to the consumer, and help sell the most radios," says Townsend-Metz. Because of the complexity of creating and modeling well-run conjoint studies, she brought in Boise, Idaho-based research firm POPULUS, Inc. In six markets across the U.S., the company conducted conjoint surveys of consumers who participated in activities, such as camping and biking, where a two-way radio would be a natural accessory. POPULUS tested 18 attributes, covering technical specifications, price points, and the appearance of the devices.

Using a conjoint methodology was especially appropriate because all the attributes were interdependent—different features, for example, would affect the look of the radio, as well as the price. "The goal was to find the combination of features that would maximize interest at the lowest production cost," says John Fiedler of POPULUS. The resulting product was right on consumers' wavelength, and the TalkAbout now leads the market for recreational and industrial two-way radios.

CONJOINT ANALYSIS IN A NUTSHELL

Conjoint analysis presents a way for researchers to understand which specific elements (i.e. parts or features) of a product, package design, or marketing message are most valued by consumers when making a decision to purchase. It involves placing a series of product concepts, composed of different elements, in front of survey respondents. The respondents express their preferences for the different concepts, and the importance of each element is determined by analyzing the pattern of the respondents' choices. The elements tested are "attributes" (such as color, brand, and price) and "levels" within those attributes (such as blue or red, Ford or Honda, $100 or $150). After the survey, "utility scores" are calculated for each level showing which ones were most preferred, and which were most important in the hypothetical purchase decision. Many researchers have created their own unique methodology for conducting this type of research, but there are three main types of conjoint analysis:

TYPE	DESCRIPTION	PROS & CONS
TRADITIONAL (a.k.a.: full-profile; preference-based; ratings-based; card-sort)	Respondents are given a series of product profiles to rate. Each profile is composed of one level for each attribute being tested (e.g. How likely are you to buy a blue Ford that costs $150?)	• Easy, straightforward design process • Can be administered on paper or by computer • Encourages respondents to evaluate the product individually, rather than in comparison to others • Because full profiles are used (a level for each attribute is included in every profile), large numbers of attributes can confuse respondents. Respondents can begin to ignore some attributes to simplify the process. This limits the number of attributes that can be successfully tested.
CHOICE-BASED (a.k.a.: discrete choice)	Respondents are given two or more profiles at once and asked to choose the one they prefer, or none (e.g., Which would you purchase: a blue Ford that costs $100 or a red Honda that costs $150, or neither?).	• Allows for measurement of "special effects" (complex interactions between utility scores across attributes and levels in certain types of analysis). • Some researchers believe this method better re-creates the real-life shopping experience, in which consumers choose among products. • Other researchers don't believe consumers always make these side-by-side comparisons and prefer the traditional conjoint rating system. • Comparisons of side-by-side full profiles, with large numbers of attributes, can lead respondents to ignore some attributes, as in traditional conjoint methods.
ADAPTIVE (a.k.a.: Sawtooth Software's ACA)	This technique is divided into three main phases. Respondents first rate or rank the levels within an attribute (e.g., Rank these brands in order of preference: Sony, Toshiba, Compaq). Second, they rate how important a certain attribute is to them (e.g., How important is brand in considering this purchase?). Respondents then rate partial profiles (two to three attributes at a time) that are chosen to test those attributes that mattered most to them.	• Because only "partial profiles" are tested, it can be easier for respondents to make accurate preference choices between different profiles. • More attributes can be tested in the first phase, and then the questions can hone in on the most important attributes. • Software, such as ACA, makes the design and administration of these surveys easier. • Can only be administered on a computer. • Some researchers dislike the adaptive methodology, as it depends largely on the first questions being answered accurately. If they are not, subsequent questions can focus on the wrong product attributes. • Cannot directly measure certain "special effects."

Source: Information compiled from reports by Maritz Marketing Research; Sawtooth Software, POPULUS, Moscowitz Jacobs, and DSS Research.

The popularity of conjoint research was greatly increased by the development of software in the 1980s that made it easier to design and run these types of studies. The leader in this field is Sequim, Washington-based Sawtooth Software, whose ACA brand of conjoint is the most widely used in the world. Other software suppliers include SPSS Inc. and SAS Systems. Prior to computer-assisted research, conjoint surveys were conducted using cards that had groups of attributes printed on them, and which were sorted by preference. The number of attributes that could be tested in this manner was severely limited, as was the concluding analysis.

The trend toward conducting survey research on the Web will further increase the use of conjoint, according to experts in the field. The Web provides an easy way to present respondents with groups of attributes, something that was much more difficult to do over the phone (people can only remember so many features at once). Fuji Film, for one, has used conjoint Web surveys to uncover the effects of price, brand, and package configurations (i.e. the number of rolls in a package) on sales. "Film is a low-involvement category, the product is standardized, and the effects of price and packaging are significant," says Doug Rose, president of Austin, Texas-based DRC Group, who worked on conjoint projects last year for Fuji.

By showing respondents side-by-side attribute profiles of different brand, price, and packaging configurations, Fuji was able to analyze their patterns of preference, and deduce what was driving their choices. The film manufacturer was further able to estimate exactly what effect a certain price point on a particular package of film would have on market share. This conjoint study was so accurate that its estimates perfectly matched ACNielsen data on price elasticity in the film sector, which appeared after the Fuji study.

One research firm taking conjoint analysis a step further on the Web is Burlingame, California-based Active Research. Its proprietary "Active Buyer's Guide" is a powerful research tool for marketers, disguised as a shopping search engine for consumers. Licensed to over 70 popular sites, such as Lycos and MySimon, it helps Web shoppers find the computers, appliances, and financial services (135 categories in all) that most closely match their needs, both online and offline. By filling out a conjoint survey that hones in on what features, price points, and attributes they are looking for, the Guide delivers a list of products that are most likely to interest the shopper.

But Active Research doesn't do this just to help out consumers. By answering the questions required by the search engine, shoppers are providing the company with a gold mine of continuous information on what kind of products they want, and at what price. In effect, Active Research is compiling 1.5 million surveys a month. What's more, these surveys are from people who are providing the most accurate information possible and are in the market, at that moment, to buy a particular product. By compiling and analyzing this data, Active Research provides up-to-the-minute information for clients such as Ford, GE, and Sony on which aspects of a product are driving consumer decisions, which demographic segments are driving sales, and who's interested in different features.

In addition, clients of Active Research can create hypothetical products and measure what their likely market share would be. Using the conjoint-produced utility scores of different product features, marketers can preview how a new product will sell in the marketplace, without the time and cost of a test launch. Because of the size of its sample, Active Research can slice-and-dice hypothetical products in an array of categories, demographics, and configurations. "It's not an exaggeration to say that what they are doing is an absolutely unique way to do primary research," says client Suzanne Snygg, futures product manager at Palm, Inc. The dual nature of their service is highlighted by the fact that Snygg herself has used Active Research data not only to shape product concepts for Palm but also to find the best mini-stereo system for her home. As the Web makes conjoint analysis more popular, it's important to note that conjoint research is still more complicated to conduct than straightforward survey research. To produce worthwhile results, it is crucial to create a pool of attributes that actually influences consumer choice. This requires careful and creative brainstorming. Researchers have to choose the correct conjoint method (there are several types, with many researchers creating their own unique variants). They have to show groupings of elements to respondents that cover many possible combinations, in a balanced and useful way. The final results are only as good as the design and analysis of the research, which can be complicated. Keith Chrzan, director of marketing sciences at Maritz Marketing Research, goes so far as to say that "a lot of people are using conjoint who shouldn't be," due to the easy-to-use software.

That said, the effectiveness and accuracy of conjoint techniques make them powerful tools for marketers who use them properly. Says Tom Pilon, the Texas-based consultant, "once a company has done it once, they always come back for more."

A BEGINNER'S GUIDE TO
Demographics

Who are your customers?
Where do they live?
How many are there?

Answering these and similar questions can help you sharpen your marketing strategy.

BERNA MILLER
WITH AN INTRODUCTION BY PETER FRANCESE

Whatever you sell, customer demographics are important to your business. Demographics can tell you who your current and potential customers are, where they are, and how many are likely to buy what you are selling. Demographic analysis helps you serve your customers better by adjusting to their changing needs. This article provides a review of the basic concepts used in such analysis.

The most successful use of demographic analysis identifies those population or household characteristics that most accurately differentiate potential customers from those not likely to buy. The second part of using demographics is finding those geographic areas with the highest concentrations of potential customers. Once potential customers are described and located, and their purchase behavior analyzed, the next step is to determine their media preferences in order to find the most efficient way to reach them with an advertising message.

It wasn't always this complicated. Until fairly recently everyone practiced mass marketing, dispersing one message via media—newspapers, radio, broadcast television—that presumably reached everyone. No special effort was made to ensure that the message would appeal to (or even reach) the most likely customers.

The result: A great deal of money was spent pitching products and services to sections of the audience who didn't want or need them. In buying a prime-time spot for its television ads, a motorcycle company would be paying to
(continued)

The most important marketing question a business faces is: "Who are my customers?" And the first **demographic*** question a business must ask about its product or service is whether it is to be sold to an individual or a **household**. Refrigerators, for example, are household products; and most households have only one or two refrigerators. On the other hand, everyone within the household has their own toothbrush and dozens of other personal-care products.

There are more than 261 million individuals in the United States and nearly 100 million households. Those classified as "**family** households" include married couples with **children** (26 percent), married couples without children (29 percent), single parents living with their children (9 percent), and brothers and sisters or other related family members who live together (7 percent). "**Nonfamily** households" include people who live alone (24 percent) and cohabiting couples and other unrelated roommates (5 percent).

Different types of households are more prevalent among certain age groups. For instance, the majority of women who live alone are over age 65, while the majority of men who live alone are under age 45. Household types differ between **generations** as well. Younger people today are much more likely to live in the other type of nonfamily household because they are moving out of their parents' reach the housebound elderly as well as the young adults for whom their product was designed. A swimsuit manufacturer that ran an ad in a national magazine would pay a premium to reach the inhabitants of Nome, Alaska, as well as Floridians. Gradually it was recognized that the "shotgun" approach is not an efficient use of marketing dollars.

Mass marketing has since given way to target marketing, whose guiding principle is Know Thy Customers. How old are they? Where do they live? What are their interests, concerns, and aspirations? Knowing the answers to questions like these gives you insight into the marketing approaches most likely to appeal to your customers—and whether you're even shooting for the right customers in the first place! (Sometimes there is more than one set of customers: for example, research shows that low-fat frozen dinners are purchased by young women wishing to stay slim and by much older retired people who just want a light meal.)

Let's say that you find out that your customers are predominantly college graduates, and that you know in which zip codes your existing customers reside. How do you use this information?

The first step is to obtain a tabulation of the number of college graduates by zip code, which is available through an information provider (see the American Demographics Directory of Marketing Information Companies for names and numbers) or the Census Bureau. Then, for any metropolitan area that you serve, establish the percent of all college graduates in the metropolitan area who reside in each zip code. Calculate the percent of existing customers who reside in each zip code. By dividing the percent of college graduates in zip 12345 by percent of customers (and multiplying by 100), we get an index of penetration for each zip code. If the index of penetration is 100 or above, the market is being adequately served. If it is below 100, there is more potential, which can be realized through direct mail to those specific zip codes.

This analysis can be done using any group of geographic areas that sum to a total market area, such as counties within a state or metropolitan areas within a region. The object is to compare the percent of customers who should be coming from each sub-market area against the percent who are actually coming from there. The resulting indexes essentially measure marketing performance zip by zip or county by county.

Not so long ago, demographic information came printed on reams of paper or rolls of computer tape. With the tremendous advances in technology in recent years, it is now readily available on your personal computer. Demographic statistics can be obtained on CD-ROM or via the Internet, complete with software for accessing the data.

Information providers can analyze these data for you, as well as provide customized data, such as how many pairs of shoes people own and how often they shop for new ones. Census demographics can't tell you how many times a week people use floor cleaners, but it does have basic demographic characteristics that will help determine who your market is, how many of them there are, and where they live. Information providers can help you take these data and merge them with customer data to form a clearer picture of your market and its potential.

—Peter Francese

Peter Francese is founding president of American Demographics Inc., and publisher of American Demographics and Marketing Tools magazines.

homes before marriage and living with friends or lovers; such living arrangements being more acceptable today, younger people are much more likely than earlier generations to do so.

The U.S. can no longer be effectively treated as a mass market, because Americans and their lifestyles have changed dramatically.

Everyone in the United States except for the homeless lives in either a household or **group quarters**. Many businesses ignore group-quarter populations, reasoning that nursing-home patients and prison inmates probably are not doing much shopping. However, if your market is computers, beer, pizza, or any number of products that appeal to young adults or military personnel, you cannot afford to overlook these populations. This is especially important when marketing a product in a smaller area where a college or military base is present. People who live in these situations may have different wants and needs from those who live in households; in addition, the area may have a much higher rate of population turnover than other **places** do.

Refining Your Customer's Profile

Once you have determined whether you want to market to households or people, the next step is to find out which segment of households or of the population would be most likely to want your product or service. Demographics allow you to refine your conception of who your market is, who it can or should be, and how it is likely to change over time. People have different needs at different ages and lifestages, and you need to factor that into your customer profile. In addition, there are both primary and secondary markets. For instance, if you were marketing baby food, you would first target married couples with young children and single parents, and then possibly grandparents.

This level of refinement was made necessary by the massive social, economic, and technological changes of the past three decades. The United States can no longer be effectively treated as a mass market, because the people who live here and their lifestyles have changed dramatically. Due to increasing divorce rates, increasing cohabitation, rising number of nonmarital births, and increased female participation in the labor force, married couples with one earner make up only 15 percent of all households. Dual-earner households have become much more common—the additional income is often necessary for the family to pay their bills. Thus, the stereotypical family of the 1950s has been replaced by two harried, working parents with much less time available.

At the same time, there has been an explosion in the number of products available to the American public, each of which, either by design or default, tends to appeal to the very different segments of the population.

Another important trend is the increasing diversity of that population. The United States has always been an immigrant nation. However, large numbers of immigrants from Latin America and Asia have increased the proportion of minorities in the country to one in four, up from one in five in 1980.

This increasing diversity is particularly noticeable in the children's market. Minorities are overrepresented in the younger age brackets due to the higher fertility and the younger population structure of these recent immigrants. The result: one in three children in the United States is black, **Hispanic**, or Asian. Nearly all of today's children grow up in a world of divorce and working mothers. Many are doing the family shopping and have tremendous influence over household purchases. In addition, they may simply know more than their elders about products involving new technology, such as computers.

The recent influx of Hispanics, who may be of any **race**, has important implications for understanding the demographic data you have on your customers. "Hispanic" is an ethnicity, not a race; a person who describes himself as Hispanic must also choose a racial designation: white, black, Asian/Pacific Islander, American Indian/Eskimo/Aleut, or "other." Confusion on this score… can result in accidentally counting Hispanics twice, in which case the numbers won't add up.

Income and education are two other important demographic factors to consider when refining your customer profile. As a general rule, income increases with age, as people get promoted and reach their peak earning years. Married couples today often have the higher incomes because they may have two earners. Married couples may also have greater need for products and services, because they are most likely to have children and be homeowners.

Income is reported in several different ways, and each method means something very different in terms of consumer behavior. Earnings, interest, dividends, royalties, social security payments, and public assistance dollars received before taxes and union dues are subtracted are defined in the **census** as money income. **Personal** income, as reported by the Bureau of Economic Analysis, is money income plus certain noncash benefits (such as food stamps and subsidized housing). **Disposable** income is the money available after taxes, while **discretionary** income is the money available after taxes and necessities (food, shelter, clothing) have been paid for.

All of these are useful measures as long as their differences are fully understood. For example, discretionary income of $30,000 has much more potential for businesses than does a personal income of $30,000. But none of these statistics measures wealth, which includes property owned. Ignoring wealth may provide a skewed picture: a 70-year-old woman with a personal income of $15,000 who must pay rent is much less able to afford additional items than a woman of the same age and income who owns a fully paid-for house, which she could sell if she needed to.

Income can be reported for people or households; household income is the most commonly used measure in business demographics since it provides the best picture of the overall situation of everyone in the household. Income is often reported as **mean income**. But mean income can be distorted by very large or small incomes, called "outliers," which are very different from most of the other values. Thus multimillionaires skew the mean income upward, overestimating the income of the population in question. Using a measure called **median** income can avoid this bias and is more widely used as a measure of income in demographics. The mean income of all United States households is $41,000. The median income is $31,200—almost $10,000 lower than the mean.

It is important to not only identify today's customers, but to predict how their wants and needs will change tomorrow.

Education is another very important and commonly used demographic characteristic—in today's increasingly technological and highly skilled economy, education makes a big difference in occupation and thus in earning power. Education is most often measured as number of years of schooling or in terms of level of education completed. Today's adults are better educated than ever before; however, only one in four adults older than age 24 has a college degree or higher. Another 23 percent have attended college. Eight in ten American adults have a high school diploma. One reason for the low percentages of college graduates is that many older people did not attend college. Therefore, we should expect to see the percentage of college graduates and attendees increase substantially in the future.

College-educated people are one of the most lucrative markets, but you may have to work extra hard to get and keep them as customers. They are more open to technology and innovation, but they are also less brand loyal, since they are more able financially to take risks. They are more likely to read and less likely to watch television than those without any college education. They like to make informed decisions about purchases; hence, they are the most likely group to request product information.

Segmenting the Market

All of these demographic data are available in easy-to-understand packages called **cluster systems** (also known as **geodemographic** segmentation systems), which are available from information providers. Cluster systems take many demographic variables and create profiles of different individual or household characteristics, purchase behaviors, and media preferences. Most cluster systems have catchy, descriptive names, such as "Town and Gown" or "Blue Blood Estates," making it easier to identify the groups most likely to be interested in what you have to sell.

Cluster systems are especially powerful when used in conjunction with business mapping. Sophisticated mapping software programs easily link demographics to any level of geography (a process called geocoding). Some software can pinpoint specific households within neighborhoods from your customer data and then create schematic maps of neighborhoods by cluster concentrations. Geocoding can be done for **block group,** counties, zip codes, or any other market area. Businesses can integrate knowledge of customer addresses and purchase decisions with basic demographic data based on geography and come up with a clearer, more informative picture of customers—and where they can be found.

Cluster analysis is sometimes confused with **psychographics**, but the two are very different. Cluster systems are based on purchase decisions and demographics that cover physical characteristics like age, sex, income, and education. Psychographics measure motivations, attitudes, **lifestyles**, and feelings, such as openness to technology or reluctance to try new products. Both demographics and psychographics need to be taken into account.

Looking to the Future

It is not only important to identify who your customers are and how many of them there are today, but how many of them there will be in five or ten years, and whether their wants and needs will change.

Projections of population or households by **marital status**, age, or income can be very useful in determining the potential of a market a few years down the road. All projections start with the assumption that the projected population will equal the current population plus births minus deaths and plus net **migration**. For example, let's take projections at the household level. New household configurations occur through in-migration of residents or through the formation of a household due to the separation of an already existing household (such as when a child moves out of a parent's home or a divorce occurs). Household losses occur when existing households are combined due to marriage, when a child moves back home, etc., or when the residents in a household move away from the area (out-migration).

Projections can vary greatly, so it is important to ask about the methodology and assumptions behind them and make sure you fully understand why these assumptions were made. Accurate demographic data can be very valuable, but data that are flawed or biased can be seriously misleading.

In general, the future population of a larger area of geography, such as the United States or a particular state, is much easier to **estimate** accurately than populations for small areas, such as neighborhoods, which often experience greater population fluctuations. In addition, the shorter the time period involved, the more accurate the projections are likely to be, because there's less time for dramatic changes to take place. There will be factors in 15 years that we cannot begin to include in our assumptions, because they do not exist yet.

You can have more confidence in your educated guesses about the future if you know a little about past population trends in the United States, especially the **baby boom** and **baby bust** cycle. It is also important to understand the difference between a generation and a **cohort**.

The events for which generations are named occur when their members are too young to remember much about them (i.e., the Depression generation includes people born during the 1930s). That's why cohort is often the more useful classification for marketers; it provides insight into events that occurred during the entire lifetimes of the people in question.

To illustrate, let's look at the baby boomers, who were born between 1946 and 1965. In their youth, they experienced a growing economy, but they also dealt with competition and crowding in schools and jobs due to the sheer number of cohort members. Their lives were shaped by events like the civil rights movement, the Vietnam conflict, the women's movement, and Watergate. Baby boomers have seen increasing diversity and technology. They're living longer, healthier lives than the cohorts that came before them.

All these factors make baby boomers very different from 32-to-51-year-olds of 20 years ago. Traditional ideas concerning the preferences of 50-year-olds versus 30-year-olds are no longer accurate; age-old adages such as "coffee consumption increases with age, and young people drink cola" are no longer as valid as they once were—people who grew up on cola often continue to drink it. The same is true for ethnic foods and a host of other products.

The received wisdom will have to change constantly to reflect new sets of preferences and life experiences. For example, baby boomers remember when the idea of careers for women was considered pretty radical. Not so for younger Generation X women; most of them work as a matter of course, just like their own mothers. As a result, ideas about marriage, family, and jobs are changing and will continue to do so.

If you are marketing a product to a certain age range, be aware that the people who will be in that range in five or ten years will not be the same as the ones who are there now. A strategy that has worked for years may need to be rethought as one cohort leaves an age range and another takes its place.

Therein lies the challenge in contemporary marketing: the fact that it is no longer advisable to treat a market as an undifferentiated mass of people with similar fixed tastes, in-

Define Your Terms

A GLOSSARY OF DEMOGRAPHIC WORDS AND PHRASES

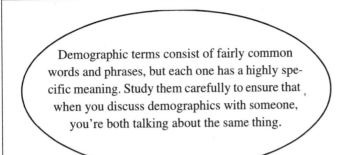

Demographic terms consist of fairly common words and phrases, but each one has a highly specific meaning. Study them carefully to ensure that when you discuss demographics with someone, you're both talking about the same thing.

demography: derived from two Greek words meaning "description of" and "people," coined by the French political economist Achille Guillard in 1855. Sometimes a distinction is drawn between "pure" demography (the study of vital statistics and population change) and "social" demography, which gets into socioeconomic characteristics. Business demography is also often understood to include consumer attitudes and behavior.

POPULATION COMPONENTS

The three things that add to or subtract from population are:
- **fertility:** having to do with births. There are several measures of fertility, mostly different kinds of annual rates using different base populations.
- **mortality:** otherwise known as death. There are different death rates, as there are for births.
- **migration:** the movement of people into or out of a defined region, like a state. It typically refers only to moves that cross county lines.

A related term is **mobility**, meaning change of residence. This usually refers to how many people move any distance in a given period of time, even if they just move across town.

HOUSEHOLDS/FAMILIES/ MARITAL STATUS

household: one or more people who occupy a housing unit, as opposed to group quarters (dorms, hospitals, prisons, military barracks, etc.). The vast majority of Americans live in households.

householder: formerly called "head of household," the householder is the one adult per household designated as the reference person for a variety of characteristics. An important thing to check when looking at demographics of households (such as age or income) is to see whether the information pertains to the householder or to the entire household. *Household composition is determined by the relationship of the other people in the household to the householder.*

family: a household consisting of two or more people in which at least one person is related to the householder by blood, marriage, or adoption. The major types of families are **married** couples (these may be male- or female-headed and with or without children), and **families without a spouse present**, which may also be headed by a man or a woman. The latter category includes single parents as well as other combinations of relatives, such as siblings living together or grandparents and grandchildren. Note that seemingly single parents may live with a partner or other adult outside of marriage.

nonfamily: households consisting of persons living alone, or multiple-person households in which no one is related to the householder, although they may be related to each other. This includes unmarried and gay couples, as well as roommates, boarders, etc.

children: The United States Census Bureau makes a distinction between the householder's own children under age 18 (including adopted and stepchildren), and other related children, such as grandchildren or children aged 18 and older. Other surveys may define children differently.

marital status: this is an individual characteristic, usually measured for people aged 15 and older. The four main categories are never married; married; divorced; and widowed. The term "single" usually refers to a person who has never married, but may include others not currently married. Likewise, the term "evermarried" also includes widowed and divorced people. "Married" includes spouse present and spouse absent. "Spouse absent" includes couples who are separated or not living together because of military service.

RACE/ETHNICITY

race: white, black, Asian and Pacific Islander, and native American (includes American Indians, Eskimos, and Aleutian Islanders). That's it. The government does not use the term African American, but many others do.

Hispanics: the only ethnic origin category in current use. NOT A RACE. Most Hispanics are actually white. Used to be called Spanish Origin. The term Latino is becoming popular, but is currently not used by the government. It is becoming more common to separate out Hispanics from race categories and talk about non-Hispanic whites, blacks, etc. This way, the numbers add up to 100 percent.
Note: The Office of Management and Budget is considering revamping the racial categories used in federal data collection, including the addition of a mixed-race group. This may happen in time for use in the 2000 census.

GENERATIONS/COHORTS

cohort: a group of people who share an event, such as being born in the same year, and therefore share a common culture and history. The most commonly used cohorts are birth cohorts, although there are also marriage cohorts, etc.

generations: more loosely defined than cohorts, typically refers to people born during a certain period of time. These examples are not definitive:

- **GI Generation:** born in the 1910s and 1920s, served in WWII. Today's elderly.
- **Depression:** born in the 1930s. Boomers' parents. Now aged 56 to 65.
- **War Babies:** born during WWII, now aged 50 to 55. Sometimes lumped with the Depression group as the "silent generation."
- **Baby Boom:** born between 1946 and 1964, now aged 31 to 49. Further introductions are probably unnecessary.
- **Baby Bust:** born 1965 to 1976. Today's twentysomethings, although the oldest turned 30 this year. Also called **Generation X**.
- **Baby Boomlet:** or Echo Boom. Born 1977 to 1994. Today's children and teens.

EDUCATION

- **attainment:** completed education level, typically measured for adults

(continued)

aged 25 and older because it used to be the case that virtually everyone was finished with school by then. This is less true today, with one-third of all college students over age 25. Until 1990, attainment was measured by years completed rather than actual degrees earned. The new categories include no high school, some high school but no diploma, high school graduate, some college but no degree, associate's degree, and other types of college degrees.

INCOME

Income can be measured for households, persons, or even geographic areas. When you look at income figures, make sure you know which kind is being referred to!

disposable: after-tax (net) income. In other words, all the money people have at their disposal to spend, even if most of it goes for things we have little choice about, like food, electric bills, and kids' braces.

discretionary: income left over after necessities are covered. This is extremely tough to measure: Who's to say what's necessary for someone else? It's generally accepted that very few of the poorest households have any discretionary income at all, but also that the level of necessary expenses rises with income.

personal and **per capita:** aggregate measures for geographic areas such as states and counties. Personal income is total income for all people in an area, and per capita divides it equally by total population, regardless of age or labor force status.

mean income: the average of all income in the population being studied.

median income: the midway point, at which half of the people being studied have higher incomes and half have lower incomes.

ESTIMATES/PROJECTIONS

census: complete count of a population.

survey: the process of collecting data from a sample, hopefully representative of the general population or the population of interest.

estimate: calculation of current or historic number for which no census or survey data are available. Usually based on what's known to have happened.

projection: calculation of future population or characteristic, based on assumptions of what might happen—a "what if" scenario. Two related terms are **prediction** and **forecast**. Both refer to a "most likely" projection—what the forecaster feels may actually happen.

MEDIA/MARKETING TERMS

The following are not defined by the government, so there are no real standards.

mature: an age segment, usually defined as those 50- or 55-plus, although some go so far as to include those in their late 40s. This is often seen as an affluent and active group, but it actually consists of several age segments with vastly diverse economic and health status. Related terms include:

- **elderly:** usually 65 and older, although sometimes narrowed down to very old (85 and older).
- **retired:** not necessarily defined by age; although most retirees are older people, not all older people are retired.

middle class: This is one of the most widely used demographic terms. it is also perhaps one of the most statistically elusive: If you ask the general public, the vast majority will claim to be middle class. It might be most sensible to start with the midpoint—that is, median income ($31,200 for households in 1993)—and create a range surrounding it (e.g., within $10,000 of the median) until you come up with a group of households that says "middle class" to you.

affluent: most researchers used to consider households with annual incomes of $50,000 or more as affluent, although $60,000 and $75,000 thresholds are becoming more popular. Upper-income households are sometimes defined more broadly as those with incomes of $35,000 or more. As of the mid-1990s, this merely means they are not lower income, suggesting that there is no middle class.

lifestyles/psychographics: these terms are somewhat interchangeable, but **psychographics** usually refers to a formal classification system such as SRI's VALS (Values and Lifestyles) that categorizes people into specific types (Achievers, Belongers, etc.). **Lifestyle** is a vaguer term, and many 'lifestyle' types or segments have been defined in various market studies. Generally speaking, these systems organize people according to their attitudes or consumer behavior, such as their involvement with and spending on golf. These data may seem soft, but they often use statistical measures such as factor analysis to derive the segments.

cluster systems/geodemographic segmentation: developed by data companies to create meaningful segments based on residence, and the assumption that people will live in areas where there are a lot of other people just like them. This geographic element is one thing that distinguishes clusters from psychographic segments. Another difference is that cluster categories are virtually always based on socioeconomic and consumer data rather than attitudinal information. Each system has at least several dozen clusters. The four major cluster systems are: Claritas's PRIZM, National Decision Systems' MicroVision, CACI's ACORN, and Strategic Mapping's ClusterPlus 2000.

GEOGRAPHIC TERMS

Census geography: areas defined by the government.

- **regions:** Northeast, Midwest, South, and West.
- **divisions:** there are nine Census Statistical Areas: Pacific, Mountain, West North Central, East North Central, West South Central, East South Central, New England, Middle Atlantic, and South Atlantic.
- **states:** note: data about states often include the District of Columbia for a total of 51.Congressional district: subdivision of a state created solely for Congressional representation; not considered a governmental area by the Census Bureau.
- **enumeration district:** census area with an average of 500 inhabitants, used in nonmetropolitan areas.
- **counties:** the U.S. had over 3,000 counties as of 1990.
- **places:** these include cities, towns, villages, and other municipal areas.
- **tracts:** these are subcounty areas designed to contain a roughly homogeneous population ranging from 2,500 to 8,000.
- **blocks** and **block groups:** blocks are what they sound like: an administrative area generally equivalent to a city block and the smallest unit of geography for which census data are published. Block groups are groups of blocks with average populations of 1,000 to 1,200 people; they are approximately equal to a neighborhood.

(continued)

- **metropolitan areas:** these are defined by the Office of Management and Budget, and are built at the county level. Each consists of at least one central city of the appropriate size (usually at least 50,000), its surrounding "suburban" territory within the same county, and any adjacent counties with strong economic ties to the city. Metros may have one or more central cities and/or counties. Stand-alone metros are called **MSAs** (Metropolitan Statisical Areas). Metros that are right next to each other are called **PMSAs** (Primary MSAs), and the larger areas that they make up are called **CMSAs** (Consolidated MSAs). The U.S. currently has over 300 metros (depending on how you count PMSAs and CMSAs) that include about three-fourths of the nation's population.
- **NECMAs** are New England Metropolitan Areas and are similar to MSAs.
- **central city:** largest city in the MSA and other cities of central character to an MSA.

zip code: subdivision of an area for purposes of delivering mail; not a census area.

Two related terms are **urban** and **rural** The essential difference between "metropolitan" and "urban" is that metros are defined at the county level, while urbanized areas are more narrowly defined by density. An **urban area** has 25,000 or more inhabitants, with urbanized zones around the central city comprising 50,000 or more inhabitants. This means that the outlying portions of counties in many metropolitan areas are considered rural. Oddly enough, suburbs are commonly defined as the portions of metro areas outside of central cities and have nothing to do with the urban/rural classification system.

—*Diane Crispell*

Diane Crispell is executive editor of American Demographics *magazine, and author of* The Insider's Guide to Demographic Know-How.

terest, and needs. In the age of target marketing, it is imperative to know who the customers are and how to reach them. When the customer's needs change, it's essential to know that, too, so you can adjust your marketing efforts accordingly. A working knowledge of demographics will keep you on top of the situation. It's a piece of marketing know-how that no one can afford to ignore.

*For definitions for this and other terms in **bold-faced type**, see the [article] glossary.

Berna Miller is a contributor to American Demographics *magazine.*

GETTING INSIDE
GEN Y

MARKETERS USE PSYCHOGRAPHIC ANALYSIS TO DETERMINE HOW TO REACH DIFFERENT GROUPS OF PEOPLE. WHAT ARE THE COMMON SENSIBILITIES, HOT BUTTONS AND CULTURAL REFERENCE POINTS OF THE NATION'S 71 MILLION GEN Ys? *AMERICAN DEMOGRAPHICS* ASKED A PANEL OF EXPERTS TO IDENTIFY THE EVENTS THAT MAY HAVE ENOUGH IMPACT TO BECOME THE DEFINING MOMENTS FOR THIS GENERATION.

BY PAMELA PAUL

A chain e-mail has been spreading like wildfire among bewildered Baby Boomers. "Can you believe this?" the subject heading reads. "Just in case you weren't feeling too old today…" What follows are some facts about today's college freshman class. Among them:

- They do not remember the Cold War and have never feared nuclear war.
- The expression "You sound like a broken record" means nothing to them.
- There's no such thing as a busy signal or no answer at all.

Baby Boomers aren't the only ones struggling to get their collective minds around Generation Y. Companies across the country are trying to understand this next big consumer market: the 71 million children of Baby Boomers who are now beginning to come of age.

Gen Y, also known as Echo Boomers, has been heralded as the next big generation, an enormously powerful group that has the sheer numbers to transform every life stage it enters—just as its parent's generation did. Already, even before all the members of this genera-

tion have reached adulthood, businesses in nearly every consumer spending category are jockeying for a piece of this market. But with a generation so complex and huge, how can a company communicate effectively with all its members? Will businesses need to market differently to the youngest members of Gen Y than the oldest, considering that this group spans 17 years?

THE BEST WAY TO FIGURE OUT AMERICA'S NEXT BIG MARKET IS TO UNDERSTAND THE IMPACT OF THEIR FORMATIVE EXPERIENCES.

After all, Gen Y's parents, the nation's 78 million Baby Boomers, have proved that the umbrella definition of a generation doesn't always makes sense, says J. Walker Smith, president of Yankelovich, a research firm based in Norwalk, Conn. In a report last year, the company argued that the most effective way to reach Boomers was to separate them into three segments. Yankelovich classified boomers into three subgroups: Leading Edge (those born between 1946 and 1950), Core (born between 1951 and 1959) and Trailing Boomers (born between 1960 and 1964).

GEN Y'S WOODSTOCK?

For Boomers, the war was in Vietnam, for Gen Y it's in Kosovo. The Clinton impeachment replaces Watergate as the government debacle of the decade.

THE TOP TEN FORMATIVE EXPERIENCES OF THE BABY BOOMERS	EVENTS THAT MADE THE BIGGEST IMPRESSION ON THE HIGH SCHOOL CLASS OF 2000
1. Women in the workplace	1. Columbine
2. Sexual revolutions of the Pill and AIDS	2. War in Kosovo
3. Economic expansion of the '60s and early '70s	3. Oklahoma City bombing
4. The Space Race	4. Princess Di's death
5. Rock 'n'roll	5. Clinton impeachment trial
6. The Vietnam War	6. OJ Simpson trial
7. The oil crisis of the '70s	7. Rodney King riots
8. The stock market boom and bust of the '80s	8. Lewinsky scandal
9. Watergate	9. Fall of Berlin Wall
10. Disney	10. McGwire-Sosa homer derby

Source: Yankelovich

Source: Class of 2000 Survey (1999). Virginia statewide poll of 655 members of class of 2000, conducted for Neil Howe and William Strauss

By studying birth patterns from the U.S. Census Bureau, *American Demographics* found that Gen Y, too, can be looked at in terms of three distinct age groups. Gen Y is usually defined as those born between the years 1977 and 1994; the youngest in this generation is 7 years old this year, the oldest 24. We found that 36 percent of this generation has reached adulthood; this year they will be between the ages of 18 and 24. Another 34 percent are teens, currently 12- to 17-years-old; 30 percent are pre-pubescent "'tweens," ranging in age from 7 to 11 this year.

"Just like Baby Boomers, Gen Y is a very large generation, so particularly at different life stages, it makes sense to look at them in terms of older and younger groups," says Susan Mitchell, demographer and author of *American Generations.* Adds Louis Pol, demographer at the University of Omaha: "It's essential to look at the different formative experiences within a generation—what they've experienced and what they've witnessed growing up."

Formative experiences are significant in that they help mold specific preferences and beliefs—psychographic tendencies that marketers use in developing messages to target varying groups of people. Yet, formative experiences and the resultant attitudes, sensibilities, hot buttons and cultural reference points can vary for members at either end of the generational spectrum. In carving up Baby Boomers into three subgroups in the 1990s, Yankelovich based the segments on how old Boomers were in 1969, which it considered to be a watershed year in Boomer lore. Arguably, a comparably significant year for Gen Y has not yet occurred—or if it has, historians have yet to put it in perspective.

But the pace of business has changed dramatically since the 1960s, and marketers are especially eager to understand this next generation of consumers. In an attempt to predict what the formative experiences and resulting psychographics may be for Gen Y, *American Demographics* interviewed a dozen demographers, sociologists and marketing experts about the cultural and historical events that have taken place so far. To help us understand this huge generation, we asked this panel of experts to name some events that have had enough impact to possibly become defining moments for this generation. While this information is less than scientific, these opinions may provide businesses with insight into creating more targeted marketing messages for this generation. According to the experts, here are some recent events that have impacted Gen Y's lives today—events that may shape the attitudes of this generation in the long run:

COLUMBINE

Although school violence actually decreased dramatically during the 1990s and the percentage of high school students carrying a weapon dropped to 19 percent in 1997 from 26 percent in 1991, according to the Centers for Disease Control, the attention paid to school violence has increased exponentially. In particular, the impact of the 1999 shootings at Columbine High School in Littleton, Colo., and the subsequent news coverage is likely to affect today's youth in two ways: Gen Ys are not only more careful and watchful about their own personal safety, but they are also more wary of the news media's interpretation of, or intrusion into, their personal sphere.

First, Columbine brought the issue of school safety and gun violence directly to families' front doors. In a 2000 *Newsweek* poll of 509 parents of teens and 306 teens nationwide, teens' top fear was violence in society: 59 percent of teens say they worry about it a lot. Among parents, the poll showed that 55 percent worried about their teenagers' safety on the street and 37 percent worried about their safety at school. Concern among college students is also quite high. According to the spring 2001 Student Monitor report, based on a national survey of 1,200 undergraduates, 19 percent of college seniors think violence is the most important domestic issue; 26 percent of freshman agree, ranking violence—alongside drugs—higher than any other issue, including AIDS and education.

(Continued)

VOICES OF THE ECHO BOOM

THE FIRST WAVE:
GEN Y ADULTS, AGES 18 TO 24

- "My earliest memories of American history was the Challenger crash when I was in second grade. And the 1984 Olympics with Mary Lou Retton."
- "I didn't start using the Internet until 11th or 12th grade. The VCR was the most influential invention during my lifetime. Huge. Every day I tape something, it's a part of my daily life."

—Caroline McClowskey, 22,
writer, Milton, Mass.

- "I envy the activists of the '60s for having the ability to unify. My generation looks out and sees a country mired in big problems and we don't know where to begin. We don't have one thing to rally around like Vietnam or segregation. So we don't have the same urge or impetus to coalesce as a generation."
- "I remember the whole OJ Simpson thing. I thought the trial was very frustrating—a lot of money and attention spent for no real reason. It was a circus."

—Caitlin Casey, 20,
Harvard junior, Washington, D.C.

- "My first recollection of American history is the first Bush being inaugurated. I don't remember Reagan in office and I don't remember Challenger. I remember the Gulf War, but it didn't seem important at the time; it didn't really affect America that much. I definitely remember the L.A. riots though—that seemed kind of frightening—people in an uproar, fighting in the streets."
- "When were CDs invented? I don't remember using records. I guess CDs were the invention that had the biggest impact on me, probably more than the Internet."

—David Plattsmier, 18,
high school senior, Fort Worth, Texas

THE SECOND WAVE:
GEN Y TEENS, AGES 12 TO 17

- "The Berlin Wall came down when I was only 6 years old, but I remember the Gulf War pretty clearly. I was completely under the impression that we were going to save the Kuwaitis. But I was annoyed because my parents watched CNN every night and I just wanted to watch baseball."
- "I think the most important invention during my lifetime was the cell phone. I just got one for Christmas. I got like 7,000 calls a day because I have the easiest number to remember of all my friends. Everyone calls to find out what's going on."

—Tanner Rouse, 17,
high school senior, Phoenixville, Pa.

- "With my parents' generation, you had to save money because nobody had money. But our generation always finds a way to spend money. Even if we don't need something. Even if we don't have money to spend."
- "I loved *The Phantom Menace*. I saw the other Star Wars movies on video but they weren't that good. Technologically, they just weren't there yet."

—Bill Callahan, 16,
high school junior, Huntington Valley, Pa.

- "I wish I had been more aware of the Gulf War at the time. I've never been around for a real war. Some people don't count the Gulf War as a real war, but I do. I'm interested in what happens to your state of mind during wartime. World War II and the Vietnam War totally fascinate me."
- "Kids are exposed to more adult things earlier. In the media, on the street, everywhere. People aren't as secret anymore about what they do; they're not as discreet. So kids today are much more aware of what's going on in the world."

—Peter Cohen, 15,
high school sophomore, New York City

THE THIRD WAVE:
GEN Y KIDS, AGES 7 TO 11

- "I think the best invention during my lifetime was the scooter."
- "Clinton is the earliest president I can remember."

—Chris Callahan, 10,
fifth-grader, Huntington Valley, Pa.

- "I don't remember Clinton. Bush is the president now."
- "My parents say to me, 'You know, we didn't even have computers when we were your age.'"

—Anna Orens, 8,
third-grader, Fort Bragg, Calif.

- "I have my own iMac. My dad says to me, 'You're so lucky. We didn't have iMacs when I was little.' I don't use the Internet at home because my Dad thinks I'm not old enough yet."
- "I don't know if they were invented when I was born or before, but I think scooters are the best invention during my lifetime."

—Samantha French, 7,
third-grader, New York City

FORMATIVE EXPERIENCES SHAPING GENERATION Y

TALKIN' 'BOUT MY GENERATION

WHAT WAS HAPPENING:	GEN Y ADULTS BORN 1977–1983 AGE 18–24	GEN Y TEENS BORN 1984–1989 AGE 12–17	GEN Y KIDS BORN 1990–1994 AGE 7–11
WHEN THEY WERE BORN	1977–1983	1984–1989	1990–1994
Around the World	Pope John Paul II ordained; Iranian revolution and hostage crisis; Soviets invade Afghanistan	Lockerbie; Tiananmen Square; Berlin Wall falls; U.S. invades Panama; Chernobyl	Cold War officially over; Warsaw Pact dissolved; Germany reunited; apartheid repealed
In the States	President Carter pardons Vietnam draft dodgers; Three Mile Island; Reagan shot	1987 stock crash; Bush/Quayle beat Dukakis/Bentsen; Oliver North testifies and is convicted	Bush pardons Iran-Contra convicts; Clinton/Gore elected; World Trade Center bombed; Nixon dies; L.A. earthquake
Culturally	*Star Wars; Saturday Night Fever; Raiders of the Lost Ark; Grease; Animal House; Roots* miniseries; Billy Joel wins Grammy; Norman Mailer, Tom Wolfe and William Styron best-sellers	*Rain Man; Back to the Future; Beverly Hills Cop; Indiana Jones and the Last Crusade; Fatal Attraction;* Toni Morrison's *Beloved;* Madonna's "Like a Virgin" tour; *Thirtysomething* debuts	*Jurassic Park; Home Alone 2; Dances with Wolves; Pretty Woman;* Nirvana hits big and Kurt Cobain kills himself; Dr. Seuss dies, Woodstock 94 concert; *Friends* debuts
Socially	Elvis, Chaplin, Groucho Marx, Norman Rockwell and John Lennon die; *Kramer vs. Kramer; Ordinary People;* 10% unemployment; affirmative action affirmed; Michael and Jennifer most popular names	U.S. first officially observes Martin Luther King day; life expectancy passes 75 years; homelessness crisis; Andy Warhol dies; Michael and Jessica most popular names	Jim Henson dies; Pee-Wee Herman arrested; "Don't Ask; Don't Tell" policy instituted; Michael Jackson accused of sexual harassment; first black woman elected to Senate; Michael and Ashley most popular names
In Science/ Technology/ Business	CNN and MTV launch; Pac-man; dawn of AIDS; first IBM PC; NutraSweet; artificial heart implant; Mount St. Helens erupts; Walkmans introduced	Prozac debuts; CDs start to outsell vinyl; Apple Mac with mouse debuts; Bell phone system broken up	Gopher Internet interface; CDs outsell cassettes; tuberculosis resurfaces; human cells cloned; Microsoft sales hit $1 billion
WHEN THEY ENTERED GRADE SCHOOL	1982–1988	1989–1994	1995–1999
Around the World	Falklands; Grenada attack; Princess Grace and Brezhnev die	Gorbachev becomes president; Deng Xiaoping resigns; Persian Gulf invasion; Mandela freed	Panama Canal turned over; bailout of Mexico; Rwanda massacre; Rabin assassinated
In the States	Challenger explodes; "Star Wars" bill nixed; Iran-Contra; Bork borked	Bush inaugurated; NAFTA approved; Clinton accused of sexual harassment	Columbine shooting; Oklahoma City bombing; Clinton impeached; Unabomber arrested
Culturally	*E.T.; Tootsie; The Big Chill; Ghostbusters; Return of the Jedi;* Michael Jackson's "Thriller," *Cats* opens; *The Cosby Show* debuts; Cabbage Patch kids	*Home Alone; Batman; The Lion King; Aladdin;* Lucille Ball, Frank Capra, Fellini and Greta Garbo dies; *The Simpsons* debuts; Beanie Babies	*Titanic; The Sixth Sense; Toy Story; Babe;* Jerry Garcia, Sinatra and Ella Fitzgerald die; TV ratings system debuts; *Harry Potter* fever; Pokemon; Tamagochi and Teletubbies

(continued)

Socially	ERA fails; crack hits U.S.; Band Aid; Rock Hudson dies; Oprah syndicated nationwide; Sally Ride	Robert Bly's *Iron John*; Anita Hill accuses Clarence Thomas; L.A. riots; Woody-Mia-Soon Yi triangle; Jackie O dies	WWW becomes ubiquitous with 150 million Americans online; Million Man March; Pope John Paul II visits U.S.; OJ Simpson acquitted; welfare reform
In Science/ Technology/ Business	CDs introduced; Microsoft Windows debuts; dawn of desktop publishing; New Coke; Nintendo debuts; PC Magazine launches	First WWW server, Hubble launched; Earth summit in Rio; home video games sales reach 40 million; Apple II discontinued; Isaac Asimov dies	PlayStation introduced; Dolly the sheep cloned; Melissa virus; Hale-Bopp comet
WHEN THEY ENTERED JUNIOR HIGH	**1989–1995**	**1996–2001**	**2002–2006**
Around the World	Ayatollah denounces Salman Rushdie; U.S.S.R. collapses; Thatcher resigns; E.U. formed	Netanyahu elected; Madeleine Albright first female U.S. secretary of state; Hong Kong returned to China; The Euro debuts	
In the States	Exxon Valdez; Clean Air Act; OJ Simpson arrest and trial	Timothy McVeigh sentenced to death; Monica Lewinsky scandal	
Culturally	*Sex, Lies and Videotape, Forrest Gump; Philadelphia; Schindler's list; Seinfeld* and *ER* debut; Howard Cosell and Mickey Mantle die	*Independence Day; Mission Impossible; The Ice Storm; The Full Monty*; Philip Roth, Rick Moody and Frank McCourt bestsellers	
Socially	R.D. Laing, Bette Davies and Laurence Olivier die; flag burning banned; *Backlash* published; NC-17 rating debuts; Waco siege; River Phoenix overdoses	Americans go online in vast numbers; Matthew Shepard and James Byrd murders; JFK Jr. dies; Ellen DeGeneres comes out	
In Science/ Technology/ Business	"Virtual reality" debuts; White House Web site built; approval of first genetically engineered food; Sega and Power Macs debut	Carl Sagan dies; made cow disease breaks out; Mars exploration; Viagra approved; John Glenn revisits space	

SOURCE: AMERICAN DEMOGRAPHICS

Tim Coffey, CEO and Chairman of the Wonder Group, a Cincinnati-based youth marketing firm, says that Columbine showed how fears have changed for this generation. Whereas for Boomers and Gen Xers, threats came from beyond our shores in terms of communism and nuclear annihilation, today it's more local. "There's more of a threat from within. It's in *my* school, *my* house," Coffey says. "And that has created a bit more risk-averseness with kids. The size of the backyard, psychologically, is a lot smaller than it was before. Yesterday's kids ventured from one yard to the next to play after dark. They rarely do that anymore."

Second, Columbine not only made kids more fearful within their communities, it's made teens more mistrustful of the media. "I would say that even more important than the event itself was the way in which it was handled," says Michael Wood, vice president of the Northbook, Ill.-based market research firm, Teenage Research Unlimited (TRU). "It's made teens today very skeptical of the news and has led them to really question the news. I think they felt like the media exploited the situation and handled it as a media opportunity." In their 2000 report, "A Psychographic Analysis of Generation Y College Students," Marquette University advertising researchers Joyce Wolburg and Jim Pokrywczynski found Gen Ys to be alienated from and wary of the mainstream media, in large part because they felt their views had been misrepresented on important issues. In a 2001 Northwestern Mutual poll of 2,001 college seniors, "Generation 2001," conducted by Harris Interactive, a mere 4 percent gave the the people running the press and media an "A."

BOOM, ECHO BOOM

In a certain way, Gen Ys may not be so different from their parents' generation after all.

BABY BOOMERS	LEADING BOOMERS	CORE BOOMERS	TRAILING BOOMERS
YEAR BORN	1946-1950	1951-1959	1960-1964
CURRENT AGE	52-55	42-51	37-41
PERCENT OF GROUP	23%	49%	28%
ECHO BOOMERS	GEN Y ADULTS	GEN Y TEENS	GEN Y KIDS
YEAR BORN	1977-1983	1984-1989	1990-1994
CURRENT AGE	18-24	12-17	7-11
PERCENT OF GROUP	36%	34%	30%

Source: Yankelovich Monitor, U.S. Census Bureau, American Demographics

ECHOING THE DIVIDE

Generation Y birth rates trend similarly to that of the Baby Boom generation.

Source: U.S. Census Bureau

MTV

Having recently celebrated its 20th anniversary, MTV is almost as old as Gen Y itself. For most Gen Ys, MTV is as natural and ubiquitous as the Big Three Networks were for the generations before them. After all, even most Gen Xers didn't have cable TV in their households until they were in their early teens. Not only does this fundamentally change the way this generation thinks about music (remember when it was about LPs and concert tours?), according to demographer Susan Mitchell, it's created a way of thinking that impacts many aspects of Gen Y's daily lives.

In a spring 2001 Lifestyle and Media poll of 1,200 college students, MTV was by far the favorite cable channel, with 39 percent of students calling it their top choice. The influence of MTV on all kinds of media, especially those created by or targeted to this younger demographic has been dramatic. Mitchell thinks that MTV and video games have created a propensity toward a type of visual style that speaks specifically and effectively to Gen Ys: loud graphics, rapid edits, moving cameras, etc. "That MTV style of editing is impossible for adults to follow," she says. "But I suspect that there's some difference in today's kids' hard wiring now because they've had this rich, rapid visual growing up."

Mitchell says the impact of MTV visuals extends beyond marketing and advertising messages in the media—into the classroom and workplace. She cites as an example an employer who told her he had to to turn to a

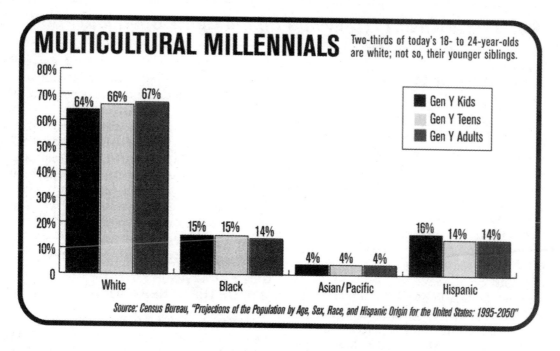

MULTICULTURAL MILLENNIALS Two-thirds of today's 18- to 24-year-olds are white; not so, their younger siblings.

- Gen Y Kids
- Gen Y Teens
- Gen Y Adults

White: 64%, 66%, 67%
Black: 15%, 15%, 14%
Asian/Pacific: 4%, 4%, 4%
Hispanic: 16%, 14%, 14%

Source: Census Bureau, "Projections of the Population by Age, Sex, Race, and Hispanic Origin for the United States: 1995-2050"

video game format for training purposes because his new Gen Y employees didn't respond to a traditional training manual or lecture method. Others think that the MTV video style leads to shorter attention spans, stimulation overload, chronic boredom, and even attention deficit disorder. In *Next: Trends for the Near Future,* Ira Matathia and Marian Salzman point out that for Generation 2001, such "millennial afflictions" are widely thought to be "symptoms of an Information Age in which kids are weaned on computers, consumer electronics and the high-octane programming of MTV."

CELEBRITY SCANDALS (MONICA, OJ, ETC.)

The 1990s were racked by major scandals that made national spectacles of formerly unimpeachable heroic figures—an African American football hero/spokesman and the U.S. president. According to William Strauss, co-author of *Millennials Rising: The Next Great Generation,* these scandals have deeply influenced Gen Y values, which are different from, and in many ways more conservative than, those of their Boomer parents.

While public opinion polls showed Boomers to be more tolerant of former President Clinton's misbehavior, teenagers thought Clinton was a hypocrite who dishonored his office, Strauss says. "That's the impact of the Clinton scandals. They liked the things he said, but not how he upheld his own words. They were much more judgmental of Clinton than the public at large."

The net effect: extensive media coverage of celebrity scandals during the 1990s further demystified celebrities as heroes, says Michael Wood of TRU. "Today's teens no longer have an unquestioning admiration for public figures," he says. "The scandals with athletes and celebrities have made teens realize that though these people are

leaders, they're also very human. It's broken down the facade that existed between celebrities and regular people, which I think makes them much more realistic about who they look up to." The Northwestern Mutual poll of college seniors proves the point. According to the survey, 57 percent cited a parent as the person they admired and respected the most; an additional 8 percent named a grandparent.

Wood sees the impact of celebrity scandals playing out in the long run in terms of an increasing emphasis on privacy among today's youth. "I think the media coverage of these celebrities' personal lives has made teens today much more conscious of their own privacy and has heightened their concerns about protecting their information. They do not like the idea of companies collecting information and knowing things about them." This may have started to play out already—at least in terms of online behavior. In the spring 2001 Lifestyle and Media poll, four out of 10 said they were extremely or very concerned about the safety and security of transmitting personal information online; only 8 percent were not at all concerned.

DIVERSITY

Today's kids live in a world where diversity prevails. Not only is society increasingly multicultural, but kids today are used to a range of global viewpoints, an array of nontraditional family types and different sexual alignments from an early age.

"Look at *The Real World*—there's always a gay teen on there," says Wood. While in the Gen X '80s, homophobia in high school was rampant, many high schools today have lesbian and gay clubs. "A lesbian was named prom king in one high school this year," Wood says. "Then

SHOW ME THE MONEY: (*Divvying Up the Gen Y Spending Pool*)

THE FIRST WAVE:
GEN Y ADULTS, AGES 18 TO 24
(36% OF THE GENERATION)

The biggest distinction between leading Gen Ys and their Gen X predecessors is probably their attitude toward money. Today's leading Gen Ys are optimistic about their earning power. In a March 2001 Northwestern Mutual poll of college seniors, 73 percent said they thought it very likely they would be able to afford the lifestyle they grew up in; and 21 percent said it was somewhat likely. They expect to have money because they want it: Asked in the same poll to choose one thing that would improve their lives forever, most chose "having more money" (26 percent).

At the same time, they like to spend. According to the Northwestern Mutual study, 37 percent currently own three or more credit cards, while only 13 percent claim none. The fall 2000 Lifestyle & Media Student Monitor reports that overall, college students today have a purchasing power of $105 billion, and that 6 out of 10 earn this money through a part-time job. According to Student Monitor's spring 2001 report, the average monthly discretionary spending of full-time undergraduate college students is $179; their average annual personal earnings, $5,140.

THE SECOND WAVE:
GEN Y TEENS, AGES 12 TO 17
(34% OF THE GENERATION)

According to Teenage Research Unlimited (TRU), teens spent $155 billion in 2000—$2 billion more than they did in 1999—an increase of 1.3 percent, and the fourth annual increase in a row. (Previous annual growth was in the 9 percent to 18 percent range.) TRU estimates the average teenager's weekly spending at $84, $57 of which is

their own money. In large part, they are spending money on clothing: According to Harris Interactive, 75 percent of the girls' expenditure and 52 percent of boys' goes toward apparel.

Yet they also have longer-term plans: An astounding 18 percent own stocks or bonds. In a study of 2,030 12- to 19-year-olds nationwide, TRU found that 30 percent of teens are interested in getting their own credit card and of the 18- and 19-year-olds, 42 percent already have cards in their own name. In the meantime, they use a variety of debit cards and pre-loaded cards such as American Express's Cobalt Card.

THE THIRD WAVE:
GEN Y KIDS, AGES 7 TO 11
(30% OF THE GENERATION)

'Tweens may have even more spending power. According to the Wonder Group, today's 'tweens spend an average of $4.72 a week of their own money, typically from an allowance. In addition, these 'tweens get a lot of money through cash gifts—mostly from their grandparents. That amounts to $10 billion a year out-of-pocket—with either their own allowances or with money acquired through gifts. In addition, there's the spending they influence, estimated by the Wonder Group at $260 billion annually.

"This is the most influential youth segment," says Dave Siegel, president of the Wonder Group. "Unlike teens, they still have to rely on their power to influence their parents in order to get the goods and services they want. And today's parents are different from yesterday's. Instead of being the gatekeeper that puts off their kids' nagging, they've become cooperative partners in this endeavor. We call them the '4 eyed, 4 legged consumer.' The 'tween and mom act as one consumer."

there was a big story about a high school football player who brought his boyfriend to the prom." Public opinion polls bear out this growing tolerance. In a June 2000 Medill News Service poll of 1,008 18- to 24-year-olds, 66 percent favored allowing gays into the military and only 25 percent opposed the measure outright.

"I would say the single biggest influence on this generation has been the increasing diversity of America," says Yankelovich's J. Walker Smith. "It's changed their sense of what they have permission to do, where they look for cultural styles, their whole sense of possibility. Because it's not just ethnic and linguistic diversity—it's different household types. It's a global mix and match of cultures. Marketers who don't speak that language should go to their high school yearbook and flip through them page by page next to a child's yearbook today to see the transformation."

Gen Y attitudes reflect an interest in and acceptance of diversity in all areas of life—in the private realm as well as in the public arena. Several major polls have shown young people have a broader definition of what constitutes a family; they tend to be more tolerant of cohabitation, single parenting and extended families. The spring 2001 Lifestyle and Media Monitor study reveals that half of today's college students believe we will have a black president in the next 20 years and 58 percent think there will be a female president.

THE ELECTION CRISIS

The presidential election crisis of 2000 will not only go down in history, it is also likely to influence the next generation of voters in several ways. William Strauss believes the election will have a long-term impact on today's youth. "I think it's going to make them vote more," says Strauss. "They say they're going to vote more than Gen Xers. Some of them are already starting to register." Indeed, the spring 2001 Student Monitor study of college students found that a majority has strong feelings about the need for political reform.

Strauss sees Gen Y's reaction to the election crisis as illustrating generational differences. "One teenager I know said to me, 'This just goes to show what happens when two Baby Boomers who took drugs when they were young run against each other in an election.'" The 2001 Northwestern Mutual poll of college seniors found that 44 percent are very concerned about the political leadership in this country. Compare this with other issues that fall low on their radar, such as nuclear war at 19 percent, a meager 3 percent gave the people running the election process an "A." This was the lowest rating among America's social and political institutions.

Before the election, Gen Ys seemed cynical about their impact on the political landscape. In the Medill News Service poll, 68 percent of 18- to 24-year-olds said they had an important but unheard voice. Yet the crisis may change their perception of the importance of voting: only 53 percent agreed before the election that their vote would make a difference. After the debacle, that view shifted dramatically. In the spring 2001 Monitor report, 85 percent of college students said we need a uniform and consistent method to count votes. And 81 percent agreed with the statement, "My vote matters."

TALK SHOWS/REALITY TV

For Gen Y, anybody can be a star. We can all have our 15 minutes of fame. Everyone deserves to have their say. According to New York-based market research firm, the Zandl Group, "There's a sense that everyone can be a star. It's very populist. Talk shows, reality TV and the Internet have created a mindset in which every voice gets an equal hearing."

Where does this belief come from? According to TRU's Wood, in an Oprah-infused culture, everyone's voice deserves to be heard. And with so many different points of view out there, not only in the public arena as articulated in TV shows, but also on the Internet, teens today are less likely to believe there's one right answer. Wood says the talk show mentality has even affected the way in which today's teenagers learn. "What's changed the whole classroom atmosphere are shows like *Jerry Springer*," he explains. "They think it's OK to be disruptive and to challenge what's being said. There's this 'prove it to me' mentality. And teachers and everyone in the school environment are struggling right now with figuring out how to teach to that mentality."

For young people, getting heard, having your say, and becoming well known are not only easy, they seem natural. You can create your own Web site, make a movie with your own webcam or digital camera; post your thoughts, pictures and writings online; even be on television. Part of the draw of reality TV shows like *The Real World, Survivor* and *Temptation Island*, is that "real people" can become stars. The Northwestern Mutual poll found that college seniors' ideal careers centered around fame: 19 percent dreamed of being a movie actor, 15 percent a professional athlete, and 13 percent president of the United States.

Another result of the talk show/reality transformation of television programming (as well as the convergence of TV, the Internet and the use of the remote control), is that for this generation, TV has become a more interactive, rather than passive, experience. In their psychographic portrait of Gen Y, advertising professors Joyce Wolburg and Jim Pokrywczynski describe today's 18- to 24-year-olds as being "active channel surfers" who have "personalized technology as it developed."

THE MULTICULTURAL REPORT

Nearly a quarter of the U.S. population identifies itself as something other than white alone. The multicultural marketplace has reached critical mass, and it requires a new business approach.

BY JOAN RAYMOND

TWENTY YEARS AGO THE MOST EXOTIC condiment you could find in your local grocery store was garlic. Today, one of the toughest decisions you'll make is choosing among 30 varieties of salsa—the Mexican condiment that has become a staple on American tables, outselling ketchup since the early 1990s. Even kimchi, couscous and samosas have edged into the mainstream.

These choices reflect not only our increasing emphasis on ethnic pride but also a clear change in the demographics of our nation. Over the past decade, census data shows that multiculturalism has moved from an emerging trend to a concrete reality. Today, nearly 70 million Americans identify themselves as something other than white alone—that's nearly a quarter of the population. While these numbers are not directly comparable to 1990 census figures due to methodological changes, it's clear that companies can no longer consider diversity a side issue: Minorities now control nearly $900 billion in annual spending—an increase of more than $420 billion since 1990, according to the Selig Center for Economic Growth at the University of Georgia.

For businesses that seek to tap this bulging consumer purse, the latest census data paints a portrait of a multicultural marketplace that's more diverse than ever. Businesses can no longer assume that all minorities are concentrated in a handful of metropolitan areas—or that one strategy for a particular ethnic group will be effective in reaching all members of the same group. The multicultural marketplace has reached critical mass, and it requires a new approach. "The entire composition of America is shifting," says demographer

Lynn Wombold of CACI Marketing Systems, based in Chantilly, Va. "It's important for marketers to recognize that the numbers and the stories behind the numbers are important."

Here's a snapshot of each group, and how it has aged over the past decade:

AFRICAN AMERICANS
Growing Fast and Upwardly Mobile

AS ONE OF THE NATION'S LARGEST minority groups, the African American population has grown even larger over the past decade. In 2000, more than 36 million people identified themselves as black alone or black in combination with another race. Although Census 1990 and Census 2000 numbers are not directly comparable, growth in the black population far outpaced growth in the population overall. The Census Bureau estimates that the black population grew between 16 percent and 22 percent throughout the 1990s, compared with a 13 percent growth in the total population.

At the same time, black consumers have moved up the economic ladder, as median household income hit historic highs—a fact that can be traced directly to a steady increase in educational attainment. African Americans had a median household income of $30,439 in 2000, up from $18,676 in 1990. By the end of the decade, more than 27 percent of black households had incomes of more than $50,000, and 51 percent of married African Americans had incomes at $50,000 or above.

With increased wealth, many blacks moved out of the inner city and into the

suburbs, creating a larger upscale segment for marketers to target. Between 1990 and 2000, the share of blacks who live in the suburbs climbed from 34 percent to 39 percent, a total of nearly 14 million people, according to the bureau's 2000 Current Population Survey (CPS). While many blacks who live in the suburbs fall in the middle-class category, a substantial share are affluent, CPS data reveals: 10 percent of black suburbanites have household incomes of $100,000 or more.

The black population boomed in the suburbs against the backdrop of a migration trend of historical note: After a century of leaving the South in search of better jobs in the manufacturing metros of the Midwest and Northeast, African Americans started to return en masse to Dixie. Between 1990 and 2000, the black population in the South rose by 3.5 million, according to census data. A 54 percent majority of blacks now live in the South, census figures reveal.

HISPANICS
Unprecedented Growth

BY FAR, THE BIGGEST STORY TO COME out of Census 2000 is the remarkable growth in the Hispanic population. Over the past 20 years, fueled by immigration and high birth rates, the share of Hispanics in the United States has soared from under 7 percent in 1980 to nearly 13 percent in 2000. Now totaling 35 million people, Hispanics rival African Americans for the title of "largest minority group" in the nation.

The umbrella term "Hispanic" encompasses people of many different backgrounds, according to Census 2000.

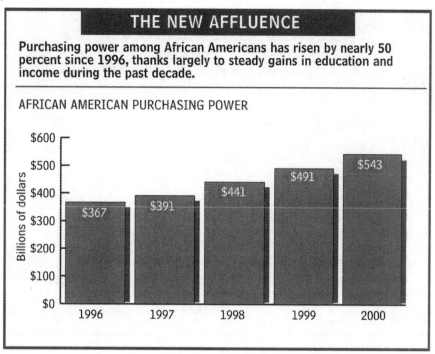

THE NEW AFFLUENCE

Purchasing power among African Americans has risen by nearly 50 percent since 1996, thanks largely to steady gains in education and income during the past decade.

AFRICAN AMERICAN PURCHASING POWER

Year	Billions of dollars
1996	$367
1997	$391
1998	$441
1999	$491
2000	$543

Source: Target Market News, "The Buying Power of Black America" 1997-2001

Nearly 60 percent of Hispanic Americans are of Mexican descent. The next largest group, Puerto Ricans, make up just under 10 percent of Hispanics. Other groups, including Central Americans, Dominicans, South Americans and Cubans account for less than 5 percent of all Hispanics.

Hispanics are becoming more diverse within their own communities, Census 2000 reveals. Historically, Hispanics have been highly concentrated by ethnic background: Mexicans tended to cluster in the South and West, while Puerto Ricans tended to live in the Northeast and Cubans in Florida, for example. While this pattern still holds true today, Hispanic subcultures are penetrating into former ethnic strongholds. For example, in Houston, long dominated by Mexican Americans, a sizable Dominican and Guatemalan population has taken root, says José Villaseñor, vice president of the U.S. Hispanic Markets Group at Ketchum Inc., in Dallas.

Hispanics are also scattering throughout the country, according to Census 2000. While more than 75 percent of Hispanics live in the West or South, small but rapidly growing Hispanic populations are cropping up in all regions of the country. For example, the Hispanic population in the Midwest nearly doubled over the past decade. In Minnesota alone, the Hispanic populace grew by 166 percent, from a tiny 53,884 in 1990 to 143,382 today.

Many companies are trying to target Hispanics—witness McDonald's Corp. re-

cent test of a Cuban sandwich and dulce de leche caramel sundae in select restaurants in South Florida. However, pushing ethnicity in flavors, music, language or commercial "face time," may not translate to success among the Latino population, says Loretta H. Adams, president of TNS Market Development, a research firm in San Diego. She says that marketers must become aware of the subcultures of the Hispanic population. "For businesses to be successful in penetrating the market, they will have to delve into the cultural and psychographic differences of the Hispanic population."

ASIAN AMERICANS
Rapid Growth, Increasing Segmentation

As ONE OF THE NATION'S SMALLEST ethnic groups, Asian Americans are much like other minority groups in one respect: they are rapidly growing in number. In 2000, 12 million Americans identified themselves as Asian alone, or Asian in combination with other races. That's up from just 6 million in 1990. But trends in the Asian American community are markedly different from other racial and ethnic groups in an important way: Asians have become increasingly segmented within their own communities.

Population growth in the Asian community over the past decade varied widely by ethnic subgroup. The number of Asian

Indians in the U.S. shot up by 106 percent between 1990 and 2000, to 1.7 million; the number of Vietnamese rose by 83 percent to 1.1 million; while the number of Japanese actually decreased by 6 percent to just under 800,000. Accounting for these differences: varying rates of immigration, and different rates of acculturation. More Japanese Americans, for example, who have been in the country for a longer period of time than other Asian subgroups, may have selected two or more races on their census forms.

"There really isn't one Asian American market," says Nancy Shimamoto of San Francisco-based Hispanic & Asian Marketing Research, Inc. a division of Cheskin. What marketers must recognize, she says, is the cultural and linguistic differences among the Chinese American, Filipino, Japanese, Vietnamese, Korean, Indian and Pakistani markets. "There is absolutely no common language or culture, and to find the ties that bind is extraordinary difficult," she says.

Businesses might find it worth the effort, however, because Asian households are far more affluent on average than all U.S. households and all other minority households. About 32 percent of Asian households have incomes of more than $50,000 compared with 29 percent in the entire U.S. population; and 39 percent have incomes topping $75,000, compared with 27 percent of the total population, according to the CPS. All told, Asian Amer-

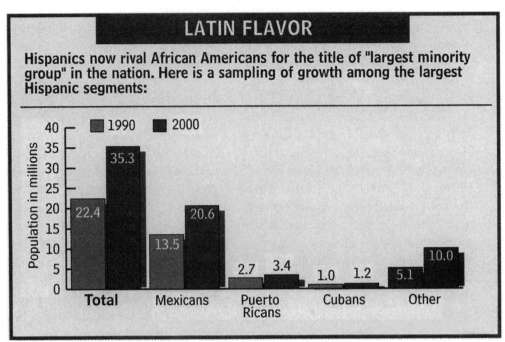

LATIN FLAVOR

Hispanics now rival African Americans for the title of "largest minority group" in the nation. Here is a sampling of growth among the largest Hispanic segments:

Source: U.S. Census Bureau

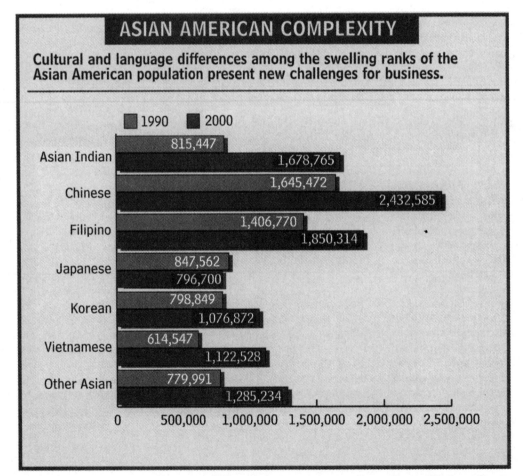

ASIAN AMERICAN COMPLEXITY

Cultural and language differences among the swelling ranks of the Asian American population present new challenges for business.

Source: U.S. Census Bureau

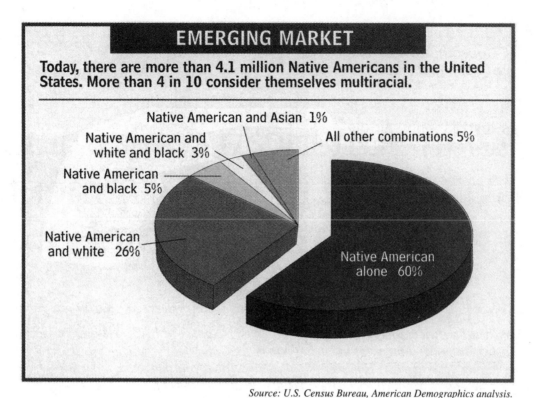

EMERGING MARKET

Today, there are more than 4.1 million Native Americans in the United States. More than 4 in 10 consider themselves multiracial.

Native American and Asian 1%

All other combinations 5%

Native American and white and black 3%

Native American and black 5%

Native American and white 26%

Native American alone 60%

Source: U.S. Census Bureau, American Demographics analysis.

icans' purchasing power is estimated at $254 billion this year, according to the Selig Center for Economic Growth.

NATIVE AMERICANS
On the Radar Screen

In THE MULTICULTURAL MARKETPLACE, the smallest minority group has actually called this continent home for a longer time than any other cultural group. There are just 2.5 million Native Americans in the U.S. today, although the number swells to over 4.1 million when you count the 2 million people who said they were Native American and a member of some other racial group.

Among Native Americans, the story of the past decade is increasing prosperity. Although historically plagued by poverty, this ethnic group has seen its financial power rise throughout the 1990s, thanks to an increase in earning power. Native American businesses, such as casinos, are changing the financial landscape of the

Native American population. Reservation-based casinos and other gaming took in more than $5 billion last year, and some members of Native American tribes earned an estimated $600,000, according to census figures. Native Americans are also benefiting from the service, construction and retail sectors. Native American–owned companies are growing faster than other U.S. companies, with $34 billion in revenue in 1997, a 179 percent increase over 1992, according to the 2001 Economic Census.

MULTIRACIALS
A New Minority Emerges

MANY AMERICANS CONSIDER THEM-selves to be members of more than one race, and census data has never been able to capture this multiracial identity. That is, until Census 2000, which gave people the option of selecting more than one race.

While this has made data difficult to compare with previous census statistics, it

does provide a first look at the demographics of multiracial America. Some 7 million identified with two or more races, refusing to describe themselves as only white, black, Asian, Korean, Samoan or one of the other categories listed.

Although the number of those who indicated more than one race was seemingly insignificant—less than 3 percent of the population—their action was nothing short of momentous. Multiracials are a growing community composed largely of young people. Nearly 42 percent of multiracials are under 18 years of age, compared with 26 percent of the total population. The challenge for businesses, says CACI's Wombold, is that acculturation among ethnic groups has created a society that is more than the sum of its various cultures. The population that best reflects this trend: the multiracial. For businesses who use the census information to formulate plans, the data abyss is a "huge challenge," she says. "The numbers are just so difficult to grasp since there is no basis for comparison." At least until the next census.

From *American Demographics,* November 2001, pp. 53-54, 56. © 2001 by Media Central Inc., a Primedia Publication. All rights reserved. Reprinted by permission.

Asian-American consumers as a unique market segment: **fact or fallacy?**

Keywords *Consumer behavior, Market segmentation, Consumer marketing, Ethnic groups*

Abstract *The Asian-American consumer group is thought to be the fastest-growing market in the USA. Asian-Americans are thought to be well-educated, generally affluent, and geographically concentrated. However, significant cultural and language differences among Asian subgroups are often overlooked. These include patterns of information gathering, use of promotional media, and methods of household decision making. This article presents a comparative marketing examination of the similarities and differences among five of the largest Asian-American groups and develops implications for marketing strategies.*

Carol Kaufman-Scarborough
Associate Professor of Marketing, School of Business,
Rutgers University—Camden, New Jersey, USA

Introduction

Fastest growing population

Marketers today are attracted by the Asian-American consumer market as growing numbers of Asians emigrate to the USA. In fact, Asian-Americans are the fastest growing population in the USA, with a 99 percent increase since the 1980 census (Paisano, 1993). Currently, they account for 9.8 million of the US population. By the year 2050, they are expected to account for 10 percent of the total US population. If the Asian-American population in the USA were viewed as a separate country, it would be ranked the 85th largest country out of 220 nations (*Marketing Review*, 1994). With spending power estimates of over $200 billion, and tendencies toward brand loyalty, Asian-American consumers form a desirable market (Edmondson, 1997).

Some analysts, particularly in the popular press, have suggested that this group of consumers can be treated as one large segment, without analyzing the key acculturation issues that may be particular to each specific subgroup. Others have focused on each specific market without identifying the similarities among them that are useful to marketers. Still others have argued that Asian-Americans are over-stereotyped in ads, overemphasizing business settings, while downplaying home settings and family relationships (Taylor and Stern, 1997). Industry's eagerness to capitalize on their substantial spending power may compromise the need to identify and examine areas in which the Asian-American "market" is really composed of numerous submarkets, with neglected similarities and critical differences to take into account (Campanelli, 1995).

Similarities and differences

The present paper will present an examination of the similarities and differences among five of the largest Asian-American segments with a focus on key consumer behaviors. These groups are Chinese, Filipino, Asian Indian, Japanese, and Korean-Americans. Numerous background sources on each group's homeland consumer behaviors and immigration consumer behaviors are examined to present a summary of areas which likely to require specific subgroup attention. In addition, key similarities will also be derived, and recommendations for marketing to Asian-Americans as a unified group will be discussed.

Method of investigation

The goals of the present article are:
1. to compare and contrast existing "definitions" of Asian-Americans;
2. to summarize prevalent misconceptions in marketing regarding Asian-Americans;
3. to investigate and present some of the under-represented household aspects of consumer behavior; and
4. to describe key areas of consumer behavior and media use which are thought to differentiate one Asian subcultural group from another.

Factors which impact cultural influence

Key concepts: socialization, consumer acculturation and traditional assimilation

Many Asian-Americans have lived in the USA for numerous years and have blended their households with persons from the USA and from other cultures. Over time, second- and third-generation families have emerged, with their own particular blends of traditional and "new" consumer habits. Asian-Americans are thought to learn and use US culture in relation to the length of time they have been in the USA and their level of involvement in the workforce. Motivation for moving to the new culture or reason for being influenced by the new culture (e.g. fleeing the takeover of one's home country, searching for the "good life" in another country, traveling to acquire education or as part of one's employment) are also thought to impact cultural influence (Wallendorf and Reilly, 1983).

Less need to assimilate

Assimilation. Assimilation is generally known as the process of transforming aspects of a nondominant (in this case, immigrant Asian) culture into a status of relative adjustment to the form of the dominant culture. Changes in behavior may be deliberately undertaken, as each new

generation of immigrant attempts to better fit into the dominant host culture. A critical point when considering Asian-Americans is that, given their familiarity with US life from travel, education, and global communications, they may not feel the need to assimilate in the same ways that prior generations of European immigrants did. Moreover, their ability to live in ethnically dominant Asian communities makes it possible to retain one's home country behaviors, habits, and preferences.

Socialization. Socialization occurs when people learn socially relevant behaviors from their surrounding environment. This initial "view of the world" is called primary socialization. However, as new environments are encountered, individuals learn new ways through "secondary" socialization (Penaloza, 1989). Immigrants gradually learn a new culture as they increase their contact with it; this is called the "traditional assimilation model" (Wallendorf and Reilly, 1983).

Acculturation. Acculturation can be defined as the process of learning and adopting cultural traits, different from the ones with which the person was originally reared (Berelson and Steiner, 1967; Ownbey and Horridge, 1997; Sturdivant, 1973; Valencia, 1985). New symbols and new customs are experienced, new foods are consumed, and new ways of thinking are learned. Social and cultural changes occur when people from different cultures come in direct contact with each other. That is, they learn each other's behaviors and customs.

Shaping consumer behavior

Consumer acculturation. As part of these processes, people acquire skills, knowledge, and attitudes relevant to their functioning as consumers in the marketplace. This is called consumer acculturation (Penaloza, 1989). New ways of shopping are tried, and new products are encountered. Several possibilities are thought to occur in shaping the consumer behavior that emerges. Consumers can learn and adopt all new consumer behaviors, they can maintain their consumer practices from their homeland or heritage, or they can form completely new patterns of behavior that are hybrids of both homeland and the new culture (Wallendorf and Reilly, 1983).

Contradictory themes

Misconceptions regarding the Asian-American consumer segment

Several misconceptions and contradictory themes are sometimes found in the popular press in their discussions of marketing to Asian-Americans. These misconceptions appear to overgeneralize on certain similarities among Asian-Americans, while apparently overlooking the differences which occur because of national origin, language habits, level of acculturation, reason for immigration, and so forth. While this list is not exhaustive, it is thought to be representative of some of the overly simplistic approaches which can create problems, rather than efficiencies, in marketing to Asian-American consumers. Eight misconceptions are identified as follows:

Misconception 1: Asian-Americans can be grouped together into a single segment. In this review, I argue that such an overall grouping can be useful for some aspects of consumer behavior, but may cause the manager to overlook other key differences.

Misconception 2: Since English is a common language across Asian-American subgroups, translating an English message into an Asian language will communicate the intended message. While English may be relatively common as a second language, its use, idioms, and meanings are not likely to be conceptually equivalent nor appropriate for all Asian-American groups.

Misconception 3: Since English is a common language across Asian-American subgroups, it is efficient and effective to advertise to them in English, with adjustments and inclusion of specific Asian themes. Such an approach is likely to miss the significant numbers of Asian-Americans who are not fluent in "consumer English."

Misconception 4: Asian-Americans constitute too small a percentage of the US population to target for specific messages. The overall Asian-American group is growing rapidly and will continue to do so.

Significant media differences

Misconception 5: Targeting the Asian-American market is not necessary because they can be reached through the mass media. Significant media differences are found across Asian-American subgroups.

Misconception 6: There are too many Asian-American cultures and languages to create different marketing strategies for each. Different strategies may not be necessary in all product areas; many common needs can be found. Moreover, while over 800 Asian languages are thought to exist, dominant tongues do occur within each subgroup.

Misconception 7: There are numerous similarities among Asian-American cultures; common advertising themes are always desirable. Researchers have identified both

similarities and differences among preferred and acceptable themes across Asian groups.

Misconception 8: There are numerous differences among Asian-American cultures; common advertising themes aimed at Asian-Americans will not be possible. Researchers have identified both similarities and differences among preferred and acceptable themes across Asian groups.

Classification of Asian groups

Just who is an Asian-American?

There are numereous similarities that characterize persons of Asian descent. These include a strong emphasis on family and education, ties to the homeland, geographic concentration in the USA, and relative affluence in relation to the general population. However, it is often unclear just which Asian groups are included in the term "Asian-American." Several studies were consulted in identifying commonly-used methods of classification.

Problems with definitions

Depending on which study is consulted, Asian-Americans include over 30 ethnic groups who trace their roots to Asia and the islands located in the Pacific Ocean. Some definitions include a different combination of countries than others. The inconsistency in definitions creates a research nightmare, since it is essential to create a consistent understanding across researchers about which national groups are actually under consideration. Table I summarizes five different definitions that are found in the literature.

Growth of population

General characteristics

The Asian-American population has grown from 3.8 million in 1980, to 7.3 million, which is an increase of 95 percent, comprising 3 percent of the US population. The US Census Bureau statistics as of August 1, 1997, estimate that the Asian-American population is over 10 million, which constitutes 3.8 percent of the total US population. By the years 2010 and 2050, it is estimated that Asian-Americans will number over 12 million and 40 million respectively, equal to 6 percent and 10 percent of the total projected population (Natividad and Gall, 1996).

According to Ho (1997), Asians may actually be underrepresented in the annual US census. Reasons cited for this problem include:

Table I. Selected definitions used in Asian-American classification schemata

1. Persons whose ancestors came from one of over 20 Asian nations: Bangladesh, Bhutan, Cambodia (including Hmong), China (including Hong Kong or Taiwan), India, Indonesia, Japan, Korea, Laos, Malaysia, Mongolia, Myanmar (Burma), Nepal, Pakistan, the Philippines, Singapore, Sri Lanka, Thailand, and Vietnam (Baron and Gall, 1996).

2. A member of one of over 30 ethnic groups from different parts of Asia: Cambodia, China, India, Indonesia, Japan, Korea, Malaysia, Pakistan, the Philippines, Singapore, Vietnam, American Samoa, Northern Mariana Islands, Micronesia, Guam, Marshall Islands, Palau, and Hawaii (Natividad and Gall, 1996).

3. The Census Bureau's category Asian and Pacific Islander covers more than 17 countries. The Immigration and Naturalization Service counts people from more than 29 countries, ranging from the Middle East to Taiwan (Edmondson, 1997).

4. Asian-Americans are defined as persons whose ancestry is rooted in any Asian country, other than of the Indian Subcontinent (Cohen, 1992).

5. Asian-American is a term that is used to describe people who were born in the USA such as American-born Chinese, and those people who emigrated from Asian countries long ago (Ho, 1997).

1. Asian groups may distrust information collected by the government;
2. Asian persons may be unwilling to divulge personal information on black and white official forms (even if they are in their native language); and
3. illegal immigrants tend to avoid census-takers, but are still part of the consumer market.

Geographical concentration

Asian-Americans also tend to be concentrated geographically. The ten states that have the largest Asian-American population are: California, New York, Hawaii, Texas, Illinois, New Jersey, Washington, Florida, and Massachusetts. In addition, Asian-Americans tend to locate in or near major metropolitan centers. The ten cities with the largest Asian-American population are Los Angeles, New York, Honolulu, San Francisco, Oakland, San Jose, Orange County, Chicago, San Diego, and Washington D.C.

Household characteristics

Asian-Americans are recognized and often stereotyped as being technically competent, hardworking, serious, well assimilated, with a high value on education and family (Taylor and Lee, 1994; Taylor and Stern, 1997; Natividad and Gall, 1996). They have a higher average income, education, and occupational status than the average American. Of Asian-Americans 38 percent have achieved

a bachelor's degree or higher by 1990, versus 20 percent of the total population.

Of Asian households 53 percent have at least two earners, which is a higher proportion than other racial groups. The median household income of Asian-Americans is higher than that of the overall market: $38,540 versus $29,943. In contrast, their poverty rate is also higher than the national average, given at 14 percent versus 13 percent.

Strong cultural ties

Asian-Americans have strong ties to their native cultures and continue to keep their identities within the host culture of the USA. One force, which appears to link all of the Asian cultures, is Confucian ethics, which can be represented by two terms: filial piety and loyalty to authority. These are manifested in the family structure that is strong throughout each group (Larson and Kleiner, 1992). For instance, Asian-American marriages are less than half as likely to end in divorce compared to the national average (Braun, 1991).

Asian-Americans hold their families in high regard, which is a value strongly held in the homelands. Family is a source of individual identity, and a strong sense of connectedness to heritage and tradition is maintained. Asian Americans value achievement, since achievements will reflect well on one's family and group. Traditional household decision making attempts to consider the relative roles of husband and wife in understanding how purchase decisions are made, or not made. Since children and teenagers may be the dominant English-speakers in Asian-American households, their roles may be more influential than those of children/teens in US households.

Significant language differences

Language

Language is possibly one of the most significant areas of difference. Experts report that there are 800 or more different languages used in Southeast Asia. While many Asian-Americans do share the English language in common, their own native tongues are often used in a variety of situations. Because of improvements in technology, worldwide educational programs, and the ease and frequency of international travel, recent immigrants are not finding the need to assimilate into US culture, as they had in the past. Fifty-six percent of the 4.1 million Asian-Americans five years old and older do not speak English fluently, nor do they use English in everyday situations. Approximately 35 percent of those are "linguistically isolated." That is, they live in homes where no one over age 14 speaks English (Fisher, 1994). Such a situation might significantly alter the role of children in household decision making.

In many Asian-American families, younger family members use English as their primary language, whereas parents or older relatives are likely to use their native tongues as primary. Thus, when they interact, conversations are likely to be a mixture of English and the native tongue. As a result, many younger Asian-Americans can understand their native language, and can respond to it in English, but they themselves cannot speak it (Ho, 1997). In addition, many Asian-Americans prefer to use their native tongues in many situations, such as reading, entertainment, and making consumer evaluations. In fact, more than half of Asian-Americans are more comfortable speaking their native language, and 24 percent primarily use their native language.

Attraction to brand names

Brands and consumer behavior

Asian-American consumers are intensely brand-loyal and cost-conscious (Cohen, 1992). They will not buy the cheapest item, but the best item for the cheapest price. Doing business with an Asian-American means establishing a relationship. Basically, Asian-Americans do business with people, not with product attributes (Ho, 1997). A recent survey of 1,600 Asian-Americans showed that this group has a strong attraction to brand names, with 72 percent reporting that brand names are a strong influence on their purchase decisions, in contrast with 34 percent of

the general population. They also like to purchase premium products (Berkowitz, 1994). Automobiles, for instance, represent status to Asian-Americans, and they are more likely to own autos in the $20,000 to $30,000 price range.

Different motivations for coming to USA

Key similarities and differences among the five Asian-American subgroups

Although Asian-Americans come from the same area of the world, their subgroups vary in the usual ways that nationalities vary from each other. Asian Americans come from countries which differ in languages, cultural values, traditions, beliefs, religions, personality characteristics, occupational skills, and so forth. In addition, many of the Asian groups had different motivations in their move to the USA, which often has affected their desire and need to assimilate. The issues investigated across the five cultures were consumer spending and price sensitivity, household purchase decisions, language use, and advertising habits and preferences.

Chinese-Americans

About 1.6 million Chinese people live in the USA; four out of ten Chinese-Americans live in California. There are concentrations in major cities: for example, most live in New York, San Francisco, and Los Angeles. They are a hard-working people, operating numerous small businesses, and owning and developing real estate. Chinese-Americans are somewhat older than the national average. However, the China-born, compared to the American-born, are less likely to have a regular income. Seven out of ten Chinese immigrants are foreign-born. Chinese immigrants were among the first Asians to enter the USA and to establish distinct cultural communities, staying mainly on the West Cost. These "Chinatowns," as they have come to be known, have served to preserve the culture, tradition and lifestyle of China.

Chinese-American society has historically emphasized family, societal interests, and collective actions, while de-emphasizing personal goals and accomplishments (Zhang and Gelb, 1996). Immigrants from several years ago and students can be characterized by "Americanized" household decision making, in which both husband and wife participate in the decision. This is also true of recent immigrants from Hong Kong and Taiwan, but newcomers from Mainland China still practice traditional decision making, with the husband deciding large purchases (Pounds, 1998). A mid-range possibility also occurs, in which the wife makes suggestions, but the husband makes the final purchase.

Prefer ethnic markets

Chinese shoppers are typically price-sensitive, and tend to prefer ethnic markets. However, since they are bargain seekers, Chinese-Americans will shop in American discount stores as well. They often use coupons from direct mail. Moreover, they rely on advertising to provide straightforward information. Belittling or disparaging other competitors' products may be considered to be unlawful or at least unacceptable (Zhou and Belk, 1993).

Language use and learning is also a complex issues. Eighty-three percent report wanting in-language advertising, yet the language issue is quite complex. For instance, recent immigrants regularly read and watch in-language media, reinforcing both reading and hearing their homeland tongues. In contrast, US-born Chinese speak the language but do not read or write it. Thus, print messages provided in Chinese may be confusing for those born in the USA, while audio ads may be effective. While the Chinese population has several distinct language groups and dozens of dialects, Cantonese is the most accepted form of Chinese in the USA.

Racial and cultural mix

Filipino-American

Approximately 1.4 million Filipino-Americans reside in the USA, primarily in California. Los Angeles, Chicago, and New York-Newark are major cities. Filipinos may be of Chinese, Spanish, or Malayan lineage, which determines physical characteristics and subsequently influences choice and purchases of cosmetics and other appearance-related items. Lineage is also thought to determine food tastes, art and decorative preference. Thus, a variety of learned preferences is found across Filipino-Americans.

The history of the Philippines shows a nation that has been dominated by other nations for hundreds of years. The Spanish, the Americans and the Japanese have ruled over the Filipinos. Other influences include the Germans and the Chinese. Thus, there is a significant racial and cultural mix in the Philippines that is not easily captured into one uniform group of cultural behaviors. There are three major ethnolinguistic groups, which are each well-represented in the USA, as well as several smaller ones.

Acculturation is a key factor in which Filipino-Americans are likely to buy. A Filipino's level of integration into the American mainstream is greatly determined by the social class that his family belonged to back in the homeland. Class distinctions in the Philippines are similar to those underlying social class in the USA. Those who lived in large cities in the Philippines are likely to be fluent in English before coming to the USA. They are also likely to have established patterns of shopping in large depart-ment stores and be knowledgeable regarding brands (Pounds, 1998).

Like other Asian-Americans, Filipinos place a high value on education and family. However, unlike other segments, Filipinos lack a "visible and cohesive community" (Larson and Kleiner, 1992). In families with medium to high acculturation, and where the wife also works, the wife will make most purchase decisions. Large purchases are decided jointly with the husband. Children may dominate American food and toy purchases. Newcomers with lower acculturation may depend on input from relatives or friends who have been in the USA for a while.

An interesting point is that Filipino-Americans will tend to look for the "made in the USA" mark on products while shopping in their homeland (Pounds, 1998). This can be explained by the presence of factories in the Philippines that contract the manufacturing of top name brands such as Nike and Lacoste. The Phillipine-made products are cheaper than the US-made counterparts, so Filipinos tend to prefer the US-made versions as a sign of status. Upon migrating to the USA, they tend to continue this pattern and seek products made in the USA, as assurances of quality and status. Filipinos feel that promotional efforts to their group should still include in-language media, even though a majority of them read and write English. Sixty-six percent prefer in-language media advertising. Filipino-Americans are very price-sensitive, since they often have low income and low spending power in the USA. They tend to comparison shop for quality and for bargains. They frequent discount-type stores.

Varying food shopping preferences

Filipino food shopping preferences are related to their level of acculturation. Those who have a low level of acculturation, perhaps coming from rural Philippine provinces and speaking little English, tend to avoid US grocery stores in favor of oriental food and specialty stores. Those with high acculturation prefer the convenience of one-stop shopping at American supermarkets, but will visit oriental food stores for those items that they cannot find elsewhere.

Most affluent group

Asian-Indians

Over 1 million Asian-Indians are estimated to live in the USA, with concentrations on the Eastern seaboard and the West Coast. The top three states are California, New York, and New Jersey. Metro areas such as New York, Chicago, and Los Angeles are popular. Asian-Indians are the most affluent of the five groups considered in this manuscript, and can be analyzed in terms of three identifiable periods of immigration proposed by Arun Jain of SUNY-Buffalo (Edmondson, 1997). The first group, who came to the USA in the 1960s, are generally well-educated successful men, with homemaker wives and adult children. The second group came in the 1970s and are also well-educated. However, both the husband and wife are employed, and they typically have young children. The third group is generally less-educated, and typically own motels and convenience stores (Mogelonsky, 1995).

India is a country of diverse classes with many ethnic subgroups. Indian society is characterized by a distinct division between the upper and lower classes. Because labor is cheap, most households in India can afford live-in domestic help. Since they are accustomed to conveniences in the home, products that promise to be labor-saving are popular with Indian customers who migrate to the USA. Asian-Indians are typically interested in comparison shopping, seeking to attain security, financial stability, and good value. They prefer to shop in areas that are convenient.

Importance of education

Asian-Indians believe highly in education for their children, and thus invest in computers and technological items. They traditionally value money and wealth, and thus invest in stocks, bonds, CDs, and insurance. Since banking and savings are high in importance, they seek banks and investment firms which will cater specifically to them and offer the best value. They also tend to invest in businesses, paying particular heed to franchise businesses, such as gas stations and convenience stores.

Older immigrant families adhere to traditional Indian custom, in which the male head of household makes most of the purchase decisions. Newcomers to the USA, in contrast, tend to follow a more typical American style of decision making, in which both husband and wife are eligible to take part in the decision. Thus marketing campaigns that appeal to traditional norms are likely to miscommunicate with some Asian-Indian groups.

Acceptability of English in advertising

In contrast to Chinese and Filipinos, Asian Indians find English to be highly acceptable for advertising. However, they also welcome use of the Indian language in promotional messages, with 55 percent preferring in-language media. Word-of-mouth is also important in transmitting consumer information. Given these preferences, the marketer must also consider both acceptable and unacceptable thematic presentations. For instance, advertisements to Indians should avoid sales arguments, which may be interpreted as confrontational or highly impolite. Ads

should also avoid trying to motivate the consumer by using psychological appeals. Direct, clear information is best, with an emphasis on verbal messages. India is a country that does not place much emphasis on using visual information in advertising (Zandapour, 1994).

Japanese-Americans

The Japanese originally began to immigrate to the USA in the late nineteenth century due to hard economic times in Japan at that time. When Japan relaxed emigration laws in the early twentieth century and allowed women to emigrate, many Japanese families moved to the USA. As a result, a large portion of Japanese-Americans are older and better established than other Asian-Americans. Many Japanese immigrants own and operate their own businesses, from large corporations to small stores. They value land ownership and investment in real estate.

The 1990 Census states that about 850,000 Japanese Americans live in the USA, with the top states being California, Hawaii and New York. Many Japanese-Americans, especially in California, come for experience, training, or education. They do not plan to stay in the USA, but instead leave once their goals are complete. Thus, learning behaviors and norms of US cultures is not as important as it is to those who plan to stay permanently in the USA. An important characteristic of these "temporary" Japanese-Americans is that the husband usually speaks English, while the wife does not speak English. Since their stay is considered short-term, the wife often does not consider it to be necessary that she learn English. That is, the traditional assimilation model breaks down under conditions of short-term residence plus isolation from mainstream culture.

Distinct cultural characteristics

The Japanese have many distinct cultural characteristics that are thought to shape their behavior. They value conformity, as expressed in the statement *hitonami consciousness*, which roughly translates to "aligning oneself with other people." They are also reserved and extremely polite. The household decision roles are somewhat more complex. The wife typically researches products and ads, making suggestions of what to buy. However, the husband generally makes the final decision on major purchases.

Emphasis on quality

Quality is a must for the Japanese shopper. They look for signals of quality in packaging and branding, and shop at specialty stores to obtain what they want. For example, they loyally patronize Asian food stores for their cooking ingredients, gadgets, small appliances, and other items and brands from Japan. They insist on products such as noodles, dried fish and seaweed, and various types of fish and fish parts for their traditional recipes.

Like ads in their native Japan, Japanese-American consumers prefer short ads that include humor, celebrities, and indirect messages (Di Benedetto *et al.*, 1992). Important themes include the company's loyalty to the customers, with product quality being less emphasized. Product quality is taken for granted. In-language media are preferred by 42 percent, especially on Asian television and in print. Japanese consumers prefer to see young people in ads, for any product or service.

Indirectness, subtlety, and symbolism have always been important in Japanese cultures (Graham *et al.*, 1993). Printed material is considered to be impersonal and perhaps insincere. Although there is a definitive preference in US advertisements for critical, realistic impressions, this is not the case with the Japanese-American consumers. The Japanese-American consumers are likely to have developed expectations that advertisements should resemble those from their home country that are typified by illustrations and cartoon figures.

Three pillars of marketing in Japan

Marketers in the USA may also want to consider incorporating themes of ads that occur in Japan. For instance, as much as 70 percent of all Japanese print ads mention the price of the advertised item (Javalgi *et al.*, 1994). In addition, emotional rather than informational appeals are used (Lin, 1993). Customer service along with product quality and after-sales service are the three pillars of marketing and selling in Japan. It would be reasonable to assume that careful attention and detail must be paid to quality and service when targeting Japanese-American consumers.

More homogeneous group

Korean-American consumers

In contrast to several of the other Asian-American groups, Koreans are homogeneous and consider themselves to be one big family. They speak only one language and, interestingly, there are only 25 predominant surnames. The overwhelming majority of Korean immigrants, 82 percent, were foreign-born, with most having immigrated since 1965. Unlike other groups, Koreans are largely Christian. The churches serve a dual purpose of a religious center and that of a center for maintaining Korean social and cultural bonds. Over 800,000 Korean-Americans live in the USA, according to the 1990 Census, with 44 percent living in the West, 23 percent in the

Northwest, 19 percent in the South, and 14 percent in the Midwest. They are possibly one of the most geographically-diverse of the Asian Americans groups under consideration.

Husband and wife roles in household decision making tend to vary by age. Thus, younger Koreans tend to make purchases independently, while older Korean-Americans are more traditional, with the male head of household making major purchase decisions. Children tend to influence their fathers in American food and toys. While the male tends to make most of the decisions, Korean-American couples tend to shop together.

Korean-Americans have a strong interest in quality products and in well-established brand names. They shop with the goal of getting the most for their money, using top-of-the-line products and services. Korean-Americans indicate a preference for in-language advertising. Many ignore mainstream media altogether. Ads are most popular which feature young to middle-aged males, unless the product is specifically for females. Korean-Americans appreciate participation in their communities by companies.

Easy to reach

Managerial implications and applications

Asian-Americans consumers represent a growing market, with spending power and identifiable purchasing and media habits. They are generally easy to reach, since they concentrate in major metropolitan markets. Asian-American media rates are generally less expensive than mainstream media. Newer media, such as Asian-American Web sites, attempt to address the needs of several Asian groups, while maintaining the cultural identities of each. In addition, many Asian-Americans live in extended family situations. Influence throughout the family helps to extend advertising reach. Communicating with immigrants who have settled permanently in the USA is critical since they become influencers to newly-arrived immigrants who are unaware and unsure of which brand to purchase.

Common set of variables

When attempting to counter the misconceptions listed above, there are no absolute rules of thumb that can be confidently applied to Asian-American consumers. Instead, there is a common set of variables that can affect whether it is appropriate to try to reach "the" Asian-American group as a whole, or whether subgroups or even an individual group needs to be targeted independently. The issue of language, similarly, becomes an "it depends" issue, based on the level of assimilation and acculturation of the subgroups or parts of subgroups whose needs are being addressed. The following list presents a summary of guidelines:

1. Asian-Americans have been over-stereotyped in promotional media. Numerous other common characteristics have been overlooked, such as extended household cohesiveness and interaction. Use of these themes can be beneficial in presenting accurate images of Asian-American households (Taylor and Stern, 1997).

2. Desire to assimilate and degree of cultural learning are related to the reason for migration and intended length of stay in the USA.

3. While, on the average, all Asian-American groups are similar in preferring to receive advertising in their own languages (Wiesendanger, 1993), those who are more highly-acculturated and those who are second- and third-generation often prefer English messages.

Acceptable themes in advertising

4. Acceptable themes in advertising to Asian-Americans are related to acceptable interpersonal interaction and inherent "truthworthiness" of certain types of media.

5. Shopping gender roles and shopping opinion leadership are related to length of time in the USA and to consumers' acculturation levels (Ownbey and Horridge, 1997).

6. Certain Asian-American groups are composed of various subgroups and subclasses, which determine rank and privilege in their homeland societies. While less familiar in the USA, there are carried-over shared feelings that may affect behavior.

Shared needs

7. Certain needs are shared among Asian-American groups. For instance, all groups are likely to need to contact families in their homelands. Thus, long-distance service, Internet providers, and airlines are strong contenders for the Asian-American business. Messages may require adjustments for specific subgroups.

8. Other needs are specific to any given Asian-American subgroup. Food ingredients and preparation methods may be native to a specific subgroup, although there may be some cross-over of foods with other Asian-American subgroups.

Marketing to Asian-Americans requires careful balance. There are often parts of a specific marketing process that can target Asian-Americans as a mass market, and other parts in which a specific subgroups' needs must emerge. When needs are common, creating a standardized advertising campaign can be possible. However, the decision process and household interaction may differ among subgroups. Similarly, the purpose for immigration and consequent degree of acculturation are likely to affect the language used and the media selected.

References

Baron, D. and Gall, S. (Eds.) (1996), *Asian-American Chronology*, UXL, New York, NY.

Berelson, B. and Steiner, G. A. (1967), *Human Behavior: An Inventory of Scientific Findings*. Harcourt, Brace, Jovanovich, New York, NY.

Berkowitz, H. (1994), "Concerning a market," *Newsday*, December 5, p. 4.

Braun, H. D. (1991), "Marketing to minority consumers," *Discount Merchandiser*, February, pp. 44–6.

Campanelli, M. (1995), "Asian studies," *Sales and Marketing Management*, March, Vol. 147, No. 3, Part 1, p. 51.

Cohen, J. (1992), "White consumer response to Asian models in advertising," *Journal of Consumer Marketing*, Vol. 9, Spring, pp. 17–27.

Di Benedetto, C. A., Tamate, M. and Chandran, R. (1992), "Developing creative advertising strategy for the Japanese marketplace," *Journal of Advertising Research*, January/February, Vol. 32, No. 1, pp. 39–48.

Edmondson, B. (1997), "Asian Americans in 2001," *American Demographics*, Vol. 19, No. 2, pp. 16–17.

Fisher, C. (1994). "Marketers straddle Asian-American curtain," *Advertising Age*, Vol. 65, No. 47, pp. 2, 18.

Graham, J. L., Kamis, M. A. and Oetomo, D. (1993), "Content analysis of German and Japanese advertising and print media from Indonesia, Spain, and the USA," *Journal of Advertising*, June, Vol. 22 No. 2, pp. 5–15.

Ho, B. (1997), "Communicating with the Asian-American traveler," unpublished manuscript.

Javalgi, R., Cutler, B. D. and White, S. D. (1994), "Print advertising in the Pacific Basin: an empirical investigation," *International Marketing Review*, Vol. 11, No. 6, pp. 48–64.

Larson, H. H. and Kleiner, B. H. (1992), "Understanding and effectively managing Asian employees," *Equal Opportunity International*, pp. 18–22.

Lin, C. A. (1993), "Cultural differences in message strategies: a comparison between American and Japanese television commercials," *Journal of Advertising Research*, July/August. Vol. 33 No. 4, pp. 40–8.

Marketing Review (1994), Vol. 50, pp. 6–18, 22–5.

Mogelonsky, M. (1995), "Asian-Indian Americans," *American Demographics*, Vol. 17, No. 8. pp. 32–6+.

Natividad, I. and Gall, S. B. (Eds) (1996), *Asian-American Almanac*, UXL, Detroit, MI.

Ownbey, S. F. and Horridge, P. E. (1997), "Acculturation levels and shopping orientations of Asian-American consumers," *Psychology and Marketing*, Vol. 14, No. 1, January, pp. 1–18.

Paisano, E. L. (1993). *We the Americans: Asians*, US Department of Commerce, Bureau of the Census, Washington, DC.

Penaloza, L. (1989), "Immigrant consumer acculturation," *Advances in Consumer Research*, Vol. 16, pp. 110–18.

Sturdivant, F. D. (1973), "Subculture theory: poverty, minorities and marketing," in Ward, S. and Robertson, T. S. (Eds), *Consumer Behavior: Theoretical Sources*, Prentice-Hall. Englewood Cliffs, NJ.

Taylor, C. R. and Lee, J. Y. (1994), "Not in vogue: Portrayals of Asian-Americans in US advertising," *Journal of Public Policy and Marketing*, Vol. 13, Fall, pp. 239–45.

Taylor, C. R. and Stern, B. B. (1997), "Asian-Americans: television advertising and the 'model minority' stereotype," *Journal of Advertising*, Vol. 26, No. 2, pp. 47–61.

Valencia, H. (1985), "Developing an index to measure Hispanicness," in Hirschman, E. and Holbrook, M. (Eds) *Advances in Consumer Research*, Vol. 12, Association for Consumer Research, Ann Arbor, MI, pp. 118–21.

Wallendorf, M. and Reilly, M. D. (1983), "Ethnic migration, assimilation, and consumption," *Journal of Consumer Research*, Vol. 10, December, pp. 292–302.

Weisendanger, B. (1993), "Asian-Americans: the three biggest myths," *Sales and Marketing Management*, September, pp. 86–8, 101.

Zandapour, F. (1994), "Global reach and local touch: achieving cultural fitness in television advertising," *Journal of Advertising Research*, September/October, Vol. 34, No. 5, pp. 35–63.

Zhang, Y. and Gelb, B. D. (1996), "Matching advertising appeals to culture: the influence of product use conditions," *Journal of Advertising*, Fall, Vol. 25, No. 3, pp. 29–46.

Zhou, N. and Belk, R. (1993), "China's advertising and the export marketing learning curve: the first decade," *Journal of Advertising Research*, November/December, Vol. 33, No. 6, pp. 50–66.

The author wishes to extend appreciation to Bryan Ho, Darwin Lacorte, William Mason, Celeste Pounds, Karen Parikh, and Meredith Roash for detailed literature reviewing and integration.

ATTENTION, SHOPPERS!

Paco Underhill knows what they look at, what they buy and why, so get ready to put a huge dent in the concept of customers' free will.

BY SCOTT S. SMITH

PACO UNDERHILL IS THE FOUNDER AND MANAGING DIRECTOR of Envirosell Inc., a New York City-based research consulting company that studies the interaction between customers and their environment. If Dalai Lama is right that "shopping is the museum of the 20th century," then Underhill is the curator. Part cultural anthropologist and part spy, Underhill has innovated commercial research with his scientific studies of purchasing behaviors. When he talks, everyone interested in consumer spending habits listens. Especially during an economic downturn, when it's ever more critical to persuade customers to spend money despite widespread budget-tightening.

60% *of men who take jeans into a fitting room end up buying them, compared with just 25 percent of women.*

His 150 clients worldwide include retailers such as The Gap and CVS Drug Stores as well as Fortune 500 banks, restaurants and product manufacturers, including Citibank, Coca-Cola, Estee Lauder, Hewlett-Packard and McDonald's. Plus, any business owner can benefit from the ideas Underhill expounds in his bestselling book, *Why We Buy: The Science of Shopping* (Simon & Schuster).

Underhill's ideas aren't purely theory; he and his "trackers" have closely watched shoppers (currently 50,000 to 70,000 of them per year) for more than two decades. In addition to discreetly following shoppers around stores, Underhill's staff studies thousands of hours of footage from in-store video cameras for each project. Underhlll's research yields conclusions you won't find with traditional consumer focus groups, because when people know they're being studied, they tell researchers what they think the researchers want to know.

86% *of women look at price tags when they shop, compared with 72 percent of men.*

Understanding consumers' shopping habits has become increasingly critical, as the amount of selling space per U.S. shopper has more than doubled in the past 25 years. Meanwhile, the average time per visit a person spends at a shopping mall is down to about an hour, the lowest ever recorded. Purchasers, Underhill has found, spend an average of 11.27 minutes in a store, nonbuyers 2.36. Converting browsers into spenders greatly depends on store design and displays, because 60 to 70 percent of purchases are unplanned.

But that's just at the store level. Consumers are bombarded with thousands of marketing messages daily. How do you get them to respond, especially during troubled economic times? Underhill recently agreed to let us shop his brain for a few of the answers.

HOW DO RETAILERS GET PEOPLE WHO SEE THE STORE TO COME IN?

PACO UNDERHILL: Look at all the sightlines. Do a 180-degree tramp around to see the exposures, what someone might see at an angle and a distance. There's a difference in being in a strip mall, in a shopping center or on an urban street.

A store window needs to communicate beyond the people immediately in front of it. Windows should have one message, not 15. They need to change no less than every two weeks to get people coming back. People should look forward to window

SELLING POINTS

NO MATTER THE ECONOMIC CLIMATE, YOU'LL NEVER GET CONSUMERS INTO YOUR STORE, MUCH LESS TO THE REGISTER WITH BIG PURCHASES, UNLESS YOU PAY CLOSE ATTENTION TO PACO UNDERHILL'S GOLDEN RULES.

1. BREAK IT DOWN. Generational gaps have an effect on how consumers interpret your marketing campaigns so target each demographic as a distinctive group.

2. WOMEN RULE. "Women are an important part of the consumer economy," says Underhill "Pay attention to them."

3. THE TIMES THEY ARE A-CHANGIN'. "Understand that the way we shop in 2001 is different from the way it was 10 years ago." Says Underhill "Recognize the value of convenience"

4. MARKET TO MINORITIES. "We are a nation of immigrants," says Underhill "You outreach to those customers to whom English is not a first language is just good business."

5. HAVE FUN. "If it isn't fun, people aren't going to come back." Says Underhill. "If you're having fun doing what you're doing, and your employees are having fun doing what they're doing, then it means your customers are going to have fun [spending money]."

—*Peter Kooiman*

displays as a place to have fun. MTV has shown us the importance of focusing on icons rather than words, using visual puns and symbols of having a good time.

WHAT ARE THE RULES ONCE CUSTOMERS STEP INSIDE?

UNDERHILL: [Someone] should greet everyone, but don't ask if they need help because that provides an opportunity to say no. In the entrance of any retail environment, you have a decompression zone where the shopper is in transition and not inclined to take in much information. Asking questions is an intrusion at that point.

"People want something more from the shopping experience than simply an exchange of money and merchandise."

You also don't want to stack people up there interfering with traffic into the store. This isn't a place for a lot of messaging or browsing. Also think about the zone in terms of exiting customers.

YOU SAY WE'RE TRAINED TO GO TO THE RIGHT WHEN WE GO INTO A STORE BECAUSE MOST OF US ARE RIGHT-HANDED. WHAT ABOUT LEFTIES?

UNDERHILL: They're 10 to 15 percent of the population and have been well-trained. Older people will be especially conditioned this way. The point is, know that as a rule, people will start their circulation of the store by going right.

WHAT CONSTITUTES GOOD OR BAD STORE DESIGN?

UNDERHILL: A lot of women are uncomfortable in narrow aisles—what I call the "butt-brush" factor. If you want them to stop and browse where there's a high rate of conversion to purchase, you need to have wide aisles.

On the other hand, don't put a product for men in places where an alpha male will be perfectly comfortable blocking traffic while he examines it.

DO MEN AND WOMEN SHOP DIFFERENTLY?

UNDERHILL: Women are more patient and get more out of the search. Men want to go in for the quick kill. You want to turn guys into drunken sailors, getting them excited about the fun of shopping. They love sampling and trials. If you're selling something for kids, aim the merchandising at them so they'll push Dad for it, since he'll have a harder time saying no than Mom. I don't understand why McDonald's doesn't put the kiddie menu on the floor, which is where the kids are.

For women, create the reality and the illusion that you're making shopping efficient, since they're being pressured [by men]. Less waiting time at the register is critical. Also, hardware and technology retailers need to make women feel welcome, since they're increasingly the customers.

Given that stores often appeal to one sex or the other, they should have comfortable, strategically placed chairs for the uninvolved party to relax, because the more they get distracted, the more time the shopper will have to browse, which is the most important factor in purchase size. Too often, chairs are placed as an afterthought. Put out reading material that is appropriate. You can even leave out merchandising materials to give them ideas for gifts.

HOW SHOULD RETAILERS ACCOMMODATE SENIORS?

UNDERHILL: If you're going to sell to older people, who are an increasing part of the population, you need good lighting. If you're selling packaged goods, you might want to follow the lead of Eckerd's drugstores in Florida, which put magnifying glasses on chains at points of purchase. Also, the lenses of our eyes yellow as we age, so colors look different.

If you put something below 28 inches, seniors may have trouble stooping down to get it. On the other hand, that's a great place for stuff for kids; you don't want to put products for them too high.

WHAT ABOUT SELLING TO ETHNIC GROUPS?

UNDERHILL: They often aren't well-served. Look around your neighborhood and see what products might sell to ethnic customers. Also, most retailers are completely missing the huge number of offshore visitors who would love to buy things here they can't get in their own countries at the prices we can offer.

DOWN TIME

To illustrate our current state of affairs, Paco Underhill points to the written Chinese word for "chaos," which is composed of two characters—danger and uncertainty. For entrepreneurs, however, all is not lost. Despite widespread fears, Underhill insists that consumer confidence is not at an all-time low, nor will it be. Underhill offers his view of our current situation as well as advice on how entrepreneurs should deal with troubled times and business slowdowns.

Consumers may be holding onto their dollars tighter, but people still need to shop. Meeting the five basic needs (see "Selling Points") will continue. Nor will leisure and entertainment spending come to an end. Underhill notes that during past war times, people still went to the movies. He also doesn't see an abrupt halt in vacationing, although a shift in consumer interest from air travel to cruise lines will be evident.

In the aftermath of the terrorist attacks, consumers' attentions have been greatly distracted, which is to be expected. One stark result is that some businesses, large and small, will disappear. Businesses heavily dependent on advertising will be most affected, as their revenue streams mirror the declining incomes of the businesses advertising with them.

How can you persuade customers to buy when money is tight and the future is uncertain? You may need to reposition your approach. "Position your product or service as cost-effective or smart," says Underhill, who adds that convincing customers that your product is a good investment or that now is the best time to buy may also lure them.

Underhill cautions entrepreneurs to be a little more fiscally conservative and adds, "Companies that had trouble before September 11 are the ones having more trouble now. I think this is the issue of everyone being a gunslinger, in the sense that they've leveraged [in the past], always assuming markets are going to go up. They haven't gotten a war chest or have neglected it."

While dealing with the sting of slow sales, Underhill stresses the importance of using this time wisely. "Meet with your employees, undertake small projects, polish areas [that need it] and realize things aren't always up," Underhill says. "Use your downtime to your best advantage."

—*April Pennington*

ANY OTHER THOUGHTS ON MAXIMIZING THE TIME CUSTOMERS ARE IN THE STORE?

UNDERHILL: Think about adjacency sales. For every primary purchase made, there should be one secondary purchase added to it. If someone buys a dress, you want to sell [pantyhose] to go with it. It always blows my mind [when the] obvious isn't apparent to [merchants]: They put the wrong things together or miss obvious opportunities.

This is particularly true at the register. Amateur retailers don't put any design into the register area. They should work merchandising into the original plan for the cash wrap area rather than slapping something on afterward. Also, if the owner is usually the only one there, he or she should always be able to keep eyes on the floor, not have to turn around to work the credit card machine or take a phone call.

Everything should be for sale in the store. When you go into Restoration Hardware, they're selling you not only the item on the table, but also the table. If you sell books, sell bookcases, too; if you offer jewels, then price the boxes holding them.

IF SOMEONE DOESN'T MAKE A PURCHASE, ARE THEY LOST TO YOU?

UNDERHILL: Even if they don't buy, you want them to walk out with a better sense of what your store offers and where things are—reference points for the future when they need something. Look at your store's design through the eyes of the first-time visitor who is breezing through for an introductory tour.

SCOTT S. SMITH *writes about business issues for a variety of publications, including* Investors Business Daily.

THE LURE OF SHOPPING

In her book, *Why People Buy Things They Don't Need*, the author explores the trends that drive consumer spending.

BY PAMELA N. DANZIGER

What does the future hold for companies in the business of manufacturing, marketing and selling discretionary products—those things that people desire but don't need? How can new insights about why people buy things they don't need help companies sell more of their products? How can companies divine the future for the sales of discretionary products and develop plans for action that will increase sales and build market share? Tracking trends is one method many businesses use to foresee the future. Here are the major trends on the horizon that will have the strongest impact on discretionary product manufacturers.

A SHIFT FROM BUYING THINGS TO BUYING EXPERIENCES

Part of our popular cultural mythology says that when people reach middle age, they undergo a personal identity crisis, the "midlife crisis," that often is played out in the consumer marketplace. Stereotypically, a man may address his midlife crisis by buying a little red sports car or, more sinisterly, trading in his middle-aged wife for a new, younger model. A woman may get a face-lift, dye her hair, find a younger man or, empowered by "menopausal zest," find new energy to pursue a career or hobby. When grandchildren come along, the new grandparents may shower presents on their grandchildren to make up for some of the inadequacies their children may have experienced because money was tighter when their kids were growing up. This is the life stage that the Boomer generation is now approaching en masse, and it will change the fortunes of many companies that sell and market to people who buy things they don't need.

In their middle years, the members of the Baby Boom generation will face the inevitability of their mortality. In doing so, they will try to make up for lost time and the things they may have missed, by directing their energy and money toward experiences and away from the continued acquisition of material things. With the attitude of

"been there, done that" in buying more things, Boomers will turn away from a consuming focus on things, to a hunger for experiences and personal development. Service industries that satisfy the mature Boomer's craving for personal enhancement will fare well after 2010. These include travel providers, especially adventure travel modified for aging Boomers' health and fitness levels; health and beauty spas; and colleges and adult-education experiences, including training such as cooking or language schools.

I predict Boomers will eschew the big, bulky, luxurious RV models so admired by today's mature generation in favor of more simplified, environmentally friendly models that can take them off the highway. Think modified VW bus concept crossed with an SUV, equipped with bed, kitchen and bath, with a powerful engine and four-wheel drive.

As Boomers pursue new experiential passions, they will need tools, equipment and accessories to support their new pursuits. Discretionary product providers can position themselves for success by offering new products to enhance Boomers' experiences and adventures. Durable goods providers, such as automobile manufacturers, will fill such a need, as will those who manufacture and market sporting goods, personal care items, books, housewares and entertainment. For example, Boomers will need new recreational vehicles to take them on their new adventures. I predict they will eschew the big, bulky, luxurious RV models so admired by today's mature generation. Instead, they will favor more simplified, environmentally friendly models that can take them off the highway. Think modified VW bus concept crossed with an SUV: equipped with bed, kitchen and bath, and with a powerful engine and four-wheel drive.

Since the future focus in consumer behavior will be about buying the experience, manufacturers and marketers must think beyond the features and benefits of the product they are selling, to how that product supports or enhances an experience. If you came of age in the 1960s, as I did, you will remember the strong antimaterialism ethic running through the youth culture. At the same time, 1960s youth hungered after new, mind-opening experiences. Some members of the Boomer generation self-destructively turned to sex, drugs and rock'n'roll to fulfill much of this craving for experience. I sincerely hope that Boomers learned from their youthful excesses, as I foresee that they will participate in a second adolescence in their senior years.

Some Boomers will turn away from the pursuit of materialism and excessive consumption and save their money for adventures. New and exciting experiences in their second adolescence could include climbing Mount Everest or at least trekking to base camp. They might decide to travel to China, hike the Appalachian Trail, learn to cook in Paris or get an advanced degree in English literature. Some may take up painting or photography, set off cross-country on a Harley, or learn to fly, skydive or balloon. Closer to home, others may take up a second language, join a theater group, form a "garage" band, or, like me, take piano lessons after 30-odd years without touching a keyboard.

CONSUMERS WILL CRAVE REALITY

Our society is undergoing a digital revolution. The Internet is playing a bigger role in our lives. Schoolchildren today learn about computers right along with their lessons in reading, writing and arithmetic. The Internet is also playing an increased role in the commercial side of consumers' lives. In 2000, roughly $27 billion in sales were conducted over the Internet. While this is just slightly less than 1 percent of total retail sales of $3.1 trillion, it is a significant contribution to the overall economy.

As our world goes more cyber, consumers will feel the need to surround themselves with things that will bring them back to reality. This will manifest itself in many different areas of our lives, from how we dress to how we decorate our homes, how we play and how we entertain ourselves.

As we turn away from buying things and focus more of our spending on experiences, nature travel and history travel will grow. What connects us with the real world more than nature? What grounds us in our cultural reality better than history? History travel, especially travel focused on Civil War sites, is already a booming business and destined to grow. History travel will encompass Colonial America, Revolutionary War sites, western expansion and native cultural attractions as well. Foreign travel will take consumers overseas to the homelands where their ancestors originated.

Grounding through nature will express itself in the garden. Outdoor living space will grow, with consumers building elaborate garden getaways where they can shut out the modern world and enjoy the sounds, smells and sights of nature. We will populate our gardens with birds, turtles, frogs, toads, peaceful snakes, squirrels, bats and even other furry mammals that will connect us better to the real world.

With an emphasis on reality, our home decorating focus will expand to include all five senses. While color and style (i.e., sight) may always dominate our home decor, consumers are broadening their focus to texture (i.e., touch), background music or sounds or running water in indoor fountains (i.e., hearing) and home fragrances (i.e., smell). The sense of taste is indulged in our kitchens, now the center and focus of the home.

As we stimulate our senses through the things with which we surround ourselves, we will pay particular attention to the feel of fabrics in our upholstered furniture, rugs, pillows, throws, bed linens, curtains, towels, and kitchen and dining linens. Shoppers have always been "touchy-feely" when buying these products, but in the future they will become even more so.

Our taste in home furnishings, including the colors we use to decorate and the art we choose for our walls, will also become more soothing, more natural and more beautiful. Our taste in color will not fade into pastel nothingness. Rather, we will look for stronger, bolder colors that appear in nature. Think of the bright, bold colors found in a spring garden filled with tulips, daffodils and other flowers. Moreover, we will combine colors not to contrast, but to complement.

In the home of the future, sound will play a more central role. Music that is created to stimulate a mood or a feeling will grow in demand as consumers enhance their homes with new entertainment systems that give the effect of surround sound. Designers will figure out ways to bring the sounds of nature into our homes, from simple tabletop fountains that recycle tap water to other, more complex, fountain designs. Expect architectural design to incorporate a Spanish influence by introducing inner courtyards with natural fountains. Silence itself may become a new luxury and status symbol, with architects incorporating more sound-blocking features in new homes.

Home fragrance will become an essential element of the home. While candles are the preferred means for home-fragrance delivery today, more flexible mechanisms, such as heated waxes, potpourri boilers and misters, will give consumers more control of the fragrance and the mood the fragrances are intended to set. Aromatherapy technology will be applied to home fragrances; recipes for combining different scents to achieve desired emotional effects will become popular.

The trend toward realism and naturalism will also play out in fashion. We will strive to achieve multisensory looks that combine color and style with texture and scent. Cosmetics and personal care products will satisfy our sensual cravings for indulgences. Fashion designers will experiment with new fiber technologies, even combining new man-made fibers with natural ones that achieve ultra-comfort in our clothes while enhancing feminine curves with fabric that floats and swings rather than clings. We will look for more washable fabrics, rather than having to dry-clean with all those dangerous chemicals. Consumers will have signature fragrances that are individually hand blended to capture the essence of the personality. Personal fragrances will be developed for different moods, allowing the individual to coordinate his or her signature scent with activities for the day or their feelings.

As we ground ourselves more and more in reality, we will want our "techno-toys" to be decidedly *Jetsons* 21st century. For TVs, home entertainment systems, major appliances and computers, we will favor an ultra-high-tech look: lots of chrome and steel, lights and buttons and sleek curves. Our desire for the ultra-high-tech look for technology products will play out in our favorite toy: cars. Today's consumers are enamored of the retro-looking Chrysler PT Cruiser, Ford Thunderbird and the new GM Chevy Bel Air Concept Vehicle, but car design will take a decidedly high-tech turn soon. The designs will look forward by looking back to the future vision of motor vehicle transportation, as conceived in the 1940s and 1950s.

TIME IS THE NEW SHOPPING CURRENCY

If the rising economy of the 1990s taught us anything, it was that anyone who is willing to get the right education and work hard at the right job can make more money. However, we also discovered that no matter how rich or poor we were, no one could add one second more to one's life. Time is the great social equalizer. A new priority of making the most of the limited time we have is taking over. Consumers are looking at all the ways they spend their time, including shopping, and demanding a more time-efficient, time-conscious way to shop.

The amount of time consumers are willing to shop has declined steadily over the past decade, and it can be expected to collapse even more as consumers are confronted with new concerns about safety in public places. America's Research Group found that consumers who visited 2 to 3 stores in 1990, to buy home furnishings, electronics and major appliances, had cut the number of visits back by 0.5 stores by the end of the decade. Today, shoppers are going to only 1.8 stores to make the same purchases.

Further, as consumers retreat into the safety and comfort of their homes, they want to spend less time at the store, especially a store that is not satisfying their craving for a unique and emotionally satisfying experience. They will do more of their weekly shopping in a single trip, so they can get back home and to safety more quickly. More shopping will also be done from the home, with consumers turning to the Internet, mail-order catalogs and even party-based and other direct-selling businesses.

Party plans and other forms of direct selling will be the next guerrilla marketing method to grab share while giving fits to traditional retailers in the years to come. This retailing methodology has everything going for it in today's emotional climate. You get a chance to meet and greet your friends in the safety of a friend's home, thus providing social experiences that people desire. Over appetizers and a glass of wine, you get to look at new, interesting products presented by your friend, a spokesperson you can really trust. While seeing the new products, you can learn how to use them or display them in innovative ways, thus providing the enhancement of education and information. You gain access to special sales offers, and you can pay for the products later, when they are delivered to your home. It is the perfect retailing method for the new millennium. Longaberger Baskets, Blyth's PartyLite candles, Pampered Chef, Discovery Toys, Avon, Mary Kay and many others have known it for years, and soon many other smart marketers will be exploring opportunities to sell in this way. Word of warning: It only works with women, at least so far.

Television shopping mimics the intimacy of party plans. We are already conditioned to think of the television celebrities we invite into or homes every day as our "friends." As a result, the television shopping channels, with their personally engaging show hosts, will become a more powerful retailing medium in the future.

THE COMING RETAIL CRISIS

Office real estate is facing a crisis of excess inventory. After years of creating new office space, coupled with overly optimistic tenants who grabbed more office space than they needed, nearly 40 million square feet of office space will return to the market in 2002, according to Torto Wheaton Research. As new office buildings remain vacant and existing tenants fail to renew their leases, rents will fall and overall office vacancy rates will rise.

Contributing to the coming retail crisis is the shifting pattern of consumer shopping. Consumers are turning away from traditional department stores and shopping more at mass merchants, discounters and warehouse marts. While the sales from general merchandisers in total rose 64 percent from 1992 to 2000, the key driver of growth in this segment was the category of "other" general retailers, including Wal-Mart, Kmart, Target, Costco and Sam's Club. Posting growth of 141 percent from 1992 to 2000, the other general retailers, composed of discounters and warehouse clubs, reached $170.9 billion in retail revenue. In the same eight-year period, traditional department stores' sales grew only 34 percent, not even matching growth of the retail industry as a whole. Non-store retailers also posted triple-digit growth from 1992 to 2000. Non-store retailers include catalogers and mail-order marketers, television shopping, direct sales, party-plan marketers and e-tailers. This segment rose 121 percent, from $73.4 billion in sales in 1992 to $162 billion in 2000. Growth of these two segments—other general merchandisers and non-store retailers—is expected to outpace that of the retail industry as a whole. These two segments will continue to grab market share by siphoning sales away from competing classes of retailers.

A bright spot in the retail marketplace has been the explosive growth of large national specialty chains, including Bed Bath & Beyond, Linens 'n' Things, Pier 1, Pottery Barn, Williams-Sonoma, Restoration Hardware, Home Depot, Lowe's and so forth. These national specialty retailers are literally "eating the lunch" of small independent specialty retailers that focus on gift and home products. Yet the national specialty chains have an Achilles' heel that may soon start to trip them up. Many of these companies have become retail "darlings" by posting consistent annual growth rates in the range of 7 percent to 15 percent. However, that growth has come from opening new stores rather than increases in existing store sales. The trouble is that with only about 225 U.S. cities boasting a total population of 100,000 or more, the new markets where the national specialty retailers can open is shrinking. Many of the chains have between 200 and 300 individual stores, and behemoth Pier 1 has just topped 900 outlets. Inevitably, revenue growth for these chains will return to earth as their "frontier" markets evaporate. Their new store openings will be slated for existing markets, where they will start to cannibalize their own stores' sales.

The coming retail shakeout will have an impact on all retailers, large and small. Clearly, some big-name department stores will be unable to stay the course as the department store sector continues to distance itself from the shopping needs of consumers. More small independent retailers, those shops that line small-town America's main streets, will fold as Wal-Mart, Kmart or Target open up on the town's bypass. The national specialty chains will have to work harder for every percentage point of revenue growth as their building expansion programs slow. They may well start to close some of the unproductive stores in favor of larger stores in growing urban or suburban centers. Many older malls will fold as consumers start to patronize the new, unenclosed, lifestyle malls that are sprouting up throughout the country. They are designed to mimic small-town ambience while showcasing national, upscale and specialty chain stores.

HOW TO SURVIVE THE RETAIL SHAKEOUT

Understanding why people buy applies equally to manufacturers and retail businesses in anticipating consumer behavior now and in the future. Retailers need to explore with their consumers why people shop in their stores. What features, products, attributes, benefits, needs and consumer desires does the store meet? In what areas does it fail to satisfy? Retailers need to dig deeper than simply "customer service" and "quality." Too many retailers imagine their point of difference is "customer service" or "quality" products, but if you sit in a room for five minutes with consumers, you discover that these terms are meaningless. Retailers have to understand the heart, mind and emotions of their customers. They need to figure out what experiences consumers expect and desire to have while shopping in the store and then develop strategies to give them more of those experiences.

Customer service has to be more than answering a question, wrapping a package or escorting the customer to an aisle. Retail salespeople need to participate in the shopping experience with their customers. They have to be shopping partners, not salespeople or clerks. They have to have authentic enthusiasm. They need to be real and honest. They need to be likable. They need to like their customers.

Retailers can also enhance the shopping experience by providing information. Why should Home Depot have a monopoly on teaching people how to use their products? Any retailer selling home products can figure out hundreds of ways to provide information to its customers. Just watch HGTV, The Learning Channel or Discovery to figure out how. The same theory applies to retailers of electronics, books, pet supplies, cosmetics and personal care items, gourmet foods, housewares, sporting goods, hobby items and crafts supplies. Consumers are eager to learn about their passion and willing to participate with retailers in this process. The key to launching a successful experiential retailing program is to provide valuable information without substituting a sales presentation for a learning experience. Consumers are too savvy today. They will immediately see through the hoax.

Defining Moments: Segmenting by Cohorts

Coming of age experiences influence values, attitudes, preferences, and buying behaviors for a lifetime.

By Charles D. Schewe, Geoffrey E. Meredith, and Stephanie M. Noble

Cohorts are highly influenced by the external events that were happening when they were "coming of age" (generally between the years 17–23). For example, those now in their late seventies and early eighties lived through the Great Depression while baby boomers witnessed the assassination of JFK, saw other political assassinations, shared the Vietnam War, and lived through the energy crisis. Such shared experiences distinguish one cohort from another.

Today, many call marketing to birth groups generational marketing. Generations differ from cohorts. Each generation is defined by its years of birth. For example, a generation is usually 20 to 25 years in length, or roughly the time it takes a person to grow up and have children. But a cohort can be as long or short as the external events that defines it. The cohort defined by World War II, for example, is only six years long.

Consider how different cohorts treat spending and saving. Today's Depression cohort, those ages 79 to 88 in 2000, began working during the Great Depression. Their conduct with respect to money is very conservative. Having experienced the worst of economic times, this age group values economic security and frugality. They still save for that "rainy day." Those, however, in the 55 to 78 age category today were influenced by the Depression, but also experienced the boom times of the Post-World War II period. This group has attitudes toward saving that are less conservative; they are more willing to spend than the older group. In sharp contrast to the "Depression-scarred" is the free-wheeling generation that grew up during the "hippie revolution." Russell (1993) calls this birth group the "free agents," since its members defied the establishment, sought individualism, and were skeptical of everything. This cohort can be characterized as "buy now, pay later" and its members will carry this value into the century ahead as they journey through middle age and on into old age.

Cohort effects are life-long effects. They provide the communality for each cohort being targeted as a separate market segment. And since these cohorts can be described by the ages of their constituents, they offer an especially efficient vehicle for direct marketing campaigns.

Six American Cohorts

In 2000, American adults can be divided into six distinct cohorts, or market segments, ranging in age from the Depression cohort (age 79–88) to what many people are calling Generation X (age 24–34). This division is based on intensive content analysis of a wide range of publications and studies scanned over a 10-year period. The roughly 4 million people who are age 89 and older are not included for two reasons. First, this group is much smaller than other cohorts. Also, much of their consumption behavior is controlled by physical need. There also are more than 72 million persons under the age of 24. This newly emerging cohort can be referred to as the "N-Gen," since the impact of the internet revolution appears to be the key defining moment shaping this group's values. Yet it is too early to know their "defining moment-driven" values, preferences, and attitudes because external forces take some time to influence values. A brief description of each of the six cohorts follows.

The Depression Cohort

This group was born between 1912 and 1921, came of age from 1930 to 1939, and is age 79–88 today. Currently this cohort contains 13,054,000 people, or 7% of the adult U.S. population.

This cohort was defined by the Great Depression. Maturing, entering the workforce, trying to build and support families during the '30s had a profound influence on this cohort in so many areas, but most strongly in finances: money and savings. To many of today's business managers, the Depression seems like ancient history, almost apocryphal, like the Great Flood. Yet to this cohort, it was all too real. To put the Depression in perspective, the S&P 400 (the broadest measure of the economy as a whole available at that time) declined 69% between 1929 and 1932 in a relentless and agonizing fall. It wasn't until 1953—24 years and a World War later—before the S&P index got back to where it had been in 1929! People starting out in this environment were scarred in ways they carry with them today. In particular, financial security still rules their thinking as reflected in the following example.

A Depression Cohort Marketing Example. One savings and loan bank on the West Coast took a cohort perspective to boost deposits from this cohort. They used an icon familiar to this age group, George Feneman (Groucho Marx's television sidekick on *You Bet Your Life*), who assured this cohort of the safety of their money. He stressed that the financial institution uses their money for mortgages. "We build houses," he says, which is just what this cohort can relate to, since preserving their homes was central to the financial concerns of this age group.

EXECUTIVE
briefing

Cohorts are groups of individuals who are born during the same time period and travel through life together. They experience similar external events during their late adolescent/ early adulthood years. These "defining moments" influence their values, preferences, attitudes, and buying behaviors in ways that remain with them over their lifetime. We can identify six known American cohorts that include those from age 88 to those coming of age in 2000. While generational cohorts are far from the final solution for marketers, they are certainly a relevant dynamic. Marketers should seriously consider targeting these age groupings, especially in their marketing communications.

The World War II Cohort

Born 1922–1927, this cohort came of age from 1940 to 1945. Its members are age 73–78 today. Currently 9,465,000 people, it represents 5% of our adult population.

World War II defined this cohort. Economically it was not a boom time (the S&P 500 gained 50% from 1940 to 1945, but it was still only half of what it had been in 1929), but unemployment was no longer a problem. This cohort was unified by a common enemy, shared experiences, and especially for the 16 million in the military, a sense of deferment and delayed gratification. In World War I, the average duration of service was less than 12 months; in World War II, the average was 33 months. Marriages, careers, and children were all put on hold until the war was over.

This sense of deferment made the World War II cohort an intensely romantic one. The yearning for loved ones left behind, and for those who left to fight is reflected in the music and literature and movies of the time (e.g., *I've Got My Love to Keep Me Warm, Homesick, That's All, 'Til Then,* and *You'd Be So Nice to Come Home To*). And, while for many the war was an unpleasant experience, for many others it was the apex of their lives. They had a defined role (frequently more important in status than any other they would ever have), a measure of freedom from their particular social norms, and an opportunity to travel, some to exotic foreign shores, others just away from the towns and cornfields of their youth. The horrors and heroism experienced by our soldiers imbedded values that stay with them still. And this influence was clearly depicted in the award-winning and highly acclaimed movies of 1998: *Saving Private Ryan* and *The Thin Red Line*.

A World War II Cohort Marketing Example. Using cohort words, symbols, and memories can bring substantial rewards for marketers. A direct marketing campaign designed for a cable television provider to increase subscriptions is just such an example. Postage stamp-sized pictures of Douglas McArthur were put on the corner of the envelope with the copy "If you remember V-J Day, we've got some new programs you're going to love." This attention-getter immediately communicated that the content is for members of the targeted cohort. When this approach was used, subscription response rates surged from 1.5% to more than 10%.

The Post-War Cohort

Members of this cohort were born from 1928 to 1945, came of age from 1946 to 1963, and are age 55 to 73 in 2000. Currently 42,484,000 people, 22.7% of the adult population are Post-Wars.

This cohort is a very long one—18 years span the youngest to the oldest members. They were the beneficiaries of a long period of economic growth and relative social tranquility. Economically the S&P 500, which had struggled until 1953 just to get back to where it had been before the Depression, then tripled over the next 10 years. There were dislocations during this time—the Korean War in the early '50s, Sputnik in 1957, the first stirrings of the civil rights movement, a brief recession in 1958—but by and large, at least on the surface, things were pretty quiet.

The tenor of the times was conservative, seeking the comfortable, the secure, and the familiar. It was a time that promoted conformity and shrank from individual expression, which is why the overt sexuality of Elvis and the rebellion of James Dean were at once popular and scandalous.

A Post-War Cohort Marketing Example. The Vermont Country Store, highly successful marketers of nostalgic products difficult to find, uses cohort images and memories to target market segments. To capture the attention of Post-War cohort customers, it peppers its catalog with pictures from the '50s and value-reflective copy along the outside of various pages such as:

"When I was young, I knew kids who were allowed in their living rooms only on special occasions—and usually under adult supervision. Now, instead of a chilly room used only to entertain on holidays, we can really relax in our living rooms."
and
"In high school, buying clothes was easy. The more we dressed according to the conventions of the day, the better. If we'd known then what we know now, we could have looked every bit as good—and been a lot more comfortable. But then, that wasn't the point of being a teenager."

Boomers—I

The Baby Boom is usually defined as the 76 million people born between 1946 and 1964, since this is indeed when the annual birthrate bulged to more than 4 million per year. However there are two boomer cohorts. The first of these are the leading-edge boomers and they are 32,531,000 people strong, 17.4% of the adult population. They were born from 1946 to 1954, and came of age from 1963 to 1972. They are age 46 to 54 today.

Due to their numbers, the baby boomers as a whole have dominated marketing in America since they first appeared on the scene. When they were truly babies, they made Dr. Spock's *Infant and Child Rearing* the second best-selling book in the history of the world, after the Bible. As pre-teens, they dominated the media in shows like *Leave It to Beaver* and in merchandising with fads like Davy Crockett caps and Hula Hoops. As teens they propelled Coke, McDonald's, and Motown into corporate giants, and ensured the success of Clearasil.

The "Boomer I" cohort began coming of age in 1963, the start of a period of profound dislocations that still haunt our society today. It ended shortly after the last soldier died in Vietnam. The Kennedy presidency seemed like the natural extension of continued good times, of economic growth and domestic stability. It represented a liberated and early transfer of power from an older leader to a much younger one.

The Kennedy assassination, followed by that of Martin Luther King and Robert Kennedy, signaled an end to the status quo and galvanized a very large boomer cohort just entering its formative years. Suddenly the leadership (LBJ) was no longer 'theirs,' the war (Vietnam) was not their war, and authority and the establishment which had been the bedrock of earlier cohorts disintegrated in the melee of the 1968 Democratic National Convention in Chicago.

However, the Boomer I cohort continued to experience economic good times. Despite the social turmoil, the economy as a whole, as measured by the S&P 500, continued an upward climb. The Boomer I cohort wanted a lifestyle at least as good as they had experienced as children in the '50s, and with nearly 20 years of steady economic growth as history, they had no reason not to spend whatever they earned or could borrow to achieve it.

The Boomer I cohort still heavily values its individualism (remember, they were and are the "Me Generation,") indulgence of self, stimulation (a reflection of the drug culture they grew up with), and questioning nature. Marketing to this cohort demands attention to providing more information to back up product claims and to calm skeptical concerns. And these boomers prize holding on to their youth as the following example shows.

A Boomer I Cohort Marketing Example. The California Prune Board recommended to its plum producers that they plant many more trees, since large numbers of baby boomers were turning 50 and the 50+ age bracket (indeed, the 65+) was the heaviest consumer of prunes. However, boomers did not relate to prunes; they did not come of age with prunes as part of their consumption lives. Why, then, would they eat prunes in later life? In fact, prunes reflect cohort preferences of their parents—those same parents boomers did not want to trust ("Don't Trust Anyone Over 30").

Research into the chemical composition of prunes, however, found that they naturally stimulate the body's production of testosterone and estrogen... just the ingredients aging boomers desire to hold on to their sexual vitality and sense of youth. Clinical studies to provide advertising claim support for the estrogen and testosterone benefits were being undertaken. This approach could lead to, for example, a radio or television commercial featuring Adam and Eve in the Garden of Eden. Eve requests some fruit for sustenance, since they have a big night ahead populating the earth. She is delighted to receive a platter including one lonely prune (no apples, please). Her comment as she gulps the prune: "Well, this should get us through Asia, at least!"

Boomers II

The trailing-edge boomers were born between 1956 and 1965, came of age from 1973 to 1983, and are age 35 to 45 today. Currently 46,794,000 people are Boomer II's, 26% of the adult population.

The external events that separate the Boomer I from the Boomer II cohort were less dramatic than The Depression or World War II, but were just as real. They were composed of the stop of the Vietnam War (it never really ended—just stopped), Watergate (the final nail in the coffin of institutions and the establishment), and the Arab Oil Embargo that ended the stream of economic gains that had continued largely uninterrupted since 1945.

By 1973, something had changed for a person coming of age in America. While faith in institutions had gone, so had the idealist fervor that made the Boomer I cohort so cause-oriented. Instead, those in the Boomer II cohort exhibited a narcissistic preoccupation with themselves which manifested itself in everything from the self-help movement (*I'm OK—You're OK*, and various young and aging gurus imported from India) to self-deprecation (*Saturday Night Live, Mary Hartman, Mary Hartman*).

The change in economic fortunes had a more profound effect than is commonly realized. Throughout their childhood and as they came of age, the Boomer I cohort members experienced good times; their expectations that these good times would continue were thus reinforced, and the cohort mindset formed at that time can be seen today in a persistent resistance to begin saving for retirement. Things had been good, and they were going to stay good—somehow.

For the Boomer II cohort, the money mindset was much different. The Oil Shock of 1973 sent the economy tumbling: the S&P 500 lost 30% of its value between 1973 and 1975! At the same time, inflation began to resemble that of a banana republic. During this period, the real interest rate (Prime minus the CPI) hit a record low of -4%. In those circumstances, debt as a means of maintaining a lifestyle makes great economic sense. And a cohort with a 'debt imprint' will never lose it. Boomers II are spenders just like the Boomer Is, but for a different reason. It's not because they expect good times, but because they assume they can always get a loan, take out a second mortgage on the house, get another credit card, and never have to "pay the piper."

A Boomer II Cohort Marketing Example. A major finance company is currently aggressively promoting home equity loans with radio advertising directly oriented toward this cohort mindset. The commercial in essence states "Everyone else has a BMW, or a new set of golf clubs, and they're not any better than you are. Even if you don't think you can afford them, you can have them, now—with a home equity loan from XYZ company. And, while you're at it, why not take the Hawaiian vacation, too—you deserve it!" The copy brings on severe anxiety attacks for the World War II and Depression cohorts, but it makes perfect sense to the Boomer IIs.

Generation X

Born 1966–1976, Gen Xers came of age from 1984 to 1994. They are age 24 to 34 today. Currently 41,119,000 people, they represent 21.9% of the adult population.

Much has been written about Generation X, most of it derogatory in tone: "Slackers" (from the movie of that name); "Whiners"; "a generation of aging Bart Simpsons," "armed and possibly dangerous." That seems to be unfair. The generation of F. Scott Fitzgerald was widely characterized as "Lost," and that describes Generation X. This cohort has nothing to hang on to—not the institutions of the Post-War cohort, not the Boomer I's idealism and causes and institutions to resist, not the narcissism of the Boomer IIs. These were the children of divorce and daycare, latch-key kids of the 1980s; no wonder they exhibit so little foundation. The fact that they are searching for anchors can be seen in their seemingly contradictory "retro" behavior—the resurgence of proms, coming-out parties, and fraternities that Boomers rejected.

It can be seen in their political conservatism, which is also motivated by a "What's in it for me?" cynicism that repudiates liberal redistribution tendencies. And they feel alienated, reflected in the violence and brutal sex of the popular culture, and resigned to a world that seems to have little hope of offering them the lifestyles of their parents.

A Generation X Cohort Marketing Example. So how does a marketer reach a cohort with no defining moments? One way is with irreverent, rebellious, self-mocking, and sassy portrayals—which helps explain the popularity of South Park, the Simpsons, and the infamous Married With Children. Commercials like Maybelline's ad for Expert Eyes Shadow with Christy Turlington also exemplifies this sassiness. The ad shows the stunning model with beautifully made-up eyes illuminated by moonlight. A voice-over says: "Was it a strange celestial event... that gave her such bewitching eyes?" Then Turlington, sitting on her living room sofa, laughs and says, "Get over it."

Managerial Implications

Cohort segmentation provides a most intriguing additional method for separating consumer markets. Age has long been a segmentation variable, but this innovative approach shows it is defining moments that shape mindsets and provide the true value of age targeting. While not a key behavior driver for all product categories, cohort segmentation is particularly appropriate for food, music, apparel, automotive, financial and insurance, as well as entertainment products. Product creation and management over its life cycle is clearly ripe for cohort implementation.

Cohort analysis can help in designing communication campaigns. Determining music, movie stars, or other icons that cohorts identified with in their past is an effective selling technique. These tactics work because they rely on nostalgia marketing, that is, tapping deep, pleasurable memories of what seemed simpler, better times. They also work by calling out the target in an implicit way. "This message is for you!" Many companies have already engaged in this tactic as evidenced by the growing number of songs, logos, and actual commercial footage from the past.

Additionally, the changing nature of values across cohorts has important implications for marketers. As new cohorts enter the marketplace, organizations need to keep apprised of their changing value structures. In particular, as the age distribution in the United States changes, so will consumers' wants and needs. A cohort analysis can help track and forecast these wants and needs. In the 1980s, for example, the age segment of 50–65 years was comprised mostly of Depression and World War II cohort consumers. Today, it is made up mostly of the Post-War cohort and in 2010 it will be all Boomers. The demographic age segmentation—age 50 to 65—is the same, but the composition of that segment is constantly changing. It's a moving target.

Final Thought

Cohort segmentation works in the United States. But what about outside of the United States? Would cohorts be the same as here? Our research has found cohort values derived from defining moments indeed do exist abroad. Germany, for example, witnessed no Depression as Hitler's war effort energized the economy. In Brazil, the 1970s found a dictatorship imposing severe censorship, which created the need for personal freedoms in individuals coming of age during that time. In Jordan,

the Six-Day War in 1967 dramatically displaced Jordanians from their homeland and they now long for stability in maintaining a place to live. As these examples illustrate, cohort segmentation offers a rich opportunity here… and around the world.

Additional Reading

Meredith, Geoffrey and Charles D. Schewe (1994), "The Power of Cohorts," *American Demographics*, December, 22–31.

Rentz, Joseph O. and Fred D. Reynolds (1991), "Forecasting the Effects of an Aging Population on Product Consumption: An Age-Period-Cohort Framework," *Journal of Marketing Research*, 28, (3), 355–60.

——, ——, and Roy G. Stout (1983), "Analyzing Changing Consumption Patterns With Cohort Analysis," *Journal of Marketing Research*, 20, 12–20.

Russell, Cheryl (1993), *The Master Trend: How the Baby Boom Generation Is Remaking America*, Plenum, New York.

Schewe, Charles D. and Stephanie M. Noble (forthcoming), "Market Segmentation by Cohorts: The Value and Validity of Cohorts in America and Abroad," *Journal of Marketing Management* (Scotland).

Schuman, Howard and Jacqueline Scott (1989). "Generations and Collective Memories," *American Sociological Review*, 54, (3), 359–381.

Smith, J. Walker and Ann Clurman (1997), *Rocking the Ages*, Harper Business, New York.

Strauss, William and Neil Howe (1997), *The Fourth Turning*, Broadway Books, New York.

About the Authors

Charles D. Schewe is professor of marketing at the University of Massachusetts and a principal in Lifestage Matrix Marketing. Focusing on the marketing implications of the aging process, Schewe has advised such companies as Coca-Cola, Kellogg's, Kraft General Foods, Time-Life, Lucky Stores, Grand Metropolitan, and K-Mart. He may be reached at schewe@mktg.umass.edu.

Geoffrey E. Meredith is president of Lifestage Matrix Marketing, located in Lafayette, Calif. Formerly a senior vice president at Olgivy & Mather, Ketchum Communications, and Hal Riney and Partners, he also spent two years with Age Wave (see V1,N3 MM). He may be reached at Lifestage@aol.com.

Stephanie M. Noble is a doctoral candidate at the University of Massachusetts. She may be reached at smevans@som.umass.edu.

From *Marketing Management*, Fall 2000, Vol. 9, No. 3, pp. 48-53. © 2000 by the American Marketing Association. Reprinted by permission.

UNIT 3
Developing and Implementing Marketing Strategies

Unit Selections

Key Points to Consider

- Most ethical questions seem to arise in regard to the promotional component of the marketing mix. How fair is the general public's criticism of some forms of personal selling and advertising? Give some examples.

- What role, if any, do you think the quality of a product plays in making a business competitive in consumer markets? What role does price play? Would you rather market a higher-priced, better-quality product or one that was the lowest priced? Why?

- What do you envision will be the major problems or challenges retailers will face in the next decade? Explain.

- Given the rapidly increasing costs of personal selling, what role do you think it will play as a strategy in the marketing mix in the future? What other promotion strategies will play increased or decreased roles in the next decade?

 **Links: www.dushkin.com/online/**
These sites are annotated in the World Wide Web pages.

American Marketing Association Homepage
http://www.marketingpower.com

Consumer Buying Behavior
http://www.courses.psu.edu/mktg/mktg220_rso3/sls_cons.htm

Product Branding, Packaging, and Pricing
http://www.fooddude.com/branding.html

Marketing management objectives, the late Wroe Alderson once wrote, "are very simple in essence. The firm wants to expand its volume of sales, or it wants to handle the volume it has more efficiently." Although the essential objectives of marketing might be stated this simply, the development and implementation of strategies to accomplish them is considerably more complex. Many of these complexities are due to changes in the environment within which managers must operate. Strategies that fail to heed the social, political, and economic forces of society have little chance of success over the long run. The lead article in this section provides helpful insight suggesting a framework for developing a comprehensive marketing plan.

The selections in this unit provide a wide-ranging discussion of how marketing professionals and U.S. companies interpret and employ various marketing strategies today. The readings also include specific examples from industry to illustrate their points. The articles are grouped in four sections, each dealing with one of the main strategy areas: product, price, distribution (place), and promotion. Since each selection discusses more than one of these areas, it is important that you read them broadly. For example, many of the articles covered in the distribution section discuss important aspects of personal selling and advertising.

Product Strategy. The essence of the marketing concept is to begin with what consumers want and need. After determining a need, an enterprise must respond by providing the product or service demanded. Successful marketing managers recognize the need for continuous product improvement and/or new product introduction.

The articles in this subsection focus on various facets of product strategy. The first article reveals that there is more to product positioning than just features and benefits. The second article describes a new generation of digital tools that can improve the odds of a successful new product launch. The last article in this subsection suggests the world's top 100 brands.

Pricing Strategy. Few elements of the total strategy of the "marketing mix" demand as much managerial and social attention as pricing. There is a good deal of public misunderstanding about the ability of marketing managers to control prices, and even greater misunderstanding about how pricing policies are determined. New products present especially difficult problems in terms of both costs and pricing. The costs for developing a new product are usually very high, and if a product is truly new, it cannot be priced competitively, for it has no competitors.

"Kamikaze Pricing" scrutinizes the tremendous pricing pressures that companies face and suggest some ways to make better pricing decisions. In "Pricing Practices That Endanger Profits," the authors discuss how buyers perceive and respond to pricing.

Distribution Strategy. For many enterprises, the largest marketing costs result from closing the gap in space and time between producer and consumer. In no other area of marketing is efficiency so eagerly sought after. Physical distribution seems to be the one area where significant cost savings can be achieved. The costs of physical distribution are tied closely with decisions made about the number, the size, and the diversity of marketing intermediaries between producer and consumer.

The three articles in this subsection scrutinize ways retailers can create value for their customers, the importance of designing a trust-based e-business strategy, and the dynamics of online retailing.

Promotion Strategy. The basic objectives of promotion are to inform, persuade, or remind the consumer to buy a firm's product or pay for the firm's service. Advertising is the most obvious promotional activity. However, in total dollars spent and in cost per person reached, advertising takes second place to personal selling. Sales promotion supports either personal selling and advertising, or both. Such media as point-of-purchase displays, catalogs, and direct mail place the sales promotion specialist closer to the advertising agency than to the salesperson.

The three articles in this final unit subsection cover such topics as evaluation of the effective use of Web advertising, suggestions for creating a good ad, and some examples of various ad campaigns.

THE VERY MODEL OF A
MODERN MARKETING PLAN

SUCCESSFUL COMPANIES ARE REWRITING THEIR STRATEGIES TO REFLECT CUSTOMER INPUT AND INTERNAL COORDINATION

SHELLY REESE

IT'S 1996. DO YOU KNOW WHERE YOUR MARKETING PLAN IS? In a world where competitors can observe and rapidly imitate each other's advancements in product development, pricing, packaging, and distribution, communication is more important than ever as a way of differentiating your business from those of your competitors.

The most successful companies are the ones that understand that, and are revamping their marketing plans to emphasize two points:

1. Marketing is a dialog between customer and supplier.

2. Companies have to prove they're listening to their customers by acting on their input.

WHAT IS A MARKETING PLAN?

At its most basic level, a marketing plan defines a business's niche, summarizes its objectives, and presents its strategies for attaining and monitoring those goals. It's a road map for getting from point A to point B.

But road maps need constant updating to reflect the addition of new routes. Likewise, in a decade in which technology, international relations, and the competitive landscape are constantly changing, the concept of a static marketing plan has to be reassessed.

Two of the hottest buzz words for the 1990s are "interactive" and "integrated." A successful marketing plan has to be both.

"Interactive" means your marketing plan should be a conversation between your business and your customers by acting on their input. It's your chance to tell customers about your business and to listen and act on their responses.

"Integrated" means the message in your marketing is consistently reinforced by every department within your company. Marketing is as much a function of the finance and manufacturing divisions as it is the advertising and public relations departments.

Integrated also means each time a company reaches out to its customers through an advertisement, direct mailing, or promotion, it is sending the same message and encouraging customers to learn more about the product.

WHY IS IT IMPORTANT?

The interaction between a company and its customers is a relationship. Relationships can't be reproduced. They can, however, be replaced. That's where a good marketing plan comes into play.

Think of your business as a suitor, your customers as the object of your affection, and your competitors as rivals. A marketing plan is your strategy for wooing customers. It's based on listening and reacting to what they say.

Because customers' priorities are constantly changing, a marketing plan should change with them. For years, conventional wisdom was 'prepare a five year marketing plan and review it every year.' But change happens a lot faster than it did 20 or even 10 years ago.

For that reason, Bob Dawson of The Business Group, a consulting firm in Freemont, California, recommends that his clients prepare a three year plan and review it every quarter. Frequent reviews enable companies to identify potential problems and opportunities before their competition, he explains.

ILLUSTRATION BY KELLY KENNEDY

"Preventative maintenance for your company is as important as putting oil in your car," Dawson says. "You don't wait a whole year to do it. You can't change history but you can anticipate what's going to happen."

ESSENTIAL COMPONENTS

Most marketing plans consist of three sections. The first section should identify the organization's goals. The second section should establish a method for attaining them. The third section focuses on creating a system for implementing the strategy.

Although some plans identify as many as six or eight goals, many experts suggest a company whittle its list to one or two key objectives and focus on them.

"One of the toughest things is sticking to one message," observes Mark Bilfield, account director for integrated marketing of Nissan and Infiniti cars at TBWA Chiat/Day in Los Angeles, which handles national advertising, direct marketing, public relations, and promotions for the automaker. Bilfield argues that a focused, consistent message is easier to communicate to the market place and to different disciplines within the corporation than a broad, encompassing one. Therefore, he advises, "unless there is something drastically wrong with the idea, stick with it."

SECTION I: GOALS

The goals component of your plan is the most fundamental. Consider it a kind of thinking out loud: Why are you writing this plan? What do you want to accomplish? What do you want to achieve in the next quarter? The next year? The next three years?

Like taping your New Year's resolution to the refrigerator, the goals section is a constant reminder of what you want to achieve. The key difference between a New Year's resolution and your marketing goals, however, is you can't achieve the latter alone.

To achieve your marketing goals you've got to convince your customers to behave in a certain way. If you're a soft drink manufacturer you may want them to try your company's latest wild berry flavor. If you're a new bank in town, you need to familiarize people with your name and convince them to give your institution a try. Or perhaps you're a family-owned retailer who needs to remind customers of the importance of reliability and a proven track record in the face of new competition.

The goals in each of these cases differ with the audiences. The soft drink manufacturer is asking an existing customer to try something new; the bank is trying to attract new customers; the retailer wants to retain existing customers.

Each company wants to influence its customers' behavior. The company that is most likely to succeed is the one that understands its customers the best.

There's no substitute for knowledge. You need to understand the demographic and psychographic makeup of the customers you are trying to reach, as well as the best methods for getting their attention.

Do your research. Learn as much as possible about your audience. Trade associations, trade journals and government statistics and surveys are excellent resources, but chances are you have a lot of data within your own business that you haven't tapped. Look at what you know about your customer already and find ways to bolster that information. Companies should constantly be asking clients what they want and how they would use a new product.

"If you're not asking people that use your end product, then everything you're doing is an assumption," argues Dawson.

In addition, firms should ask customers how they perceive the products and services they receive. Too often, companies have an image of themselves that they broadcast but fail to live up to. That frustrates consumers and makes them feel deceived.

Companies that claim to offer superior service often appear to renege on their promises because their definition of 'service' doesn't mesh with their customers', says Bilfield.

"Airlines and banks are prime offenders," says Bilfield. "They tout service, and when the customers go into the airport or the bank, they have to wait in long lines."

The problem often lies in the company's assumptions about what customers really want. While an airline may feel it is living up to its claim of superior service because it distributes warm towels and mints after a meal, a business traveler will probably place a higher value on its competitor's on-time record and policy for returning lost luggage.

SECTION II: THE STRATEGY

Unfortunately, after taking the time and conducting the research to determine who their audience is and what their message should be, companies often fail by zooming ahead with a plan. An attitude of, "OK, we know who we're after and we know what we want to say, so let's go!" seems to take over.

More often than not, that gung-ho way of thinking leads to disaster because companies have skipped a critical step: they haven't established and communicated an internal strategy for attaining their goals. They want to take their message to the public without pausing to get feedback from inside the company.

For a marketing plan to work, everyone within the company must understand the company's message and work cooperatively to establish a method for taking that message to the public.

For example, if you decide the goal of your plan is to promote the superior service your company offers, you'd better make sure all aspects of your business are on board. Your manufacturing process should meet the highest standards. Your financial department should develop credit and leasing programs that make it easier for customers to use

GETTING STARTED

A NINE-STEP PLAN THAT WILL MAKE THE DIFFERENCE BETWEEN WRITING A USEFUL PLAN AND A DOCUMENT THAT GATHERS DUST ON A SHELF

by Carole R. Hedden and the *Marketing Tools* editorial staff

In his 1986 book, *The Goal*, Eliyahu M. Goldratt writes that most of us forget the one true goal of our business. It's not to deliver products on time. It isn't even to manufacture the best widget in the world. The goal is to make money.

In the past, making money depended on selling a product or service. Today, that's changed as customers are, at times, willing to pay for what we stand for: better service, better support, more innovation, more partnership in developing new products.

This section of this article assumes that you believe a plan is needed, and that this plan should weave together your desires with those of your customers. We've reviewed a number of marketing plans and come up with a nine-step model. It is perhaps more than what your organization needs today, but none of the steps are unimportant.

Our model combines some of the basics of a conventional plan with some new threads that we believe will push your plan over the edge, from being satisfactory to being necessary. These include:

• Using and improving the former domain of public relations, image, as a marketing tool.
• Integrating all the business functions that touch your customers into a single, customer-focused strategic marketing plan.
• Borrowing from Total Quality theories to establish performance measures beyond the financial report to help you note customer trends.
• Making sure that the people needed to deliver your marketing objectives are part of your plan.
• "Selling" your plan to the people whose support is essential to its success.

Taking the Plan Off the Shelf

First, let's look at the model itself. Remember that one of the primary criticisms of any plan is that it becomes a binder on a shelf, never to be seen again until budget time next year. Planning should be an iterative process, feeding off itself and used to guide and measure.

Whether you're asked to create a marketing plan or write the marketing section of the strategic plan for your business, your document is going to include what the business is trying to achieve, a careful analysis of your market, the products and services you offer to that market, and how you will market and sell products or services to your customer.

1. Describe the Business

You are probably in one of two situations: either you need to write a description of your business or you can rely on an existing document found in your annual report, the strategic plan, or a capabilities brochure. The description should include, at minimum:

• Your company's purpose;
• Who you deliver products or services to; and
• What you deliver to those customers.

Too often, such descriptions omit a discussion about what you want your business to stand for—your image.

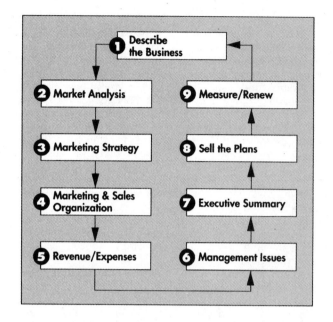

1. Describe the Business
2. Market Analysis
3. Marketing Strategy
4. Marketing & Sales Organization
5. Revenue/Expenses
6. Management Issues
7. Executive Summary
8. Sell the Plans
9. Measure/Renew

This is increasingly important as customers report they are looking for more than the product or service; they're in search of a partner. The only way to address image is to know who you want to be, who your customers think you are, and how you can bridge the gap between the two.

Part of defining your image is knowing where you are strong and where you are weak. For instance, if your current yield rate is 99.997 percent and customers rate you as the preferred supplier, then you might identify operations as a key to your company's image. Most companies tend to be their own worst critic, so start by listing all your strengths. Then identify weaknesses or the threats you face, either due to your own limitations or from the increased competency of a competitor.

The description also includes what your business delivers to its owners, be they shareholders, private owners, or employees. Usually this is stated in financial terms: revenue, return on investment or equity, economic value added, cash generated, operating margin or earnings per share. The other measures your organization uses to monitor its performance may be of interest to outsiders, but save them for the measurement section of your plan.

The result of all this describing and listing is that you should have a fairly good idea of where you are and where you want to be, which naturally leads to objectives for the coming 6, 12, or 18 months, if not longer.

2. Analyze the Market

This is the section you probably believe you own. *Marketing Tools* challenges you to look at this as a section jointly owned by most everyone working with you. In a smaller company, the lead managers may own various pieces of this section. In a

(continued)

smaller company, the lead managers may own various pieces of this section. In a larger organization, you may need to pull in the ideas and data available from other departments, such as logistics, competitor intelligence, research and development, and the function responsible for quality control or quality assurance. All have two things in common: delivering value to customers, and beating the competition.

Together, you can thoroughly cover the following areas:

•**Your target markets**. What markets do you currently compete in? What do you know about them in terms of potential, dollars available, and your share of the market? Something frequently prepared for products is a life cycle chart; you might want to do the same for your market. Is it embryonic, developing, mature or in decline? Are there new markets to exploit?

•**Customer Knowledge**. Your colleagues in Quality, Distribution, Engineering, or other organizations can be helpful in finding what you need. *The customer's objectives.* What threats do your customers face? What goals does the customer have? Work with your customer to define these so you can become a partner instead of a variable component. *How is the customer addressing her or his markets?* Do you know as much about your customer's position as you know about your own? If not, find out. *How big is each customer, really?* You may find you're spending more time on a less important customer than on the customers who can break you. Is your customer growing or in decline? What plans does the customer have to expand or acquire growth? What innovations are in development?

What does your customer value? Price, product quality, service, innovation, delivery? The better you know what's driving your customer's purchasing decision, the better you'll be able to respond.

•**Clearly identify the alternatives your customer** has. As one customer told employees at a major supplier, "While you've been figuring out how to get by, we've been figuring out how to get by without you." Is backward integration—a situation in which the customer develops the capability inhouse—possible? Is there an abundance of other suppliers? What is your business doing to avoid having your customers looking for alternatives?

•**Know your competition**. Your competitors are the obvious alternative for your customer, and thus represent your biggest threat. You can find what you need to know about your competitors through newspaper reports, public records, at trade shows, and from your customers: the size of expansions, the strengths that competitor has, its latest innovations. Do you know how your competition approaches your customers?

•**Describe the Environment**. What changes have occurred in the last 18 months? In the past year? What could change in the near future and over a longer period of time? This should include any kinds of laws or regulations that might affect you, the entry or deletion of competitors, and shifts in technology. Also, keep in mind that internal change does affect your customers. For instance, is a key leader in your business planning to retire? If so, decision making, operations or management style may change—and your customer may have obvious concerns. You can add some depth to

this section, too, by portraying several different scenarios:
•What happens if we do nothing beyond last year?
•What happens if we capitalize on our strengths?
•What might happen if our image slips?
•What happens if we do less this year than last?

3. The Marketing Strategy

The marketing strategy consists of what you offer customers and the price you charge. Start by providing a complete description of each product or service and what it provides to your customers. Life cycle, again, is an important part of this. Is your technology or product developing, mature or in decline? Depending on how your company is organized, a variety of people are responsible for this information, right down to whoever is figuring out how to package the product and how it will be delivered. Find out who needs to be included and make sure their knowledge is used.

The marketing strategy is driven by everything you've done up to this point. Strategies define the approaches you will use to market the company. For instance, if you are competing on the basis of service and support rather than price, your strategy may consist of emphasizing relationships. You will then develop tactics that support that strategy: market the company vs. the product; increase sales per client; assure customer responsiveness. Now, what action or programs will you use to make sure that happens?

Note: strategy leads. No program, regardless of how good it is, should make the

cut if it doesn't link to your business strategies and your customer.

The messages you must craft to support the strategies often are overlooked. Messages are the consistent themes you want your customer to know, to remember, to feel when he or she hears, reads, or views anything about your company or products. The method by which you deliver your messages comes under the heading of actions or programs.

Finally, you need to determine how you'll measure your own success, beyond meeting the sales forecast. How will you know if your image takes a beating? How will you know whether the customer is satisfied, or has just given up complaining? If you don't know, you'll be caught reacting to events, instead of planning for them.

Remember, your customer's measure of your success may be quite different from what you may think. Your proposed measures must be defined by what your customer values, and they have to be quantifiable. You may be surprised at how willing the customer is to cooperate with you in completing surveys, participating in third-party interviews, or taking part in a full-scale analysis of your company as a supplier. Use caution in assuming that winning awards means you have a measurable indicator. Your measures should be stated in terms of strategies, not plaques or trophies.

4. The Marketing and Sales Organization

The most frequently overlooked element in business is something we usually rele-

(continued)

gate to the Personnel or Human Resources Office—people. They're what makes everything possible. Include them. Begin with a chart that shows the organization for both Marketing and Sales. You may wish to indicate any interdependent relationships that exist (for instance, with Quality).

Note which of the roles are critical, particularly in terms of customer contact. Just as important, include positions, capabilities, and numbers of people needed in the future. How will you gain these skills without impacting your cost per sale? Again, it's time to be creative and provide options.

5. Revenue and Expense

In this section, you're going to project the revenue your plan will produce. This is usually calculated by evaluating the value of your market(s) and determining the dollar value of your share of that market. You need to factor in any changes you believe will occur, and you'll need to identify the sources of revenue, by product or service. Use text to tell the story; use graphs to show the story.

After you've noted where the money is coming from, explain what money you need to deliver the projected return. This will include staff wages and benefits for your organization, as well as the cost for specific programs you plan to implement.

During this era of budget cuts, do yourself a favor by prioritizing these programs. For instance, if one of your key strategies is to expand to a new market via new technologies, products, or ser-

vices, you will need to allocate appropriate dollars. What is the payback on the investment in marketing, and when will revenues fully pay back the investment? Also, provide an explanation of programs that will be deleted should a cut in funding be required. Again, combine text and spreadsheets to tell and to show.

6. Management Issues

This section represents your chance to let management know what keeps you awake at night. What might or could go wrong? What are the problems your company faces in customer relations? Are there technology needs that are going unattended? Again, this can be a collaborative effort that identifies your concerns. In addition, you may want to identify long-term issues, as well as those that are of immediate significance.

To keep this section as objective as possible, list the concerns and the business strategy or strategies they affect. What are the short-term and long-term risks? For instance, it is here that you might want to go into further detail about a customer's actions that look like the beginnings of backward integration.

7. Executive Summary

Since most senior leaders want a quick-look reference, it's best to include a one-page Executive Summary that covers these points:

- Your organization's objectives
- Budget requirements
- Revenue projections
- Critical management issues

When you're publishing the final plan document, you'll want the executive summary to be Page One.

8. Sell the Plan

This is one of the steps that often is overlooked. Selling your plan is as important as writing it. Otherwise, no one owns it, except you. The idea is to turn it into a rallying point that helps your company move forward. And to do that, you need to turn as many people as possible into ambassadors for your marketing efforts.

First, set up a time to present the plan to everyone who helped you with information and data. Make sure that they feel some sense of ownership, but that they also see how their piece ties into the whole. This is one of those instances where you need to say your plan, show your plan, discuss your plan. Only after all three steps are completed will they *hear* the plan.

After you've shared the information across the organization, reserve some time on the executive calendar. Have a couple of leaders review the plan first, giving you feedback on the parts where they have particular expertise. Then, present the plan at a staff meeting.

Is It Working?

You may think your job is finished. It's not. You need to convey the key parts of this plan to coworkers throughout the business. They need to know what the business is trying to achieve. Their livelihood, not just that of the owners, is at stake. From their phone-answering technique to the way they pro-

cess an order, every step has meaning to the customer.

9. Measure/Renew

Once you've presented your plan and people understand it, you have to continuously work the plan and share information about it. The best way to help people see trends and respond appropriately is to have meaningful measures. In the language of Total Quality, these are the Key Result Indicators—the things that have importance to your customers and that are signals to your performance.

For instance, measure your ability to deliver on a customer request; the amount of time it takes to respond to a customer inquiry; your productivity per employee; cash flow; cycle time; yield rates. The idea is to identify a way to measure those things that are critical to you and to your customer.

Review those measurements. Share the information with the entire business and begin the process all over again. Seek new ideas and input to improve your performance. Go after more data and facts. And then renew your plan and share it with everyone—all over again.

It's an extensive process, but it's one that spreads the word—and spreads the ownership. It's the step that ensures that your plan will be constantly in use, and constantly at work for your business.

Carole Hedden is a writer and communication/planning consultant living in Elmira, New York.

---

your product. Finally, your customer relations personnel should be trained to respond to problems quickly and efficiently, and to use the contact as an opportunity to find out more about what customers want.

"I'm always amazed when I go into the shipping department of some company and say, 'What is your mission? What's the message you want to give to your end user?' and they say, 'I don't know. I just know I've got to get these shipments out on time,'" says Dawson.

Because the success of integrated marketing depends on a consistent, cohesive message, employees throughout the company need to understand the firm's marketing goals and their role in helping to fulfill them.

"It's very important to bring employees in on the process," says James Lowry, chairman of the marketing department at Ball State University. "Employees today are better than any we've had before. They want to know what's going on in the organization. They don't want to be left out."

HELP IS ON THE WAY

THREE SOFTWARE PACKAGES THAT WILL HELP YOU GET STARTED

Writing a marketing plan may be daunting, but there is a variety of software tools out there to help you get started. Found in electronics and book stores, the tools are in many ways like a Marketing 101 textbook. The difference lies in how they help.

Software tools have a distinct advantage: They actually force you to write, and that's the toughest part of any marketing plan. Sometimes called "MBA In a Box," these systems guide you through a planning process. Some even provide wording that you can copy into your own document and edit to fit your own business. Presto! A boiler plate plan! Others provide a system of interviewing and questioning that creates a custom plan for your operation. The more complex tools demand an integrated approach to planning, one that brings together the full force of your organization, not just Sales or Advertising.

1. Crush

Crush, a modestly named new product from a modestly named new company, HOT, takes a multimedia approach. (HOT stands for Hands-On Technology; *Crush* apparently stands for *Crushing the Competition*)

Just introduced a few months ago, *Crush* is a multimedia application for Macintosh or Windows PCs. It features the competitive analysis methods of Flegis McKenna, marketing guru to Apple, Intel and Genentech; and it features Mr. McKenna himself as your mentor, offering guidance via on-screen video. As you work through each section of a complete market analysis, McKenna provides germane comments; in addition, you can see video case studies of

marketing success stories like Intuit software.

Crush provides worksheets and guidance for analyzing your products, customers, market trends and competitors, and helps you generate an action plan. The "mentor" approach makes it a useful

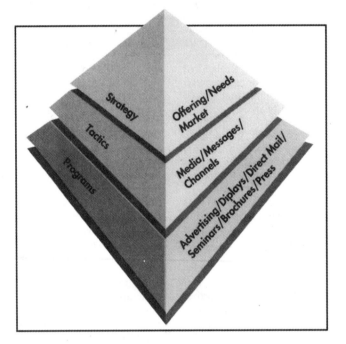

Pyramid Power: Plan Write's pyramid approach asks the user to define the messages for a business as part of the tactics.

tool for self-education; as you work through the examples and develop your company's marketing plan, you build your own expertise.

2. Marketing Plan Pro

Palo Alto's *Marketing Plan Pro* is a basic guide, useful for smaller businesses or ones in which the company leader wears a number of different hats, including marketing. It includes the standard spreadsheet capability, as well as the ability to chart numerical data. *Marketing Plan Pro* uses a pyramid process.

I liked the pyramid for a simple reason: It asks you to define messages for your business as part of your tactics. Without a message, it's easy to jump around, reacting to the marketplace instead of anticipating, leaving customers wondering what really is

significant about your company or your product.

The step-by-step process is simple, and a sample plan shows how all the information works together. The customer-focus aspect of the plan seemed a little weak, demanding only sales potential and buying capacity of the customers. Targeted marketing is increasingly important, and the user may want to really expand how this section is used beyond what the software requires.

The package displays, at a glance, your strategy, the tactics you develop for each

strategy, and the action plan or programs you choose to support the strategy. That could help when you're trying to prioritize creative ideas, eliminating those that really don't deliver what the strategy demands. Within each of three columns, you can click on a word and get help. Click on the heading program: a list of sample actions is displayed. They may not be what you're looking for, but if this is your first plan, they're lifesavers.

I also really liked *Marketing Plan Pro's* user's manual. It not only explains how the software works with your computer, it helps with business terms and provides a guide to planning, walking you through step-by-step.

3. Plan Write

Plan Write, created by Business Resource Software, Inc., is exponentially more powerful than *Marketing Plan Pro*. *Plan Write* brings together the breadth of the business, integrating information as far flung as distribution systems and image. And this software places your marketing strategy within the broader context of a business plan, the approach that tends to prove most effective.

As with *Marketing Plan Pro*, *Plan Write* provides a sample plan. The approach is traditional, incorporating a look at the business environment, the competition, the product or service mix you are offering, the way you will tell customers about that mix, pricing, delivery, and support.

Among the sections that were particularly strong was one on customer alternatives and people planning. Under the heading of customer alternatives, you're required to

(continued)

incorporate competitive information with customer information. If you don't meet the customer's needs, where could he or she go? Most often we look only at the competition, without trying to imagine how the customer is thinking. This exercise is particularly valuable to the company who leads the market.

The people part of planning too often is dumped on the personnel guy instead of being seen as a critical component of your organization's capabilities. *Plan Write* requires that you include how marketing is being handled, and how sales will be accomplished. In addition, it pushes you to define what skills will be needed in the future and where the gaps are between today and the future. People, in this plan, are viewed as a strategic component.

Plan Write offers a fully integrated spreadsheet that can import from or export to most of the popular spreadsheet programs you may already be using. Another neat feature allows you to enter numerical data and select from among 14 different graphing styles to display your information. You just click on the style you want to view, and the data is reconfigured.

Probably the biggest danger in dealing with software packages such as *Marketing Plan Pro* and *Plan Write* is to think the software is the answer. It's merely a guide.

—Carole Hedden

Employees are ambassadors for your company. Every time they interact with a customer or vendor, they're marketing your company. The more knowledgeable and helpful they are, the better they reflect on your firm.

At Nordstrom, a Seattle-based retailer, sales associates are empowered to use their best judgment in all situations to make a customer happy.

"We think our sales associates are the best marketing department," said spokeswoman Amy Jones. "We think word of mouth is the best advertising you can have." As a result, although Nordstrom has stores in only 15 states, it has forged a national reputation.

If companies regard marketing as the exclusive province of the marketing department, they're destined to fail.

"Accounting and sales and other departments have to work together hand in hand," says Dawson. "If they don't, you're going to have a problem in the end."

For example, in devising an integrated marketing campaign for the Nissan 200SX, Chiat/Day marketers worked in strategic business units that included a variety of disciplines such as engineers, representatives from the parts and service department, and creative people. By taking a broad view of the business and building inter-related activities to support its goals, Chiat/Day was able to create a seamless campaign for the 200SX that weaves advertising, in-store displays, and direct marketing together seamlessly.

"When everybody understands what the mission is, it's easier," asserts Bilfield. "It's easier to go upstream in the same direction than to go in different directions."

After bringing the different disciplines within your company on board, you're ready to design the external marketing program needed to support your goals. Again, the principle of integrated marketing comes into play: The message should be focused and consistent, and each step of the process should bring the consumer one step closer to buying your product.

In the case of Chiat/Day's campaign for the Nissan 200SX, the company used the same theme, graphics, type faces, and message to broadcast a consistent statement.

Introduced about the same time as the latest Batman movie, the campaign incorporates music and graphics from the television series. Magazine ads include an 800 number

potential customers can call if they want to receive an information kit. Kits are personalized and include the name of a local Nissan dealer, a certificate for a test drive, and a voucher entitling test drivers to a free gift.

By linking each step of the process, Chiat/Day can chart the number of calls, test drives, and sales a particular ad elicits. Like a good one-two punch, the direct marketing picks up where the national advertising leaves off, leveraging the broad exposure and targeting it at the most likely buyers.

While the elaborate 200SX campaign may seem foolproof, a failure to integrate the process at any step along the way could result in a lost sale.

For example, if a potential client were to test drive the car and encounter a dealer who knew nothing about the free gift accompanying the test drive, the customer would feel justifiably annoyed. Conversely, a well-informed sales associate who can explain the gift will be mailed to the test driver in a few weeks will engender a positive response.

SECTION III EXECUTION

The final component of an integrated marketing plan is the implementation phase. This is where the budget comes in.

How much you'll need to spend depends on your goals. If a company wants to expand its market share or promote its products in a new region, it will probably have to spend more than it would to maintain its position in an existing market.

Again, you'll need to create a system for keeping your employees informed. You might consider adding an element to your company newsletter that features people from different departments talking about the marketing problems they encounter and how they overcome them. Or you might schedule a regular meeting for department heads to discuss marketing ideas so they can report back to their employees with news from around the company.

Finally, you'll need to devise a system for monitoring your marketing program. A database, similar to the one created from calls to the 200SX's 800 number, can be an invaluable tool for determining if your message is being well received.

It's important to establish time frames for achieving your goals early in the process. If you want to increase your market share, for instance, you should determine the rate at which you intend to add new customers. Failing to achieve that rate could signal a flaw in your plan or its execution, or an unrealistic goal.

"Remember, integrated marketing is a long-range way of thinking," warns Dawson. "Results are not going to be immediate."

Like any investment, marketing requires patience, perseverance, and commitment if it is to bear fruit. While not all companies are forward thinking enough to understand the manifold gains of integrated marketing, the ones that don't embrace it will ultimately pay a tremendous price.

MORE INFO

Software for writing marketing plans:

Crush, Hands-On Technology; for more information, call (800) 772-2580 ext. 14 or (415) 579-7755; e-mail info@HOT.sf.ca.us; or visit the Web site at http://www. HOT.sf.ca.us.

Marketing Plan Pro, Palo Alto Software: for more information, call (800) 229-7526 or (503) 683-6162.

Plan Write for Marketing, Business Resource Software, Inc.: for more information, call (800) 423-1228 or (512) 251-7541.

Books about marketing plans:

Twelve Simple Steps to a Winning Marketing Plan, Geraldine A. Larkin (1992, Probus Publishing Co.)*
Preparing the Marketing Plan, by David Parmerlee (1993, NTC Business Books)*
Your Marketing Plan: A Workbook for Effective Business Promotion (Second Edition), by Chris Pryor (1995, Oregon Small Business Development Center Network)*
Your Business Plan: A Workbook for Owners of Small Businesses, by Dennis J. Sargent, Maynard N. Chambers, and Chris Pryor (1995, Oregon Small Business Development Center Network)*

Recommended reading:

Managing for Results, Peter Drucker
The One to One Future: Building Relationships One Customer at a Time, by Don Peppers and Martha Rogers, Ph.D. (1993, Currency/Doubleday)*
"Real World Results," by Don Schultz *(Marketing Tools* magazine, April/May 1994)*
* Available through American Demographics; call (800) 828-1133

Shelly Reese is a freelance writer based in Cincinnati.

Got
Emotional
Product
Positioning?

There's more to positioning than just features and benefits.

By Vijay Mahajan and Yoram (Jerry) Wind

EXECUTIVE briefing

It's not vitamins and minerals that sell milk these days, but rather "affective" emotional relationships, with celebrities sporting milk moustaches. From pedestrian products, such as milk, to online relationships, emotion is becoming more important in product positioning. In this article, the authors explore the rising importance of "affect," explain when it's most important, and point out some possible pitfalls in applying it.

Marketers of perfume, fashion, liquor, and high-quality image products have always known there wasn't a logical argument that could convince a buyer to purchase their brand of scent, champagne, luggage, or jewelry. They appealed to emotions. They associated their products with fashionable and attractive people and situations. While emotion has long been recognized as an important aspect of positioning, the appeal to the heart instead of the head is now increasing in a wide range of markets. Given product proliferation, information overload, a focus on customer relationships, and consumers' increased use of Web-based search engines and decision tools, companies need to do more than appeal to the head in positioning products. They must also appeal more than ever to the heart.

Approaches using emotional appeals have swept out of the fashion stores into a wide range of industries. Volkswagen positions its new Beetle with '60s retro associations and psychedelic colors, and the company has created an online radio station to reinforce the importance of music to the brand. Similarly, BMW has created a series of short online movies by famous producers that only peripherally feature its automobiles. And Swatch has created an interactive online store where visitors not only look at products, but also actually "design" their own personal store clerk as part of the overall experience. Nike's "Just do it" campaign doesn't even tell our logical

heads what "it" is, but we all get the emotional messages of achievement and courage. POWERade uses glowing colors and associations with Shaquille O'Neal, and Budweiser has emphasized associations with fun through advertising featuring frogs and lizards.

Even milk is positioned by painting its mustache on every celebrity lip that stands still for a few moments. While the "Got milk?" and "Milk mustache" campaigns continue to offer a subtext of the health and lifestyle benefits of drinking milk, all these cognitive messages are sweetened and permeated by the syrup of an emotional appeal.

Messages are becoming more vague while the emotions are becoming more vivid. The overriding message is that if you're not using emotion to position your products and services—any product or service—you're missing a tremendous opportunity. Your position also may be vulnerable to competitors who recognized this potential first.

When Visa International launched an advertising campaign claiming that seven million merchants who accept Visa don't accept American Express credit cards, American Express countered with its own ad dismissing the claim. American Express countered that Visa charges cardholders "$1.5 billion in unnecessary interest." The cognitive arguments led to a public shouting match that did more to confuse than win new customers. In contrast, Visa's "Everywhere you want to be" campaign was based on the same argument as before, but it used affect to associate its card with exciting events and locations (such as the Olympics and upscale restaurants) rather than proving its point with statistics. Consumers who have an emotional link with a brand also are likely to be less price-sensitive so long as they continue to derive their emotional satisfaction from the brand.

In advertising its disposable cameras, Kodak could have made logical arguments for the superiority of its cameras. But the company didn't discuss low price or argue how the camera is ideal for risky situations when a camera may be damaged or stolen. Instead it showed straight-laced maids and butlers frolicking while the mistress of the house was away—taking pictures with disposable cameras the whole time. The ads associate the camera with risk and excitement, but through an emotional appeal.

Cognitive and Affective Positioning

Positioning can be based on a combination of cognition and affect. Cognition depends on logical arguments in favor of the product. It focuses on problems, solutions, or benefits sought by customers and how the product features help to solve the problems or achieve the benefits. (For example, "milk builds healthy bones.") At the extreme, this includes comparative advertising, which compares the features of the product or service directly with those of rivals.

In contrast to cognitive approaches, affect goes straight to the heart by focusing on emotions, feelings, or drives associated with a product or service. Milk is associated with athletes, actors, and other role models that create an emotional association with the product or service. The emotions that can be drawn on in positioning products range from joy to fear to desire to sadness. While both cognition and affect are important, the battle-field of positioning is shifting to affect.

To illustrate how these cognitive and affective strategies are combined, consider an advertisement for milk featuring television host Joan Lunden. The four sentences of copy below Lunden's photo read as follows:

"Most people think I must drink at least 10 cups of coffee to be so perky in the morning. But the truth is, I like skim milk first thing. It has all the same nutrients as whole milk without all the fat. And besides, my husband got the coffee maker."

Along with Lunden's smiling milk mustache, this simple ad succinctly units its cognitive and affective components to exploit the six major strategies of product positioning:

- **Based on product features**. The "same nutrients as whole milk without the fat" describes features of the product.

- **Based on benefits, solutions, or need**s. Skim milk makes her "perky" and it is implied that it also helps keep a trim figure.

- **For a specific usage occasion**. Lunden drinks milk first thing in the morning.

- **For a specific user category**. As a successful, independent woman, Lunden shows that milk is not just for kids.

- **Against another product**. She drinks milk instead of drinking 10 cups of coffee.

- **For product class disassociation**. The advertisement differentiates skim milk from whole milk, showing it is healthier.

In this single ad, the six major positioning strategies are combined in a tight package. It really is a marvel of engineering, but that's not the whole story. What's less evident, and perhaps more significant, is the addition of affect to the cognitive positioning contained in the copy. The ad uses some of these six strategies in its affective positioning. For example, Lunden's appearance in the ad is associated with benefits such as health, success, and energy. Her presence also helps to target a certain group of users (young professional women). The questions used in the campaign: "Got milk?" and "Where's your milk mustache?" also convey an attitude that targets a set of contemporary and savvy customers.

When It Matters

Although all products and services can and should use affect to some degree, it makes the most sense in the following situations:

Big-ticket items. If customers are motivated to buy products based on emotions, they usually have a reduced need for cognitive information during the prepurchase stage. Consumers in general have surprisingly little interest in detailed prepurchase information, even when buying expensive or socially risky goods. It's far easier to purchase a car that gives you the latest technology or makes you look "smart" than to read all the fine print on engines and transmissions. Acquiring customers by affect also can help reduce post-purchase "buyer's remorse." So long as the purchase lives up to the affective promises, the customer will be less likely to feel dissatisfied based on cognitive dissonance. Mercedes-Benz, for example, used analogies to great writers, ballplayers, and historical events in the United States in its advertising to differentiate its product from an ordinary "car." (A photo of Hemingway is shown with the caption "a writer.") The tag line for the campaign is a direct reference to the limitations of cognition: "Sometimes words can be hopelessly inadequate." There may ultimately be no rational argument to cause a customer to part with that much money. It has to be the emotions.

Commodity products. Almost by definition, commodity products have very little to say for themselves. Cognitive arguments are pointless if there's little to distinguish one product from another. It's the emotional associations with the commodity product that make it cease to be a commodity. In addition to the milk campaign, spring water is the ultimate example of how affect can turn a commodity into a brand worth a dollar or two a bottle. Aside from the shape of the bottle and the affective positioning, what is it that distinguishes one spring water product from another? The de-commoditization of a product can also be seen in Absolut Vodka's shift from focusing on the spirits inside the bottle to affective associations with the bottle, and its artistic execution, which helped it rise above the shelves of generic vodka. Emotions can lift commodities from sameness and position them as something different.

Technologically complex products. Among the most complex products or services to sell are those based on high technology. Affective approaches may provide a motivation for purchase without getting lost in the complexity of the cognitive arguments. Apple's famous "1984" campaign and IBM's Charlie Chaplin campaign for its PC were early examples. Apple Computer's more recent "Think different" campaign associates itself with radical thinkers throughout society, without one mention of either the hardware or software (although these are described in more cognitively focused advertising).

Southwestern Bell marketed a new voice messaging system by showing a young woman fruitlessly trying to retrieve an invitation for a date from an old-fashioned answering machine. A second ad shows a man professing his love to a date in his home while a message from a second woman is audible in the background on his answering machine. The association is not with technology but with personal privacy, love, embarrassment, and lost opportunity. One Philadelphia-area stereo retailer stressed that it sold "goosebumps" rather than trying to explain the quality of its highly technical merchandise.

Multiple generations of products. For products such as chips, software, and automobiles, with planned obsolescence of each version of the product, affective approaches can bring continuity to the customer relationship. Even when cognitive benefits and features are rapidly changing, affect remains. For example, Intel's use of its "Intel Inside" branding, along with a distinctive set of musical tones and cool-looking, clean-room-suited representatives, uses an affective strategy as the connective tissue for a set of products with shifting features and benefits. Affect is used to create an emotional link, so customers will continuously upgrade based on the relationship.

Service. Service comes from the heart, so it's particularly important to use affect in positioning service. When American Express tried to sum up the impact of its credit card and related services, it used affective relationships with celebrities to make its point. Its "profiles" campaign focused on how the card improved the lives of high-profile individuals. This allows the company to pull together a complex bundle that includes a less tangible service component. Affect fuses together a wide range of features and benefits that are not, or cannot be, clearly articulated. Insurance companies show hurricanes and other disasters to make an emotional appeal.

Credence goods. Products can be divided into search goods (e.g., clothing and furniture) whose quality can be judged before consumption; experience goods (e.g., travel or restaurant meals) that have to be experienced to be evaluated; and credence goods (e.g., medical diagnosis and auto repair) that customers cannot evaluate even after experience. Because of the trust needed for credence goods, affective positioning may be even more important.

Familiar products. Affect can help ensure that a familiar product remains among the limited consideration set from which customers make their purchases. The emotions associated with the brand or product become part of the consumer's autobiographical memories, making them stronger and more accessible. For example, the powerful affective associations with Coke or Pepsi are often the determining factor in purchases. In contrast, unfamiliar products that tend to evoke more cognitive effort on the part of the customer are less susceptible to affective approaches.

To develop strong brands. Affect helps strengthen brands because it adds another distinction to the brand. If a Home Depot builds its brand identity only around broad selection, high quality, and lower prices, its customers may quickly defect if another competitor moves in with a larger selection or lower prices. But if the brand also has an affective association—there are some relationships, emotions, or warm feelings associated with the store (i.e., friendly personal service)—the brand becomes a more powerful force in holding customers. For example, the Traveler's umbrella or Prudential's Rock of Gibraltar are designed to appeal more to the feeling of security than to any specific benefit.

Discontinuous innovations. Discontinuous innovations require customers to change their current behavior to adopt the innovation. For example, online grocery shopping and using video telephones require substantial changes in behavior. Because their attachment to the old product or service may be based on sound reasons, affect can be a way to break through this wall of arguments and encourage more innovative behavior.

Unmentionables. Unmentionable products (e.g., condoms, hygiene products, funeral services) are generally difficult to market. Marketers may use affect to market these products because they are difficult to position in cognitive terms. A commercial for Trojan condoms uses a super hero character. A Fort James ad shows a roll of toilet paper and merely says, "Imagine your life without it." If a product is unmentionable, you need more than words to encourage customers to be comfortable considering it.

Some Pitfalls

Even as marketers begin to understand and use affective approaches, several pitfalls are worth noting. In particular, companies using affective positioning have to be careful of the following potential problems:

Dissonance between affect and cognitive messages. The affective messages are out of step with one another, the cognitive arguments, or the actual product experience. If the affective cognitive positioning is based on high quality but customer service is shoddy, the positioning will be undermined. One of the problems of the milk campaign may have been that it was very effective in positioning its product as hip and healthy, but the supermarkets still offered the product in the same old bland containers. The advertising was giving one message while the packaging and distribution strategy sent another one. Milk producers could have moved more aggressively to take milk into different packaging that would be more consonant with its milk mustache positioning.

Cultural differences. Affect is very susceptible to differences in interpretation across cultures. The Milk Processor Board's "Got Milk?" campaign became the unflattering "Are You Lactating?" when translated into Spanish for Latino audiences in the United States. This unwanted overtone and differences in family relation-ships led the advertiser to create a separate Latino campaign targeted toward mothers that asked, "And You, Have You Given Them Enough Milk Today?" Instead of athletes and models, the campaign showed mothers cooking traditional milk-rich Latin foods such as flans in the family kitchen. On the other hand, Latino focus groups found that teens may identify more with English language "Got Milk?" campaigns than with those specifically targeted toward Latinos. (Wartzman, Rick (1999), "When You Translate 'Got Milk' for Latinos, What Do You Get?" *Wall Street Journal*, June 3.) As in all cross-cultural marketing, defining where the global market ends and the local market begins is an art.

Lack of credibility. To be effective, any positioning (cognitive or affective) requires the marketer to understand what's important to the customer and to show that the product or service delivers on those expectations better than anyone else. The message has to be credible to be believed.

Confusion. Even though affect can be effective in reaching out to diverse, heterogeneous segments, it's also more open to interpretation than cognitive arguments. Not everyone relates to the same humor and mood of the advertising. What one person finds hilarious, another may find baffling or shocking. Most marketing research is limited to testing the cognitive impact of marketing and doesn't generally address the affective dimension of positioning. We need to develop and employ better techniques for testing the effectiveness of affect. Sometimes, even without cultural differences, the message doesn't come across. What the advertiser intended with the affect approach is not received that way. Some of this

can be avoided through careful testing, but by its nature affect is less precise than cognitive approaches.

Unwanted overtones. Affective relationships can be very hard to manage because they are highly personal and emotionally charged. When American Express used Body Shop founder Anita Roddick as a profile in its advertising campaign, there may have been a disjoint between the images of the Body Shop and American Express. While some potential customers would be positively moved by the association, others might find it a negative association. When partnering with other companies and seeking to evoke certain emotions, managers need to carefully consider whether the affect of one product is compatible with the other.

Winning Hearts and Minds

Affect has a powerful role to play in product positioning today. With care, affect can be a powerful addition to positioning based on features and benefits. It should be in the arsenal of every marketer, no matter what their product or service. In fact, it can be powerful in an industry where this approach has not been used extensively in the past.

In a world of information overload, rapid change, and complexity, increased need to build relationships with customers, and the growing availability of Web-based product and service comparison data on any attribute from performance through style to price, affect has never been more important.

We need more experimentation in this area. If you're not already using affect, how can you add it to your positioning? If you are using it, how can you increase the affective appeal of your positioning? How can you make it more effective by avoiding the mistakes discussed previously? If you are overlooking affect, you may be missing out on an opportunity to make a more powerful impact with your positioning and to forge deeper and more enduring relationships with your customers. It is the affective, rather than the cognitive, story of and about your offerings that will win customers' hearts and minds, and this is what companies need to do to create, manage, and harvest emotional brand loyalty.

About the Authors

Vijay Mahajan is the John P. Harbin Centennial Chair in Business and professor of marketing at The University of Texas, Austin. He may be reached at vmahajan@mail.utexas.edu.

Yoram (Jerry) Wind is the Lauder Professor and professor of marketing at the Wharton School at the University of Pennsylvania and Director of the SEI Center for Advanced Studies in Management. He may be reached at windj@wharton.upenn.edu

GET TO
MARKET FASTER

Half of all new products are destined to fail. Don't let yours be one of them.

A new generation of digital tools improves your odds of success—and pushes products out the door in record time.

BY DESIREE DE MYER

A year ago, 3Com unveiled Audrey, a Net appliance for the 21st century. Audrey would bring high-tech to the kitchen by organizing shopping lists, e-mail, and the Web on a counter-space-saving 8-inch screen. Designed by the celebrated Silicon Valley design house IDEO, the curvy gizmo looked supercool.

Five months later, Audrey was dead. 3Com overestimated consumer readiness for kitchen computing, and this March the company quietly began giving full refunds to customers who'd brought the $499 appliance. With that Audrey joined the Edsel in the graveyard of failed new products.

They're not buried alone. About half of all new products brought to market fail, according to the Product Development & Management Association. For household consumer items, the odds are even worse. For each smash hit like Polaroid's i-Zone camera, there are at least eight flops like Kellogg's Breakfast Mates. Most new product ideas never get to market at all. Why? Danger lurks at every turn of the new product development process—from the fuzzy front end where a company identifies customer needs and the initial concept takes shape, through product and process design, to manufacture and delivery.

Still, companies can't afford not to gamble on new products. With competition for shelf space and market share fierce, rivals keep upping the ante on research. An annual forecast by the Battelle Memorial Institute and *R&D Magazine* predicts that spending on R&D will rise 5 percent by $277 billion in 2001.

In today's economy, speed to market is the Holy Grail. Some call it "time to value"—and in the world of *new*, time really is money. With time to market shrinking by as much as 50 percent over the last five years, according to AMR Research, the challenge is to push good ideas out the door faster than the competition. Studies have shown it's more profitable to get a product out in time but over budget by 50 percent than it is to be six months late and within budget.

A new generation of Internet and digital tools can improve the odds of success, make failures less costly, and help get the right products to market, at the right price, at the right time. Online tools foster collaboration that can both shorten time to market and ensure product quality. Collaboration can't make people think faster, but it can make the "ideation" process faster and more fruitful, automating the tasks of capturing and implementing the best ideas. On the Web, employees from engineering, marketing, and manufacturing departments in different offices—even different countries—can share concepts, design files, product specifications, and late-breaking changes. These cross-functional product teams are key: If you let engineers control a product's development; no one will know if it's going to sell. Let the marketing department run the show, and a product might sound like a winner—but try getting it to work.

The Net also improves access to customer feedback. The new product graveyard is full of ideas that seemed brilliant but no one was ready to by: Maalox Whip, anyone? A traditional focus group program might cost up to $45,000 and take 16 weeks to set up and analyze. By contrast, for $20,000 a month the online consumer-feedback service Recipio can draw opinions from many more respondents—and have useful results available in days.

Whether a product succeeds or fails, information about it is still useful. Old ideas, suggestions, and designs can prove valuable—if they're readily available. With past projects archived on the Net, product teams can quickly learn what worked—and what didn't—before. Innovating is a must, but reinventing the wheel just wastes time and money. Aren't the odds bad enough?

ENVISION IT

What's the Big Idea?

Online collaboration kick-starts the creative process.

WHERE DO GREAT NEW PRODUCT ideas come from? The same place all ideas come from: people's heads. The challenge is coaxing the concepts out.

"We were getting a little burned out with the typical ideation," says Mike Mitchell, a former brand director for cordials at Jim Beam Brands Worldwide. The cordials market is extremely fashion-conscious. Though apple flavor may be hot today, in another year mocha could be the thing. In just two years, most cordials are ready for the scrap heap. To keep up with flavor fads, Mitchell and his team—a mix of marketing, sales, and packaging pros, and even professional bartenders—would get together once or twice a year, looking to re-create the huge success of Jim Beam's DeKuyper Sour Apple Pucker or invent the next Watermelon Schnapps.

"We were always looking for different techniques within ideation to create something new," says Mitchell. So he asked Synectics, a Cambridge, Massachusetts-based creativity consulting firm (www.synecticsworld.com), for help with the process.

Synectics had just the tool: a beta version of online ideation software InSync (slated for release this year; site licenses range from $250,000 to $500,000). Not just another free-form, collaborative workspace, InSync is a Web-based creativity tool that digitizes Synectics' widely imitated step-by-step problem-solving process to stimulate and guide brainstorming. It allows problem-solving and brainstorming meetings to occur at any time, from anywhere.

"The ideal size group to do invention is eight," says Terry Gilliam, a partner at Synectics. You need experts who know the topic inside and out, but also people who know absolutely nothing about it. You need somebody with a checkbook to green-light good ideas, and you need leaders who can champion projects. But often, with too many smart people together, airtime becomes a problem. With InSync, however, everybody can talk at once.

An InSync session starts with a group task headline that defines the problem, then lets people type ideas and build on them. Because participants are anonymous, they don't have to worry about looking stupid for suggesting

Another Tool for The Perfect Brainstorm

IdeaFisher brain-picking software has fans ranging from Global 1000 marketing managers to comedian Drew Carey. Developed in the late 1980s by Century 21 cofounder Marshall Fisher, the single-user PC software is built around a huge database of thousands of words and the thousands of concepts associated with them—for example, it offers 700 connotations just for "red."

"It's really just enabling you to remember what you know," which is the essence of brainstorming, Fisher says. An add-on module for new product development adds hundreds of questions like, "What corporate image must your product uphold?" that help you generate words ripe for association. The software has no Internet component, though creative types seeking to capture that latest buzz often run the concepts it generates through online search engines. Available for Windows or Macintosh. IdeaFisher Pro cost $209, plus $54 for add-on modules. For more, go to www.ideafisher.com.

glow-in-the-dark liqueur or a schnapps named Fuzzy Monkey Toes. "If you think of a name, sometimes it's embarrassing to bring it up because names don't immediately strike everybody as being good," says Mitchell. With the fear factor gone, those crazy—and sometimes brilliant—ideas get out in the open where they can be discussed, improved, and acted on. "I didn't care where all those wacky names came from. Likewise, I didn't care what name I thought of because it didn't come from my mouth, it appeared on the screen," says Mitchell.

Next, participants pick their favorite ideas anonymously. InSync tallies and ranks votes. It's a secret ballot, so there are no hurt feelings and no sucking up to the boss by voting for her horrible idea. The software also takes participants through other steps, including a phase called "excursion" that encourages them to think about everything *but* the problem they're trying to solve. Out of nowhere, a freight train may rumble across the screen or they'll be asked to imagine themselves trying to land a hot-air balloon. Gilliam explains, "Einstein said no problem can be solved in the context in which it was created."

Though product teams can hook up and generate ideas with InSync even if they're a world and several time zones apart, Mitchell's cordials crew met in a single room as they usually did. The difference? This time they had laptops—and were much more jazzed than usual. "The technique brought an air of intensity and newness to the room, and that was important at that time because we were starting to get into a grind," he says.

Jim Beam produced dozens of ideas worth considering using InSync, according to Mitchell, but the company won't disclose what those ideas were—the cordials market is *that* cutthroat. Other InSync users are talking, however. William A. Hamlin, vice president of Americas region operations for shipping company APL, used the software from Europe to brainstorm with his company's finance, operations, and systems employees in North America and Asia. Their online session saved on travel expenses and led to ideas that helped whittle $60 million in costs across several business areas.

Hamlin says the software allows more ideas to be considered. On the Web, there are no time limits. "I've been in InSync sessions where we've generated over a hundred [ideas] in 35 or 40 minutes," says Hamlin. In a face-to-face meeting "with a traditional facilitator, a good one who's a hell of a fast writer, you might get 30."

TEST IT

The Sweet Sound of Feedback

Wiretap your customers' minds—and improve your product—with online feedback.

REPLAY NETWORKS HAD A PROBLEM. Users complained that its new ReplayTV digital video recorders conked out when they were left on for extended periods. The root of the problem was a glitch in the memory circuitry that Replay's engineers hadn't discovered.

Replay had just signed its first contract to deliver its equipment to the mass consumer market, and the deal was a biggie: Consumer-electronics giant Panasonic was about to market a line of digital video recorders, labeled ShowStoppers, based on Replay's technology.

"To be ready to launch a product with Panasonic and to have them say, 'No, this bug is unacceptable,' and then to take another four to eight weeks to fix and test—that's expensive," says Kimberly Wiefling, a business management consultant who was acting program manager for ReplayTV at the time. "The whole marketing engine is ready to go, the stores are ready to receive it, and if you miss your market window to get into retail, they give away your shelf space."

Luckily for Replay, the users who found the bug were part of a Web-based test market: They spotted the problem early in the cycle, so Replay could fix it before it was too late and too costly. To set up the test market, Wiefling had enlisted the help of BetaSphere (www.betasphere. com), which typically charges between $100,000 and $250,000 to organize early-product-testing groups via the Internet. BetaSphere rounded up more than 100 consumers from its pool of 70,000 participants to test and critique the new ReplayTV unit.

What Do They Want?

Besides the BetaSphere Feedback Management Server, these two online tools will take your customers' temperature.

Perseus Development Survey Solutions Enterprise

www.perseus.com ($2,495)
What It Does Net-based tools let you design your own questionnaire using Microsoft Word, upload it to Perseus's Web server, and integrate it into your site. Provides detailed, Web-based reports.
Customers American Express, Microsoft, NASA. Weather.com used Perseus to get a real-time take from visitors on its revised home page design.

Recipio Brand Connection

www.recipio.com (Starts at $25,000)
What It Does Hosts customer feedback pages that integrate with a company's own site, then provides a Web-based analysis tool, Dashboard, to interpret it.
Customers NBC, Procter & Gamble, and General Motors have used Recipio's "inbound marketing" system to solicit consumer opinion. NBC got feedback about *The West Wing* and the ill-fated XFL football league. P&G lets consumers become P&G Advisors and chat with other customers.

The first group to test the digital recorder were hackers. "We wanted to send our first units to people who were going to rip 'em to bits and find all the dirty laundry," recalls Wiefling. BetaSphere identified about 40 hackers, and Replay sent them test models of the machine. Acting as an extension of the company's quality assurance department, they looked for hard-to-find, idiosyncratic bugs in the machines. Some even "wrote white papers on usability improvement required by the remote control," Wiefling says.

Next came compatibility testing. Replay's labs didn't have the resources to test the digital recorder in every time zone with every make and combination of TV, VCR, and DVD player. So BetaSphere provided a geographically dispersed group of customers with a wide variety of TV models and other electronic devices. Unlike the hackers, this second wave of testers didn't care what made the machine tick; they just wanted to record their favorite shows. Replay wanted to know how the average customer used the machine, if he could get it to work, and what he did—and didn't—like about it.

With BetaSphere's Feedback Management Server, it was easy. A midpoint or end-of-test survey could be sent out to all the customers, and within a day or two, says Wiefling, she'd have 80 responses. The software automatically tallied survey responses and converted them into charts and graphs—a process that could take a week without the Web. Because that data was delivered online, no one at Replay had to waste time making sense of it all.

The feedback helped settle debates about the various feature and enhancement ideas up for consideration. Engineers are sometimes accused of having the attitude, "If customers are too dumb to understand our products, they shouldn't be buying them." The results from Replay's BetaSphere tests made sure this mindset didn't sink its product. "Feedback from real, live customers outweighs anyone's gut feel," Wiefling says. "The endless conversations can be brought to a close with some facts."

PROTOTYPE IT

The Shape of Things to Come

Rapid prototyping adds a dimension to product previews.

SO YOU'VE GOT A KILLER PRODUCT DESIGN—HOW DO YOU give the marketing department a feel for it? Try rapid prototyping with a futuristic 3D printer. Z Corporation's Z406 System takes digital models of objects designed using CAD software and creates prototypes you can pass around the room. Z Corp. customers include Porsche, Adidas, and Fisher-Price.

How's it work? The printer's software slices a digital design into hundreds of cross sections, then prints each section using starch- or plaster-based powder and a binding chemical, piling up the layers atop one another until the object takes shape. Powder is also laid down around the model to support it, but it isn't chemically treated, so it falls away and can be recycled. It takes an hour to produce one to two vertical inches—in full color. The printer costs $67,500, but output materials are cheap—from 40 cents to $1 per cubic inch. Find out more at www.zcorp.com.

POSITION IT

Strike the Right Tone

His product was fine. But this business owner needed a new marketing strategy—fast.

FOR MOST PEOPLE, WIND chimes are whimsical garden decorations, ranking right up there with garden gnomes and gazing globes. For Peter Baker, they're serious business, and for 10 years business boomed. His company, based in Hunter River, Prince Edward Island, sold the only musically tuned chimes on the Canadian market.

But in 1991, Island Winds' monopoly ended. American-made Woodstock Chimes—and Woodstock knockoffs—started moving in. Customers preferred the imports because they were prettier than the hefty, stainless steel-alloy chimes that Baker's brother Chris had originally created in 1978. By 2000, sales were down about two-thirds from their high in 1990.

Baker toyed with the idea of changing his chimes, going head-to-head with the competition. "We wanted to make a chime similar to the Woodstock Chime from New York, which is the one that everyone copies," says Baker.

Then Doug Hall came to town with a better solution. Hall is a former master marketing inventor at Procter & Gamble and founder and CEO of Eureka Ranch in Cincinnati, an "innovation spa" where corporations pay hundreds of dollars for multiday sessions that inspire them to think up new products and ideas. Eureka had helped Frito Lay concoct snack food flavors and Nike envision shoe designs. Baker was simply in the right place at the right time. Hall vacationed regularly on Prince Edward Island and took a liking to Baker's little company.

Hall had recently put some of his expertise into a software program called Merwyn (www.eurekaranch.com/merwyn). The software takes a product concept and analyzes its probability of success. It does its match based on seven marketing criteria: overt benefit, real reason to believe, dramatic difference, clarity of communication, executional synergy, focus, and ratio of value versus cost to customers. Until this year, Merwyn was available only to Eureka Ranch clients such as PepsiCo and Nike. Now it's on the Web, and within about 24 hours anyone with a bright idea and $500 can get a Merwyn Idea Scan, which is a subset of its analysis.

Hall and Baker wrote a concept statement for Baker's wind chimes and sent it to Merwyn over the Internet. In about an hour they had an answer: Baker's chimes had only a 34 percent overall chance of success.

Then Hall advised Baker to turn what he thought was a product problem—the industrial strength of his chimes—into a selling point. Once more they wrote up a concept statement. This time they focused on the durability of the chimes and Island Winds' unique lifetime guarantee. When Merwyn tested the new, improved concept, it came back with a 69 percent probability of success.

Since then Baker has renamed his chimes—they're Nor'easters now—and has started to reposition them in the market. Summer sales are up about 50 percent.

BUILD IT

You're Gonna Make It After All

P&G gets new product data to the factory on time—online.

PROCTER & GAMBLE IS PRACTICALLY synonymous with "new and improved." But that new bleach additive in Tide—a P&G Product that becomes new or improved about once a year—doesn't only get gym socks whiter, it also requires changes in the manufacturing equipment that makes the detergent.

Depending on the formula change, sometimes it's just a single machine part that needs alteration. Other times, pipes and storage facilities have to be repurposed for a new chemical additive. Since Tide, like other P&G products, is manufactured in different plants around the world, those equipment changes must be made in multiple locations. If one plant falls behind in modifications, it slows down the product's time to market. To avoid delays, they've got to work together no matter how far apart they are.

With a portfolio of more than 300 products, 164-year-old P&G has a lot of experience in product design and manufacturing. But with manufacturing facilities in more than 70 countries, sharing that experience and knowledge isn't headache-free. Often, information never gets exchanged, and time is wasted as engineers go it alone: starting from scratch to design new parts, machines, and even facilities to bring that product to market.

Pulling It All Together

A growing class of integrated software helps manage the entire product development process, from conception to launch and beyond.

Project management systems like **Primavera Systems' Enterprise** (primavera.com) let managers schedule deadlines, juggle resources, and keep an eye on budgets. **Speed to Market's Concerto** (speedtomarket.com) goes further, using algorithms to predict which tasks will need attention first to meet deadlines.

Product data management tools like **PTC's Windchill** (www.windchill.com) share product-specific information such as part numbers and bills of materials. Prices for such systems vary widely—starting as low as $400 per user but potentially costing thousands per user and upward of $1 million enterprisewide.

Product lifecycle management systems tie everything together, letting engineering, manufacturing, marketing, and outside suppliers and channel partners coordinate activities. According to AMR Research, these systems can cut development costs 20 to 30 percent by fostering collaboration, reducing remakes, and eliminating duplicate information. **SAP's mySAP Product Lifecycle Management** (mysap.com/plm) has among the widest capability of any big-player solution; it can track products after they hit the market, tying into customer-relations and marketing systems. **MS2's Accelerate** (ms2.com), designed for high-tech product development, provides scheduling along with product and marketing data. PLM systems can cost from $50,000 to $500,000.

"There will be times where we're making changes to our manufacturing process and not know if we're already making that change somewhere else in the world," says Tom Massung, P&G associate director of product lifestyle management. To get its worldwide facilities working together, P&G uses SDRC's Metaphase knowledge management system (www.sdrc.com) to put CAD drawings, technical documentation and specifications, and operational procedures all in one place—the Internet.

With Metaphase, information about the facilities that manufacture P&G's Tide, Tampax, Pampers, and Pringles products are available online so that "everybody is on the same page at the same time and changes can be made synchronously," says Massung. The benefit? When working on a new product, P&G can get different factories up to speed simultaneously, allowing the company "to put products all around the world more quickly," says Massung.

Metaphase also allows P&G plants in Pennsylvania and Germany to learn from each other by reusing data about manufacturing equipment and raw materials such as plastics and fabrics. For example, while reengineering a machine part, one business unit used Metaphase to pull information from a sister plant that had already faced the same problem, netting a 90 percent rework reduction.

A year after putting Metaphase to work, P&G had realized a 10 percent reduction in engineering costs for the processes entered in the database. Massung says the setup was "incredibly easy." Training consisted of telling employees, "Don't store your drawings over there in the corner anymore. Put them in this computer system."

PACKAGE IT

Thinking *About* the Box

Good packaging sells a product, protects it during shipment to customers, and minimizes freight costs.

HEWLETT-PACKARD'S core business is making printers and desktop computers, not cartons. Still, the boxes that contain HP's LaserJet printers are incredibly complex. There are literally hundreds of specifications for the packaging, and each element—from custom-molded foam to accessory trays—has to be built to the precise dimensions of the product. The last thing anyone wants is to slow down a product's delivery because the box isn't ready. "As a packaging engineer, you never want packaging to be in the critical path," says Tim Lalley, corporate packaging engineer for Hewlett-Packard.

Last November HP began using webPKG (www.webpkg.com), a Web-based hub created to help companies connect the dispersed parties involved in package creation. WebPKG provides a browser-based hosted space where product design engineers can share requirements with package designers, package creators can share design documents with manufacturing facilities, and outside contractors that may be supplying the cardboard or producing package ideas can see what they need to see, whether it's CAD drawings or marketing graphics.

HP designs its LaserJet shipping cases in Boise, Idaho, where it designs the printers. Packaging engineers work with CAD files supplied by HP printer designers and, in some cases, outside package designers. But once the boxes are conceived, they're manufactured somewhere else, generally where the printers themselves are completed. For printers it sells in Germany, for example, HP buys finishing components like power cords and does final packaging there. That's where it produces boxes for those units. "All of those places need to get this information to buy tooling, print the boxes, plan floor space, and find the suppliers they need for manufacturing," says Lalley. "WebPKG gets the information into their hands sooner."

Though webPKG can't get the product out the door faster, it can help improve the quality of the package. Traditionally in a nine-month period HP might do five or six package-design revisions, says Lalley. "Now, we can do 10 design revisions in that time frame—to get a finer product."

Once it's fully implemented—HP piloted the online tool with LaserJets that hit the streets in May—webPKG is expected to cut other costs. Without the online database, Lalley says he's in Boise "kind of working in my own world, and even though there might be a box that already exists that was created in Singapore, I don't know about that." With webPKG, he can search for a package design by packaging style, dimensions, creation date, material type, and even the number of colors printed on it. "If it already exists, I can use it," he says.

The company also can use the tool to calculate how much cardboard it needs. "We can find all the corrugated components loaded into the system and calculate the square footage," Lalley explains. "Now we can go to International Paper, for example, and say, 'Next year we're going to buy x million tons of corrugated material. What kind of price break can you give us?'"

DESIRÉE DE MYER *is a New York–based business writer.*

From *Smart Business*, October 2001, pp. 62-68, 70-71. © 2001 by Desiree De Myer.

THE BEST GLOBAL BRANDS

BusinessWeek and INTERBRAND tell you what they're worth

Wireless phones. Consumer electronics. Memory chips. Could you pick three tougher lines of business to be in right now? Somehow, with just such a portfolio, Samsung Electronics Co. managed to more than double its profits in the most recent quarter, to $1.6 billion.

How? Once a humdrum manufacturer of commodity electronics largely sold under other companies' names, South Korea-based Samsung is reaping the rewards of moving aggressively into higher-end products that carry fatter profit margins. It has invested heavily to produce cutting-edge designs, from flat-panel TV monitors that can be hung on walls like paintings to an elegantly thin DVD player. The company moved up the memory-chip price chain to sell more devices to video game makers. And it became the No. 3 producer of cell phones, with a premium-priced line that includes handsets with color screens.

But just as critical as the turnover in product was the face-lift Samsung gave its brand. Last year, it took a first stab at creating a new image with visually arresting ads such as one that posed an impossibly stylish woman in blue makeup, yellow nail polish, and ostrich feathers next to one of its TV monitors. This year, it plans to spend $200 million on ads focused on the company's promise to provide a "DigitAll Experience." That's an attempt to drive home the link between Samsung's new upscale image and the lifestyle its customers crave, says Eric B. Kim, executive vice-president for global marketing operations. Says Kim: "This is our first attempt to be at the leading edge rather than being a follower."

Now more than ever, companies see the power of a strong brand. At a time when battered investors, customers, and employees are questioning whom they can trust, the ability of a familiar brand to deliver proven value flows straight to the bottom line. If, shaken by the plummeting stock market and concerned about the security of their jobs, consumers start cutting back on spending, they're more likely to stick with names they know they can rely on. "When a brand earns our trust, we not only re-peat our purchases, but we also tell all of our friends about it," says David Martin, U.S. president of New York-based Interbrand Corp., a pioneering brand consultant that teamed up with *BusinessWeek* to create our second annual ranking of the most valuable global brands.

The World's 10 Most Valuable Brands		
RANK	**BRAND**	**2002 BRAND VALUE ($BILLIONS)**
1	COCA-COLA	69.6
2	MICROSOFT	64.1
3	IBM	51.2
4	GE	41.3
5	INTEL	30.9
6	NOKIA	30.0
7	DISNEY	29.3
8	McDONALD'S	26.4
9	MARLBORO	24.2
10	MERCEDES	21.0

Data: Interbrand Corp., J.P. Morgan Chase & Co.

Brands usually aren't listed on corporate balance sheets, but they can go further in determining a company's success than a new factory or technological breakthrough. That's because nurturing a strong brand, even in bad times, can allow companies to command premium prices. Purveyors of products ranging from Budweiser beer to BMW cars have been able to keep growing without succumbing to the pricing pressures of an intensely promotional environment. A strong brand also can open the door when growth depends on breaking into new markets. Starbucks Corp. , among the fastest-growing brands, recently

	Winners			
RANK	BRAND	2002 BRAND VALUE ($BILLIONS)	2001 BRAND VALUE ($BILLIONS)	% CHANGE
34	SAMSUNG	8.3	6.4	+30
91	NIVEA	2.1	1.8	+16
46	HARLEY-DAVIDSON	6.3	5.5	+13
31	DELL	9.2	8.3	+12
93	STARBUCKS	2.0	1.8	+12

Samsung used bold designs to transform itself into a premium seller of consumer products. Baby boomers, meanwhile, pay Harley top dollar for a dash of rebel independence.

Data: Interbrand Corp, J.P. Morgan Chase & Co.

	Losers			
RANK	BRAND	2002 BRAND VALUE ($BILLIONS)	2001 BRAND VALUE ($BILLIONS)	% CHANGE
71	ERICSSON	3.6	7.1	-49
11	FORD	20.4	30.1	-32
17	AT&T	16.1	22.8	-30
82	BOEING	3.0	4.1	-27
25	MERRILL LYNCH	11.2	15.0	-25

The telecom debacle cut the legs out from under Ericsson and AT&T. Boeing still hasn't recovered from September 11, and Merrill Lynch got mauled by the bear market.

Data: Interbrand Corp., J.P. Mortan Chase & Co.

set up shop in Vienna, one of Europe's cafe capitals, and says 400 of its planned 1,200 new store openings this year will be overseas.

To sort out which global brands are holding their ground and which are crumbling, Interbrand and *BusinessWeek* created a ranking of the top 100 by dollar value. The list by Interbrand, a unit of Omnicom Group Inc. , is based on the idea that strong brands have the power to lift sales and earnings. Interbrand attempts to figure out how much of a boost each brand delivers, how stable that boost is likely to be, and how much those future earnings are worth today. The value that is assigned is strictly for the products with the brand on them, not for others sold by that company. Therefore, Coca-Cola Co. —easily the top brand again this year, with a value approaching $70 billion—is ranked just on those products carrying the Coke name, not Sprite or Powerade.

SAMSUNG Heavy investment in design R&D has brought fatter profit margins

Because Interbrand relies on a rigorous analysis of cash flows rather than mere consumer perceptions to calculate brand values, changes in the business climate or a category's economics can have a strong impact on those values. An economic downturn can erode values even among companies that have resisted the temptation to cut marketing budgets, slash prices, or compromise on quality. In today's perilous economic climate, it's no surprise, then, that 49 out of the 100 brands on our list— and 7 of the top 10—fell in value this year. That compares with 41 that dropped in value in our 2001 ranking. Some of the hardest-hit brands represent industries—telecommunications, finance, travel, and luxury goods—that have been body-slammed by the downturn.

Take Boeing Co., whose ambitious brand-influencing efforts—from advertising to relocating its headquarters from Seattle to Chicago—helped put it on the list last year at $4 billion.

But September 11's devastating impact on air travel almost instantly put on hold airlines' plans to expand their fleets, causing Boeing's hard-won brand value to plunge 27% this year, to $3 billion—a billion dollars of value wiped out.

Still, some companies compounded the problems of a down economy with management missteps. AT&T plunged 30% in value, losing its place among the top 10 brands. The company spent hundreds of millions on aggressive, youth-oriented ads and upgraded the range of licensed products that bear the AT&T name in order to shed its stodgy Ma Bell image. But it didn't deliver enough exciting new products and services fast enough to sell customers on a "new" AT&T.

Amid the carnage, though, many companies found ways to add value to their brands. Samsung was easily the fastest-growing, its value rising an estimated 30% to $8.3 billion. While Coke continues to struggle to get back its rhythm in the U.S., its sales are still growing in the developing world, buttressed by a strong global marketing effort behind the World Cup. Thus, Coke eked out a 1% gain, adding $700 million in brand value. Despite losing some highly publicized battles in the courtroom over its tobacco liability, Philip Morris Cos. saw its venerable Marlboro brand push into the Top 10, adding 10% to its value. The company used deep pockets to squeeze rival brands out of prime display positions in stores.

DELL The enthusiastic "Steven" of recent ads helped boost the brand's value 12%

Other winners exploited their strong brands by launching extensions into new products and categories. Too often, new flavors, formulations, and packages wind up as barren exercises in market positioning that clog retail shelf space while offering consumers nothing truly different. But this year's ranking offers proof that the right line extensions can make a difference. H.J. Heinz Co. boosted its brand value by 4% with ingenious ways of driving consumer interest in ketchup, from squeezable bottles to versions spiced up with flavors such as Smokey Mesquite. Diageo PLC's once-tired Smirnoff vodka brand scored a 5% gain thanks to the success of a citrus-flavored, single-serve drink, Smirnoff Ice. Positioned as a sophisticated alternative to beer, Ice not only became a hit with younger consumers but also enticed them into giving a second glance to the core brand, which got a lift.

The Nivea skin-care line shows how to strengthen a brand by branching out. Beiersdorf went further than a line extension or two in garnering a 16% brand-value rise for its unit. Starting with women's skin-care products and a carefully nurtured image of wholesomeness and natural ingredients, Nivea has moved into men's products, including deodorants, shampoos, and even a moisturizer dispensed from an electric razor. Nivea has dozens of products today, vs. a handful five years ago. "They are a classic example of how far you can go with brand extensions," says Jan Lindemann, Interbrand's global director for brand valuation.

Advertising, of course, is one of the most direct ways to build a brand. But the danger in tough times is that you advertise price breaks and wind up cheapening a brand. That's why Dell Computer Corp.'s ability to see a 12% increase in brand value is so impressive. The PC maker gave its promotional ads an additional brand-building role. They feature an enthusiastic young character, "Steven," congratulating customers with "Dude, you're getting a Dell!"—driving home the point that customers can get exactly what they want at low prices. After years of making that point in a dry way, Steven brought "real personality to Dell," says Scott Helbing, the company's vice-president for global brand strategy.

But ads can take a brand only so far. And if their claims are not backed up by performance, the ads erode value. For that reason, employees are a crucial link to the consumer. If employees are motivated to reflect the core brand values in all their activities, that radiates out to customers, and on to friends and family. Such word-of-mouth endorsements—which in the Internet era can circle the globe instantly—can be far more convincing than any marketing campaign. Brand winners usually "have inculcated what's great about their companies up and down the organization," says Scott Bedbury, a former top marketer at Nike Inc. and Starbucks who now runs consultant Brandstream in Seattle.

Even the best corporate names are under attack these days. Still, those companies are reaping the benefits of years they spent building customer trust and honing images of quality and dependability. To weather an extended bout of distrust and instability, strong brands are crucial. Companies also will have to work doubly hard to keep them intact.

By Gerry Khermouch in New York

Kamikaze Pricing

When penetration strategies run amok, marketers
can find themselves in a dive-bomb of no return.

by Reed K. Holden and Thomas T. Nagle

Price is the weapon of choice for many companies in the competition for sales and market share. The reasons are understandable. No other weapon in a marketer's arsenal can be deployed as quickly, or with such certain effect, as a price discount. The advantage is often short-lived, though, and managers rarely balance the long-term consequences of deploying the price weapon against the likely short-term gains.

Playing the price card often is a reaction to a competitor and assumes that it will provide significant gain for the firm. Usually, that's not the case. Firms start price wars when they have little to lose and much to gain; those who react to the initiators often have little to gain and much to lose. The anticipated gains often disappear as multiple competitors join the battle and negate the lift from the initial reductions.

Managers in highly competitive markets often view price cuts as the only possible strategy. Sometimes they're right. The problem is that they are playing with a very dangerous weapon in a war to improve near-term profitability that ends in long-term devastation. As the Chinese warrior, Sun Tzu, put it, "Those who are not thoroughly aware of the disadvantages in the use of arms cannot be thoroughly aware of the advantages."

If marketers are going to use low prices as a competitive weapon, they must be equally aware of the risks as well as the benefits (see "The Prisoner's Dilemma"). They also must learn to adjust their strategies to deploy alternatives when pricing alone is no longer effective. Failure to do so has put companies and entire industries into tail spins from which they never fully recover.

Pricing Options

Marketers traditionally have employed three pricing strategies: skim, penetration, and neutral. Skim pricing is the process of pricing a product high relative to competitors and the product's value. Neutral pricing is an attempt to eliminate price as a decision factor for customers by pricing neither high nor low relative to competitors. Penetration pricing is the decision to price low relative to the product's value and to the prices of similar competitors. It is a decision to use price as the main competitive weapon in hopes of driving the company to a position of market dominance.

EXECUTIVE *BRIEFING*

Penetration pricing is perhaps the most abused pricing strategy. It can be effective for fixed periods of time and in the right competitive situation, but many firms overuse this approach and end up creating a market situation where everyone is forced to lower prices continually, driving some competitors from the market and guaranteeing that no one realizes a good return on investment. Managers can prevent the fruitless slide into kamikaze pricing by implementing a value-driven pricing strategy for the most profitable customer segments.

All three strategies consider how the product is priced relative to its value for customers and that of similar competitors. When Lexus entered the luxury segment of the automobile industry, the car's price was high relative to

EXHIBIT 1

Experience curve effects

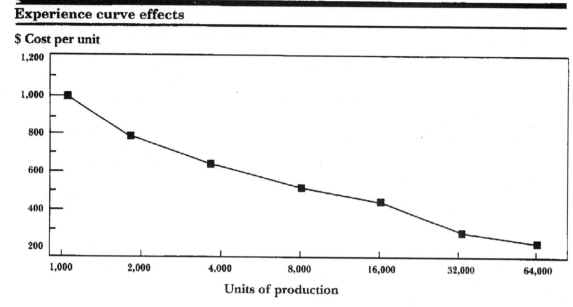

$ Cost per unit

Units of production

standard vehicles but low relative to Mercedes and BMW. The penetration strategy was defined not by the price but by the price relative to the value of the vehicle and to similar competitive products.

The main ingredient to successful penetration pricing is a large segment of customers for whom price is the primary purchase motivation.

Any of these strategies can be associated with a variety of cost structures and can result in either profits or losses. To understand when each strategy is likely to be successful, managers should evaluate their current and potential cost structure, their customers' relative price sensitivities, and their current and potential competitors. All three areas must be carefully considered before employing any pricing strategy.

Penetration Strategies Can Work

If a firm has a fixed cost structure and each sale provides a large contribution to those fixed costs, penetration pricing can boost sales and provide large increases to profits—but only if the market size grows or if competitors choose not to respond. Low prices can draw additional buyers to enter the market. The increased sales can justify production expansion or the adoption of new technologies, both of which can reduce costs. And, if firms have excess capacity, even low-priced business can provide incremental dollars toward fixed costs.

Penetration pricing can also be effective if a large experience curve will cause costs per unit to drop significantly. The experience curve proposes that, as a firm's production experience increases, per-unit costs will go down. On average, for each doubling of production, a firm can expect per-unit costs to decline by roughly 20%. Cost declines can be significant in the early stages of production (see Exhibit 1).

The manufacturer who fails to take advantage of these effects will find itself at a competitive cost disadvantage relative to others who are further along the curve. This is often the case with new technologies and innovative products, where relatively small increments in units sold yield substantial decreases in unit costs. This is also the case for many new entrants to a market who are just beginning to see experience curve cost reductions.

However, the main ingredient to successful penetration pricing is a large segment of customers for whom price is the primary purchase motivation. This can be the case in business markets where original equipment commodities are sold to the production process of a customer's business, but it rarely occurs in consumer markets where image is an important part of the use of a product.

When Omega watches—once a brand more prestigious than Rolex—was trying to improve market share in the 1970s, it adopted a penetration pricing strategy that succeeded in destroying the watch's brand image by flooding the market with lower priced products. Omega never gained sufficient share on the lower price/lower image competitors to justify destroying its brand image and high-priced position with upscale buyers. Similar outcomes were experienced by the Cadillac Cimarron and Lacoste clothing.

A better strategy would have been to introduce a totally new brand as a flanking product, as Heublein did with the Popov, Relska, and Smirnoff vodka brands and Intel did with microprocessors in 1988. After the introduction of the 386 microprocessor, Intel adopted a skim price strategy for the high value and proprietary 386 chips. It also wanted to market a circuit in the 286 market that could compete with AMD and Cirrus on a nonprice, value-added basis. The 386SX was introduced as a scaled down version of the 386, but at a price only slightly higher than the 286. The net result was to migrate price sensitive customers more quickly to the proprietary 386 market with the 386SX, while still capturing increased profit from the high value users with the 386.

In its marketing of the 486, Pentium, and Pentium Pro circuits, Intel continues this flanking strategy with dozens of varieties of each microprocessor to meet the needs of various market segments.

For penetration pricing to work, there must be competitors who are willing to let the penetration pricer get away with the strategy. If a penetration price is quickly matched by a competitor, the incremental sales that would accrue from the price-sensitive segment must now be split between two competitors. As more competitors follow, smaller incremental sales advantages and lower profits accrue to both the initiator and the followers.

Fortunately, there are two common situations which often cause competitors to let penetration pricers co-exist in markets. When the penetration-pricing firm has enough of a cost or resource advantage, competitors might conclude they would lose a price war. Retailers are beginning to recognize that some consumers who are unconcerned about price when deciding which products and brands to buy become price sensitive when deciding where to buy. They are willing to travel farther to buy the same branded products at lower prices. Category killers like Toys 'R' Us use penetration pricing strategies because they are able to manage their overhead and distribution costs much more tightly than traditional department stores. Established stores don't have the cost structure to compete on this basis, so they opt to serve the high-value segment of the market.

When the penetration-pricing firm has enough of a cost or resource advantage, competitors might conclude they would lose a price war.

The second situation conducive to penetration pricing occurs when large competitors have high-price positions and don't feel a significant number of their existing customers would be lost to the penetration pricer. This was the case when People's Express entered the airline industry with low priced fares to Europe in the 1970s. The fares were justified with reduced services such as no reservations or meal service. People's also limited the ability of the high value business traveler to take advantage of those fares by not permitting advanced reservations or ticket sales. This was a key element of their strategy: Focus only on price sensitive travelers and avoid selling tickets to the customers of their competitors.

Major airlines didn't respond to the lower prices because they didn't see People's Express taking away their high value customers. It was only when People's began pursuing the business traveler that the major airlines responded and quickly put People's out of business.

The same strategy is being repeated today by Southwest Airlines in the domestic market far more skillfully. Southwest has a cost and route structure that limits the ability of major airlines to respond. In fact, when United Airlines, a much larger competitor, did try to respond with low-cost service in selected West Coast markets, it had to abandon the effort because it couldn't match Southwest's cost structure.

Penetration or Kamikaze?

An extreme form of penetration pricing is "kamikaze" pricing, a reference to the Japanese dive bomber pilots of World War II who were willing to sacrifice their lives by crashing their explosives-laden airplanes onto enemy ships. This may have been a reasonable wartime tactic (though not a particularly attractive one) by commanders who sacrificed single warriors while inflicting many casualties on opponents. But in the business world, the relentless pursuit of more sales through lower prices usually results in lower profitability. It is often an unnecessary and fruitless exercise that damages the entire dive-bombing company—not just one individual—along with the competitor. Judicious use of the tactic is advised; in as many cases as it works, there are many more where it does not.

Kamikaze pricing occurs when the justification for penetration pricing is flawed, as when marketers incorrectly assume lower prices will increase sales. This may be true in growth markets where lower prices can expand the total market, but in mature markets a low price merely causes the same customers to switch suppliers. In the global economy, market after market is being discovered, developed, and penetrated. High growth, price sensitive markets are quickly maturing, and even though customers may want to buy a low-priced product, they don't increase their volume of purchases. Price cuts used to get them to switch fail to bring large increases in demand and end up shrinking the dollar size of the market.

A prominent example is the semiconductor business, where earlier price competition led to both higher demand and reduced costs. But in recent years, total demand tends to be less responsive to lower prices, and most suppliers are well down the experience curve. The net result is an industry where participation requires huge investments, added value is immense, but because of a penetration price

The Prisoner's Dilemma

A popular exercise in seminars and executive briefings we hold is to ask executives to participate in a prisoner's dilemma pricing game. Each team must decide whether to price its products high or low compared to those of another team in 10 rounds of competition. The objective is to earn the most money; results are determined by the decision that two competitors make in comparison with each other.

The game fairly accurately simulates a typical profit/loss scenario for price competition in mature markets. The objective is to impart several lessons in pricing competition, the first being that pricing is more like playing poker than solitaire. Success depends not just on a combination of luck and how the hand is played but also on how well competitors play their hands. In real markets, outcomes depend not only on how customers respond but, perhaps more important, on how competitors respond to changes in price.

If a competitor matches a price decrease, neither the initiator nor the follower will achieve a significant increase in sales and both are likely to have a significant decrease in profits. In developing pricing strategy, managers need to anticipate the moves of their competitors and attempt to influence those moves by selectively communicating information to influence competitive behavior.

The second lesson is that managers must adopt a very long time horizon when considering changes in price.

Once started, price wars are difficult to stop. A simple decision to drop price often becomes the first shot in a war that no competitor wins. Before initiating a price decrease, managers must consider how it will affect the competitive stability of markets.

Philip Morris discovered this when it initiated a price war in the cigarette business by cutting the prices of its top brands. Competitors followed, and the net result was a $2.3 billion drop in operating profits for Philip Morris, even as the Marlboro brand increased its market share seven points to 29%. The manufacturer of Camels experienced a $1.3 billion drop in profits.

The third lesson from the prisoner's dilemma is that careful use of a value-based marketing approach can reverse a trend toward price-based marketing. This is accomplished through signaling, a nonprice competitive tactic that involves selectively disclosing information to competitors to influence their behavior. The steel and airline industries provide prominent examples of the signaling strategy's use. They often rely on announcements that conveniently appear on the front pages of the Wall Street Journal to signal competitors of pending price moves and provide them with opportunities to follow. The strategy takes time to implement, but it provides a far better long-term competitive position for marketers who employ it.

Most managers who play the prisoner's dilemma adopt a low-price strategy. This mirrors the real world, where 63% of managers who adopt an identifiable strategy use low price, according to an ongoing research project in which we are engaged. In the game, low-price teams fail to earn any profit in a majority of cases. The strategy works in round one, but competitors quickly learn to respond and both parties end up losing any chance for profit.

Executives rationalize that, if their firm can't make money, competitors shouldn't, either. Managers quickly forget that the objective of this game—and the game of business—is profit. Price cuts in the real world can be devastating. A current example is the personal computer business, where Packard Bell sets the low price standard that many competitors follow.

Packard Bell's management is less concerned with profit than with achieving a volume of sales and market share in a growing industry. But unless the company has operational characteristics that distinguish it from competitors and permit Packard Bell to deliver a quality product at those low prices, its ability to leverage market share will be limited. Analysts estimate that Packard Bell has only made $45 million in net profit over the past 10 years and is staying afloat through loans granted by suppliers and massive cash infusions from its Japanese and European co-owners.

—Reed Holden and Thomas Nagle

mentality, suppliers can't pull out of the kamikaze death spiral.

There was a time when large, well-entrenched competitors took a long time to respond to new low-price competitors. That is no longer true; domestic automobiles are now the low priced brands, and even AT&T has learned to respond to the aggressive price competition of Sprint and MCI. The electronics, soft goods, rubber, and steel companies that ignored low-price competitors in the 1970s and '80s have become ruthless cost and price cutters. The days of free rides from nonresponsive market leaders are gone.

Another risk comes in using penetration pricing to increase sales in order to drive down unit costs. Unfortunately, there are generally two reasons managers run into trouble when they justify price discounts by anticipated reductions in costs. First, they view the relationship between costs and volume as linear, when it actually is exponential—the cost reduction per unit becomes smaller with larger increases in volume. Initial savings are substantial, but as sales grow, the incremental savings per unit of production all but disappear (see Exhibit 2). Costs continue to decline on a per-unit basis, but the incremental cost reduction seen from each additional unit of sale becomes insignificant. Managers need to recognize that experience curve cost savings as a percentage of incremental sales volume declines with increases in volume. It works great in early growth phases but not in the later stages.

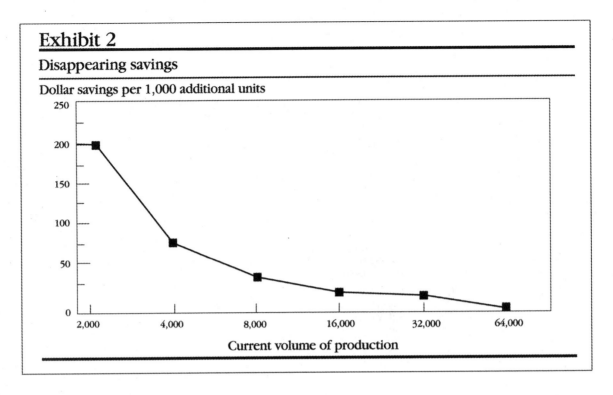

Exhibit 2

Disappearing savings

Dollar savings per 1,000 additional units

[Line graph: Y-axis labeled from 0 to 250 in increments of 50. X-axis labeled "Current volume of production" with values 2,000; 4,000; 8,000; 16,000; 32,000; 64,000. The curve starts near 200 at 2,000 units, drops to about 75 at 4,000, about 35 at 8,000, about 20 at 16,000, about 18 at 32,000, and about 7 at 64,000.]

Many managers believe that sales volume is king. They evaluate the success of both their sales managers and marketing managers by their ability to grow sales volume. The problem is that their competitors employ the exact same strategy. Customers learn that they can switch loyalties with little risk and start buying lower priced alternatives. Marketers find themselves stuck with a deadly mix of negligible cost benefits, inelastic demand, aggressive competition, and no sustainable competitive advantage. Any attempt to reduce price in this environment will often trigger growing losses. To make matters worse, customers who buy based on price are often more expensive to serve and yield lower total profits than do loyal customers. Thus starts the death spiral of the kamikaze pricers who find their costs going up and their profits disappearing.

Penetration pricing is overused, in large part, because managers think in terms of sports instead of military analogies. In sports, the act of playing is enough to justify the effort. The objective might be to win a particular game, but the implications of losing are minimal. The more intense the process, the better the game, and the best way to play is to play as hard as you can.

This is exactly the wrong motivation for pricing where the ultimate objective is profit. The more intense the competition, the worse it is for all who play. Aggressive price competition means that few survive the process and even fewer make reasonable returns on their investments. In pricing, the long-term implications of each battle must be considered in order to make thoughtful decisions about which battles to fight. Unfortunately, many managers find that, in winning too many pricing battles, they often lose the war for profitability.

Value Pricing

To avoid increasingly aggressive price competition, managers must first recognize the problem and then develop alternate strategies that build distinctive, nonprice competencies. Instead of competing only on price, managers can develop solutions to enhance the competitive and profit positions of their firms.

In most industries, there are far more opportunities for differentiation than managers usually consider. If customers are receiving good service and support, they are often willing to pay more to the supplier, even for commodities. A client in India produced commodity gold jewelry that was sold into the Asian market at extremely low penetration prices. Because of the client's good relationships with wholesale and retail intermediaries, we recommended a leveraging of those relationships to increase prices to a more reasonable level. Despite much anxiety, the client followed suit and major customers accepted the increases.

Opportunities to Add Value

Marketers often fail to recognize the opportunity for higher prices when they get caught up in kamikaze pricing. To avoid this, they need to understand how their customers value different product and company attributes. The objective is to identify segments of customers who have problems for which unique and cost-effective solutions can be developed. Sometimes it's as simple as a minor adjustment in packaging.

Know what customers want. Loctite Corp., a global supplier of industrial adhesives, introduced a specialty

Exhibit 3

Customer purchasing agenda

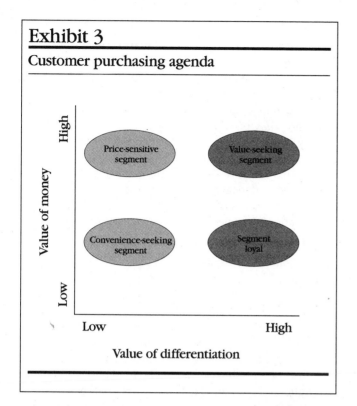

liquid adhesive in a 1-oz. bottle for use in emergency applications. Unfortunately, sales were less than spectacular. After a number of customer interviews, Loctite discovered that the liquid was difficult to apply and the bottle was difficult to carry. What customers really wanted was an easy-to-apply gel in a tube. The product was reformulated to meet these criteria and saw huge success. In the process, Loctite almost doubled the price.

Firms that attract value customers get the loyal buyer as part of the bargain and sell to the price buyer only when it is profitable and reasonable.

Managers should identify features that they can add more cost effectively than their competitors can. IBM has been under intense price pressure in the personal computer segment. Besides introducing lower-priced flanking products (with limited success), IBM also has introduced computers with more internal memory. This feature had significant appeal because of the higher memory demands of the Windows 95 operating system. The value of this feature was greater than a price cut because IBM is arguably the most cost-effective producer of random access memory in the world. It also forced low-price competitors to incur higher relative costs to match IBM, thereby undercutting their ability to price their PCs below IBM's.

In the process of adding value to their products, firms should remember that value is achieved not only from the products themselves, but from the services associated with their use. The manufacturer of a heavy-duty truck oil broke out of commodity pricing when it began analyzing the oil from its customers' trucks to determine if there were excessively high temperatures or metal in the oil that would indicate a breakdown of the internal components of engines. The service was promoted in a mailer included with each large drum of oil. The cost of this service was minimal, and a large segment of small- and owner-operator customers placed a huge value on it. This tactic helped the firm to differentiate its product with a valued service connected to the product.

Offer complete benefits. Another way to avoid downward pricing is to offer complete product benefits, which is especially useful in the early phases of a new product's life. This tactic is not as effective when products mature and customers no longer need as much service support. However, when customers are still developing their expertise, they require complete systems to achieve the maximum benefit to their organization. This is often an expensive affair that needs to be justified by the future business and profit potential that a customer represents.

When marketers correctly assess this type of situation, they often develop a sustainable competitive advantage that makes them impervious to competitive erosion. This was the strategy that Intel employed when it introduced the 8086 microprocessor to the PC industry in the early 1980s. Although the 8086 was slightly inferior technically to Motorola's 6800, Intel adopted sophisticated customer support programs that permitted new PC manufacturers to introduce new products quickly. This and other services were backed by a strong sales and marketing program that focused on specific customer adoptions. The net result was the beginning of Intel's dominance in PC microprocessors.

Understand customer agendas. Marketers make a serious mistake when they assume that all their customers are willing to sacrifice quality to obtain low prices. A few are, but most really want to get high-quality products at the lowest possible price. The seller of a high-quality product can compete against a low-price, low-quality product by recognizing that, despite the words of the purchasing agent, pricing need not be too aggressive.

Sellers who understand why customers buy their products often find that there is a fairly uniform set of reasons underlying purchasing behavior. Price is often important, but it seldom is the sole motivation. In most business situations, there are four types of agendas with regard to the pricing of products and a buyer's desired relationship with the supplying firm (see Exhibit 3). One of the best ways for marketers to avoid the trap of excessive price competition is to develop market- and customer-level strategies that reflect those behaviors.

For example, loyal customers highly value specific things that a supplier does for them, such as technical support, quality products, and customer-oriented service agents. These customers are less concerned about the price than about the care they receive. They often have a single supplier and have no intention of qualifying another. Understanding who the loyal customers are and keeping their loyalty is critical.

The purpose of sales is not to use a lower price to close a sale, but to convince the customer that the price of a product is fair.

Conversely, price buyers care little about a long-term relationship with a supplier and want the lowest possible price for products. These commodity buyers have multiple vendors and encourage them to dive into kamikaze price wars. For consumer marketers, price shoppers who switch allegiances at the drop of a coupon provide few incremental dollars to the retailers who cater to them. For business-to-business sellers, these tend to be the buyers who scream loudest and dictate pricing and selling strategies. Unfortunately, the profits they generate rarely justify the attention they demand.

The price buyer's agenda is to get products at the lowest possible prices, so he or she uses tactics that force marketers to employ kamikaze pricing tactics even when it might not be the wisest thing to do. For the marketer, the trick is only to do business with the price buyer when it is profitable to do so and when it doesn't prompt a more profitable customer to purchase elsewhere.

Convenience buyers don't care whose product they purchase, and have little regard for price. They simply want it readily available. This often is the most profitable market segment, provided marketers can deliver their products at the locations preferred by these buyers. Unfortunately, this group exhibits little brand loyalty and provides sellers with no sustainable competitive advantage beyond their distribution systems.

Offer the best deal. Value buyers evaluate vendors on the basis of their ability to reduce costs through lower prices or more efficient operations, or to make the buyer's business more effective with superior features or services. From a customer perspective, this is the place to be; while both price and loyal buying have unique costs, value buying comes with the assumption that these customers are getting the best deal possible, given all factors of consumption. From a marketing perspective, firms that attract value customers get the loyal buyer as part of the bargain and sell to the price buyer only when it is profitable and reasonable.

Organizations that employ kamikaze pricing have a poor understanding of how their products create value for customers. This lack of understanding results in excessive reliance on price to obtain orders. Successful marketers use price as a tool to reflect the value of the product and implement systems in the organization to assure that value is delivered to customers and captured in the pricing.

The Five Cs

"Sell on quality, not on price" was once a popular marketing aphorism. Unfortunately, while product quality can reduce the seller's rework and inventory costs, it does little for customers. Selling the quality of a product is often not enough because buyers have difficulty quantifying its value and may be unwilling to pay for it. By focusing on quality, we miss the opportunity for customers to understand the true value that quality brings to the buyers of our products. Instead, resolving to "sell on value, not on price" focuses on understanding how pricing really should work. To avoid the rigors of price-based competition, marketers should adopt the five "Cs" of the value-based approach:

- Comprehend what drives customer value.
- Create value in product, service, and support.
- Communicate value in advertising.
- Convince customers of value in selling.
- Capture value in pricing strategy.

How a product provides customer value and which value-creation efforts best differentiate a product from the competition must be understood by marketers. When there is additional value that can be created, marketers need to do a better job creating it in their products, service, and support activities. Once a firm provides differentiating value to its customers, the primary responsibility of the marketer is to set up a communications system, including the salesperson, that educates the customer on the components of that value.

The purpose of sales is not to use a lower price to close a sale, but to convince the customer that the price of a product, which is based on its value in the market, is fair. Of course, most sales compensation systems do just the opposite, rewarding salespeople for closing a sale, regardless of the price. Salespeople who lack an understanding of a product's value often bend to a buyer's wishes and match a lower-value competitor's price. Product prices should reflect a fair portion of their value, and they should be fixed so salespeople will have to sell on the basis of value.

Companies that approach pricing as a process rather than an event can effectively break the spiral of kamikaze pricing.

Penetration pricing gains ground in markets against competitors, but extended use of this offensive tactic inevitably leads to kamikaze pricing and calamity in markets as competitors respond, cost savings disappear, and customers learn to ignore value. Good marketers employ such weapons selectively and only for limited periods of time to build profitable market position. They learn how to draw from a broad arsenal of offensive and defensive weapons, understanding how each will affect their overall long-term market conditions, and never losing sight of the overall objective of stable market conditions in which they can earn the most sustainable profit.

Additional Reading

Darlin, Damon (1996), "The Computer Industry's Mystery Man," *Forbes*, (April 8), 42.

Nagle, Thomas and Reed Holden (1995), *The Strategy and Tactics of Pricing*. New York: Prentice Hall.

Reichheld, Frederick F. (1996), *The Loyalty Effect*. Boston: Harvard Business School Press.

Shapiro, Eileen C. (1995), *Fad Surfing in the Boardroom*. Reading, Mass.: Addison-Wesley Publishing.

Taylor, William (1993), "Message and Muscle: An Interview with Swatch Titan Nicolas Hayek," *Harvard Business Review*, (March–April), 99–110.

Tzu, Sun (1988), *The Art of War*, translated by Thomas Cleary. Boston: Shambhala Publications.

About the Authors

Reed K. Holden is President of the Strategic Pricing Group Inc., Marlborough, Mass., where he has conducted numerous industry seminars in the United States and Asia on pricing and competitive strategy, business market research, and loyal buyer behavior. He also works with corporate clients as an educator and strategic analyst. Reed has more than 11 years of experience as a sales and marketing manager in the electrical and electronics industries. During that time, he specialized in the development and implementation of sales training and industrial marketing programs. He also was an Assistant Professor at Boston University's Graduate School of Management for nine years. He coauthored the second edition of *The Strategy and Tactics of Pricing* and "Profitable Pricing: Guidelines for Management" which was published in the third edition of the *AMA Management Handbook*.

Thomas T. Nagle is Chairman of the Strategic Pricing Group Inc., which helps firms in such diverse industries as telecommunications, pharmaceuticals, computer software, semiconductors, wholesale nursery, consumer retailing, and financial services develop pricing strategies. His seminars are offered in public programs and at major corporations in North and South America and in Europe. The second edition of Tom's book, *The Strategy and Tactics of Pricing: A Guide to Profitable Decision Making*, is used extensively as a text on the subject. He is the author of "Managing Price Competition," published in *MARKETING MANAGEMENT* (Spring 1993), and "Financial Analysis For Profit-Driven Pricing," published in *The Sloan Management Review* (1994). His articles also have appeared in the *AMA Handbook of Business Strategy*. Tom has taught at the University of Chicago and at Boston University and is currently on the executive program faculties of the University of Chicago.

pricing practices That endanger profits

How do buyers perceive and respond to pricing?

EXECUTIVE briefing

Some companies are starting to embrace a proactive pricing strategy, but many still cling to old misconceptions about markets and the entire pricing process. Understanding and overcoming the pricing fallacies that continually plague managers, the pricing process, and price perceptions among buyers requires a truly proactive pricing approach. Once managers understand these problems, they can better develop and implement a product and market strategy for the current economic and competitive environment.

By Kent B. Monroe and Jennifer L. Cox

Pricing decisions can be complex and difficult, but they're also some of the most important marketing decision variables a manager faces. Companies that make profitable pricing decisions take what may be called a proactive pricing approach. By considering how pricing decisions affect the way buyers perceive prices and develop perceptions of value, these companies manage to leave less money on the table and successfully raise or reduce prices.

Eight Pricing Fallacies

Many companies continue to develop their pricing strategies and tactics naively and, consequently, don't get the results they expect. Tradition-bound solutions and outdated practices have helped perpetuate a number of pricing misconceptions that can cause problems for companies. We outline eight of the most common ones here.

1. Most companies have a serious pricing strategy based on serious pricing research. On the contrary. A recent study found that only about 8% of the companies surveyed could be classified as conducting serious pricing research to support developing an effective pricing strategy. In fact, 88% of them did little or no serious pricing research. McKinsey & Company's Pricing Benchmark Survey estimated that only about 15% of companies do serious pricing research. A 1997 Coopers & Lybrand study found that, in the previous year, 87% of the surveyed companies had changed prices. However, only 13% of the price changes came after a scheduled review of pricing strategy.

These numbers indicate that strategic pricing decisions tend to be made without an understanding of the likely buyer or competitive response. Further, it shows that managers often make tactical pricing decisions without reviewing how they may fit into the firm's overall pricing or marketing strategy. The data suggest that many companies make pricing decisions and changes without an existing process for managing the pricing activity. As a result, many of them do not have a serious pricing strategy and do not conduct pricing research to develop their strategy.

2. Prices can be set annually, typically during the budgeting exercise, and don't require continuous managerial attention between annual reviews. To understand a firm's approach to price management, first consider how it sets its pricing objectives; gathers, processes, and analyzes relevant information; provides for an orderly decision process; and establishes procedures for anticipating and responding to customer, market, and competitor changes. Although managers consistently identify pricing as a major pressure point or marketing headache, organizations have been slow to develop a proactive approach to pricing. This state of affairs exists partly because managers have misconceived price management as setting prices per se rather than as a process.

By not considering pricing as a process, companies fail to distinguish between pricing strategy and pricing tactics; to coordinate pricing decisions across departments; and to have an organizational unit responsible for regularly monitoring price adjustments and price policies. For example, a survey of the 20 largest pharmaceutical companies revealed that companies with an organized pricing function approached pricing as an ongoing process. Those without a permanently assigned pricing responsibility, however, treated pricing decisions episodically, with little or no continuity.

3. Buyers compute price differences easily and unambiguously. This misconception leads to a host of strategic pricing errors. Failing to consider the complex underlying psychology of how people encode, perceive, learn, and retrieve numbers (i.e., prices) when making buying decisions can lead to several errors. What follows are some important psychological concepts as well as problems that occur when pricing managers don't understand these concepts.

Reference Prices

4. Buyers don't evaluate prices comparatively. Not quite. In fact, behavioral pricing research provides explanations of how people form value judgments and make decisions when they don't have perfect information about alternatives. Why are buyers more sensitive to price increases than to price decreases? How do buyers respond to comparative price advertisements (i.e., regular price $65, sale price $49), coupons, rebates, and other special price promotions? The common response is that buyers judge prices comparatively through the anchoring effects of reference prices.

The reference price for a specific product category is a function of the frequency of different prices for that category (i.e., the distribution of prices). Further, the reference price is a function of the relative magnitude of the prices, the range of prices, and the dispersion of prices from the average price. A buyer's reference price is influenced by practice and past experience and by the sequence in which the buyer observes the prices for the category. A reference price may be an external price in an advertisement or the shelf price of another product. It may also be an internal price the buyer remembers from a previous purchase, an expected price, or some belief about the price of a product in the same market area.

The concept of reference price supports the notion that buyers judge or evaluate prices comparatively. Managers who ignore this point make the mistake of not distinguishing between pricing strategies and pricing tactics. The marketing group manager of Frito-Lay Inc. told the story of a local tortilla chip producer in the Phoenix market that did not understand this relationship. The local tortilla chip enjoyed a competitive advantage until Frito-Lay upgraded its Tostitos chip. Instead of raising its monetary price to continue to reflect a perceived quality/value relationship similar to Tostitos, the local producer reduced its quality and costs, but maintained the monetary price to protect its margin. Customers soon recognized that the local chip was now an inferior product and shifted their purchases to Frito-Lay. In this case, the local tortilla producer tactically maintained price to be competitive on price with Frito-Lay but ignored the important strategic issue of competing on perceived value.

Absolute Price Thresholds

5. There is just one acceptable price for a product or service.
The truth is that buyers typically have lower and upper price thresholds, or a range of acceptable prices for a purchase. The upper and lower price limits are not constant and shift as buyers obtain more information about the actual price range in the market or about the range of prices in a specific product line. Plus, a lower price threshold implies that positive prices greater than $0 exist and are unacceptable because they are considered to be too low, perhaps because buyers are suspicious of the product's quality at prices below the lower price threshold.

A number of factors influence the varying levels and widths of buyers' acceptable price ranges. For a specific product category the upper price threshold will be lower if buyers recognize the availability of similar alternative offerings. However, if customer satisfaction increases or buyers become more loyal, the upper threshold tends to increase. Conversely, if customer satisfaction declines, leading to lower buyer loyalty, then buyers' upper price thresholds decrease.

When buyers are relatively uncertain about prices for a product category, their acceptable price ranges tend to be relatively narrow and their lower and upper acceptable price limits tend to be lower than those of more knowledgeable buyers. Buyers who infer quality on the basis of price usually have higher acceptable price levels, higher upper acceptable price limits, and wider acceptable price ranges. On the other hand, price-conscious buyers typically tend to have lower acceptable price levels, lower upper acceptable price limits, and narrower acceptable price ranges. The sidebar on this page illustrates the pricing error made when French buyers were unwilling to pay more than a specific amount to enter Disneyland Paris.

Differential Price Thresholds

Usually a buyer selects from among alternative choices available for a contemplated purchase. The prices of these alternative choices may provide cues (or information) to facilitate the decision process. However, even if the numerical prices are different, we can't assume prices are perceived to be different. Hence, the problem becomes one of determining how perceived price differences affect buyer choice. The two most relevant concepts when considering this are price elasticity and cross-price elasticity of demand.

6. Absolute price is more important than relative price. The experience of a major snack food producer illustrates the error of not recognizing the difference between absolute and relative price. Several years ago, a specific size of this brand's potato chips was priced at $1.59 while a comparable size of the local brand was $1.29, a difference of 30 cents. Over time, the price of the national brand increased several times until it was being retailed at $1.89. In like manner, the local brand's price increased to $1.59. However, while the local brand was maintaining a 30–cent price differential, the national brand obtained a significant gain in market share. The problem was that buyers perceived a 30-cent price difference relative to $1.89 as less than a 30-cent price difference relative to $1.59.

As this example shows, relative price is a more important concept than absolute price. The concept of price elasticity of demand indicates the sensitivity of buyers to a price change for a particular product. Thus, if buyers perceive the product's price as different from the last time they purchased it, then the issue is whether this perceived price difference alters their purchasing behavior. For example, a price reduction from $1.30 to $1.25 may not be sufficient to induce buyers to buy more of the product, whereas reducing the price to $1.15 might lead to increase demand. Conversely, a price increase from $1.30 to $1.35

might not deter some buyers from purchasing it, but an increase to $1.40 might lead to noticeably decreased demand.

Perceived Value vs. Price (Mickey Goofed!)

Disneyland Paris, formerly known as Euro Disney, opened in April 1992 on the eastern outskirts of Paris. However, this new venture didn't fare well at first. In fact, it got so bad that by 1994, losses were averaging $1 million a day. Prior to the April 1995 opening, a market research survey discovered that French consumers were unwilling to spend more than 200ff (French francs) for a single adult to enter the park. So Disneyland Paris set the 1995 admission price for a single adult at 195 francs. The number of visitors increased by approximately 23% in 1995 and by 33% by the end of the 1996 season. Importantly, by 1996, 40% of the visitors were French, half of them from the Paris area. In 1995, the park operated at a profit for the first time.

So what's the lesson here? Apparently, managers at Disney did not immediately understand that the relationship between price, perceived quality, and perceived value has limits or absolute thresholds. Disney initially failed to recognize the important link between perceptions of quality and perceptions of value.

---

7. The way price information is communicated can't change buyers' preferences between products. The differential price issue examines how the price of one product is perceived to differ from the price of another alternative offering. These alternative products could be sold by different competitors or they could be model variations sold by a single seller. For example, Kodak cameras compete with Minolta, Polaroid, and other brands as well as with different models within the Kodak camera line. From a managerial perspective, it's important to know how to price the different cameras within the product line as well as how to price the cameras relative to the competitors' cameras. Perhaps the most important strategic aspect of a pricing manager's job is to learn how to manage the price differentials within a product line as well as relative to competitors' products.

Take a look at the sidebar "A Competitor Lends a Helping Hand." Can you figure out why sales of B increased after a competitor introduced a much higher-priced version? First consider how buyers would evaluate B relative to A when they were the only two products in this category available for purchase. On a subjective scale, B would be judged as expensive, or perhaps high-priced. However, after the competitor had introduced C, then B would be judged as not expensive, or perhaps moderately priced. Second, the $16 price difference between C and B made the $4 price difference between A and B perceptually smaller than it was before. The competitor's pricing caused a product that had been perceived as expensive to be perceived as not expensive. Third, it's well-known that people usually don't choose extremes when there is a middle option. Indeed, we found that when buyers have multiple choices, their preferences tend to gravitate toward the "middle-priced" brands. Thus, for these three reasons, consumers who had previously preferred A now purchased B. This example clearly indicates that when buyers cannot evaluate quality, the strategic use of price information can influence preferences and choices.

Decomposing Price Elasticity

8. Price elasticities are constant. In reality, price elasticities vary according to the direction of a price change, a brand's price position, and the magnitude of the price change. Buyers, in general, are more sensitive to perceived price increases than to perceived price decreases. In practical terms, this difference in relative price elasticity between price increases and price decreases means it's easier to lose sales from current buyers by increasing price than it is to gain sales from new buyers by reducing price. For example, price elasticity for local telephone calls following a price decrease was estimated to be -0.022, while the price elasticity following a price increase was -0.215. In this case, the ratio of price increase elasticity to price decrease elasticity was 9.77. Other researchers have estimated this ratio to vary between 1.3 and 4.0 for different products.

Research also confirms that price elasticity of demand varies over brands within the same product category. In one product category, elasticity varied from -0.84 to -4.56. However, price elasticity is not independent of the relative price level. The further a brand's price is from the product category's average price, in either direction, the lower its price elasticity will be. If a brand's price is already at the extreme end of the price-market range, then a more substantial price change will be needed to produce a perceived price change. And extreme prices, high or low, will become more price-elastic as the prices are changed toward the market average or as competitors' pricing moves the brand's price toward the market average. Further, price elasticity will be relatively higher for offerings positioned in the middle of a category because such a position makes it more difficult to establish either a low price or high-quality image.

How price-elastic or inelastic the demand for a product or brand is depends on its cross-price elasticity relative to competing products. Moreover, a brand's price-quality positioning relative to its competitors influences its price elasticity. These competitive effects not only are asymmetric relative to price increases or decreases, but also are relative to the price-quality positions of the competing

products. That is, price promotions by a higher-priced brand affect the market share of a lower-priced brand more than the reverse. Also, brands closer to each other in price have larger cross-price effects than brands that are priced further apart.

A Competitor Lends a Helping Hand

A producer of a consumer packaged good developed and marketed two versions of a product, A and B. The two versions were quite similar except that the label used for B and the packaging gave it an image of being a better product. Initially A and B were the only two products in the market, and the firm priced them as follows:

A	B
$14.95	$18.95

As would be expected, the lower-priced version, A, was the firm's best-selling product in this line. However, after a time, a competitor introduced its version of the product, C, positioning it as a high-price, high-quality product. Now the prices of the three products were:

A	B	C
$14.95	$18.95	$34.95

In a very short time, version B became the first firm's best-selling product in this product category! The product manager was mystified and sought help to figure out what had happened.

In summary, price elasticities are not constant and they can be managed over products, brand, and time to a greater extent than previously recognized. Managers need to pay attention to the nature and duration of a price change and to how extensively the price change will be communicated or promoted to the market. Unfortunately, most companies do not make sufficient efforts to track the sensitivity of demand from their products to price changes and to price differences over time.

Becoming Proactive Pricers

The pricing misconceptions we've discussed here can prevent managers from becoming proactive pricers. Too often, companies fail to conduct proper research to guide their pricing strategy. They base price setting on annual budgeting exercises and misunderstand how buyers compute price differences and form value judgments.

To overcome these hurdles, managers need to understand the realm of pricing, including their customers' perceptions of prices, price changes, and price differences. To become proactive pricers, managers should take certain steps. First, research your pricing environment to understand the factors that influence the dynamics of supply and demand. Next, recognize that strategic pricing decisions define an organization's value image in the eyes of customers and competitors. In fact, one of the most important statements a firm can make about a product or service is its price. Finally, understand that tactical pricing decisions concern the day-to-day management of the pricing process and must be made within the firm's overall pricing strategy. By mastering these three principles, management can leave behind reactive or stagnant pricing practices and fully embrace a new era of proactive pricing.

Additional Reading

Monroe, Kent B. and Angela Y. Lee (1999), "Remembering Versus Knowing: Issues in Buyers' Processing of Price Information," *Journal of the Academy of Marketing Science*, 27(2), 207–225.

Sivakumar, K. (2000), "Price-Tier Competition: An Integrative Review," *Journal of Product & Brand Management Featuring Pricing Strategy & Practice*, 9(5), 276–290.

Urbany, Joel E. (2001), "Justifying Profitable Pricing," *Journal of Product & Management Featuring Pricing Strategy & Practice*, 10(3),141–157.

About the Authors

Kent B. Monroe is the J. M. Jones professor of marketing, department of business administration, University of Illinois, Champaign, Ill. He may be reached at k-monroe@uiuc.edu.

Jennifer L. Cox is a marketing specialist with John Deere, Worldwide Commercial & Consumer Equipment Division, Raleigh, NC. She may be contacted at jCoxUI@aol.com.

From *Marketing Management*, September/October 2001, pp. 42-46. © 2001 by the American Marketing Association. Reprinted by permission.

The Old Pillars of New Retailing

*Looking for the silver bullet that will solve your retailing woes? It doesn't exist.
The best retailers lay a foundation for success by creating
customer value in a handful of fundamental ways.*

by Leonard L. Berry

EVERYONE WHO GLANCES AT A newspaper knows that the retailing world is brutally competitive. The demise of Montgomery Ward in the realm of bricks and mortar as well as the struggles of eToys on-line—to choose only two recent examples—make it clear that no retailer can afford to be complacent because of previous successes or rosy predictions about the future of commerce.

Despite the harsh realities of retailing, the illusion persists that magical tools, like Harry Potter's wand, can help companies overcome the problems of fickle consumers, price-slashing competitors, and mood swings in the economy. The wishful thinking holds that retailers will thrive if only they communicate better with customers through e-mail, employ hidden cameras to learn how customers make purchase decisions, and analyze scanner data to tailor special offers and manage inventory.

But the truth of the matter is, there are no quick fixes. Yes, technology can help any business operate more effectively, but many new advances are still poorly understood—and in any case, retailing can't be reduced to tools and techniques. Over the past eight years, I've analyzed dozens of retail companies to understand the underlying differences between outstanding and mediocre performers. My research includes interviews with senior and middle managers and frontline employees, observations of store operations, and extensive reviews of published and internal company materials. I've found that the best retailers create value for their customers in five interlocking ways. Doing a good job in just three or four of the ways won't cut it; competitors will rush to exploit weakness in any of the five areas. If one of the pillars of a successful retailing operation is missing, the whole edifice is weakened.

The key is focusing on the total customer experience. Whether you're running physical stores, a catalog business, an e-commerce site, or a combination of the three, you have to offer customers superior solutions to their needs, treat them with real respect, and connect with them on an emotional level. You also have to set prices fairly and make it easy for people to find what they need, pay for it, and move on. These pillars sound simple on paper, but they are difficult to implement in the real world. Taking each one in turn, we'll see how some retailers have built successful operations by attending to these commonsense ways of dealing with customers, and how others have failed to pay them the attention they require.

Pillar 1: Solve Your Customers' Problems

It has become commonplace for companies to talk about selling solutions rather than products or services. But what does this really mean for retailers? Put simply, it means that customers usually shop for a reason: they have a problem—a need—and the retailer hopes to provide the solution. It's not enough, for example, just to sell high-quality apparel—many retailers do that. Focusing on solutions means employing salespeople who know how to help customers find clothing that fits and flatters, having tailors on staff and at the ready, offering home delivery, and happily placing special orders. Every retailer hopes to meet its customers' pressing needs; some do it much better than others.

The Container Store provides its customers with superior solutions. The 22-store chain, based in Dallas, averages double-digit annual sales growth by selling something that absolutely everyone needs: storage and organization products. From boxes and trunks to hangers, trays, and shelving systems, each store carries up to 12,000 different products.

The Container Store's core strategy is the same today as it was in 1978, when the company was founded: to improve customers' lives by giving them more time and space. The company accomplishes this mission well. It starts with the selection of merchandise, which must meet criteria for visibility, accessibility, and versatility. The company's philosophy is that its products should allow people to see what they've stored and get at it easily. The merchandise must also be versatile enough to accommodate customers' particular requirements.

Store organization is another key ingredient of superior solutions at the Container Store. The merchandise is organized in sections such as kitchen, closet, laundry, office, and so on. Many products are displayed in several sections because they can solve a variety of problems. A sweater box, for example, can also store office supplies. Plastic trash cans can also be used for dog food and recyclables. Individual products are often combined and sold as a system—thus, parents in the store who want to equip their children for summer camp may find a trunk filled with a laundry bag, a toothbrush case, a first-aid pouch, leakproof bottles, a "critter catcher," and other items.

Great service is another component of the Container Store's ability to solve its customers' storage prob-

lems. The company is very careful about hiring; it patiently waits until it finds just the right person for a position. Container Store employees are well trained to demonstrate how products work and to propose solutions to complex home organizational problems. They are also treated very well, both in terms of pay and in less tangible ways. In fact, the Container Store was ranked the best place to work in the country in 1999 and 2000 by *Fortune* magazine.

A relentless focus on solutions may sound simple, but it's not. The Container Store has many imitators, but none have matched it. Many businesses have only the fuzziest concept of selling solutions. Department store chains, for example, have stumbled in recent years. They lost their one-stop shopping advantage by eliminating many merchandise categories outside of apparel and housewares. And even as they focused on apparel, they lost ground both to specialty retailers that have larger category selections and to discounters that have lower prices. Finally, they lost their customer service advantage by employing salespeople who often are little more than poorly trained order takers. As a result, these stores do a relatively poor job of solving customers' problems. That's probably why only 72% of consumers shopped in department stores in 2000 compared with 85% in 1996.

Clearly, the lesson here is that you must understand what people need and how you're going to fill that need better than your competitors. The Container Store has figured this out; many department stores and other struggling retailers must go back to the beginning and answer these basic questions.

Pillar 2: Treat Customers with R-e-s-p-e-c-t

The best retailers show their customers what Aretha Franklin sang about: respect. Again, this is absolutely basic, and most retail executives would say that of course they

treat customers with respect. But it just isn't so.

Everyone has stories to tell about disrespectful retailing. You're in an electronics store, looking for assistance to buy a DVD player or a laptop computer. You spot a couple of employees by their uniforms and badges, but they're deep in conversation. They glance in your direction but continue to ignore you. After awhile, you walk out, never to return.

Or you're in a discount store, looking for planters that have been advertised at a low price. You go to the store's garden center but cannot find the planters. This time, you succeed in flagging down an employee. You ask about the planters, but she just mumbles "I dunno" and walks away. Frustrated, you go to the customer service desk and ask the clerk where you might find the advertised planters. He suggests that you try the garden center. Once again, you head for the exit.

It's easy to go on. Stories about women trying to buy cars, as everyone knows, are enough to make your hair curl. The fact is, disrespectful retailing is pervasive. In the 2000 Yankelovich Monitor study of 2,500 consumers, 68% of those surveyed agreed with the statement that "Most of the time, the service people that I deal with for the products and services that I buy don't care much about me or my needs."

Disrespectful retailing isn't just about bored, rude, and unmotivated service workers. Cluttered, poorly organized stores, lack of signage, and confusing prices all show lack of respect for customers.

The best retailers translate the basic concept of respect into a set of practices built around people, policies, and place:

- They select, prepare, and manage their people to exhibit competence, courtesy, and energy when dealing with customers.
- They institute policies that emphasize fair treatment of customers—regardless of their age, gender, race, appearance, or size

of purchase or account. Likewise, their prices, returns policy, and advertising are transparent.

- They create a physical space, both inside and outside the store, that is carefully designed to value customers' time.

In 1971, a 30-year-old entrepreneur named Len Riggio bought a floundering Manhattan bookshop called Barnes & Noble. Today, Barnes & Noble is the nation's largest bookseller, with fiscal 1999 sales of $3.3 billion. Respect for the customer has been at the heart of the company's rise.

Riggio's biggest idea was that books appeal to most everyone, not just to intellectuals, writers, and students in cosmopolitan cities. Riggio listened to prospective customers who wanted bigger selections of books, more convenient locations, and less intimidating environments. He put superstores in all types of communities, from big cities like Atlanta and Chicago, to smaller cities like Midland, Texas, and Reno, Nevada. His respect for the customer led him to create stores with spacious and comfortable interiors, easy chairs for relaxing with a book, and Starbucks coffee bars. To this day, he considers his best decision the installation of easy-to-find public restrooms in the stores. As he said in a recent speech, "You work so hard and invest so much to get people to visit your store, why would you want them to have to leave?"

Besides the large selection of books, the stores also have an active calendar of author signings, poetry readings, children's events, and book discussion groups. Many Barnes & Noble superstores have become a social arena in which busy consumers—who normally rush in and out of other stores—linger.

Riggio sees the Internet as much more than a way to deliver books to customers; it's another opportunity to listen to them and thus show respect for them. He views the store network and Barnesandnoble.com as portals to each other. Customers can ask salespeople at Internet ser-

vice counters to search Barnesandnoble.com for out-of-stock books, for customer reviews of titles that interest them, and for information about authors, such as other books they've published. Customers in a superstore can order the books they want on-line and have them shipped either to that store or to any other address. If a return is necessary, customers can bring their on-line purchase back to the store.

The value of respect often gets little more than lip service from retailers. Some companies wait until it's too late to put words into action.

Pillar 3: Connect with Your Customers' Emotions

Most retailers understand in principle that they need to connect emotionally with consumers; a good many don't know how to (or don't try to) put the principle into practice. Instead, they neglect the opportunity to make emotional connections and put too much emphasis on prices. The promise of low prices may appeal to customers' sense of reason, but it does not speak to their passions.

Many U.S. furniture retailers are guilty of ignoring consumers' emotions. Although the average size of new homes in the country has grown by 25% since 1980, furniture accounts for a lower percentage of total U.S. consumer spending today (1%) than it did in 1980 (1.2%). Making consumers wait up to two months to receive their furniture contributes to these poor results. How can consumers get emotionally involved in products they know they won't see for weeks?

Poor marketing also hurts the industry. Most furniture stores focus strictly on price appeals, emphasizing cost savings rather than the emotional lift that can come from a new look in the home. "We don't talk about how easy it can be to make your home more attractive," says Jerry Epperson, an investment banker who specializes in the furni-

ture industry. "All we talk about is 'sale, sale, sale' and credit terms."

Great retailers reach beyond the model of the rational consumer and strive to establish feelings of closeness, affection, and trust. The opportunity to establish such feelings is open to any retailer, regardless of the type of business or the merchandise being sold. Everyone is emotionally connected to some retailers—from local businesses such as the wine merchant who always remembers what you like; to national companies like Harley-Davidson, which connects people through its Harley Owners Group; to catalog retailer Coldwater Creek, which ships a substitute item to customers who need to make returns before the original item is sent back.

One retailer that has connected especially well with its target market in recent years is Journeys, a Nashville, Tennessee-based chain of shoe stores located primarily in shopping malls. The chain focuses on selling footwear to young men and women between the ages of 15 and 25. Started in 1987, Journeys didn't take off until 1995 when new management took over. The chain has achieved double-digit comparable-store sales increases in five of the six years since then and is now expanding by as many as 100 new stores per year.

Journeys has penetrated the skepticism and fickleness that are characteristic of many teens. By keeping a finger on the pulse of its target market, the company consistently has the right brands available for this especially brand-conscious group of consumers. Equally important, it creates the right store atmosphere—the stores pulsate with music, video, color, and brand merchandising.

A Journeys store is both welcoming and authentic to young people; it is simultaneously energetic and laid-back. Journeys' employees are typically young—the average age of a store manager is about 25—and they dress as they please. Customers frequently visit a store in groups just to hang out; salespeople exert no pressure to buy. And everyone, whether they've made a purchase or not, usually leaves with a giveaway—for instance, a key chain, a compact-disc case, a promotional T-shirt, or one of the 10 million or so stickers the stores give out over the course of a year. The stickers, which usually feature one of the brands Journeys sells, often end up on backpacks, skateboards, school lockers, or bathroom mirrors. Journeys also publishes a bimonthly magazine, *Dig*, that is available in the stores, and it runs a Web site that seeks to replicate the atmosphere of its stores. The number of site visits explodes whenever the company's commercials appear on MTV.

Journeys works in large part because it has created an atmosphere that connects emotionally with the young people it serves. Other retailers should bear in mind that it takes more than a room full of products with price tags on them to draw people in.

Pillar 4: Set the Fairest (Not the Lowest) Prices

Prices are about more than the actual dollars involved. If customers suspect that the retailer isn't playing fair, prices can also carry a psychological cost. Potential buyers will not feel comfortable making purchases if they fear that prices might be 30% lower next week, or if certain charges have only been estimated, or if they are unsure whether an advertised sale price represents a genuine markdown.

Consider some of the pricing tactics commonly used by certain home improvement retailers. One well-known company advertises products as "special buys" even though it has not lowered the regular prices. Another purposely misrepresents a competitor's prices on price-comparison signs within its stores. Still another company promotes lower-grade merchandise implying that it is top quality. One retailer puts a disclaimer in its ads that reads: "Prices in this ad may be different from the

actual price at time of purchase. We adjust our prices daily to the lumber commodity market." The disclaimer paves the way for the retailer to raise its prices regardless of the advertised price.

Excellent retailers seek to minimize or eliminate the psychological costs associated with manipulative pricing. Most of these retailers follow the principles of "everyday fair pricing" instead of "everyday low pricing." A fact of retail life is that no retailer, not even Wal-Mart, can truthfully promise customers that it will always have the lowest prices. An uncomfortable truth for many retailers is that their "lowest price anywhere" positioning is a crutch for the lack of value-adding innovation. Price is the only reason they give customers to care.

Retailers can implement a fair-pricing strategy by clearing two hurdles. First, they must make the cultural and strategic transition from thinking value equals price to realizing that value is the total customer experience. Second, they must understand the principles of fair pricing and muster the courage needed to put them into practice. Retailers who price fairly sell most goods at regular but competitive prices and hold legitimate sales promotions. They make it easy to compare their prices with those of competitors, and they avoid hidden charges. They don't raise prices to take advantage of temporary blips in demand, and they stand behind the products they sell.

Zane's Cycles in Branford, Connecticut, is one of the most successful independent bicycle retailers in the United States. Zane's has grown its one-store business at least 20% every year since it was founded in 1981, selling 4,250 bicycles in 2000 along with a full array of accessories. The company's success illustrates the appeal of fair pricing.

Zane's sells better bike brands with prices starting at $250. It stands behind what it sells with a 30-day test-drive offer (customers can return a bike within 30 days and ex-

change it for another) and a 90-day price protection guarantee (if a buyer finds the same bike in Connecticut at a lower price within 90 days, Zane's will refund the difference plus 10%). Zane's also offers free lifetime service on all new bicycles it sells; it was likely the first bicycle retailer in the United States to take this step. The promise of lifetime service includes annual tune-ups, brake and gear adjustments, wheel straightening and more.

Zane's holds only one promotional sale a year, a three-day spring weekend event featuring discounts on all products. Vendors and former employees come to work at the huge event—some even fly in to participate. Customers who purchase a bicycle at Zane's within 90 days before the sale are encouraged to return during the event for a refund based on the discounted price of their bike. The company refunded about $3,000 during the 2000 sale, but most of that money remained in the store because customers bought more gear. Zane's sold 560 bicycles during the 2000 sale—that's more than the typical one-store U.S. bicycle retailer sells in an entire year. And yet the limited duration of the sale means that Zane's sells about 85% of its bicycles at the regular price.

When Connecticut passed a bike-helmet law in 1992, Zane's sold helmets to kids at cost rather than take advantage of legislated demand. Owner Chris Zane convinced area school administrators to distribute flyers to students under 12 announcing that policy. "We sold a ton of helmets and made a lot of new friends for the store," Zane says. "Our customers trust us. They come in and say, 'I am here to get a bike. What do I need?' They have confidence in our ability to find them just the right bike at a fair price and to stand behind what we sell."

Constant sales, markdowns on over-inflated prices, and other forms of pressure pricing may boost sales in the short term. Winning customers' trust through fair pricing will pay off in the long term.

Are Your Retailing Pillars Solid—or Crumbling?

	Inferior Retailers...	Superior Retailers...
Solutions	gather products, stack them on shelves, put price tags on them, and wonder where their customers are.	consider what people really need and how they can meet that particular need better than competitors can.
Respect	are staffed by people who don't know what customers want and aren't about to interrupt their conversations to find out.	actually train and manage the salespeople they hire so that they are courteous, energetic, and helpful to customers.
Emotions	act as if their customers are Spock-like Vulcans who make purchases solely according to cold logic.	recognize that everything about a retail experience sends a message to customers that goes to the heart, not just the brain.
Pricing	focus exclusively on their supposed low prices, often because they have nothing else of value to offer customers.	focus on having fair prices instead of playing mind games with "special offers," fine print, and bogus sales.
Convenience	are open for business when it's convenient for them, close checkout lanes when it's convenient for them, deliver products when it's convenient for them, and so on.	understand that people's most precious commodity in the modern world is time and do everything they can to save as much of it as possible for their customers.

Pillar 5: Save Your Customers' Time

Many consumers are poor in at least one respect: they lack time. Retailers often contribute to the problem by wasting consumers' time and energy in myriad ways, from confusing store layouts to inefficient checkout operations to inconvenient hours of business. When shopping is inconvenient, the value of a retailer's offerings plummets.

Slow checkout is particularly annoying to busy people. Managers usually know how much money they are saving by closing a checkout lane; but they may not realize how many customers they've lost in the process. For a food shopper waiting behind six other customers in the "10 Items or Fewer" lane to buy a carton of milk, the time invested in the purchase may outweigh the value of the milk. The shopper may follow through this time but find another store next time. Studies by America's Research Group, a consumer research company based in Charleston, South Carolina, indicate that 83% of women and 91% of men have ceased shopping at a particular store because of long checkout lines.

To compete most effectively, retailers must offer convenience in four ways. They must offer convenient retail locations and operating hours and be easily available by telephone and the Internet (access convenience). They must make it easy for consumers to identify and select desired products (search convenience). They need to make it possible for people to get the products they want by maintaining a high rate of in-stock items and by delivering store, Internet, or catalog orders swiftly (possession convenience). And they need to let consumers complete or amend transactions quickly and easily (transaction convenience).

ShopKo, a discount chain based in Green Bay, Wisconsin, illustrates how shopping speed and ease can create value. ShopKo's more than 160 large discount stores operate in 19 midwestern, mountain, and northwestern states; 80% of the customer base is working women. With fiscal 1999 sales of $3.9 billion (including its small-market subsidiary, Pamida), ShopKo is much smaller than Wal-Mart, Kmart, or Target, yet it competes successfully against all three. Since 1995, following the arrival of new management a year ear-

lier, ShopKo has more than doubled sales and achieved record earnings growth.

ShopKo takes possession convenience seriously and is in-stock 98% of the time on advertised and basic merchandise. Search convenience is another strength. ShopKo stores are remarkably clean and neat. Major traffic aisles are free of passage-blocking displays. Customers near the front of the store have clear sight lines to the back. Navigational signs handing from the ceiling and on the ends of the aisles help point shoppers in the right direction. Clothing on a hanger has a size tag on the hanger neck; folded apparel has an adhesive strip indicating the size on the front of the garment. Children's garments have "simple sizing"—extra small, small, medium, and large—with posted signs educating shoppers on how to select the proper size.

ShopKo has a "one-plus-one" checkout policy of opening another checkout lane whenever two customers are waiting in any lane. Ready-to-assemble furniture is sold on a pull-tag system. The customer presents a coded tag at checkout and within three minutes the boxed merchandise is ready to be delivered to the customer's car. These ways of operating give ShopKo an edge in transaction convenience.

ShopKo is succeeding in the fiercely competitive discount sector by focusing on the total shopping experience rather than on having the lowest prices. Shopping speed and ease combined with a pleasant store atmosphere, a well-trained staff, and a carefully selected range of merchandise creates a strong mix of customer value.

While ShopKo creates real convenience for its customers, the term is often used carelessly in retailing. Consider that Internet shopping is commonly referred to as convenient. The Internet does indeed offer superior convenience for some stages of the shopping experience; it is inferior for other stages. On-line shoppers who save a trip to a physical

store must wait for delivery. Christmas shoppers who receive gifts ordered on-line *after* the holiday learn a lesson about possession inconvenience. This is one reason that the most promising path for most retailers is a strategy that combines physical and virtual stores. Increasingly, the best-managed retailers will enable customers to take advantage of the most effective features of physical and virtual shopping, even for the same transaction.

Retail competition has never been more intense or more diverse than it is today. Yet the companies featured in this article, and hundreds of other excellent retailers, are thriving. They understand that neither technology nor promises of "the lowest prices anywhere" can substitute for a passionate focus on the total customer experience. These retailers enable customers to solve important prob-

lems, capitalize on the power of respectfulness, connect with customers' emotions, emphasize fair pricing, and save customers time and energy. In an age that demands instant solutions, it's not possible to combine those ingredients with Redi-Mix, crank out a concrete-block building, and hope the structure will stand. But retailers who thoughtfully and painstakingly erect these pillars will have a solid operation that is capable of earning customers' business, trust, and loyalty.

Leonard L. Berry is Distinguished Professor of Marketing and holds the M.B. Zale Chair in Retailing and Marketing Leadership at Texas A&M University in College Station, Texas. He founded Texas A&M's Center for Retailing Studies and directed it from 1982 to 2000. He is the author of Discovering the Soul of Service *(Free Press, 1999).*

designing a trust-based e-business strategy

trust will make or break an e-business.

EXECUTIVE briefing

Trust determines the success or failure of many companies. Unless they feel a sense of trust, buyers will not return to a business, and this situation holds true whether the business is offline or online. To enjoy sustained success in e-business, companies need to understand how trust is defined and then incorporate the factors that influence perceptions of trust in their online strategies.

By Fareena Sultan and Hussain A. Mooraj

IN RECENT YEARS, NO OTHER TECHNOLOGY HAS affected marketing and business activities as significantly as the Internet. While the popular press has focused on the demise of many dot-coms, online B2B activity has continued to grow. The Gartner Group predicts that B2B e-commerce will hit $8.5 trillion by 2005. Of this, 42% or $3.6 trillion will be North America's share. At the same time, dot-coms that were promising to overthrow age-old established players have lost their sting or are no more. E-business is awash with change.

We contend that the development of trust between all the stakeholders is crucial for fueling the expansion of e-business. A December 2000 Jupiter Media Metrix survey found that trust issues were the number one priority for firms seeking new partners. Trust is especially critical for developing and sustaining new relationships. So it stands to reason that trust is going to be a key differentiator in determining the success or failure of many e-business companies.

Conventionally, companies have preferred to interact with parties that they know. However, in today's business environment, interaction with new entrants is inevitable. Many companies are interacting with unfamiliar players, particularly with small- to medium-sized firms. Using trust as the foundation for new relationships is a way to retain value in a business.

We interviewed managers to try to determine how trust is defined and examined factors that influence perceptions of trust in B2B interactions. (See Exhibit 1.)

Defining Trust in E-Business

We know from the offline world that a business can't have liquidity without returning buyers and there will be no returning buyers without trust. This rule holds true for the Internet as well. Trust is imperative for success in e-business and to ensure repeat customers. According to the TRUST-EC project, which was conducted in 2000 on behalf of the European Commission, e-business can be defined in a broad sense as the carrying out of business activities that lead to an exchange of value, where the parties interact electronically, using network or telecommunications technology. The question arises: How do various players engaged in e-business define trust? Trust is an elusive concept and has varied definitions depending on the discipline and the stakeholders investigating trust relationships.

We found that managers distinguish between two types of trust environments they encounter: (1) trust in the relationship among businesses, consumers, and other stakeholders; and (2) trust in the B2B Web site and its functionality.

In each of these two cases, respondents in our study articulated a variety of definitions of trust. For example, Mamoon Yunus, global systems architect at webMethods, a B2B integration firm, states that trust in e-business can be defined as "the ability to do business reliably, in a repeated fashion and securely with non-repudiation." In his opinion, trust is all about fulfilling the promise to the customer and is a fundamental aspect of any successful Internet strategy.

EXHIBIT 1 The study

•Thirteen one-on-one interviews with senior managers and executives

•Seven companies with a high level of involvement with the Internet in various capacities

•Interviewees included senior management, technology managers, sales and marketing executives, and Internet consultants

Company	Sample Business Focus	Respondent
1. ZEFER	Internet consulting	1. Managing director
		2. Director business consulting
		3. Principal business consulting
2. webMethods	B2B integration software provider	4. Global accounts architect
		5. Regional Sales Manager
3. KeyCommerce Inc.	E-marketplace solutions provider	6. CEO
4. Anchorsilk Inc.	B2B platform provider and ASP	7. President and CEO
5. State Street Corp.	Global financial services	8. Sr VP e-business incubator
		9. VP mkt. communication
		10. VP technology acquisition and corporate procurement
		11. Senior purchasing officer
6. Compaq	Computer hardware	12. Director Internet and e-business
7. NetNumina	E-business systems integrator	13. CTO

Definitions of trust are contingent on the nature of e-business being conducted. Much of e-business between firms starts first with online procurement. According to Albert Hofeldt, a principal at ZEFER, an Internet strategy consulting firm, the definition of trust varies depending on whether we are dealing with direct or indirect procurement. He is of the view that in indirect procurement, the factor that matters most is the price, whereas in direct procurement the more critical factors are availability and order fulfillment. Thus, dimensions of trust can include such elements as offering a good price, having products available, and fulfilling orders in a timely manner.

Todd Alcock, regional sales manager at webMethods, says that "trust is defined by the brand and promise to the customer, and how you back your promise." He also states that trust in technology vendors is defined by the perception of confidence that their people, processes, and technology are going to be capable in driving the success of your company. Peter DeBruin,

senior purchasing officer at State Street Corp., has yet another definition. He defines trust as "the ability to deliver on implicit or explicit statements and to execute the activity in a manner that the client wants it to be and is promised."

What Influences Trust?

Understanding the factors that influence customer perceptions of trust can help managers make better decisions. Our study unveiled seven factors that influence trust. (See Exhibit 2.) These factors, explained below, form a "circle of trust" that is necessary for success in e-business. To establish trust you need to have a good brand and good ratings. To operationalize and maintain trust, you need management domain knowledge, good security and clear privacy policies, current and functional technology, good order fulfillment, and responsive customer service.

Brand. We found that trust in the brand name is one of the most important factors when buying online. Brand recognition and reputation play important roles in instilling trust and helping businesses succeed online. For new entrants, it's important to leverage other known brands and associate with them in some form to create a sense of stability and longevity. This can be done through partnerships. For example, ZEFER leveraged the Sun Microsystems brand by forging a close working partnership.

According to Mansoor Khan, CEO of Key Commerce, "Trust will be created only if there is a pre-existing business relationship. However, if there is no prior business relationship, then brand becomes the single most important trust cue. This is especially true for small- and medium-sized firms."

EXHIBIT 2 The circle of trust

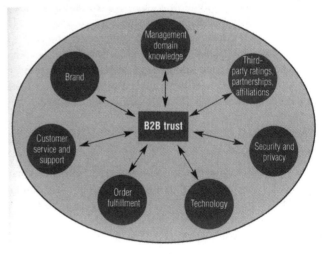

Management domain knowledge. Our study shows that building a trusting B2B relationship is predicated on having a dedicated management team. Anne Bowen, senior executive vice president of State Street Corp., explains that "Clients want to integrate their back-end systems with State Street because they perceive us to be experts in our domain."

Relatively new entrants such as e-marketplaces have to cross a hurdle stemming from the lack of any track record of suc-

Questions to Help Establish Trust With Unknown Parties

1 Who are the backers and participants? Are they large corporations or a VC?

2 Do they have the resources to ensure the transaction and aid in troubleshooting?

3 Do they have a dedicated management team?

4 How technically savvy are they?

5 Do they have the infrastructure to support the transactions?

6 Will the company survive in the long term?

cessful business relationships. They have to encourage participants by displaying the management team's domain expertise. In such cases, executive bios and "about us" buttons on Web sites are important trust cues.

Third-party ratings, partnerships, and affiliations. Our study indicates that new firms that have no proven track record to fall back on would be wise to incorporate certification by third parties and include customer testimonials on a Web site. Investors should be clearly identified and brands of partners and affiliates should be leveraged.

One trust cue that has been proposed for e-marketplaces is supplier performance ratings. Open Ratings and Dun and Bradstreet offer supplier performance ratings to e-marketplaces like the "Buyer Insight" ratings program. While this product may help build B2B trust, Forrester Research reports that widespread adoption will require several years.

However, in some industries like aerospace and medicine, no amount of certification will compensate for existing tried and tested relationships to invoke trust because the consequences of product failure are immense. In these instances, working first on establishing a personal relationship offline and then moving to the online world may be necessary.

Security and privacy. Successful B2B transactions can only take place in a secure environment that also protects customer privacy. To increase the level of trust, our study recommends that companies incorporate security in software such as firewalls. This would typically have functionality like Secure Socket Layer (SSL), which prevents interception of data and packet sniffing, authentication (to conform your identity), and authorization (to prevent unauthorized access to information). Digital certificates and repudiation logs also ensure security and can act as trust indicators.

Omar Hussain, CEO of Anchorsilk, a B2B platform provider, says, "Whereas in B2C e-commerce consumers worry about putting their credit card information on the Web, in B2B e-commerce one of the biggest fears is that sellers' prices will become available to competition." Today, technological security is taken for granted. However, privacy policies and the level of security still need to be clearly specified on the Web site.

Technology. In an e-marketplace, being technology agnostic depicts neutrality, which in turn creates trust. The level of IT so-

phistication within a company and personalization options also contribute to the overall trust environment.

Max Grasso, chief technology officer at NetNumina, a system integration company, is of the opinion that "Internet technology itself does not change the nature of trust relationships. However, a repeated failure of technology does affect this relationship." Successful companies must not only have current technology on a Web site, but also one that functions as expected.

Order fulfillment. We believe that making a commitment to deliver flawless execution and fulfillment helps engender trust. This commitment should be communicated clearly on Web sites. The site should also clearly articulate the intention to measure customer service and rectify mistakes. The technology on a Web site, at the very least, should allow the buyer to control the time of delivery of orders. In addition, Web sites should have the capability to check the status of an order with tracking functionality. Toffer Winslow, former director of business consulting at ZEFER, states, "Without flawless execution and order fulfillment there can be no trust."

Customer service and support. Our study found that poor online customer service is holding back the growth of B2B e-business and preventing companies from building trust on the Web. In the next generation of online commerce, companies must provide a high quality, consistent level of service across all channels (e-mail, wireless, call centers). This would entail personalized marketing, service, sales and support to win the trust of the customer. According to Ed Jay, former managing director of the Boston office at ZEFER, trust is eroded if you have different service levels across different channels.

Studies at the E-business Center at MIT have established the role of "virtual advisors" in establishing trust on the Internet. These are software programs that offer support to customers in complex buying decisions.

Private vs. Public E-Marketplaces

Is there a difference between trust in private and public e-marketplaces? Our study found that in private e-marketplaces the trust issue is solved to a large degree because you know the suppliers and membership is usually restricted. Michael Podavano, director of Internet and e-business at Compaq, says, "When a customer is part of a community, there is even more reason to build trust; in private e-marketplaces you have to have absolute trust or risk banishment." Having a sense of community leads companies to further integrate their business processes. This in turn enhances trust between parties.

Large corporations that have their own private marketplace need a single interface that's integrated with the various divisions. Stephen Dill, vice president of marketing at State Street Corp., states, "Trust implications are that all Web initiatives should be under one umbrella, which gives an impression of being customer-centric (e.g., having a single sign on)."

One aspect of public e-marketplaces that encourages trust is the sharing of perfect information. Here, participants are looking for price and order fulfillment and e-marketplaces

Steps to Create B2B Trust

In relationships with unknown parties
- Check with companies the unknown party has dealt with
- Use authenticated processes for checking financial backgrounds and confirm ability to pay bills
- Have conceptual discussions about the technology before entering into transactions
- Meet top executives and sales engineers
- Examine whether you can 'identify' with the individual or firms
- Ask for proof of concepts, trial installations, and conduct usability testing
- Develop an explicit contract that has recourse for eventualities
- Evaluate the level of effort being put into maintaining the relationship
- Keep feelers out in industry to find out what is going on

On Your Web site
- Ensure there are no "trustbusters"
- Leverage other brands by displaying partnerships and affiliations
- Exhibit management teams, explains domain expertise, and display job listings
- Have third parties rate your site
- State clearly privacy/security policies and specify security level
- State commitment to measure customer service and rectify mistakes
- Display customer testimonials
- Provide tools to allow control of time of delivery and order tracking
- Allow product comparisons of competitors' products on own Web site
- Establish a multi-layer process; buyer can contact many parties in one firm

might have contracts and SLAs (Service Level Agreements) to enforce compliance with agreements. Public e-marketplaces give a price advantage and guarantee fulfillment. What they do not always give are operational and relationship benefits.

Create Trust

There's usually a learning period before two entities start transacting with each other online. We recommend checking references in order to establish trust with unknown parties. It's important to identify companies that the unknown party has dealt with and to examine their experience with goods and services. Authenticated processes should be used for checking financial backgrounds. Given the state of affairs in the technology sector these days, the ability to pay bills is one of the main criteria for screening companies.

Industry feelers play an important role in identifying trustworthy B2B firms that you would want to do business with. It's best to validate any vendor claims with current users. Before transacting with the firm, have conceptual discussions with their team, meet their sales engineers, ask for demos and trial products, carry out extensive usability testing, and meet their executive team. Finally, develop an explicit contract with recourse for any eventualities.

Assisting the customer in the buying process can create trust. According to Gary Beaudreau, vice president corporate procurement at State Street Corp., "There is a need to enforce that the customer's B2B decision is the right one. Suppliers can help accomplish this in a number of ways, including initially guiding customers through the transaction process in order to establish trust and confidence and providing detailed information on the products and services in order to simplify the overall experience."

To enhance customer service and support, e-business firms need to form multi-layer processes whereby customers can contact many parties in one firm. Allowing input from customers on a B2B Web site through the free flow of information in chat rooms and forums can also create trust. Even if it hurts, a democratic aspect instills trust. Live advisers, text chat, audio, and 1-800 numbers all help create an environment conducive to building trust.

Another way to create trust is to take a customer perspective and allow product comparisons. To maintain true neutrality, it's a good idea to allow the customer to compare competitors' products on the Web site.

In our study nearly all the participants indicated the need to establish *relationship trust* before trust in the B2B Web site can be achieved. To do this, examine whether you can "identify" with the individuals within the other firm. If so, you're more likely to build trust. Review the level of effort put in by the parties to maintain the relationship, such as responsiveness to e-mail and level of preparation for meetings.

Consistency Is Key

Trust generally is built over time and with experience. However, with more and more businesses going online, the need to work with new and unfamiliar entities is coming to the fore-

Trustbusters

We identified 10 "trustbusters" that can make or break a company in the B2B space. Firms need to take a proactive stance to avoid these trustbusters.

- Inferior quality of the product
- Poor Web site content
- Complex Web site navigation and outdated links
- Slow response time of Web pages (i.e., more than three to seven seconds per page)
- Repeated failures of technology
- Lack of customization/personalization
- Lack of advisers (live chat, text chat, audio, 1-800 numbers)
- Inferior customer service
- Different service levels over different channels (in person vs. online)
- Poor order fulfillment

need to be established anew in the electronic environment. Just because a company is successful at gaining customers' trust in offline transactions doesn't mean this trust will automatically be translated online. However, existing offline trust can facilitate the process. While the Internet as a new technology may not influence existing B2B relationships, B2B transactional relationships are affected.

In today's business environment, companies have to acquire, retain, and service customers in a multi-channel environment. Consistent interactions and service in a multi-channel environment are critical factors in building trust. The ability to provide products and services in a trustworthy manner, across multi-channels, is a new challenge for customer-oriented firms in e-business. Only through trust-based strategies can a firm be successful in e-business.

Additional Reading

Jones, Sara, Marc Wilkens, Phillip Morris, Marcelo Masera (2000), "Trust Requirements in E-Business," *Communications of the ACM*, 43(12), 81–87.

Urban, Glen L., Fareena Sultan, and William Qualls (2000), "Placing Trust at the Center of Your Internet Strategy," *Sloan Management Review*, 42(1), 39–48.

front. Companies need these new customers to enable growth in e-business transactions. However, buyers and sellers still need to establish an element of trust before any B2B transactions can take place.

Online trust is hard to establish because people have trouble assessing intentions over the Internet. Customers who have been through a similar online transaction might come away with different notions as to whether an experience was trustworthy. Firms need to ensure that a maximum number of trust cues are presented online.

To create trust, a company must have the seven elements from the circle of trust in place. To maintain trust, a company must eradicate "trustbusters." Many of the trust factors are not easily carried over from the bricks-and-mortar environment and

About the Authors

Fareena Sultan is an associate professor in the College of Business Administration at Northeastern University and consults on technology issues. She may be reached at f.sultan@neu.edu.

Hussain A. Mooraj is an MBA candidate at Northeastern University. Mooraj was formerly an Engagement Leader with ZEFER Corp. in Boston. He may be reached at h.mooraj@neu.edu

Revolution Retail report

10 top stores put to the test

What makes a successful online retailer? Revolution tries out some of the online giants to figure out why they're attracting customers, and then parting them from their money

Just because Wall Street held a barbecue of internet retailers the other week doesn't mean the internet is dead as a retail medium. People are still shopping online, and will continue to do so in growing numbers. But it is becoming clear that in many sectors not all the current retailers are going to survive. They are insufficiently differentiated, and in many cases the brick and mortar world is biting back with its own online offerings.

So what makes a winning internet retailer? What is it that makes people buy things from one store and not another? It's a question that has been exercising retailers ever since retailing was just dusty market squares in mud-walled villages. And you only have to look at the number of stores that go out of business in main streets and local malls every year to know that we don't have all the answers yet, by any means. And online, things are more complicated, because the elements that make people prefer one store to another in the physical world do not necessarily have the same importance online.

Shopping is as much about the experience of buying things as it is about the products you're buying. In the brick-and-mortar world, it's everything from the layout of the store, the signposting and lighting, to the smiles on the faces of the shop assistants. Online, the essential ingredients of the shopping experience are to do with web site navigation, ease of finding what you're looking for, the clarity of reassurance that your personal and credit card details are secure, how well the business handles queries or unusual requests, and other related issues.

Internet retailers have to figure out new rules, and they're all still learning. But some are definitely doing better than others. The question is why. We decided to take 10 of the top internet retailers and try them out firsthand.

We talked to them to find out a little bit about their marketing strategy, how they're attracting customers and turning them into cash. And where possible, we bought something. But as you'll see, that was an occasion easier said than done. In the process we tried to figure out whether they're living up to the promise of their marketing, and how. And where they have a physical world presence, how comfortably does their online business sit with that? What is it that they're doing well? What can other retailers learn from them?

You may well disagree with some of our choices. This is not a league table, and choosing who to write about for reports like this is always somewhat subjective. These aren't flawless online stores (in this game nobody's perfect), but each is a giant in its space, with a powerhouse brand and serious numbers of customers. All of them are doing things that we think are interesting, so no matter what your line of business, we think they're worth your spending a bit of time with.

EBAY

Proposition

Founded by the supportive husband of a Pez dispenser collector, eBay's mission is simple: "We help people trade practically anything on Earth." And with some four million items on sale on any given day, practically everything is just what consumers will find. The company has grown profitable with its online version of the classic auction model: a commission on every single item sold on the site.

The company acquired San Francisco-based traditional auctioneer Butterfield & Butterfield in the fall of last year. The resulting auctions of high-end items have been joined by other niche plays, such as eBay Motors, a collaboration with Autotrader.com. Local auctions mean more yard-sale level merchandise is now available and further serve to erode classified advertising revenues for local newspapers. People are selling all types of household items through the site.

As perhaps the original online business-to-business trading service, the company has also sought to cash in on the investor cachet of an explicit B-to-B play. "EBay Business Exchange is a natural evolution of the eBay business model, enabling businesses to obtain new, used and refurbished business merchandise and providing businesses of varying sizes a targeted way to reach buyers of business items," says eBay chief operating officer Brian Swette.

Marketing

eBay built its user base during The Great Beanie Baby Craze. Indeed, tens of thousands of its daily auctions are still accounted for by Beanie Baby traders. The site consistently tops Media Metrix's ranking of e-commerce destinations. An online-centric approach to building its brand has concentrated on affiliate stores, where other online retailers (including Buy.com) are able to offer a co-branded version of the auction site, putting auctions of their own products to the fore.

User Experience

Buying and selling on eBay is not for the fainthearted. The site's huge number of concurrent auctions make navigation a nightmare. EBay does a good job of enabling searches and making popular categories easy to access. But registration is close to indispensable, and over 10 million have already signed up. A My eBay page is a necessity for tracking multiple auctions. And for the truly active (and addicted), eBay a-go-go is a service for wireless devices that lets traders keep track of when they are outbid, when a bid has been successful and when an item sells.
While online fraud remains at a level comparable with traditional sales channels, every user who has lied about his or her age, hair color or profession in an online chatroom will feel justified in worrying about buying on eBay. But those worries are dissipated by eBay's user-feedback feature: sellers are ranked according to the comments of previous customers, indicating whether they were satisfied or not.

Mark Dolley

AMAZON

Proposition

Amazon is still based on "our founding commitment to customer satisfaction and the delivery of an educational and inspiring shopping experience." It has, however, thrown in a dozen new categories since it started as a books-only site in 1996. With the boast of Earth's Biggest Selection to uphold, this marriage of selection and service is watched from Wall Street to Main Street.

Amazon puts its money where its mouth is. All of its 13 product areas offer a well-presented and wide array of brands, price points and personalities. For example, the look and feel of the art and collectibles site is more upscale than the book area. But the same accessible layout and graphic scheme pervades.

"We want to be less about push and more about inviting the consumer in," says marketing director Bill Curry. "We have a rich amount of information that helps consumers find what they want, rather than having someone tell them what they should buy."

What Amazon.com will tell consumers about next is anyone's guess. The company has actively added new categories and services. About the only hot e-commerce area they've stayed out of is financial services. Stay tuned.

Marketing

Amazon has built arguably the most extensive and active affiliate network of any online retailer. It is the official book retailer of Excite@Home and the official link for Yahoo!Search, as well as myriad other revenue producing alliances. Because it has expanded into so many areas, it has a huge audience target to hit. Marketing is accomplished more through specific areas than through the overall site. For example, full-page ads in regional Sunday newspaper book review sections only advertise the site's book business. The kitchen store may find its best audience in women 35 to 54 years of age, but the music audience may skew much younger. According to Curry, the site experience has to be a key marketing element to make sure the wide audience comes back to Amazon. "The nature of the business is that we want to get to anyone who is online and has a credit card," he says. "The individual areas need to appeal to each demographic group through their offerings and the way the site is navigated.

User Experience

We decided to take Amazon up on its claims by searching for a recent record release from a critically acclaimed but under-distributed artist, Neko Case. The site definitely invites more than pushes, as Curry says. After registering information (privacy policy plainly displayed), we entered "Neko Case" in the search box and got a quick page featuring the artist's most recent release, *Furnace Room Lullaby*. The page showed many different ways to learn about the artist and the release. Front and center were reviews from Amazon staff. More intelligent, complete and absent of hype were the user reviews.

When we clicked the selection into the shopping cart and hit continue to place the order, it was clear the order was "secure" and stored on Amazon's servers. Everything about the process was clearly explained, including what to expect in terms of shipping times and costs. On the final order confirmation page, big thank you messages were prominently posted at the top and the bottom. And you could even sign up for more information via email on artists like Neko Case.

John Gaffney

PRICELINE

Proposition

Priceline's value to online consumers is based on a business model protected by US Patent No. 5,794,207. Granted in 1998, it reads: "The present invention allows prospective buyers of goods and services to communicate a binding purchase offer globally to potential sellers, for sellers conveniently to search for relevant buyer purchase offers, and for sellers potentially to bind a buyer to a contract based on the buyer's purchase offer." In plain terms, it's a name-your-price model, where you can trade off naming a lower price against the correspondingly lower chance of getting what you want.

The company's initial focus was airline tickets. By signing up 34 airlines, Priceline was able to provide compelling deals on domestic and international fares and claims to have picked up some three percent of the US leisure fare market.

But even on the airline front, Priceline has found itself challenged by Microsoft's Expedia.com. Showing scant regard for Priceline's patent, Expedia.com offers an identical service, its Flight Price Matcher ("Flights At A Price You Like: Yours!").

Expansion has brought new categories of goods and services to Priceline's home page, including hotel stays, cars, mortgages and even groceries and telephone calls. "Further down the line, we'll add cruises, vacation packages and more. You can also expect priceline.com to begin its international expansion, beginning with Asia, later this year," says CEO Dan Schulman.

Despite charging a commission on every successful bid, the venture remains unprofitable.

Marketing

Priceline's advertising will forever be remembered for two things: making William Shatner very rich, and resurrecting radio as a means to promote dot-coms. The company combined Shatner's well-known voice with the bombardment of an uncluttered medium to earn almost overnight recognition.

Shatner cleverly chose to emulate savvy Silicon Valley landlords and take payment in equity, netting him an eight figure sum. With national radio now overrun by dot-com commercials, Priceline's more recent campaigns (still featuring Shatner) have concentrated on national TV. Local cable buys have been added in markets where the company offers specific services, such as its WebHouse Club grocery shopping scheme.

User Experience

Bidding on Priceline is no guarantee of satisfaction. In measuring its own success, the company looks at "reasonable" bids falling within 30 percent of the regular price for a product or service. In the first quarter of 2000, it was only able to satisfy 43.5 percent of those bids.

Even where users win on price, they lose on convenience. Online status checking, real-time online customer support and other helpful features abound. But to achieve maximum scalability with minimum investment, Priceline.com makes consumers sweat for their savings. For instance, first-time grocery buyers must compile their list, make their bids, pay up via credit card and then wait for a WebHouse Club Card to arrive in the mail before trekking to a participating store.

Mark Dolley

BUY.COM

Proposition

Buy.com was started as one of the truly visionary business models of the web. Its premise was one of buying computer hardware and software from Ingram Micro (a wholesaler that supplies many other dot-coms) and then selling those products at a loss. The company hoped to make up that loss with revenues from advertising shown to its customers as they shopped. Now though, post reality check, the company is regularly mentioned in reports of impending dot-com demise.

In fairness, the company widely diversified its offering. Books, CDs and DVDs form part of an online superstore that now numbers some 850,000-plus SKUs. But it still relies heavily on Ingram Micro as a supplier (for all its books, for example), and competition has driven margins to razor-thin levels. With a low price guarantee, Buy.com locked itself into the business of stacking product high and selling it cheap, though this is no bad thing for the consumer.

International expansion has seen Buy.com affiliates open in the UK, Australia and Canada. The company has also gone beyond the web, with a compact version of the store accessible on various wireless devices, including the Palm VII and Sprint PCS phones with the Wireless Web option. "Buy.com is increasing its presence within the wireless sector, says CEO Greg Hawkins. "We're catering to the growing number of consumers, professionals and corporations that recognize the importance of extending data access into the mobile, wireless internet environment."

Marketing

Buy.com tried it all: from billboards to banners and even Super Bowl ads. And not without success. The company has served more than two million unique customers. Unfortunately, those customers proved costly to acquire and as fickle as one might image for a store whose main claim has been cheapness.

User Experience

Buy.com's eSearch facility, combined with separate store departments for the main categories (book, computers, music etc.), make navigation relatively easy. But with such a breadth of items, Buy.com doesn't offer the depth of product descriptions users of other sites take for granted. Try buying a book, and you'll only find detailed information for the top 25 sellers. Lower down the list, you'll be lucky to find a one-line synopsis.

Shipping times, a key piece of information determining online purchases, are present throughout Buy.com. And for those who want to make extra sure, an ordertracker is available. The company boasts about its Anytime Customer Service, and a telephone call in the middle of the night was answered within two minutes.

Mark Dolley

EGGHEAD

Proposition

The name "Egghead" enjoys almost 70 percent brand recognition among online users, largely the by-product of Egghead's brick and mortar days gone by. The firm wants to parlay that advantage into a top place in the hierarchy of web retailers.

"We want to become the leading internet destination for technology products and services," says Bari Abdul, senior VP of marketing for the site. While online retailers have been aggressive in their fight for supremacy over the book and toy categories, which together represent a $25-billion-a-year industry, there still is no clear online leader in the $150-billion-a-year computer supplies market, Abdul says. Egghead may soon be able to claim that crown for itself. In 1999 it was the third-largest e-commerce site by sales volume after Amazon and Buy.com, with some $515 million in sales.

Marketing

The site's advertising promotes the idea of a "computer store inside a computer." Its print campaign has targeted the *Wall Street Journal, USA Today* and business publications such as *Inc.* and *Entrepreneur* magazine. Online ads have appeared on small-business sites and at portals such as CNET and ZDNet.

Egghead also sends out 20 million emails a month to its 3.7 million users who registered for email. These messages feature promotions such as private auctions that are listed only through email and five-percent-off deals on superstore sales.

The big sell here is variety. The site includes a retail "superstore," an auction area and a "Smart Deals" section offering surplus and overstock items at deep discounts.

"Most important is the selection," says Abdul. "At egghead.com we have up to 50,000 of the latest products on the site every day, and at the auction site we have about 10,000 more daily."

User Experience

This variety of offerings comes as the result of a deal last fall in which the auction site OnSale.com bought out Egghead and the OnSale.com leadership effectively took over management of the site.

On a recent test drive, we found variety—Egghead's chief selling point—to also be the site's main weakness. With no specific product in mind, we found it difficult to get a clear sense of what was available on the site. The superstore listed three categories of goods—computer products, software and electronics—each with a dozen or so subcategories to navigate. The auction half of the house has four categories, including (and we found this mystifying) travel and sports and fitness.

These seemingly mismatched offerings are perhaps part of a larger plan. Egghead wants to be the site of choice for small- and home-based business operators, and these categories may be aimed at that market. More logical is the site's plan to leap into the office products market this spring. "They need a place that they can go to get information and also get huge selection and good customer service. That is what the market is looking for," Abdul says.

Functionality on this sprawling site is sufficient. A search feature allows shoppers to track down products simultaneously in the retail store, in auctions and in the discount shop. If you know what you are looking for, that is helpful. In the travel section we found a large Samsonite suitcase that was going for $60, reduced from $150. It shipped the day after we ordered and arrived six business days later—a genuine bargain.

Adam Katz-Stone

TRAVELOCITY

Proposition

In March of this year Travelocity was the 30th most active site on the web, with over seven million unique visitors, according to the research group Media Metrix. The site's proud parents say they offer "a new way to plan and buy travel."

That phrase comes from Mike Stacy, senior VP of marketing, who explained that Travelocity is all about empowering consumers to research and plan their personal travel itineraries and vacation plans.

"All the airlines, all the hotels and vacation packages are surrounded by destination content information, and that presents a much different customer experience than you find in the traditional world," he says. "The consumer now is in control."

Marketing

Travelocity's TV ad campaign hawks the "control" message with emotional visuals. A grandfather arrives to see a new baby for the first time. A woman in the tropics awaits her lover.

In the online realm, Travelocity's innovative banner ads allow users to enter an origination city through an ad and immediately receive a list of the day's lowest fares to 10 or 15 destinations. The banner appears on all the major portals, at college sites and at financial sites.

With a target audience of 35- to 45-year-old homeowners whose income tops $75,000 per household, Travelocity seems to have a working formula. In 1998 the site did $285 million in gross sales. In 1999 the gross topped $1.1 billion, and in the first quarter of this year sales had already topped $500 million.

User Experience

We went to www.Travelocity.com to book a weekend room in Virginia Beach. This should have been easy, but it was not. Since we already knew where we wanted to go, we took control by going straight to "Find/Reserve a Hotel" and entered the city and state: Virginia Beach, VA.

Travelocity could not find that city, so we went to another site to track down the ZIP code for the resort town and then tried again, still without success. Eventually we queried Travelocity to search for a hotel "near a point of interest" and—lo and behold—the search engine recognized Virginia Beach as a point of interest.

Asked about the problem, a customer service representative said on the phone that the hotel booking tool gets a little funky sometimes. This is disappointing, but perhaps not surprising, since Travelocity has set its sights chiefly on the competitive arena of air travel bookings.

Stacy touted as a unique feature a "best fare finder," in which a traveler may enter a desired destination and get a report back detailing the lowest available airfares. Likewise, the "alternate airports" feature will search out less expensive fares that can be obtained by flying into nearby airports and then calculate the mileage from those airports to the traveler's destination.

Still, you'd think they could find Virginia Beach.

Adam Katz-Stone

TOYSRUS

Proposition

Despite some well-publicized stumbles last holiday season, Toysrus.com still finds itself the best-positioned toy e-commerce site going forward. As a division of the global Toys 'R' Us retail chain, Toysrus.com is able to leverage its parent company's incredible name recognition as well as its skills in managing inventories, giving it a huge advantage over pure online retailers such as eToys.

"They just have great brand awareness," notes Jupiter Communications Ken Cassar, in predicting Toysrus.com will likely lead online toy retailers this year.

Toysrus.com's weaknesses are the same ones faced by toy retailers in general—it is a seasonal and hits-driven business. The site will do as much as 70 percent of its annual revenues during the fourth quarter. That puts a lot of pressure on all aspects of Toysrus.com, from site management to fulfillment. Last year, Toysrus.com ended up alienating some consumers by failing to fulfill orders by Christmas. The site has since built two additional fulfillment centers to better meet surges in seasonal demand.

Marketing

The best thing Toysrus.com has going for its brand values. Plain and simple, Toys 'R' Us is the best known name in the lucrative US toy retail sector. "Our Q scores, measuring popularity and awareness, rank Toys 'R' Us equal with the likes of Disney and McDonalds," boasts John Barbour, CEO of Toysrus.com.

Toys 'R' Us leverages that stellar brand equity by including the site's URL in newspaper circulars and other advertisements, generating 50 million impressions during the last post-Thanksgiving shopping period. The URL is also displayed on in-store signage and shopping bags.

"All of these bricks and mortar assets allow us to spend far less on the important aspects of marketing and customer acquisition costs—which gives us a much faster track to profitability than pure online toy retailers," Barbour says.

User experience

The Toysrus.com interface is very clean looking with lots of white space to facilitate fast load times. Consumers can search for items by age group, brand, category (i.e. dolls, games) and character and theme. This search function appears on every page within the site, as does a selection of channels that include video games, Pokemon Central and collectibles. Products are displayed with age range and a small thumbnail picture, with more information available at a single click. Toysrus.com also offers "The Toy Guy," who provides brief reviews of products.

Toysrus.com offers a reasonably helpful FAQ page, as well as the ability to check on the status of an order. Customer service can be accessed through both email and 1–800 number. Both were required during initial attempts to shop, since the screen froze several times during the shipping and billing process. The site's technical support blamed the problem on later versions of the Netscape Navigator browser, adding that it was being addressed. A later attempt using Internet Explorer was completely free of problems.

David Ward

BARNES & NOBLE

Proposition

Barnes and Noble may be the internet's best example to date of using an offline brand to build an online business. Barnesandnoble.com is constructed on the brand's offline strengths, plain and simple. Barnes & Noble was the first book superstore and the first retail brand name in the book business. Since launching its online business in May 1997, it fought through the challenge of Amazon.com to become the sixth largest e-commerce site, according to Media Metrix.

Marketing

By the company's own admission, it does not do a lot in the way of unique branding for the site, or even the promise of a unique internet experience. Like its competitors in this space B&N relies heavily on affiliate marketing. In 1998 it launched a mybnlink.com program with BeFree, which essentially made every user an affiliate. For example, if you recommend a book via email to 20 of your friends and they all buy it from BarnesandNoble.com, you get 10 percent of the total revenue generated. The site relies heavily on brick and mortar power to drive online business. One recent promotion gave consumers a 10 percent discount on any online purchase in return for filling out a demographic information card in the store. B&N maintains strategic alliances with major Web portals and content sites, such as AOL, Lycos and MSN.

User Experience

More than its competitors, Barnes & Noble's approach seems to be aimed at the 35- to 54-year-old demographic. The day we shopped, users could pre-order *The Beatles Anthology* book, not due until late summer at best, but certainly an attention-getter for this age group. The featured music entry was Carly Simon's new record, when the site could easily have opted for the new Britney Spears or Pearl Jam records, released on that very day. It is definitely book-centric. Other product lines seem to get minimal attention. Links from the home page directed readers to subsets of book interests such as the Discover New Writers program and the wildly successful Oprah's Book Club. (Both are also in-store features.)

The site was unique in its grouping of books by winners of various literary awards. We clicked on the IMPAC Dublin Literary Prize and found a great description of the winner, a novel called *Wide Open* by Nicola Barker.

Upon ordering, the site seems to become more of an AOL affiliate than Barnes & Noble. Orders are handled by a co-branded AOL Quick Checkout system. New York City customers were urged to take advantage of a new home or office delivery service.

John Gaffney

CDNOW

Proposition

CDNow is trying to stress the "now" in its company's name. After making a living off its first-mover status for the past three years, the company has repositioned its brand. The site is now more in step with the broadband era of music e-commerce, content and community. In fact, its new tagline is: "Never miss a beat."

"We want to be a music destination. Buying a CD is only part of that," says senior brand marketing director Sam Liss. "We're looking to offer the user specificity. We're not looking to be the Wal-Mart of the internet. We're looking to offer an immersive experience that will make it easier for the user to find the product they're looking for and learn a lot about other product available on the way."

Marketing

CDNOW is in a state of transition financially, and that will affect its marketing plans. It has put a lot of PR muscle behind its new interview section and other broadband applications. It has also been chastised by some analysts for overpaying for some extensive portal deals. Time Warner and Sony will explore a broader strategic relationship with the company and have committed $51 million to it. CDNOW has also hired an investment banker, Allen & Company, to investigate other strategic opportunities and partnerships.

User Experience

CDNOW gets a number one with a bullet for being a fun site to surf. The company's vision of a "destination site" for music is executed with an obsessive attention to detail, presenting literally dozens of informational and commerce choices on the home page alone.

The day we shopped, the page had a broad array of artists featured (from Matchbox 20 to Jeff Buckley to Primal Scream) in the new release section. Album reviews were broken out by editor's picks, staff picks and featured reviews. Our favorite was the artist's pick, where an artist picks their top 10 records.

Looking for jazz selections, we opted for pianist Kenny Barron's picks. On the jump page his picks and an audio sample were listed together. We listened to a mid-1960s McCoy Tyner record titled *Inception*, which had a great smoky club feel.

Meanwhile, we found something else that will help CDNOW appeal to music fans: the company sells vinyl records, where available. But they're more expensive than compact discs.

The order process seemed suspiciously similar to Amazon.com's, both in the graphic interface and the actual process. One segment of the process that could stand more direct explanation is one of supreme importance: the availability of the product is not listed until you place your order. So if an item is backordered, the customer has no information, unless he or she calls the help line, as to when it will be delivered.

John Gaffney

DELL

Proposition

Founded in 1984 as a direct supplier of built-to-order computers Dell had long realized the importance of efficient fulfillment, billing and customer service even before the advent of e-commerce and the formation of Dell.com.

Thanks in part to a growing e-commerce business, Dell current ranks number two in the PC market, with a market capitalization of $130 billion and more than 35,000 employees. Dell.com now generates nearly $40 million dollars each day, a growing percentage of which is in high-end business-to-business services and infrastructure offerings.

Over the past year Dell.com intensified its efforts in the consumer space with Dell Gigabuys, which carries both PC and consumer electronics products such as digital cameras. It also launched the Dell4Me.com initiative to raise consumer awareness about the site's ability to provide everything from PCs to an ISP service. "It gives people a reason to visit the site more than once a year," comments Jupiter analyst Cassar.

Marketing

Dell.com leverages its direct mail channel to drive traffic for the web site. Catalogs sent to businesses and homes carry the URL on the cover and on inside pages. Dell.com also maintains its brand identity through print advertising in business, trade and technical publications.

Dell offers one of the most recognizable names in computing, one that many home consumers have already come in contact with at the office. "Dell projects the image of being a leader in providing customers customized solutions for their computing and internet needs," says company spokesman Bryant Hilton, adding that TV advertising is primarily the vehicle for corporate branding campaigns. Dell has also aggressively paired with companies such as America Online in promotions.

User Experience

Shopping at Dell.com is a utilitarian experience. Pages often have a cluttered look, but information is easily retrievable. The home page has multiple channels that segment users: consumers are directed to once section while government customers are sent to another. Though Dell.com primarily highlights its own products, especially in the build-to-order segment, the Gigabuys section has over 30,000 offerings, many from brands other than Dell. The site features a selection of exclusives, as well as a top-10 list chosen by customers. The most popular items were products such as laser printers, reflecting the site's business audience.

Dell.com customers can search through categories such as printers/scanners and software and accessories, or use a keyword to locate what they want. There were no attempts at cross- or up-selling, but the site does allow you to group four products together for comparison shopping. With its foundation in direct mail, Dell.com excels in fulfillment. A CD writer ordered on Sunday evening arrived on our doorstep Thursday morning via standard delivery. Repeat customers have the option of one-click checkout, and all customers have the ability to monitor the status of their order. Customer service consists of FAQs as well as an e-mail section.

David Ward

CHOICES, CHOICES

A look at the pros and cons of various types of Web advertising

By JENNIFER REWICK

For many marketers, the big question isn't whether to advertise on the Web, but how.

Do they go with horizontal banner ads or skyscrapers? Sponsorships or e-mail?

Here is a look at the kinds of Web ads currently available, along with their pros and cons.

BASIC BANNER ADS

Banner advertisements still are the staple of Web advertising. They are to the Internet what 30-second commercials are to television. Typically, banners are rectangular strips that run horizontally across the top of a Web page. Some blink; some flash; some just sit there quietly. In the late-1990s heyday of banner ads, consumers were said to be clicking on lots of these ads. But in recent years, the novelty wore off and viewers began to shrug. Now the "click-through" rate is less than 0.5%.

Banners originally were pitched as a direct-marketing tool, because consumers can click on them and be taken to another page or Web site to buy a product or get more information.

PROS: After consumers got click-resistant, some people began hailing banners as a brand-building tool—something with the same potential as a TV commercial to stick in a shopper's mind.

CONS: Banners' graphics are relatively crude. So advertisers and publishers are trying to become more aggressive, developing eye-catching ads and experimenting with new formats, not just placing the ads at the top of the page but all over it.

SKYSCRAPERS

Banners represent a lot of the real estate on a Web page. So perhaps it isn't surprising that one of the latest offshoots is known as the "skyscraper." It's simply a tall, skinny banner ad, and it can take up even more space than the pioneering top-of-the-screen rectangles.

PROS: Like real skyscrapers with their strengthening girders and beams, advertising skyscrapers have a structure that adds to their durability—namely, their vertical shape. Because a typical personal-computer monitor is wider than it is high, a skyscraper ad can perch on either side of the screen without infringing too much on the page itself.

CONS: Text in vertical ads is harder to read. And if an ad sits too far off to the side, a viewer may never even scan it.

BULKY BOXES

Banners are moving all over the place, turning into buttons and carefully positioned squares and rectangles as advertisers try to catch the reader's eye.

On the News.com Web site of San Francisco's Cnet Networks Inc., banner ads are about the size of a CD case and sit smack in the middle of the page. Instead of being taken to another site, readers who click on the ad get more information without having to leave the page. News stories wrap right around the ad box.

PROS: "It's a lot harder to ignore," says Jim Nail, an analyst with Forrester Research Inc., a Cambridge, Massachusetts, Internet market-research firm. But he adds a caveat about the ads, which Cnet likes to refer to as "Messaging Plus" ads.

CONS: The problem with the Cnet ad, says Mr. Nail, is simply this: "The reader's eye has to track around it in order to see the content. My guess is you will probably see some backlash. There probably will be some grumbling from readers."

BUTTONS AND 'BIG IMPRESSIONS'

Not all banners are so aggressive. Walt Disney Co.'s Web sites, including ESPN.com and ABC.com, now run business-card-size banners on the upper-right-hand corner of the page. Disney calls this format "the Big Impression."

PROS: Because the Disney ads sit off to the right side, they aren't interfering with other material on the screen and can remain there for a long time.

CONS: Because the ads are off in a corner on the right side, they might get overlooked. After all, people read from left to right.

Whether banners in general are a strong tool for brand campaigns also is questionable. Measurement firms are working on ways to gauge the impact. But it's much more difficult to quantify the impression a banner ad leaves with a consumer than it is to track an action, such as whether a consumer clicked on a mortgage-loan ad or bought a bath mat.

Dynamic Logic Inc., a New York ad-measurement firm, says it analyzed the brand impact of banners by comparing the responses of consumers exposed to a banner campaign with those of consumers who used the same site but weren't exposed to the ads. In a recent study, the results showed an average increase in brand awareness of 5%, says Nick Nyhan, president of Dynamic Logic.

POP-UP ADS

Some ads don't hesitate to get in your face. So-called pop-up ads appear in a second window that pops up on the screen while a Web page is loading.

Paving the way is the growth in high-speed Internet connections. These speedy connections allow for what online-ad types call "rich media" ads, which use animation, sound and streaming video. While banner ads can include rich media and are getting livelier these days, flashy content is found more often in the pop-up ads.

PROS: These lively ads fill a bigger space than most banner ads. They're more intrusive and memorable because they pop up and have to be clicked on to be gotten rid of. And they can be more entertaining, because they often use moving images. They're used primarily as a brand-building tool by auto makers, consumer-products companies and movie studios.

Unicast Communications Corp., a closely held online-ad firm in New York, says it has developed rich-media ads with an edge: technology that allows an ad to pop up without slowing down the loading of the page behind it. So, readers are less tempted to click the ads off just to keep things moving. Unicast says these ads boast a 6% click-through rate, compared with a high of 0.5% for banners and a 1% to 3% response rate generated by traditional direct-mail marketers.

CONS: Readers can click these ads off—and they do. Many banish the box from their screens even before they see the ad.

Pop-ups can be incredibly annoying to consumers, precisely because they are so intrusive. They often slow down the loading of the site you're trying to view. And even the ads that don't increase loading time tend to irritate users because they pop up unexpectedly on the screen.

Industry analysts doubt this is the next big thing and think a lot of the appeal is based on novelty and experimentation. Not to mention that high-speed Internet access has yet to penetrate the market, which means that these ads' use is not widespread. And readers are getting in the habit of reacting to a flurry of pop-ups simply by clicking them off before the ads can even start to make their point.

E-MAIL

E-mail marketing has surged in the past year. Jupiter Media Metrix Inc., a New York Internet-research firm, expects e-mail to be a $7.3 billion (8.4 billion euros) market by 2005, up from $164 million in 1999. Because recipients have to subscribe to receive e-mail newsletters and ads on topics in which they have expressed interest, marketers are guaranteed a highly targeted audience. Response rates can run as high as 5% to 15%, says Jupiter.

PROS: While it's most effective for retaining customers (61% of marketers using e-mail say that's their primary goal), e-mail marketing has proved to be a useful and cost-efficient way to acquire new customers as well. The cost of keeping customers is only one-third as much for e-mail as for direct mail.

One Low Price
What advertisers pay for spots in various media

TRADITIONAL ADVERTISING

LOCAL TV: A 30-second television commercial on a local station in a top 10 market ranges from $4,000, generally during a movie, to $45,000 for time on one of the highest-rated shows.

NETWORK TV: A 30-second spot in prime time ranges from $80,000 to $600,000, depending on how high a show is rated and the show's genre. The average is $120,000 to $140,000.

CABLE TV: A 30-second spot in prime time runs between $5,000 and $8,000, depending on the network.

RADIO: Commercials range from $200 to $1,000 for a 60-second spot, depending on criteria such as the time of day and the program's ratings.

NEWSPAPERS: A full-page ad in the top 10 markets runs an estimated $120 per 1,000 circulation.

MAGAZINE: Ads in regional editions of national magazines cost an average of about $50 per 1,000 circulation. The average cost of an ad in a local magazine is about $120 per 1,000 circulation.

DIRECT MAIL: The most common forms of direct mail include packages of coupons in letter-sized envelopes, which cost $15 to $20 per 1,000 delivered, and single-sheet newspaper inserts like fliers, which cost between $25 and $40 per 1,000 circulation.

BILLBOARDS: To place several short-term ads for one to three months on those 14x48 signs along the freeway ranges from $5,000 to $25,000 in top 10 markets.

ONLINE ADVERTISING

BANNER ADS: Banner ads range from $5 to $50 for every 1,000 ad impressions that appear on the site, depending on how targeted the ad and the site where it appears.

RICH MEDIA: Rich-media ads that appear in pop-up windows run between $40 and $50 per 1,000 ads that appear, depending on the quality and demographic of the site's audience.

E-MAIL NEWSLETTERS: Content sponsored by an advertiser in a newsletter format ranges from $15 to $25 per 1,000 e-mail addresses targeted, depending on the cost to create and develop the e-mail. An e-mail in the form of an advertisement ranges from $100 to $300 per 1,000 e-mail addresses targeted, depending on the quality and demographic of the list of addresses.

SPONSORSHIPS: A sponsorship per 1,000 viewers ranges from $30 to $75, depending on the exclusivity of the sponsorship. The more exclusive, the higher the cost.

Sources: Initiative Media North America in Los Angeles, a division of Interpublic Group; Carat Interactive Inc.

There are no postage fees, and "creative" costs are lower. The cost to create the e-mail runs about $1,000 and might take three weeks for a campaign, compared with $20,000 and three months for a traditional direct-mail campaign, Jupiter says. The research firm adds that e-mail also gets a faster response from subscribers—typically 48 hours—compared with snail mail, which takes three weeks.

CONS: As the e-mail market surges, so will the clutter in customers' in-boxes. Industry analysts warn that marketers are likely to become victims of their own success, and that it will grow increasingly difficult for advertisers to maintain response rates.

By one reckoning, the average number of e-mail messages from marketers per person in a year is expected to rise 40-fold to 1,612 in 2005, from 40 in 1999. The challenge will be to retain high response rates and low "unsubscribe" rates.

"Everybody thinks e-mail is the Holy Grail of online marketing," says Marissa Gluck, a Jupiter analyst. "It can be very effective, it's cheap and it's fast. But consumers can only manage a couple of relationships with advertisers. They don't want to have a relationship with every brand they buy."

SPONSORSHIPS

Analysts disagree about whether the online version of the old-fashioned "Brought to you by..." TV-show model is picking up speed or running out of steam. Regardless, sponsorships are still a popular form of online advertisement, especially among veteran advertisers looking for places to promote their brand names.

The idea behind a sponsorship is that a marketer pays to link its brand to an area of content on the Web such as a page, a section of a Web site or an entire site. Financial-services provider Charles Schwab & Co. became an early advertiser on women's site iVillage.com by sponsoring its finance channel. On a recent day, a message at the top of the site's investor page read: "Brought to you from the folks at Charles Schwab."

A more recent example is Verizon Communications Inc.'s $3 million deal to sponsor the Lifestyle channel of African-American Web site BET.com. As part of the deal, Verizon negotiated to be the entire site's only telecommunications advertiser.

PROS: With sponsorships, an advertiser can own a large chunk of Web "real estate" and often can work with the publisher to custom-build that area of the site.

CONS: Just like a banner ad, an advertiser's logo may be overlooked by a viewer who is focused on the Web page and trying to read an article. Second, fairly or not, sponsored pages invite some skepticism about the objectivity of the information, as people wonder whether the sponsor has an influence. Third, sponsorships don't make use of the interactivity of the Web medium. "It's tough to measure the impact" of a sponsorship, says Forrester's Mr. Nail.

Tips for distinguishing your ads from bad ads

By Bob Lamons

So you think you know a good ad?

It's one of the crosses we have to bear in advertising. Everybody is a creative expert; you may not know one thing about how to go about creating an ad, but by golly, you certainly know a good one when you see it. And conversely, you know a bad ad when you see it, too.

Or do you?

Most people, including many of us on the creative side, have a hard time remembering that our likes and dislikes aren't necessarily the same as those with whom we're trying to communicate. We reason that if the ad doesn't appeal to us, it won't be effective with our target audience, which may or may not be accurate.

But let's assume for the sake of argument that our personal tastes are much the same as the audiences we're attempting to reach. Here are a few suggestions for distinguishing a good ad from others that aren't so:

◆ Does it have a powerful visual?

The purpose of the primary visual in an ad is to stop the reader and begin the process of interesting him or her in the selling proposition. The purpose is not to show all the product's many features or its inner workings, unless by doing so, you can demonstrate something that differentiates your product from others the prospect may be considering. Too many technical managers simply want to show the product because they think clients will be as intrigued by it as they are, which usually isn't the case. They also think a beauty shot of the product will be a stopper. It's not.

Go ahead and take some liberties with your product shots. Baldor makes its electric motors shiny gold; Miller welding equipment is always blue (hence, "The Power of Blue" tagline), and its photography is always dramatically lighted. For Cooper Cameron, we use a photo-illustration technique that shows the product transitioning to a blueprint-like effect at the outer edges, because it fits with our message of technology leadership.

Producing powerful ads is more costly, but it's definitely worth any extra effort.

Some advertisers invest in sexy, diaphanous computer art showing the product's inner layers in an interesting but surreal way. There's no limit to the creative ways you can portray your products in magazine ads. Just don't use the photo you took for the technical bulletin; its boring.

◆ Does it have an intriguing headline?

I definitely subscribe to what I call the Law of Offering a Benefit in ad heads. Not only does this help the visual stop readers, but it sorts the prospects from the nonprospects.

Even writers of powerful headlines have to work a little harder to craft a benefit statement that is uniquely yours. For example, I like the way SAS Institute projects headlines on the foreheads of people in its series of thoughtful black-and-white (only the logo is four-color) ads for its data mining and e-intelligence software products. One recent headline was, "Opportunity no longer knocks. These days, it darts past the door before you can even react." And how about this one from Gartner/G2 Growth Research: "Growth opportunities reside in every nook and cranny of this economy. Be the tweezers."? I dare you not to read at least some of that ad to find out what they mean by "Be the tweezers."

There are many ways to offer a benefit. I favor writing magazine ad headlines that reach out and grab both eyeballs, because that's how you break through clutter.

♦ Is your selling proposition clear?

Too many trade ads these days are so clever, you can hardly figure out what they promote. They somehow confuse shock value with selling—or maybe it's not shocking at all, but many of them are so vague, you find yourself turning the page without even considering the message. I guess that's good, because nobody has time these days to read every ad, and these abstract concepts are actually performing a public service by making the goods ad stand out even more.

Still, I hate to see advertisers waste money; it perpetuates the myth that business-to-business advertising is superfluous and can be cancelled without repercussions. (Of course, bad advertising *is* superfluous and *should* be cancelled, but that's another story altogether.)

Here's one reason I like Harvey Studies: They provide verbatim comments about your ads—the good, the bad and the ugly. I usually go through the comments, marking the good ones in yellow and the bad ones in pink. If the yellow doesn't outnumber the pink by a wide margin, we have a problem.

♦ Is there a good call to action?

Most advertisers don't give much thought to the call to action, but I think it's just as important as the headline and primary visual. What do you want people to do as a result of reading your ad? If you said, "Call our 800 number for full details," or "Log on to our Web site at www.(fill in the blank).com," you need to go back to the drawing board.

A good call to action can actually start the selling process. Promise a test report; offer a product demonstration; direct them to a special section of the Web site where they have to log in before they see something of value. If nothing else, compare how your product stacks up to others in the field. Everyone is superbusy these days, and if you can offer something that helps them expedite or narrow their research, you're giving them something money can't buy: free time.

Power ads seek out the ideal prospects and cause them to pay attention in ways that serve the prospect's self interests ("What's in it for me?"). It will cost you more to produce a powerful ad, because you and the agency team will have to put more effort into it. But the results will be well worth the extra investment.

The real value in b-to-b advertising can only be achieved by making sure your ad pulls its share of the load. Marketers must stamp out lazy advertising, and you can help by knowing what to look for.

Bob Lamons is president of Robert Lamons & Associates in Houston. He can be reached at lamons@ama.org.

2001: Year of the Hard Sell

Struggling Ad Agencies Fought To Grasp Nation's Psyche Through Toughest of Times

BY SUZANNE VRANICA AND VANESSA O'CONNELL
Staff Reporters of THE WALL STREET JOURNAL

IN THE END, it was a lousy year to be selling much of anything.

Even before Sept. 11, Madison Avenue was hurting. Falling stock prices, dwindling consumer spending and rising unemployment all made for a bitter cocktail after the robust marketing revelry of the late 1990s. Overall advertising spending sank by about 7% this year, by some estimates. The top 200 agencies eliminated more than 21,750 jobs. And rather than spend on risky new creative efforts, some companies chose to tweak existing successful campaigns. In October, **Procter & Gamble** Co. reintroduced its 1990s ad, "Morning Gift," which shows vignettes of people waking up to fresh cups of Folgers Coffee. And this holiday marks the return of **Staples** Inc.'s "Sno-bot," a robotic snowman who falls in loves with an answering machine.

"When corporate America gets worried, there is less freedom to shoot for the stars," says Ann Hayden, managing partner, creative, at WPP Group PLC's Young & Rubicam.

Even some of the more memorable new ads stuck by tried-and-true selling formulas, including hiring familiar faces to hawk goods. Witness **PepsiCo** Inc.'s spots with singer Britney Spears and **Gap** Inc.'s holiday ads featuring actors Matthew Broderick and Nathan Lane as well as singers Alanis Morissette and Sheryl Crow. **Marriott International** Inc. tapped magician David Copperfield and celeb-tracker Robin Leach. Even **Microsoft** Corp. took a turn by invoking Madonna when it used her hit song "Ray of Light" to introduce its XP operating system.

Amid all this uncertainty and caution came the terrorists attacks, forcing ad execs to rethink, once again, what would motivate consumers to buy. One thorny question: How to sell anything after such tragedy without coming across as gauche? "We recognized that 911 was a turning point in the life of America and that it would have a significant impact on consumers attitudes," says Janet Pines, worldwide director of strategic planning at Interpublic Group's Foote, Cone & Belding. "We don't want any of our clients to look like ambulance chasers."

Ultimately, some of the most remarkable spots of 2001 were delivered in its final quarter, and felt earnest and patriotic in ways unthinkable a year ago. Soaring eagles … majestic scenery … stars-and-stripes —they were all there. One print ad for **General Electric** Co. showed the Statue of Liberty rolling up her sleeves to help New York; another for **Kmart** Corp. featured an American flag in newspapers and urged readers to display it. **General Motors** Corp., the world's biggest advertiser, implored consumers to "Keep America Rolling," through its 0% financing offer.

Here's a look at the best and worst of what Madison Avenue offered up on TV and elsewhere this year. The commercials can be viewed at www.wsj.com.

The Best Things in Life Are Free

Client: The City of New York

Agency: Omnicom Group Inc.'s BBDO Worldwide

Content: Billy Crystal dons an elaborate turkey costume while the rough and tumble Robert De Niro dresses like a Pilgrim. They then banter about why Mr. Crystal has to play the turkey. The commercial, filmed in New York's Central Park, ends with the duo riding a giant turkey float in the Macy's Thanksgiving Day Parade. Other ads in the campaign include Henry Kissinger belting an imaginary homer and sliding into home plate at Yankee Stadium, and Woody Allen skating his heart out at Rockefeller Center.

Feedback: The campaign, which is the talk of Madison Avenue, was created gratis by an ad shop known for its big budget. Mayor Rudolph Giuliani asked John Wren, Omnicom's chief executive, for a campaign to help the terrorism-scarred city. The celebrities all donated their time and GE's NBC, CNBC and MSNBC donated about $2 million in free media time to run the ads. Other networks running the ad free of charge include Viacom Inc.'s CBS. The message to potential clients: If BBDO's creative prowess can make gritty New York City look magical, imagine what it can do for a mundane consumer product.

They Shoot, They Score... They're Sued

Client: Nike Inc.

Agency: Wieden + Kennedy Inc.

Content: Basketball hot shots such as Vince Carter, Rasheed Wallace and Jason

Williams dribble and dance to a subtle hip-hop beat. The thump of their ball and the squeaks of their rubber-soled sneakers add to the rhythm. Think basketball meets the off-Broadway hit "Stomp."

In 2001, Ad Agencies Battled Poor Economy, Terrorism

Feedback: Even as the campaign was winning praise at the International Advertising Festival in Cannes, France, Nike and its agency were being sued by Game Over, a closely held New York sportswear maker. Game Over claims it developed Shakin,' a "basketball-handling competition that combines basketball, music and break dancing," to commercialize its athletic sportswear. The suit alleges Wieden and Nike stole the concept for the basketball/dance ad. The two companies say they didn't steal anything. Either way, consumers thought the commercial rocked.

Deserves a Stamp of Approval

Client: U.S. Postal Service.
Agency: Grey Global Group Inc.'s Grey Worldwide
Content: On Nov. 10, the U.S. Postal Service broadcast the 60-second spot, "Pride," which begins with a series of black-and-white portraits of postal carriers and the creed: "Neither rain, nor snow . . ." It then switches to color with images of current postal carriers as Carly Simon's "Let the River Run" plays in the background.
Feedback: This commercial replaced an ad featuring postal workers delivering computer chips needed for a monkey toy; the monkey spot was pulled after anthrax surfaced at postal facilities. Its replacement succeeds on many levels. First, it reminds Americans that the postal workers are human, heroes even, fulfilling their jobs even in times of tribulation. And resurrecting the old postal carrier creed was a deft nostalgic touch, making viewers feel almost patriotic about the mail. To tailor her song to one scene in the ad, Ms. Simon changed the lyrics of her "Working Girl" movie theme song. She cut the line "Come the new Jerusalem" for "Come the day has just begun."

If I Were a Rich Man...

Client: New York State Lottery
Agency: Omnicom's DDB Worldwide

Content: Farmers, factory workers, truck drivers and bakers deliver delightfully off-key lyrics from "If I had a $1,000,000" by the group Barenaked Ladies. Lottery ticket sales have been flat this year but in recent weeks New York State Lotto has enjoyed a "small but measurable" uptick in sales. A spokeswoman for Lotto attributes the increase to the jingle and big cash prizes and describes the commercial as a "pleasant annoyance."
Feedback: The actual Barenaked Ladies song is a gentle parody on being rich—"If I had a $1,000,000/ We wouldn't have to eat Kraft Dinner/ But we would eat Kraft Dinner/ Of course we would, we'd just eat more… " This ad struck a cord because it evoked the real, often whacky, conversations people have about what they would buy if they won the jackpot. It also catapulted the New York office of DDB, which made the ad, into the same league as DDB's gifted Chicago branch that masterminded the original "Whassup" commercials on behalf of Anheuser-Busch Cos.

'Whassup' Redux.

Client: Anheuser-Busch Cos.'s Budweiser
Agency: Omnicom's Goodby, Silverstein & Partners
Content: A wealthy trio named Brett, Ian and Chad drink imported beer and chat on the phone. They greet each other by hollering: "What are you doing"—a laughingly lame preppy version of the first "Whassup" series. The kicker: Two original "Whassup" guys watch the ad and appear dumbfounded.
Feedback: Agencies usually don't know when to move on. Yet just as the "Whassup" line was exiting our every day vernacular, Goodby took the work of its sister, DDB, and tweaked it just cleverly enough to get viewers buzzing again.

Riding in Cars With Boys

Client: Ford Motor Co.
Agency: WWP's J. Walter Thompson
Content: Two men in cars pull up to an intersection on a desert highway. One is driving a black import, the other a red convertible T-bird. With a nod, the man in the black sports car challenges the T-bird, and his girlfriend, a sexy brunette, uses her scarf as a flag to start the race. After his rival speeds ahead, the man in the Ford stays behind. "Need a lift?" he asks. She climbs in.
Feedback: This intriguing ad is a striking departure for Ford. It doesn't mention price or praise the car in any way. Instead, it plays to the conceit that some men believe they are as cool as the wheels they own. In a field where many car makers rely on rock music and landscapes to promote their brands, this was a clever effort. Too bad Ford extended the concept into new locales: It recently started showing the commercial in movie theaters, to the dismay of moviegoers.

Frank—and Frankly, Too Much.

Client: John Hancock Financial Services Inc.
Agency: Interpublic Group of Cos.'s Hill Holliday Connors Cosmopulos
Content: In its "Real life, real answers" campaign, John Hancock promotes life insurance with an unpleasant scenario: premature death. "What if something happens to you?… Where would that leave me and the kids?" a wife says to her husband during a date at a restaurant. In text, viewers are told that the average age a woman becomes a widow is 56. (Source: The National Center for Women and Retirement Research)
Feedback: Boston ad agency Hill Holliday began work on this commercial last spring, many months before terrorists put sudden death at the forefront of American consciousness. But John Hancock made the bold decision to first broadcast it during the November World Series, at a time when many TV viewers, especially men, were hoping to forget about reality and escape into the rivalry of professional sport.

AT&T Strikes Out

Client: AT&T Corp.
Agency: WPP's Young & Rubicam & The Media Edge
Content: During the recent Major League Baseball divisional playoffs, an AT&T logo appeared on screen each time a team changed its pitcher. The disruptive branding device was accompanied by the loud, irritating sound of a phone ringing.
Feedback: AT&T's work was a jarring reminder of how much advertising has intruded into content. The idea was clever, but sports fans cried foul. The ringing phone was more annoying than listening to John Madden banter on about his eight-legged turkey during the Thanksgiving football games.

This One's for the Dogs

Client: Florida Department of Health

Agency: Crispin Porter + Bogusky Inc.

Content: A man smears his tongue with brown BBQ sauce and dangles it in front of a ferocious Dutch Shepherd. The dog takes the bait and enjoys an early lunch. "If you chew tobacco you can lose your tongue, your jaw and even your life," a narrator says. The message, we think: chewing tobacco is as stupid as dangling your tongue before a hungry dog. In another spot, created for the American Legacy Foundation—a national anti-tobacco organization—a golden retriever defecates several times the street. A youngster then sticks signs in the excrement that says: "Ammonia is found in dog poop. Tobacco companies add it to cigarettes." Havas SA's Arnold Worldwide also worked on the American Legacy ad.

Feedback: Ugh. This is lowbrow stuff from the agency that hit the big time last year with its "Body Bag" commercial which showed teens piling body bags in front of the corporate offices of Philip Morris Cos. Some trade magazines called that spot one of the year's best.

Pop Off, Mr. Pop-Under.

Client: X10 Wireless Technologies

Agency: None. X10 did it themselves.

Content: If you used the Web much this year, you couldn't miss ads for the X10, a small, wireless video camera. The Seattle camera retailer blasted the Web with its "pop under" advertisements, essentially ad windows popping up behind the windows Internet users are viewing. Often they featured attractive women dressed in skimpy outfits.

Feedback: Consumers hated the X10 ads so much that after just 20 seconds, 73% of visitors left the site or window where the ad appeared, according to estimates by Jupiter Media Metrix, a market research firm. Some of X10's initial pop under ads suggested the camera could be used to videotape coeds without their knowledge. "We asked them to tone it down," says Donna Stokley director of advertising for Tribune Co.'s LATimes.com, one of the sites that ran the ad. Eventually X10 added a section to its own Web site to explain the pop under strategy, assuring that the ads were "100% legal and 100% safe." They forgot 100% annoying.

Honorable mention: Aflac Inc.'s pesky duck kept us amused this year via Bcom3 Group Inc.'s Kaplan Thaler Group. ... Gross factor worked for a "Got Chocolate Milk" ad via Interpublic's Bozell. The shot shows a teen boy gargling with milk and then doing the same with chocolate syrup.... Toyota Motor Corp. got laughs with its ad showing a bright red Celica parked on a quiet street when suddenly an old man shouts: "Slow down this is a neighborhood... punk." The tagline is "Looks Fast;" work was created by Publicis Groupe SA's Saatchi & Saatchi.... Walt Disney Co. tried to reklindle the magic with an ad from Bcom3's Leo Burnett featuring a middle-aged couple in bed. The wife laments that her husband doesn't talk to her anymore. He quacks "I love you" in a Donald Duck voice.

Not so honorable: An ad for Nintendo Co.'s squirrel "Conker" game from Bcom3's Leo Burnett featured a scantily clad blond lying on her bed and talking on the phone, detailing the wild night she just experienced with the squirrel.... AT&T and Interpublic's FCB ads featured Carrot Top, the comedian, aren't any more effective than last year's over-stimulated David Arquette.... Coke ads that used the "Life Tastes Good" tagline, created by Interpublic's McCann-Erickson Worldwide, are still flat.... Kimberly Clark Corp. makes eyes roll with ads from WPP's J. Walter Thompson that highlight wet toilet paper. The cheeky ads use a montage of rear ends: boys in a swimming pool and girls doing the hula-hoop as a voiceover chimes in "sometimes wetter is better."

From the *Wall Street Journal*, Eastern Division, December 20, 2001, pp. B1, B8 by Suzanne Vranica and Vanessa O'Connell. © 2001 by Dow Jones & Co. Inc. Reproduced with permission.

UNIT 4
Global Marketing

Unit Selections

Key Points to Consider

- What economic, cultural, and political obstacles must an organization consider that seeks to become global in its markets?

- Do you believe that an adherence to the "marketing concept" is the right way to approach international markets? Why, or why not?

- What trends are taking place today that would suggest whether particular global markets will grow or decline? Which countries do you believe will see the most growth in the next decade? Why?

- In what ways can the Internet be used to extend a market outside the United States?

 **Links: www.dushkin.com/online/**
These sites are annotated in the World Wide Web pages.

CIBERWeb
http://ciber.centers.purdue.edu
Emerging Markets Resources
http://www.usatrade.gov/website/ccg.nsf
International Business Resources on the WWW
http://globaledge.msu.edu/ibrd/ibrd.asp
International Trade Administration
http://www.ita.doc.gov
World Chambers Network
http://www.worldchambers.net
World Trade Center Association On Line
http://iserve.wtca.org

It is certain that marketing with a global perspective will continue to be a strategic element of U.S. business well into the next decade. The United States is both the world's largest exporter and largest importer. In 1987, U.S. exports totaled just over $250 billion—about 10 percent of total world exports. During the same period, U.S. imports were nearly $450 billion—just under 10 percent of total world imports. By 1995 exports had risen to $513 billion and imports to $664 billion—roughly the same percentage of total world trade.

Whether or not they wish to be, all marketers are now part of the international marketing system. For some, the end of the era of domestic markets may have come too soon, but that era is over. Today it is necessary to recognize the strengths and weaknesses of our own marketing practices as compared to those abroad. The multinational corporations have long recognized this need, but now all marketers must acknowledge it.

International marketing differs from domestic marketing in that the parties to its transactions live in different political units. It is the "international" element of international marketing that distinguishes it from domestic marketing—not differences in managerial techniques. The growth of global business among multinational corporations has raised new questions about the role of their headquarters. It has even caused some to speculate whether marketing operations should be performed abroad rather than in the United States.

The key to applying the marketing concept is understanding the consumer. Increasing levels of consumer sophistication is evident in all of the world's most profitable markets. Managers are required to adopt new points of view in order to accommodate increasingly complex consumer wants and needs. The markets in the new millennium will show further integration on a worldwide scale. In these emerging markets, conventional textbook approaches can cause numerous problems. The new marketing perspective called for by the circumstances of the years ahead will require a long-range view that looks from the basics of exchange to their applications in new settings.

The selections presented here were chosen to provide an overview of world economic factors, competitive positioning, and increasing globalization of markets—issues to which each and every marketer must become sensitive. "Segmenting Global Markets: Look Before You Leap" reflects the importance of understanding local and global issues before implementing a global market segmentation strategy. The second article stresses that international marketing research is a very serious and critical undertaking. The third article underlines the importance of e-business for the internationally active firm. "Continental Spendthrifts" reveals the importance of the formidable teenage European consumer market. "The Lure of Global Branding" provides some guidelines for proper global brand leadership, while "The Nation as Brand" reveals the complexity of marketing a brand in many different markets.

Segmenting Global Markets:
Look Before You Leap

Before implementing a global market segmentation strategy,
it's critical to understand both local and global issues.

By V. Kumar and Anish Nagpal

*"I am a citizen, not of Athens or Greece,
but of the world."*

Today we live in a global marketplace that makes Socrates' famous words more valid than ever before. As you read this article, you may be sitting on a chair from Paris, wearing a shirt made in Britain, and using a computer, without which you are handicapped, that probably was made in Taiwan. Have you ever wondered why and how this happens?

Global marketing refers to marketing activities of companies that emphasize four activities: (1) cost efficiencies resulting from reduced duplication of efforts; (2) opportunities to transfer products, brands, and ideas across subsidiaries in different countries; (3) emergence of global customers, such as global teenagers or the global elite; and (4) better links between national marketing infrastructures, which paves the way for a global marketing infrastructure that results in better management and reduced costs.

As the business world becomes more globalized, global market segmentation (GMS) has emerged as an important issue in developing, positioning, and selling products across national boundaries. Consider the global segment based on demographics, global teenagers. The sharing of universal needs and desires for branded, entertaining, trendy, and image-oriented products makes it possible to reach the global teen segment with a unified marketing program. For example, Reebok used a global advertisement campaign to launch its Instapump line of sneakers in the United States, Germany, Japan, and 137 other countries worldwide.

WHAT IS GMS?

Global market segmentation can be defined as the process of identifying specific segments—country groups or individual consumer groups across countries—of potential customers with homogeneous attributes who are likely to exhibit similar buying behavior.

The study of GMS is interesting and important for three reasons. First of all, considering the world as a market, different products are in different stages of the product life cycle at any given time. Researchers can segment the market based on this information, but the membership of the countries in each segment is fleeting. This makes it difficult to reevaluate and update the membership of each segment.

Second, with the advent of the Internet, product information is disseminated very rapidly and in unequal proportions across different countries. The dynamic nature of this environment warrants a continuous examination of the stability of the segment membership. Third, the goal of GMS is to break down the world market for a product or a service into different groups of countries/consumers that differ in their response to the firm's marketing mix program. That way, the firm can tailor its marketing mix to each individual segment.

Targeted segments in GMS should possess some of the following properties:

Measurability. The segments should be easy to define and measure. Objective country traits such as socioeconomic variables (e.g., per capita income) can easily be gauged, but the size of the segments based on culture or lifestyles is much harder to measure. Thus, a larger scale survey may be required for segmenting global markets depending upon the basis of GMS.

EXECUTIVE SUMMARY

The primary purpose of this article is to shed more light on the more complex challenges of global market segmentation (GMS). To provide a complete understanding, we discuss some of the well-known issues in segmenting foreign markets and move on to state the various properties of global target markets. We conclude that companies can implement GMS most effectively by first gaining a full understanding of both local and global concerns.

Size. Segments should be large enough to be worth going after. Britain and Hong Kong can be grouped together in the same segment, because of previous British supremacy in Hong Kong, but their population sizes differ.

Accessibility. The segments should be easy to reach via the media. Because of its sheer size, China seems to be an attractive market. However, because of its largely rural population, it has less access to technology.

Actionability. Effective marketing programs (the four Ps) should be easy to develop. If segments do not respond differently to the firm's marketing mix, there is no need to segment the markets. Certain legal issues need to be considered before implementing an advertisement campaign. For example, many countries, such as India, do not allow direct slandering of the competitor's products.

Competitive Intensity. The segments should not be preempted by the firm's competition. In fact, in global marketing, small companies often prefer entry of less competitive markets and use this as one of the segmentation criteria when assessing international markets.

Growth Potential. A high return on investment should be attainable. Typically, marketers face a trade-off between competitive intensity and growth potential. Currently, Latin American markets have good growth potential, but the instability of local currencies causes major problems.

Companies typically employ the following six-step process for implementing GMS:
- Identify purpose (by introducing a new or existing product and choosing appropriate marketing mix programs in groups of countries)
- Select segmentation criteria (traditional vs. emerging)
- Collect relevant information
- Segment the countries/consumers according to criteria
- Reevaluate the fit of the segment after implementation of the intended program
- Update/reassign segment membership

An interesting aspect of the GMS process is the need to constantly reevaluate segment membership. The process of assigning membership to countries into a segment could be done using traditional procedures, or by evaluating the countries by using emerging techniques.

TRADITIONAL SEGMENTATION BASES

The choice of the segmentation basis is the most crucial factor in an international segmentation study. That a segmentation approach is essential in international markets is no longer questioned. Rather, the basis for segmentation becomes the focus. For example, for its Lexus brand, Toyota would segment the market based upon household income. On the other hand, if Marlboro were planning to introduce a new brand of cigarettes, it would segment the market based on population.

Individual- and country-based segmentation includes the following categories:

Demographics. This includes measurable characteristics of population such as age, gender, income, education, and occupation. A number of global demographic trends, such as changing roles of women, and higher incomes and living standards, are driving the emergence of global segments. Sony, Reebok, Nike, Swatch, and Benetton are some firms that cater to the needs of global teenagers.

Culture. This covers a broad range of factors such as religion, education, and language, which are easy to measure, and aesthetic preferences of the society that are much harder to comprehend. Hofstede's classification scheme proposes five cultural dimensions for classifying countries: Individualism vs. Collectivism, Power Distance (PD), Uncertainty Avoidance (UA), Masculinity vs. Femininity, and Strategic Orientation (long-term vs. short-term). For example, Austria, Germany, Switzerland, Italy, Great Britain, and Ireland form one cluster that is medium-high on Individualism and high on Masculinity. These cultural characteristics signify the preference for "high performance" products and a "successful achiever" theme in advertising.

Geography. This is based upon the world region, economic stage of development, nation, city, city size and population density, climate, altitude, and sometimes, even the ZIP code. It is easy to form country segments using regional blocks such as NAFTA, European Union, MERCOSUR, or Asia-Pacific. However, the value of such segments may vary depending on the need. These groupings are viable for developing trade policies, but not for marketing products/services given tremendous variation in other factors.

Environment. GMS is further complicated by different political, legal, and business environments in each country. Economic indicators such as Gross Domestic Product (GDP) may be used. However, it may not be relevant to refer to country segments based on this criterion because a country can move from one level of GDP to another, making this criterion obsolete.

Behavior-based segmentation includes three categories, which are shown in Exhibit 1.

EXHIBIT 1   Traditional segmentation basis (behavior-based)

Segmentation Basis	Brief Description	Example
Psychographics	This segment groups people in terms of their attitudes, values, and lifestyles and helps predict consumer preferences in products, services, and media.	Porsche AG divided its buyers into five distinct categories: Top Guns, Elitists, Proud Patrons, Bon Vivants, and Fantasists—each group having a particular characteristic.
Benefit	This approach focuses on the problem a product solves, regardless of location. It attempts to measure consumer value systems and perceptions of various brands in a product class.	Toothpaste consumers can be segmented into Sensory, Sociable, Worrier, and Independent segments. Sociable consumers seek bright teeth; Worriers seek healthy teeth. Aqua packaging could indicate fluoride for the Worrier segment, and white (for a white smile) for the Sociable segment.
Behavior	This examines whether or not people buy and use a product, as well as how often and how much. Consumers can be categorized in terms of usage rates (heavy, medium, and light).	ABB classifies customers according to their switchability criterion—oyal customers, those loyal to competitors, and those who can be lost to or won from the competition.

EMERGING SEGMENTATION BASES

Countries also can be segmented by means of product *diffusion patterns* and *response elasticities*. Some countries are fast adopters of the product, whereas some countries require a lag period to adopt the product. With this in mind, a firm could introduce its products in countries that are innovators (fast adopters) and later in those countries that are imitators (lag countries).

Rather than using macro-level variables to classify countries, a firm might consider segmenting markets on the basis of new-product diffusion patterns. As Exhibit 2 indicates, country segments formed on the basis of diffusion patterns may differ by product.

This type of segmentation allows the global marketer to segment countries on the basis of actual purchase patterns. Having knowledge of purchase patterns can help marketers make mode-of-entry decisions and help determine the sequence of countries in which the product should be introduced.

Consumers in lag countries can learn about the benefits of the product from the experience of adopters in the lead country, and this learning can result in a faster diffusion rate in the lag markets. Thus, countries can be grouped according to the degree of learning they exhibit for a given lead country. Lag countries that exhibit strong learning ties are potential candidates for sequential entry (using a waterfall strategy). Entry into countries that exhibit weak learning effect can be accelerated since there is not much to gain by waiting. Here, a sprinkler strategy (simultaneous entry into the relevant markets) would work well.

If a firm wants to introduce its innovation into a new country, it must be aware that the diffusion rate depends upon the kind of innovation. The diffusion pattern of a continuous innovation (one that has a majority of features in common with earlier products plus some new features that improve performance or add value) is very different from a discontinuous innovation (which is new or drastically different from earlier forms in several relevant features or attributes).

In the case of continuous innovations, such as home computers, the introduction of a successive generation will influence not only its diffusion but also the diffusion of the earlier generations. In such cases, diffusion will occur more quickly since consumers have some related knowledge. Hence, when a new generation of the product is introduced in the lead market while the lag markets are still adopting the existing (older) generation, information on the added benefits of the new generation travels faster from the lead market to potential adopters in the lag markets. The users in the lag markets will be familiar with the innovation and can easily absorb the benefits of the next generation.

Another interesting way to group countries is according to their response elasticities. Consumers across countries respond in different ways when the price of the product changes. Grocerystore scanner systems store a wealth of information that can then be used to find customer buying patterns. If the data shows the customers are price sensitive toward a particular product, couponing strategies can help target that segment, where legal.

IMPLEMENTING GMS

It is important to consider some of the conceptual and methodological issues so GMS can fulfill its high potential. Exhibit 3 gives a brief description of the four critical types of equivalencies that should be taken into account when implementing GMS.

Construct equivalence refers to whether the segmentation basis has the same meaning and is expressed similarly in different countries and cultures. Different countries under study must have the same perception or use for the product being researched. Otherwise, comparison of data becomes meaningless. If, for example, a firm is studying the bicycle market, it must realize that, in the United States, bicycles are classified under the recreational-sports industry, whereas in India and China they are considered a basic means of transportation.

EXHIBIT 2 — Segments based upon diffusion patterns

Product Categories

Segment	VCRs	Cellular phones	Home computers	Microwave ovens	CD players
1	Germany, UK, France, Sweden	Denmark, Norway	Belgium, UK, Netherlands	Germany, Italy, Denmark, Austria	Belgium, Netherlands, Sweden, Austria, Finland
2	Belgium, Denmark, Spain, Austria, Finland	Finland, France	France, Italy, Sweden, Norway, Austria, Germany	Belgium, UK, Netherlands, France, Spain	Spain, Denmark, Germany
3	Italy, Portugal	Germany, UK, Italy, Switzerland	Spain, Portugal	Norway	Switzerland, Italy

Source: Kumar, V., Jaishankar Ganesh, and Raj Echambadi, "Cross-National Diffusion Research: What Do We Know and How Certain Are We?" *Journal of Product Innovation Management*, 15, 1998.

Similar activities also may have different functions in different countries. For example, for many U.S. families, grocery shopping is a chore to be accomplished as efficiently as possible. However, in India and many other countries interaction with vendors and local shopkeepers plays a very important social function.

Construct equivalence is easier to establish for the general bases, such as geographic variables. However, for bases such as values and lifestyles, construct equivalence is much harder to achieve. VALS-2 identifies eight segments based on two main dimensions: self-orientation and resources. Another VALS system was developed for Japan, presumably because the U.S.-based VALS-2 system was not appropriate for that country. Instead it identifies 10 segments based on two key dimensions: life orientation and attitudes toward social change.

Scalar equivalence means that scores from different countries should have the same meaning and interpretation. The first aspect used to determine scalar equivalence concerns the specific scale or scoring procedure used to establish the measure. The standard format of scales used in survey research differs across countries. For example, in the United States a 5- or 7-point scale is most common. However, 20-point scales are used in France.

EXHIBIT 3 — Types of equivalence

Equivalence

Construct	Scalar	Measurement	Sampling
Are we studying the same phenomena in Brazil, India, and Britain?	Do the scores on consumers in the U.S., Argentina, and Japan have the same meaning?	Are the phenomena in France, Singapore and South Africa measured in the same way?	Are the samples used in Hong Kong, China, and Romania equivalent?

The second aspect concerns the response to a score obtained in a measure. Here the question arises as to whether a score obtained in one research context has the same meaning and interpretation in another context. For example, on an intention-to-purchase scale, does the proportion of likely buyers indicate a similar likelihood of purchase from one country to another, or does a position on the Likert scale have the same meaning in all cultures?

Differences in response styles often result in a lack of scalar equivalence. Some of these response styles include "extreme" responding and "social desirability" responding. Research shows Chinese respondents show a "marked degree of agreeability," while Americans show a "marked willingness to dissent." These differences can cause problems in the data-collection process, which can lead to erroneous grouping of countries.

Measurement equivalence refers to whether the measures used to operationalize the segmentation basis are comparable across countries. For example, consider the level of education. The United States uses one educational scale while in Europe the educational system is quite different, and the term "college" is not appropriate. Also, household income is difficult to compare across countries owing to differences in the tax structure and purchasing power.

Some items of a segmentation basis have measurement equivalence, but the others do not. For example, research shows that in the U.S. consumer innovativeness is expressed both in terms of purchase of new products and in social communication about new products. In France, however, the latter does not apply. Hence, only items pertaining to the person's tendency to purchase new products have measurement equivalence across the two countries. The researcher thus faces the dilemma of either using the same set of items in each country (etic scale) or adapting the set of items to each country (emic-scale). A compromise would be a combined emic-etic scale with some core items common to all countries and some country-specific items.

Sampling equivalence deals with problems in identifying and operationalizing comparable populations and selecting samples that are simultaneously representative of other populations and comparable across countries. One aspect of sampling equivalence deals with the decision-making process, which varies across countries. For example, in the United States, office supplies are often purchased by the office secretary, whereas this decision is made by a middle-level manager or CEO in some countries.

It is also important to consider whether the sample is representative of the population. In most developed countries, information on potential markets and sampling frames is easily available. However, in Japan, the most popular residential list for sample studies was made inaccessible to researchers. Developing countries do not have extensive databases and so obtaining the sampling frame to suit the needs of the research could be difficult.

Equivalence presents a dilemma in the minds of managers. On one end, it would be wise to develop scales specifically for each culture; on the other, responses collected in this manner may not mean the same thing. This issue can be resolved to some extent by using a combination of items in the scale.

THINK GLOBALLY, ACT LOCALLY

Used effectively, segmentation allows global marketers to take advantage of the benefits of standardization (such as economies of scale and consistency in positioning) while addressing the needs and expectations of a specific target group. This approach means looking at markets on a global or regional basis, thereby ignoring the political boundaries that define markets in many cases.

The greatest challenge for the global marketer is the choice of an appropriate base for segmentation. Pitfalls that handicap global marketing programs and contribute to their suboptimal performance include market-related reasons, such as insufficient research and overstandardization, as well as internal reasons, such as inflexibility in planning and implementation. If a product is launched on a broad scale without formally researching regional or local differences, it may fail.

The successful global marketers will be those who can achieve a balance between the local and the regional/global concerns. Procter and Gamble's Pampers brand suffered a major setback in the 1980s in Japan when customers favored the purchase of diapers of rival brands.

The diapers were made and sold according to a formula imposed by Cincinnati headquarters, and Japanese consumers found the company's hard-sell techniques alienating. Globalization by design requires a balance between sensitivity to local needs and global deployment of technologies and concepts.

GMS offers a solution to the standardization vs. adaptation issue because it creates the conceptual framework for offering standardized products and marketing programs in multiple countries by targeting the same consumer segments in different countries. The formulation of a global strategy by a firm may result in the choice of one particular segment across markets or multiple segments. However, in implementing the marketing mix for maximum effect, the principle "Think globally, act locally" becomes a critical rule for guiding marketing efforts.

ADDITONAL READING

Ganesh, Jaishankar, V. Kumar, and Velavan Subramaniam (1997), "Learning Effect in Multinational Diffusion of Consumer Durables: An Exploratory Investigation," *Journal of the Academy of Marketing Science*, 25 (3), 214–228.

Hofstede, Geert (1984), *Culture's Consequences: International Differences in Work-Related Values*. California: Sage Publications.

Kotabe, Masaaki, and Kristiaan Helsen (1998), *Global Marketing Management*. New York: John Wiley & Sons Inc.

Kumar, V. (2000), *International Marketing Research*. New Jersey: Prentice Hall.

V. Kumar (VK) is Marvin Hurley Professor of Business Administration, Melcher Faculty Scholar, Director of Marketing Research Studies and Director of International Business Programs at the University of Houston, Bauer College of Business, Department of Marketing. He may be reached at vkumar@uh.edu.

Anish Nagpal is a doctoral student at the University of Houston, Bauer College of Business, Department of Marketing.

International marketing research: A management briefing

Many firms expand globally with little marketing research. But noteworthy business failures have occurred that could have been prevented with a minimal amount of study. Products and marketing campaigns usually need to be adapted overseas. The same is true for marketing research methods. Accepted approaches to conducting research are based on methods that were developed to study the U.S. market. Different conditions overseas, however, especially in emerging markets, make these methods difficult to apply. A look at typical problems in conducting research overseas can help in developing some guidelines for adapting methods in foreign countries.

Tim R. V. Davis
Professor of Management and International Business,
Cleveland State University, Cleveland, Ohio

Robert B. Young
Market Research Director, Stores Division,
ICI Paints/Glidden, Cleveland, Ohio

International marketing research is much more crucial than many managers think. With a burgeoning number of companies pursuing global strategies, managers are in great need of dependable information on foreign markets. Attempting to expand overseas without doing adequate research too often means having to face the crippling costs of business failure. Moreover, American market research techniques often don't work well abroad; managers must confront different challenges when conducting research overseas, especially in developing countries.

Corporate blunders in foreign markets frequently occur because of a lack of understanding of the Four Ps in the marketing mix—Product, Price, Place, and Promotion. Failure to investigate and, where necessary, reinterpret the Four P's abroad has proved costly.

Product and packaging problems

The failure of many products that lack acceptability overseas could have been predicted with minimal market research. Chase & Sanborn's attempt to introduce instant coffee in France failed because brewing real coffee is a cherished culinary delight for most French people. Instant coffee was considered a somewhat vulgar substitute.

In other cases, the problem may not be the product but the packaging. Snapple encountered difficulty marketing its bottled drinks through vending machines in Japan, where cans load more easily and are less fragile than glass. In China, Procter & Gamble marketed diapers in pink packaging that conveyed a preference for female babies. But many Chinese consumers shunned the product; under the country's one-child-per-family rule, the preference in many families is for a son. This type of product image problem could have been uncovered with prior research.

Pricing problems

Many companies do too little research on product or service pricing in overseas markets. In some cases, the price a company charges is simply the foreign currency equivalent of the domestic price, which may bear little relationship to what the customer is willing to pay. Ford recently tried to sell its economy model Escort car in India for more than $21,000. But in an emerging market like India, only a small percentage of the total population have incomes of $20,000 or more. So most Indians saw the Escort as a luxury automobile that very few could afford.

Even when managers are aware of acceptable pricing levels, they may still price products or services too high or too low. Exporters often set high prices to recover special labeling and packaging charges, overseas transportation, and import tariffs—costs that local competitors do not have to incur. These expenditures may prevent a company from pricing the product competitively. On the other hand, management may price products lower than the competition and be willing to take a loss early with a view to achieving profits later when more volume is achieved. Frequently, sufficient volume is never achieved and the foreign venture fails to break even. The lack of adequate cost analysis and pricing research is another major cause of business failure.

Place (distribution) problems

How products are placed or distributed in overseas markets can be the most important international business decision a company makes. Firms can try to break into established wholesale, retail, or direct sales networks, piggyback on other firms' distribution systems, or build their own channels, which can be costly and time-consuming. Neilson, Canada's largest manufacturer and marketer of confectioneries, has distributed its products successfully in such far-flung markets as Japan, China, and the Middle East. But success has eluded it in the market it would most like to succeed in: the United States. The reason for this is Neilson's choice of distributor. In the early 1990s, the company chose Pro Set, a collectible trading card producer, as its distributor. However, Pro Set's sales force lacked experience in selling confectionery and never achieved significant penetration in the US market. The firm was poorly managed and eventually filed Chapter 11 bankruptcy, leaving Neilson with a huge outstanding receivables balance and a severely damaged reputation with customers.

Promotional problems

Promotional methods and advertising media vary around the world. The lack of understanding of branding, selling, advertising, and promotion practices in different countries may also land companies in difficulty. Lincoln Electric, a US-based manufacturer of electric motors and welding equipment, acquired an arc welding firm in Germany and immediately slapped its own brand on the products that were made by the firm. Many customers had a strong "Buy German" attitude and were contemptuous of American engineering, so they immediately switched to other German products. Although Lincoln's problems in Germany ran considerably deeper, the company never recovered from its poor start and eventually had to close its operation there. Royal Applicant, an American manufacturer of small, hand-held vacuum cleaners like the "Dirt Devil," suffered a similar disaster. The company assumed that its successful domestic promotional strategy would work equally well in Europe. In the United States, expenditures on television advertising were closely correlated with predictable increases in sales volume. But in the different European countries, the growth in TV ad spending did not produce the predicted increases. Even though sales had risen to over $20 million by 1993, they never produced a return on investment. The company eventually withdrew entirely from the European market.

It is critical for managers to investigate the Four Ps in every country in which they do business and make modifications when and where they are needed. As these and other examples illustrate (see the box on the next page), mistakes are often made by well-known corporations, not just small firms. The tendency to take market knowledge for granted is the most insidious problem in international business, and often a fatal one.

Difficulties in conducting global marketing research

Even if managers are convinced of the need for foreign market research, they may have little understanding of the differences involved in carrying it out. They must become acquainted with the challenges it will bring—challenges they may not encounter at home.

More diverse research projects

The main types of marketing research projects are basically the same whether they are conducted at home or abroad. Studies typically deal with market entry, customer satisfaction, buyer behavior, and aspects of the Four Ps, and focus mainly on differences across countries. This may involve straight comparisons between a single foreign country and the domestic market or comparisons among multiple countries. But international research studies must contend with wide-ranging cultural diversity, which may include marked differences in language, religion, race, and ethnic origin that affect the sale of products and services. Domestic studies often examine regional differences, but they generally do not approach the level of diversity that is encountered in country comparisons.

More unknowns

Most managers know considerably more about their own domestic market than they do about conditions overseas. International research must shed light on more unknowns, providing insight on issues that may be clearly understood in the domestic market. Considering the lack of published information on many foreign markets, researchers have a heavy burden to bear. There are limits to the type and amount of data they can collect. The scope of what is to be studied will be constrained by the amount of time and resources available. So choices must be made about the focus of market research and what issues can be investigated.

Longer completion time

Generally, each phase of international marketing research—planning, design, execution, and interpretation of findings—requires more time to complete than in domestic research. The studies take longer to plan because they tend to be more complex and more difficult to arrange. Research designs must take into account viable data collection methods. Execution of the study will take longer if multiple countries are involved because of the separation in time and distance. In vast countries like China and India, the distance between markets makes large-scale studies extremely difficult to conduct. Interpreting the findings also takes time because of the logistics of coordinating comparison studies across countries.

Higher costs

Because of such factors as the different data collection techniques, the need for translation, and long-distance travel, conducting international marketing research is usually much more expensive than at home. Consumer telephone surveys that are a bargain in the United States cost much more abroad. In Japan, studies are mainly conducted door-to-door. In many developing countries, telephone ownership is low and interviewers must often travel vast distances to contact a representative sample of respondents. The time and cost required to collect primary data may make the research prohibitively expensive.

Suspect samples

Census data are unreliable or unavailable in many developing countries. Street maps and phone directories may not exist. Unreliable population statistics often make surveys of the general population difficult to conduct. In planning studies, market researchers need to question the accuracy of available demographic information and the study subjects: Are there any inherent biases in the sample? What proportion of the universe is covered? How are the data verified to ensure proper market coverage? Does

Gaffes, twists, and trials abroad

Many managers view foreign markets as being no different from domestic ones. They assume that successful marketing strategies and tactics used at home will work equally well overseas. But when Gerber first marketed baby foods in Africa, consumers thought the pictures of babies on the bottles meant that the jars contained ground-up babies! Research can also uncover unexpected uses to which products are put, such as the use of Jolly Green Giant sweet corn as fishing bait in Italy.

Obtaining adequate distribution for products is a real challenge when entering emerging markets, particularly transporting them over vast distances. The well-developed air, rail, and highway systems of the US and Europe that offer a variety of transportation options are virtually nonexistent in many developing countries, so research needs to be conducted on how products can reach far-flung markets. Wrigley, which has long been attempting to introduce chewing gum in China, had to face this problem. It discovered from its own market research that only about 17% of the Chinese population could be reached by conventional transportation. Bicycles, tricycles, carts, and motorbikes are used to reach small towns and villages, where products are sold through street kiosks and plywood stands. Wrigley found that many consumer products took eight months to reach the marketplace. After lengthy negotiations with state agencies, the company decided to use a combination of its own representatives and state-owned distributors to get its product to market. The typical route covered by a shipment of chewing gum consists of traveling 1,000 miles by truck, an additional leg by freighter, and finally by bicycle to small street stands. The process requires two weeks to complete, but the product is still freshly soft and sugar dusted at the time it is sold. This distribution method helped Wrigley sell more than 400 million sticks of chewing gum in China during 1999.

Some famous examples of translation errors have occurred in print, poster, TV, and radio advertising. In the late 1980s, Hispanics in the US were encouraged to fly on Braniff Airlines. A radio commercial mentioned flying Braniff *en cuero*, which means "in leather." But a very similar Spanish expression, *en cueros*, means "naked," and the two phrases sound identical when spoken quickly. Clairol, a popular marketer of hair care products, introduced a curling iron in Germany called the "Mist Stick," then discovered that the word "mist" is German slang for "manure." All these problems could have been averted with prior market research.

the sample cover all regions or cities? Is the sample source updated regularly?

Representative sampling may be less of a problem in countries with more homogeneous populations like Japan and South Korea, but it may be a serious concern in places where the population is more diverse, such as Hong Kong and Indonesia. More culturally diverse populations will require larger research samples or more subsamples. Researchers may also have to deal with population movement and migration. For instance, approximately two-fifths of the population of the gulf states of the Middle East consist of expatriate males working in the region for only four to five years. An unstable population is an additional headache when trying to establish a representative sample.

In one study, when asked to choose which of several brands of vodka she would buy, a Russian woman replied, "I would buy all of them because they won't be in the stores tomorrow."

Data collection difficulties

Few countries provide such open access and freely available information as the United States. In many countries, business, government, and the population at large may be less willing to discuss issues, share information, and open up to questioning. People may be unwilling to talk to strangers without formal introductions, referrals, or invitations. An interviewer arriving at a home unannounced may be seen as a threat and treated hostilely. Moreover, the usual data collection methods used at home may be inappropriate in other countries. High levels of illiteracy may rule out written surveys. Mail surveys may be hindered by unreliable postal delivery. Other methods of collecting data may be unavailable. The mall or shopping center interviews common in the US are rarely used in Asia because there are so few shopping malls. In India, electronic point-of-sale cash registers and scanners are virtually nonexistent, so retail checkout data must be collected manually. In most Middle Eastern countries, few women would consent to be interviewed by a man, so female interviewers must be recruited.

Gathering data on certain types of products can also be difficult. For instance, the idea of discussing grooming and personal care products with a stranger would be considered too personal and perhaps offensive in many countries. These data collection difficulties may result in the number of completed interviews and usable questionnaires being quite low.

Translation errors and unintended meanings

A common problem in international marketing research is the errors that occur in translation. The literal translation of brand names and terms from one language to another sometimes creates misunderstandings. Managers of Schweppes tonic water decided to shorten the name in Italy when they learned that the phonetic equivalent of the brand name translated to "bathroom water" in Italian. Questionnaires developed in one country may be difficult to translate because of differences in idioms, the vernacular, and phrasing. This can occur in the US as well, where a large section of the population are bilingual. But it is a much bigger problem in, say, India, where 13 major languages are spoken and salient cultural differences exist across regions. Questions may also take on an entirely different meaning in another country. In one study, when asked to choose which of several brands of vodka she would buy, a Russian woman replied, "I would buy all of them because they won't be in the stores tomorrow."

Measurement problems

Attitude measurement is not universal around the world. As the example of the Russian woman illustrates, participants' responses may be partly culturally determined. Skewed results on attitude scales are common. Products and services routinely achieve well above 60 or 70 percent approval ratings on five-point scales in Latin American countries. Indeed, a product has to be very poor to receive anything less. Latin Americans do not like to hurt others' feelings, including marketers. In contrast, a response of "not bad" in France would be almost the equivalent of "extraordinary." And a response of "somewhat interested" would represent a much stronger commitment than in England, where the term "somewhat" has a less enthusiastic connotation.

Respondent incentives and biased results

The use of incentives as a means to increase participation is another issue. A common criticism of paying respondents for their opinions is that it invites biased answers. But in many countries, incentives are necessary for getting respondents to participate at all. In some countries, such as Brazil, a drink and a willingness to socialize may be enough for an interview to be granted. In other countries, incentives may be considered somewhat insulting.

Reliance on outside research firms

MNCs must work closely with market research firms that collect data for them in different countries. Decisions must be made over how much autonomy will be given to these outside researchers and how closely their work will be supervised or monitored. MNCs with marketing research departments in foreign subsidiaries will be able to work more closely with local firms in different countries. But even large corporations do not have in-house marketing research staff in every country in which they do business. MNCs can send out their own staff to brief people in each country, but inevitably they must place considerable reliance on local researchers. Differences in data collection techniques and concerns about the comparability of findings across countries are significant issues when using various research firms in different countries.

Restrictive laws and disclosure of results

A more sinister threat may be the imposition of legal regulations that make it more difficult to keep research results confidential. For example, new laws enacted in the summer of 1999 control the conduct of market research in China, where government officials monitor questionnaire construction and insist on seeing survey results. Not only is this is in direct conflict with the required nondisclosure of proprietary research studies, in which the results are made known only to the clients commissioning the work, but the new disclosure requirements may unwittingly leak new product plans and marketing proposals to competitors. Managers need to be fully aware of such laws and regulations in various countries.

Inadequate use of findings

The real value of market research depends on how the findings are used. International research will add little value to management decision-making if the findings are not interpreted and acted upon appropriately. Reports from domestic market studies may languish on the shelf because management sees little relevance in the research, or disagrees with the findings. This tendency is greater in international research, where studies may be commissioned at the headquarters level but the findings may need to be implemented in foreign subsidiaries. When managers in the local subsidiaries conduct their own research, they will tend to have more ownership and belief in the findings. But corporate management at headquarters may want to control the questions that are investigated and compare the findings across countries or regions. In this case, local management may resent corporate interference and question the usefulness of the research.

Proposals for improving global marketing research

Given all these difficulties, what can marketers do to make their international research both efficient and effec-

tive? Most companies will need to adapt their approach to conducting research. Here are some guidelines for doing that.

Look for ways to cut costs

It is essential to stretch marketing research dollars so that the maximum benefit can be obtained from budgeted resources. Two excellent ways of doing this are by making the fullest use of published sources and tapping available government assistance.

Make extensive use of secondary sources

The United States and most of Western Europe have a wealth of secondary market data that can be accessed online at little or no cost. All market entry studies should begin by consulting published sources. Many international business texts urge managers to organize relevant macro region or country data (political stability, economic stability, currency strength, quality of infrastructure) and micro industry data (current sales by product, distribution access, raw material availability, labor costs, competitive activity) into a matrix where they can be weighed, ranked, and scored. Although the value of this assessment will depend on the availability of published sources, the objectivity of the data, and the accuracy of the rankings, it is generally a useful first pass for comparing countries, considering alternative selection criteria, and narrowing market entry choices. No attempt should be made to collect primary data before secondary sources have been thoroughly investigated and analyzed.

Seek help from government agencies

Most developed countries and many developing ones have state agencies that aid businesses. Virtually all governments try to promote the development of exports. The Export Market Information Center offers assistance to exporters in the UK. In the US, the International Trade Administration, a division of the Department of Commerce, provides a wide variety of market intelligence on different countries. It conducts low-cost market surveys and searches for sales agents and distributors for companies. Many export-driven emerging countries also provide assistance to help local businesses contribute to a balance-of-trade surplus.

Appoint a single market research coordinator for major studies

The use of a coordinating market research vendor with a network of affiliated offices around the world can improve the consistency and accuracy of results across countries and languages. One major vendor can organize and coordinate the work. With a single point of contact, special instructions and changes can be communicated and implemented simultaneously across multiple countries. Leading MNCs tend to appoint coordinating agencies that have offices in multiple countries. VeriFone uses a single vendor that has extensive experience in global market research and a network of branch offices throughout the world. The vendor's branch office personnel conduct most of the fieldwork. Project briefings, interviewer training, and pilot tests can be conducted and monitored much more easily. Other well-known MNCs like IBM, Compaq, Carrier, and Federal Express also use a single global vendor to manage large-scale research projects around the world.

Walker Information is a leading international research firm with more than 60 years of experience. Based in Indianapolis, it has a network of affiliate offices in more than 50 countries helping global clients conduct research studies that take into account cultural and language differences. Walker provides a diverse range of services, including studies of customer loyalty, employee commitment, corporate reputation, supplier relationships, and corporate philanthropy. Its clients include consumer packaged goods companies, heavy manufacturing firms, consumer and business services, trade associations, not-for-profits, and government agencies.

Pay close attention to the translation of questionnaires

The validity of market research can be improved by having strict, formalized guidelines governing questionnaire preparation and translation. Using a small number of translators can help reduce errors by lowering the potential for different interpretations of terms. Back translation—the process of translating questionnaires from one language to another, then back again with the aid of a second, independent translator—can reveal unintended losses of meaning. The back translator is usually a person whose native tongue is the language that will be used for the final questionnaire. Pilot tests can also help ensure better quality in the final study.

For many years, IBM has been conducting a strategic tracking study across its major markets in Europe, North and South America, and Asia. Conducted in 14 languages across 27 countries, this survey assesses IBM's products against competitors' offerings on such strategic issues as product demand, marketing channels, and preferred information sources. The study reveals broad information on trends rather than in-depth information on customer wants and needs. IBM uses only two translation firms to reduce inconsistency in terms, one for the various European languages and another for Asian languages. It also makes sure these firms use back translators to improve questionnaire accuracy. Local IBM employees in engineering, manufacturing, or sales may also be called upon

to double-check technical terms. All surveys are piloted in the field prior to conducting full-scale studies.

Develop a core set of questions to enhance comparability across countries

To compare countries and regions, many MNCs develop a core set of questions that will be used worldwide. At Carrier Corporation, a core set of 25 questions was used in a global study. Allowance was made for differences in each region by giving subsidiaries the opportunity to ask an additional five questions that were tailored to their area. Compaq uses a Customer Satisfaction Council to develop and maintain a consistent set of customer satisfaction measures across business units and geographic areas. Headed by the vice president of customer satisfaction and quality, this global, cross-divisional, interdisciplinary team meets regularly and invites representation from manufacturing and functions worldwide. Its goal is to establish internal metrics that are linked to customer satisfaction. Consistent validity and reliability among each customer segment across each country is a key strategic objective. Study results are used globally as well as locally. Some measures are customized and modified by market. The Council is responsible for integrating customer satisfaction information into product planning initiatives and process improvements.

In some countries, class, caste, or racial differences determine who speaks and who does not.

Use alternative data collection methods

The difficulties in collecting data overseas often mean that researchers need to adapt their approach to each country or region. Greater use may have to be made of qualitative methods in developing countries. The lack of accurate census and demographic information may sometimes rule out probability sampling. As a result, researchers may have to rely more on nonprobability sampling techniques such as convenience and quota sampling. Convenience sampling is often used for populations that are difficult to approach. The sample size gradually grows through introductions and referrals. Drawing quotas from different segments of society may help reduce sample bias (respondents with the same class, caste, or kinship ties, for example).

Methods will depend partly on the stage of the research, the market knowledge required, and the need for statistical precision. The lack of representative samples may be less of a handicap if the research is in the discovery stage and the objective is to obtain broad qualitative data. Indepth interviews and focus groups will often be the best method for exploring a broad range of issues.

Cultural differences may determine whether to use individual interviews or focus groups. American-style focus groups usually consist of eight to ten selected respondents who freely express their perceptions, attitudes, opinions, and feelings on pertinent research issues under the guidance of a moderator. Such discussion often provides rich qualitative data reflecting a diversity of opinions. Similar diverse results are often achieved in male focus groups carried out in the Middle East. The main problem there may be getting participants to show up on time and controlling the discussion when everybody starts talking at once. However, in collectivist cultures such as Japan and Southeast Asia, individuals may be reluctant to speak out, especially if their opinions are contrary to other group members. In some countries, class, caste, or racial differences may also determine who speaks and who does not. In these circumstance, individual interviews may encourage more openness and candor than focus groups.

Approaches to running focus groups may also partly reflect research traditions in different countries. American focus groups typically emphasize direct questioning, specific issues, and more direct interpretations. In Europe, discussions are more open-ended, with greater use of projective techniques and broader interpretations of the findings.

Recruit native language interviewers and moderators

Many consumers are reluctant to be interviewed for marketing research studies. Often, individual interviewers and group discussion moderators may have to build rapport with them. Companies can raise the comfort level of respondents by using native language interviewers and moderators who can converse in the local dialect. This is also a matter of courtesy. Native language interviewers and moderators can enhance the quality of interviews or focus groups when subtle nuances are important. Both telephone and personal interviews are influenced by country cultural norms. Local interviewers and moderators need to be able to interpret facial gestures and body language and to clarify respondent questions.

Select lead countries as a starting point

Lead countries should be chosen as a data collection point prior to conducting research elsewhere. These may be the wealthiest economies in the region or those with the best prospects. They can sometimes be used as proxies for other countries in the area. For instance, some broad cultural similarities have been found among Southeast Asian countries. Handled with care and prudence, this is another way firms can cut the costs of international mar-

keting research. Selected lead countries can also be used to iron out problems before rolling the research out on a broader scale. Surveys may be vetted for consistency and accuracy. A thorough debriefing following the initial research allows new learning to be taken into neighboring countries.

Test market in smaller countries to maintain secrecy

Secrecy or confidentiality can be a problem in conducting marketing research. Regulations need to be investigated in each country. Given the recently announced disclosure requirements in China, that may not be the best place to test new products. Smaller countries may sometimes be used to keep new product plans more private. Carewell Industries test-marketed its Dentax toothbrush in Singapore before introducing it in the United States because of the country's remoteness from the American market. It is also a relatively self-contained, low-cost environment for testing new products.

Use start-up offices and stores as research labs

An alternative method of collecting intelligence overseas is to establish a branch office, small-scale assembly operation, or service store as a research lab. This may be especially helpful for introducing new products and services into different countries. Marketing research studies rely heavily on people's perceptions and opinions—views that may be suspect when respondents have little direct experience with a new product or service. By establishing an office, factory, or store, management may learn a great deal more from having a direct presence in a country than simply relying on others' opinions about a product's or service's acceptability. Setting up a small-scale test site on a joint venture basis with a local partner can also lower risk and expense.

Citibank maintained a branch office in Tokyo while researching the market before setting up a successful retailing operation throughout Japan. Outpost factories have been used widely in manufacturing. Small, experimental assembly plants are often set up in developing countries to test the feasibility of manufacturing there and establishing local supplier relationships. Outpost factories may also be set up close to major competitors to gather intelligence. McDonald's and Pizza Hut opened experimental stores in Moscow to test the feasibility of selling fast food in Russia. KFC did the same thing in China. These outpost stores were used to adapt the menu, adjust store policies and procedures to local requirements, and explore alternative supplier relationships. Having established a successful, experimental prototype, management could then roll out more stores with a considerable degree of confidence.

Encourage broad participation by those who must use the findings

When corporate managers coordinate marketing research studies around the world, they need to build ownership at the local level. A wide range of stakeholders should be involved if the findings are to be interpreted and used properly. This is especially important when international studies are first conceived and when the implications of the findings are explored. It may necessitate involving general management at the central, regional, and local levels as well as sales, R&D, manufacturing, and other affected functions. Outside entities such as advertising agencies and local distributors may also need to be closely involved. More participation at critical stages in the research can help eliminate resistance and lead to fuller use of the study findings.

Capture and share findings in corporate marketing information system

By capturing research findings in the corporate marketing information system and sharing them across countries, management can build an understanding of the differences and similarities among markets. Marketing research information is not widely shared across the subsidiaries of most MNC's. Country managers know very little about the findings from studies that have been carried out in other foreign subsidiaries, or of product, pricing, distribution and promotional differences, brand names, slogans, and value propositions in other countries. Sharing such information can promote better understanding and collaboration between foreign subsidiaries.

Keep a close watch on the Net

The recent emergence of Internet-based research is making international marketing research easier to conduct. As more people go online, the Net is helping to define global user communities for different products. Direct contact with subjects in different countries over the Web may shrink the time and cost of conducting the research. The main methods of gathering research data over the Net are (1) e-mail based surveys, (2) Web site surveys, (3) online discussion groups, and (4) computer-assisted interviewing. With only a small portion of the world's population online, these methods are largely untried and untested. But online market studies could eventually help replace onsite interviewing and mail surveys for certain types of studies. Innovations in Net-based research need to be closely monitored. They have the potential to create major advances in international marketing research.

Many US firms are latecomers to doing business globally. With the munificence of the US market, most have not had to venture into foreign markets. Thus, few American managers have extensive international business experience. Many are unaware of the differences overseas. They may be surprised by how little is known about many foreign markets and how little has been written about international marketing research. Managers need to be educated about these differences as well as the research methods that can be used to uncover them. Ultimately, global business success depends on a foundation of valid foreign market information.

References and selected bibliography

Axtell, R. E. 1993. *Do's and taboos around the world*. 3rd ed. New York: Wiley.

Bartlett, C. A., and S. Ghoshal. 1989. *Managing across borders: The transnational solution*. Boston: Harvard Business School Press.

Byfield, S., and L. Caller. 1997. Horses for courses: Stewarding brands across borders in times of rapid change. *Journal of the Market Research Society* 39/4: 589–601.

Ceteora, P. R., and J. L. Graham. 1999. *International Marketing*. 10th ed. New York: Irwin/McGraw-Hill.

Childs, R. 1996. Buying international research. *Journal of the Market Research Society* 38/1: 63–66.

Craig, C. S., and S. P. Douglas. 2000. *International Marketing Research*. 2nd ed. New York: Wiley.

Crampton, M. F. 1996. Where does your ad work? *Journal of the Market Research Society* 38/1: 35–53.

Frevert, B. 2000. Is global research different? *Marketing Research* 12/1: 49–51.

Goodwin, T. 1999. Measuring the effectiveness of online marketing. *Journal of the Market Research Society* 41/4: 403–406.

Iyer, R. 1997. A look at the Indian market research industry. *Quirk's Marketing Research Review* (November): 22–26.

Jeffries-Fox, B. C. 1995. Dance with me: US firms need good international partners to keep in step. *Marketing Research* 7/2: 15–18.

Keillor, B., D. Owens, and C. Pettijohn. 2001. A cross-cultural/cross-national study of influencing factors and socially desirable response biases. *International Journal of Market Research* 43/1: 63–84.

Kent, R., and M. Lee. 1999. Using the Internet for market research: A study of private trading on the Internet. *Journal of the Market Research Society* 41/4: 377–385.

Lee, B., and A. Wong. 1996. An introduction to marketing research in China. *Quirk's Marketing Research Review* (November): 18–19, 37–38.

Leonidou, L. C., and N. Rossides. 1995. Marketing research in the Gulf States: A practical appraisal. *Journal of the Marketing Research Society* 37/4: 455–467.

Lewis, S., and M. Hathaway. 1998. International focus groups: Embrace the unpredictable. *Quirk's Marketing Research Review* (November): 36–41.

McIntosh, A. R., and R. J. Davies. 1996. The sampling of nondomestic populations. *Journal of the Market Research Society* 38/4: 431–446.

McKie, A. 1996. International research in a relative world. *Journal of the Market Research Society* 38/1: 7–12.

Meier, G. M. 1998. *The international environment of business*. New York: Oxford University Press.

Moseley, D. 1996. Information needs for market entry. *Journal of the Market Research Society* 38/1: 13–18.

Mytton, G. 1996. Research in new fields. *Journal of the Market Research Society* 38/1: 19–33.

Pawle, J. 1999. Mining the international consumer. *Journal of the Market Research Society* 41/1: 19–32.

Prahalad, C. K., and K. Lieberthal. 1998. The end of corporate imperialism. *Harvard Business Review* 76/4 (July–August): 69–79.

Ricks, D. A. 1983. *Big business blunders: Mistakes in multinational marketing.* Homewood, IL: Dow Jones Irwin.

Robinson, C. 1996. Asian culture: The marketing consequences. *Journal of the Market Research Society* 38/1: 55–62.

Root, F. R. 1994. *Entry strategies for international markets.* Rev. ed. New York: Lexington.

Rydholm, J. 1996. Leaping the barriers of time and distance. *Quirk's Marketing Research Review* (November): 10–11, 42–45.

Soruco, G. R., and T. P. Meyer. 1993. The mobile Hispanic market: New challenges in the 90s. *Marketing Research* 5/1: 6–11.

Valentine, C. F. 1988. *The Arthur Young international business guide.* New York: Wiley.

Wilsden, M. 1996. Getting it done properly: The role of the coordinator in multicountry research. *Journal of the Market Research Society* 38/1: 67–71.

Zikmund, W. 2000. *Exploring marketing research.* 6th ed. Orlando, FL: Dryden Press.

Extending the Reach of E-Business

Technology continues to change the corporate playing field.

By S. Tamer Cavusgil

EXECUTIVE BRIEFING
As a driver of globalization, e-business creates three fundamental implications for the internationally active firm. First, it beats geography and time zones. Second, it serves as a great equalizer between firms. Third, it causes discontinuous change, but on a periodic, recurring basis. Here we'll examine the competitive advantages that e-business applications create for individual firms, the underlying technologies, and the implications for business strategy.

"**We stand at the edge of a new era**, one in which technology will become even more deeply woven into the fabric of business, society, and our daily lives. As we enter this era, a new technology landscape is emerging. A landscape that is defined by truly simple personal devices that run useful Web services—e-services—across an Internet infrastructure that's always on, always available. We're heading toward a world where anything will be connected by way of a new generation of technology linked to the Net."—Carly Fiorina, chairman, president, and CEO, Hewlett Packard.

Information technology and the Internet have transformed business, and this transformation isn't just about conducting business online. It's about integrating e-business capabilities into every aspect of value creation, such as procurement and customer relationship management. Right now, myopically focused e-commerce has transformed into e-business. This is no longer about exchange of services or information over the Web—it's about total transformation of business services and product offerings. Today repeated success stories about purchasing books, toys, or movies online are giving way to more transformational examples such as virtual supply chain execution or online customer care programs.

The underlying technologies of the Internet are many and diverse. The dynamic nature of informational technology also suggests that additional enablers will surface in the future. E-business drives globalization in several ways. First, it beats geography and time zones. Physical distance disappears or is circumvented by electronic connectivity, and the scope of the marketplace is broadened beyond traditional spheres. Companies can now carry on business around the world all day every day. As such, virtual connectivity empowers the multinational firm to build a truly integrated worldwide network.

Second, e-business is a great equalizer! It creates a level playing field between small and large firms, experienced and inexperienced, and domestic and foreign. No longer does it take years and deep pockets to engage in cross-border business. Indeed, young, entrepreneurial firms, the so-called born global companies, discovered this long ago. Driven by a combination of products universally in demand and senior management commitment, these export-intensive companies go international soon after inception. Their entry and expansion abroad are facilitated by the Internet and information technology. Born global firms are among the most intensive users of the Web for customer service, promotion, and procurement.

Third, e-business causes discontinuous change, but on a periodic, recurring basis. This is because the Internet is driven by software. While the infrastructure of the Internet is fiber optics, its brains are software. As a new generation of software becomes available every two years or so, new applications surface for users.

The Many Faces of E-Business

For the individual enterprise, e-business offers at least three types of competitive advantage:

Productivity and cost reduction. E-business helps the enterprise perform value-chain activities more efficiently by helping companies engage in end-to-end integration of entire sales, production, and delivery processes electronically, across borders and time zones. For example, e-commerce in the global marketplace is widespread, with numerous online banking, stock trading, exchanges, and numerous B2B and B2C applications.

Speed. Information and knowledge can move freely within the global company and its customers, suppliers, and other constituents. Managers can implement decisions instantaneously. Real-time market signaling means that responses to market changes can be instant. E-business can also reduce time to market and other cycle times for responding to ongoing or anticipated business needs.

New opportunities and value creation. Web-enabled businesses can thrive because of flexibility, focus, and entrepreneurial initiatives brought to global operations. A prime benefit for global organizations is the ability to implement strategy on a worldwide scale, organize globally, and integrate and rationalize operations worldwide. Virtual interconnectedness cross-fertilizes ideas and best practices, standardizes business processes, and eliminates redundancies in the global network of companies.

Global Applications

For global companies, e-business applications abound. A primer would include the following areas:

Global supply chain management (SCM). Global companies use the Internet as an enabler to manage their supply chains. Cisco, for example, initiated a global supply chain network, called Hub, to conduct machine-to-machine links with its partners. The main drivers of global SCM for Cisco are receiving information from its partners on inventory availability, product specifications, purchase orders, shortages and excess stock; developing advanced planning and constraint-based optimization with its partners that will lead to dynamically re-planning; and addressing design collaboration and life-cycle management issues.

E-procurement. E-procurement systems offer cost savings through efficient transaction processing, reduction of cycle times, and leveraging supplier relations. Companies such as Texas Instruments, Owens Corning, General Electric, or Bristol-Myers Squibb are only some of the firms that enjoy the benefits of e-procurement applications. Texas Instruments processes more than 100,000 purchase orders annually for MRO and related items online. This showed its effect not only by 80% cost reduction per purchase order, but also redeployment of staff time for managing strategic supplier relations. Savings through efficiency gains are running at a level of more than $12 million annually. Purchases through reverse auctions of Owens Corning exceeded $250 million in the past year. Savings have averaged 10%, and the company plans to increase its use of auctions by 60% next year. With the e-procurement initiative, General Electric plans to save at least $500 million in purchase prices and to reduce transaction costs by up to 90%. Bristol-Myers Squibb has tripled its cost savings, which is $300 million more

than its annual U.S. expenditure of $3 billion, since implementing an e-procurement system.

E-fulfillment. Customers expect on-time delivery, along with product information, real-time order confirmation, and 24-hour-a-day customer service. Meeting these demands requires an effective e-fulfillment process, including picking, packing, labeling, and shipping. The integration with CRM applications is crucial for providing flexibility and scalability. Benefits are not only reduced warehousing and distribution expenses, but customer satisfaction as well.

> # While companies like Coca-Cola, IBM, Caterpillar, and Singer took decades to build identity around the world, today's aspiring multinational can do it much faster thanks to the transparency of information and transnational media.

Web-enabled design and product development. These applications allow teams that are scattered around the world to seamlessly create, access, and manage the product development and design process. At critical stages of a project, traditional revise and review cycles can slow the progress, whereas with Web-enabled systems participants can evaluate models in real time. Because the automotive industry uses CAD (computer aided design) models heavily and incurs more than 70% of manufacturing costs in the design stage, it became the main supporter of this initiative. For example, Ford introduced the first car—the European Mondeo—to be 100% produced within an environment that gives suppliers and engineers access to the information over the Internet. The main benefits of Web-enabled design and product development systems are improved quality that stems from collaborative engineering and reduced product design costs.

Global branding. While companies like Coca-Cola, IBM, Caterpillar, and Singer took decades to build identity around the world, today's aspiring multinational can do it much faster thanks to the transparency of information and transnational media. Thus, Sony's Play Station 2 can be an instant hit around the world. Worldwide acceptance of new products is facilitated by social and technological leapfrogging (i.e., developing country buyers' desire for the most recent and/or fashionable products, services, or know-how). One illustration is the third world's rapid adoption of cellular phones.

Customer service. Because loyalty extends only as far as the next link, customer relationship management aims to keep track of customers, learning about each one's likes and dislikes from various sources like transaction records, call-center logs, Web site clicks, and search-engine queries. Effective CRM links data received from the different channels that companies offer to their customers. CRM applications are designed primarily to reach real-time information; to forecast effectively based on individual product, market sector, or customer groups; and to identify trends to help create targeted marketing campaigns.

For the past two years, Chase Manhattan has been putting together an Internet-based CRM system for its retail banking division's marketing, sales, and service departments. It groups and analyzes the data pulled from the bank's tellers, ATM machines, Web site, and telephone service reps to mine information on its 3.5 million customers in a 720-branch network. With this, Chase can segment customers by current and potential value. Chase reports that the CRM program is directly responsible for a 4% increase in the retention of high-net-worth customers from January to June 2000 and a large increase in the amount of assets the bank manages for its most affluent customers.

Global account management. Increasingly, suppliers have to cater to their global customers' needs in the same way regardless of where in the world that customer is located. With more transparent markets, global customers are now demanding uniform and consistent prices, quality, and customer service. As a result, companies such as Hewlett-Packard, General Electric, and numerous suppliers of Wal-Mart have set up global account management systems to cater to such demands. Private portals have helped implement such systems.

Global centers of excellence. Multinational firms routinely set up best-practice centers in parts of their worldwide organization to help create, nurture, and share knowledge with the rest of the corporate network. Such centers of excellence actually facilitate cross-fertilization of ideas. Leading-edge practices are refined in one location and then transferred throughout the global network of companies. As an example, Philips locates key operations in "highest voltage" markets—ones that seem to possess the most advanced knowledge in a particular activity.

Knowledge portals for knowledge management, global knowledge repositories, and horizontal communities. In 1996 Booz-Allen implemented a knowledge portal, Knowledge On–Line (KOL), for its consultants. It gives 3,500 Booz-Allen consultants access to the company's experts in all fields, including training, marketing documents, best practices, and case studies. In fact, 83% of staff members in the company's worldwide commercial business sector access KOL on a monthly basis. It provides a knowledge repository and expert-skills database along with a client information system, a time-reporting database, and an automated digital library with links to outside private and public databases. The cost of any knowledge is not in technology, but in the content. According to Booz-Allen, only the cost of content management, not creation, was three times higher than last year's budget for technical upgrades and support for KOL.

Global talent pools. Multinational organizations such as Citibank manage the difficult task of identifying and recruiting the best talent within the worldwide organization by developing a computerized database of managers. In this way, it provides appropriate talent with worldwide professional development opportunities.

E-learning and e-training. The main advantages of online education are its flexibility and round-the-clock access to any courses. This makes it especially attractive to multinational companies for commercial or business training. Schools and universities are the other two main markets for online education. Although e-learning is a promising market, it still faces language- and bandwidth-related obstacles.

E-Business Enablers

A number of underlying technologies enable e-business applications:

Electronic data interchange (EDI). Developed before the Internet era, EDI is a collection of data transmission standards developed to enable the transfer of transaction data between different companies by electronic means. It's a point-to-point solution that's especially challenging for small companies because it requires significant resource commitment both in terms of training and IT.

EDI is now being somewhat displaced by newer and more flexible Internet-based standards, such as XML, which is expected to ease the task of exchanging data with trading partners and improve the speed, cost, and flexibility of the business applications. However, because many large companies have invested heavily in old legacy systems, EDI won't disappear. Therefore, the current focus is on getting these legacy systems to work with newer standards. IBM, for example, claims to have reduced paper invoices by 90% after linking up with more than 12,000 smaller suppliers using Web-based EDI.

Enterprise resource planning (ERP). ERP is a software–based business management system that integrates all facets of the business (functions and processes), including planning, manufacturing, sales and marketing, and supply chain. ERP implementations require major resource commitment as well as careful planning and immaculate execution. Most "canned" systems lead to lost flexibility and efficiency when the goal of an ERP system is just the opposite. SAP, PeopleSoft, Oracle, J.D. Edwards, and Baan are some of the major industry players.

Customer relationship management (CRM). CRM is also a software-based business management system that collects and interprets customer-based data from internal (marketing, sales, customer support) and external (market research, competitive intelligence) sources. It allows for better customer service by giving every employee the complete history of a customer's needs, problems, and purchases and targets potential sales by identifying the

Obstacles
Ahead

As e-business applications and technologies expand, a few obstacles stand in the way of implementation. Companies might run into the following problems as they try to implement an e-business strategy:

- Variations in infrastructure across countries
- System compatibility issues (e.g., legacy systems)
- Language
- Common standards (e.g., currency, measurement)
- Cultural barriers (e.g., high-vs. low-context cultures)
- Individual barriers (e.g., propensity to share knowledge varies across individuals and national cultures)
- Organizational barriers (e.g., centralized management, control issues)
- Legal barriers (e.g., unique rules and regulations)

most lucrative customers and designing products for them. The primary goal is to develop a process for identifying, targeting, and responding to the needs of the most profitable customers.

CRM and ERP are in a sense complementary. While ERP manages the functions and processes within the firm (back-office solutions), CRM manages the firm's relationship with the customer (front-office solutions). Major industry players are Siebel, Oracle, Clarify, Vantive, and SalesLogix.

Mercedes-Benz successfully implemented CRM across its European divisions. The main driver was to understand the customers and offer them an individualized experience of consistent quality and to shift from mass marketing to one-to-one marketing. Mercedes-Benz now has a database of 10 million customers across Europe and has improved customer retention and loyalty through improved customer care and insight. Sales effectiveness and efficiency also improved. Loyalty rates across Mercedes–Benz's markets in Europe are expected to rise as a result.

Groupware. Groupware applications are technological solutions designed to facilitate the work of groups or teams. Typically groupware aims to achieve three functions: communication (e-mail, chat, bulletin boards); collaboration (video conferencing, white boards, file databases); and coordination (project management, scheduling, workflow systems). It usually features a combination of synchronous and asynchronous tools.

Today, Web-based groupware applications are becoming more common. They allow collaborative research for teams irrespective of their locations, storage and retaining of information, efficient project management, and faster new product and services development through sharing knowledge. Lotus (Notes), Novell (Groupwise), and Microsoft (Exchange and Netmeeting) are the main industry players.

DuPont chose Lotus Notes as its groupware solution in order to integrate the tools that allow the company to communicate, collaborate, and coordinate along the company value chains. Although the project is not yet complete, DuPont has already begun to reap the benefits. For example, the time required to make changes in operating procedures has been reduced from weeks to days, even to hours. Similarly, a request for price changes can be approved in hours compared to weeks in traditional systems. This increases DuPont's flexibility to react to market changes. Likewise, DuPont's virtual teams, often operating across the world, have cut their decision cycle time down dramatically—in one case by 50%. Another important result of faster decision making was the reduced cycle time for introducing new products to the market.

Intranet. Intranets are Web-based, firewall-protected networks that connect all employees of the firm. They use existing Internet technologies to create company-specific information and communication portals. Intranets allow firm-to-employee as well as employee-to-employee communication. Intranets typically feature newsletters, HR information, calendars, product information, training modules, company forms, and numerous company-specific applications and utilities. They usually incorporate complete or partial groupware and ERP systems.

A correctly built intranet can automatically become a key component of the firm's knowledge management process. For example, KPMG consulting uses its intranet extensively for its knowledge management strategy. According to Peter Chivers, U.K. director of knowledge management at KPMG, "…there are over 100 content managers responsible for developing and maintaining intranet presence. The aim is to publish information, which users will act on. This creates a truly interactive intranet rather than simply an electronic noticeboard of information."

In order to improve the capabilities of its intranet, KPMG provided immediate access to *Financial Times (FT) Discovery,* the online news and information service of FT. This service provides critical business intelligence from more than 4,000 information sources. By providing access to a wide range of information, KPMG utilizes its intranet as a strategic tool.

Extranet. An extranet is a private network that uses the Internet protocols and public telecommunication system to securely share part of a business's information or operations with suppliers, vendors, partners, customers, or other businesses. An extranet can be viewed as part of a company's intranet that's extended to users outside the company. Extranets can be used to exchange large volumes of data using EDI, share product catalogs exclusively with wholesalers or those "in the trade," collaborate with other companies on joint development efforts, jointly develop and use training programs with other companies, and provide or access applications between companies.

Extranets play an especially important role in the supply chain activities, allowing firms to increase the efficiency and responsiveness of their complete supply chain. For example, Harley-Davidson developed an extranet, called h-dnet.com, to improve its relationships with the dealers. Dealers can make warranty claims, check recall status, and submit financial statements through h-dnet. Previously all of these transactions were available electronically only for the dealers who had client/server connection with Harley-Davidson headquarters. Now, with a Web browser, any dealer can access the necessary information.

Boeing provides another good example of how different parties on the supply chain interact through the Web. Boeing's extranet is used by 1,000 other companies, and its e-commerce site is used by 400 airline customers. Suppliers can use the extranet to coordinate shipment of materials to Boeing. Similarly, customers such as the U.S. Department of Defense can view information on the status of all the work Boeing is doing for that department.

E-commerce. For some, e-commerce is nothing more than financial transactions that use information technology. For others, e-commerce encompasses a full sales cycle—including marketing, selling, and post-sale service. However, e-commerce can typically be defined as the execution of any kind of business transaction among parties using Internet technologies (including payment systems, order processing and tracking systems, fulfillment systems, customer support applications, and EDI).

E-business continues to have a profound effect on how the modem business carries out its value–adding activities. With each transaction, e-business is changing the terms of market competition and corporate strategy.

About the Author

S. Tamer Cavusgil holds the John W. Byington Endowed Chair in global marketing at the Eli Broad Graduate School of Management, Michigan State University. He may be reached at cavusgil@msu.edu.

Continental SPENDTHRIFTS

Influential Euroteen demo has U.S. marketers' attention

By LISA BERTAGNOLI
Contributing Editor

The spending power of American teens and 'tweens is well-known, but across the pond, the 8- to 14-year-old crowd is becoming a formidable European consumer force. Furthermore, European teens wear American fashions, eat at American fast-food restaurants, listen to a lot of American music and are concerned about what their peers think.

But if this younger generation is more American than their parents or grandparents, the marketing channels most effective in reaching them are different, experts say.

European teens resent being thought of as Americans with an accent, but more than that, they harbor national loyalties that U.S. marketers may find baffling. They tend to be more tech-savvy, but they want to use that media channel in ways that differ from their American counterparts. Promotions, on the other hand, are always popular.

"Marketers have operated under the notion that young people are either North American or at least share in the habits and mindsets of their North American counterparts," says Marian Salzman, global director of strategic planning for Euro RSCG

Worldwide, a New York-based global advertising agency. In truth, "American teens aren't the only marketing game in town."

The Euroteen and 'tween market has money to spend. A survey of Germans ages 16 to 18 by Yomag.net, an online magazine for European teens, found that 60% had a job and 92% received an allowance, with a significant number receiving both. Another Yomag.net survey of teens from other European countries showed that they received a monthly allowance of about E36.74 (one euro having roughly the same value as a dollar), an amount with which they said they were satisfied.

That figure doesn't compare with the $22.68 weekly average that U.S teens receive, according to YM magazine in New York. In the United States, kids that age spend about $155 billion a year and influence another $300 billion in spending by their parents, according to various market reports. But the U.S. market may be slowing a bit: Various research reports show spending among teens rose only 1.3% in 2000 over the year earlier, compared with an 8.5% increase from 1998 to 1999.

Meanwhile, by way of example, in the United Kingdom, the value of the teen and 'tween market was about L436 million in 1998 (about $728 million using current exchange

rates)—a 28% increase over 1997. For that reason, marketers of teen-friendly products are more eager than ever to find an international outlet for their goods.

"The growing purchasing power of teens around the world, and European teens in particular, is sparking tremendous excitement among marketers," Salzman says.

Says Jonathan Patterson, a spokesman for Burger King in Europe, "The teen market is a growing and active one, and we actively promote to them," although he declined to be specific about how much business his company gets from the demographic.

The key consideration in marketing to European teens is the differences in national attitudes that affect how marketing messages are received in different countries. In just one example, while the United Kingdom encourages teens to "Just say no," the Netherlands has decriminalized marijuana and advocates teaching children about drugs at an early age, Salzman says.

"When it comes to European teens, it's virtually impossible to standardize findings across borders," she says. "Generalizations (are) highly superficial at best and grossly inaccurate at worst."

European boys and girls call the Internet 'too American.'

To understand how those differences could affect a marketing plan, consider that European teens consume much of the same media as their American counterparts, with television and the Internet topping the list of favorites, according to a survey done last year by Young & Rubicam's Intelligence Factory, a research arm of the New York-based advertising agency. But in the same survey, 67.5% of European boys and 47.1% of European girls call the Internet "too American." Just over a quarter of surveyed teens said they'd rather buy a local product over the Internet than an American one.

Promotions and giveaways, marketers note, are as effective in Europe as in North America.

"'Gimmes' for kids work the world over, and while the exact nature of the promotions vary—and must vary, to be locally relevant—a Dutch or Belgian or Spanish or Italian child wants a gift with (his) purchase the same way," Salzman says.

While tweaking the promotion by country is a challenge, the good news is that the gifts typically needn't be as elaborate as has become standard in the U.S. market.

"At McDonald's, for example, the prize may be a word puzzle on the menu tray, or a smallish stuffed animal or something, not of the magnitude we associate with a Happy Meal here," Salzman says.

In a promotion that began Aug. 17., Burger King's U.K. outlets have been running a music-based promotion that offers teens four CD singles by four popular acts with the purchase of a kid's meal, Patterson says. The promotion was a tie-in with Popworld.com, a popular music Web site.

"The challenge for brands, whether they are American or European, is to communicate brand attributes in a manner that's in tune with the (cultural) language of European teens," Burger King's Patterson says. Sometimes, the same tactics used in the United States work, but other times, "a market-by-market approach is beneficial," he says.

Some generalizations are possible. Wireless marketing is much more advanced throughout Western Europe, and many U.S. marketers are eyeing how the technology is used there for ideas on how to implement their wireless marketing plans at home. In fact, 65% of the 10- to 19-year-old market in the United Kingdom will have mobile phones by the end of this year; in the United States, that figure is less than 20%, according to AirMedia, a New York-based wireless communications company.

In Europe, however, the kids are more likely to use those phones for games and text services, such as instant messaging and short-message services. Furthermore, the gender difference in the United States, with more boys than girls using mobile technology, doesn't exist abroad, Salzman says. Also, fun mobile technology features, such as icons and ring tones that personalize their phones, are key to European teens.

"(Ring tones) give the phone personality," says Mark Bregman, CEO of AirMedia, noting that teens use team songs from their favorite soccer club or popular tunes to personalize their phones. Ring tones aren't yet as popular stateside, he says.

AirMedia plans to exploit this fondness for fun overseas by partnering with Fox Kids Europe to distribute ring tones and icons tied to the network's popular shows and characters. Via the mobile phones, Fox will send kids, at their request, information about television shows they're interested in. Kids will also be invited to visit Fox's U.K. Web site to participate in interactive games they learn about via text messages from Fox.

For Fox, this "closes the marketing loop," Bregman says. "Fox not only sends information, but they can find out who responds."

But Maurice Van Sabben, head of online and interactive business development for Fox Kids Europe, a joint venture partly owned by Fox Broadcasting Co., also notes that Fox broadcasts to 54 countries in 17 languages and operates 14 localized Web sites.

"Keep it local," he says. "Make it relevant to the kids and 'tweens in their respective countries."

From *Marketing News*, October 22, 2001, pp. 1, 15. © 2001 by the American Marketing Association. Reprinted by permission.

The Lure of Global Branding

Brand builders everywhere think they want global brands.
But global brand leadership, not global brands, should be the priority.
Successful companies follow four principles to meet that goal.

by David A. Aaker and Erich Joachimsthaler

AS MORE AND MORE companies come to view the entire world as their market, brand builders look with envy upon those that appear to have created global brands—brands whose positioning, advertising strategy, personality, look, and feel are in most respects the same from one country to another. It's easy to understand why. Even though most global brands are not absolutely identical from one country to another—Visa changes its logo in some countries; Heineken means something different in the Netherlands than it does abroad—companies whose brands have become more global reap some clear benefits.

Consolidating all advertising into one agency and developing a global theme can cause problems that outweigh any advantages.

Consider for a moment the economies of scale enjoyed by IBM. It costs IBM much less to create a single global advertising campaign than it would to create separate campaigns for dozens of markets. And because IBM uses only one agency for all its global advertising, it carries a lot of clout with the agency and can get the most talented people working on its behalf. A global brand also benefits from being driven by a single strategy. Visa's unvarying "worldwide acceptance" position, for example, is much easier for the company to manage than dozens of country-specific strategies.

Attracted by such high-profile examples of success, many companies are tempted to try to globalize their own brands. The problem is, that goal is often unrealistic. Consolidating all advertising into one agency and developing a

global advertising theme—often the cornerstone of the effort—can cause problems that outweigh any advantages. And edicts from on high—"Henceforth, use only brand-building programs that can be applied across countries"—can prove ineffective or even destructive. Managers who stampede blindly toward creating a global brand without considering whether such a move fits well with their company or their markets risk falling over a cliff. There are several reasons for that.

First, economies of scale may prove elusive. It is sometimes cheaper and more effective for companies to create ads locally than to import ads and then adapt them for each market. Moreover, cultural differences may make it hard to pull off a global campaign: even the best agency may have trouble executing it well in all countries. Finally, the potential cost savings from "media spillover"—in which, for example, people in France view German television ads—have been exaggerated. Language barriers and cultural differences have made realizing such benefits difficult for most companies.

Second, forming a successful global brand team can prove difficult. Developing a superior brand strategy for one country is challenging enough; creating one that can be applied worldwide can be daunting (assuming one even exists). Teams face several stumbling blocks: they need to gather and understand a great deal of information; they must be extremely creative; and they need to anticipate a host of challenges in execution. Relatively few teams will be able to meet all those challenges.

Third, global brands can't just be imposed on all markets. For examples, a brand's image may not be the same throughout the world. Honda means quality and reliability in the United States, but in Japan, where quality is a given for most cars, Honda represents speed, youth, and energy. And consider market position. In Britain, where Ford is number one, the company positioned its Galaxy minivan as the luxurious "nonvan" in order to appeal not only to soccer moms but also to executives. But in Germany, where Volkswagen rules, Ford had to position the Galaxy as "the clever alternative." Similarly, Cadbury in the United Kingdom and Milka in Germany have preempted the associations that connect milk with chocolate; thus neither company could implement a global positioning strategy.

For all those reasons, taking a more nuanced approach is the better course of action. Developing global brands should not be the priority. Instead, companies should work on creating strong brands in all markets through global brand leadership.

Global brand leadership means using organizational structures, processes, and cultures to allocate brand-building resources globally, to create global synergies, and to develop a global brand strategy that coordinates and leverages country brand strategies. That is, of course, easier said than done. For example, companies tend to give the bulk of their brand-building attention to countries with large sales—at the expense of emerging markets that may represent big opportunities. But some companies have successfully engaged in global brand management. To find out how, we interviewed executives from 35 companies in the United States, Europe, and Japan that have successfully developed strong brands across countries. (About half the executives were from companies that made frequently purchased consumer products; the rest represented durables, high-tech products, and service brands.)

Four common ideas about effective brand leadership emerged from those interviews. Companies must:

- stimulate the sharing of insights and best practices across countries;
- support a common global brand-planning process;
- assign managerial responsibility for brands in order to create cross-country synergies and to fight local bias; and
- execute brilliant brand-building strategies.

Sharing Insights and Best Practices

A companywide communication system is the most basic element of global brand leadership. Managers from country to country need to be able to find out about programs that have worked or failed elsewhere; they also need a way to easily give and receive knowledge about customers—knowledge that will vary from one market to another.

Creating such a system is harder than it sounds. Busy people usually have little motivation to take the time to explain why efforts have been successful or ineffective; furthermore, they'd rather not give out information that may leave them exposed to criticism. Another problem is one that everyone in business faces today: information overload. And a feeling of "it won't work here" often pervades companies that attempt to encourage the sharing of market knowledge.

To overcome those problems, companies must nurture and support a culture in which best practices are freely communicated. In addition, people and procedures must come together to create a rich base of knowledge that is relevant and easy to access. Offering incentives is one way to get people to share what they know. American Management Systems, for example, keeps track of the employees who post insights and best practices and rewards them during annual performance reviews.

Regular meetings can be an effective way of communicating insights and best practices. Frito-Lay, for example, sponsors a "market university" roughly three times a year in which 35 or so marketing directors and general managers from around the world meet in Dallas for a week. The university gets people to think about brand leadership concepts, helps people overcome the mind-set of "I am different—global programs won't work in my market," and creates a group of people around the world who believe in and understand brands and brand strategy. During the week, country managers present case studies on packaging, advertising, and promotions that were tested in one country and then successfully applied in another. The case studies demonstrate that practices can be transferred even when a local marketing team is skeptical.

Formal meetings are useful, but true learning takes place during informal conversations and gatherings. And the personal relationships that people establish during those events are often more important than the information they share. Personal ties lead to meaningful exchanges down the road that can foster brand-building programs.

In addition to staging meetings, companies are increasingly using intranets to communicate insights and best practices. (Sharing such information by e-mail isn't as effective—there is simply too much e-mail clutter. E-mail is useful, however, for conveying breaking news about competitors or new technology.) The key is to have a team create a knowledge bank on an intranet that is valuable and accessible to those who need it. Mobil, for example, uses a set of best-practice networks to do just that. The networks connect people in the company (and sometimes from partner organizations) who are experts on, for example, new product introduction, brand architecture, and retail-site presentation. Each network has a senior management sponsor and a leader who actively solicits postings from the experts. The leader ensures that the information is formatted, organized, and posted on an easy-to-use intranet site.

Field visits are another useful way to learn about best practices. Honda sends teams to "live with best practices" and to learn how they work. In some companies, the CEO travels to different markets in order to energize the country teams and to see best practices in action.

Procter & Gamble uses worldwide strategic-planning groups of three to 20 people for each category to encourage and support global strategies. The teams have several tasks. They mine local knowledge about markets and disseminate that information globally. They gather data about effective country-specific marketing efforts and encourage testing elsewhere. They create global manufacturing sourcing strategies. And they develop policies that dictate which aspects of the brand strategy must be followed everywhere and which ones are up to country management.

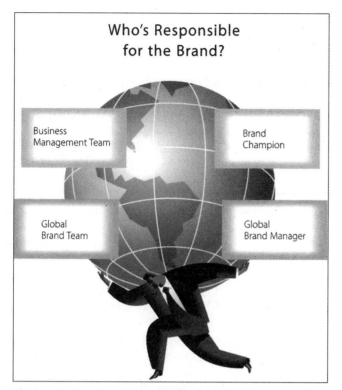

Who's Responsible for the Brand?

Business Management Team

Brand Champion

Global Brand Team

Global Brand Manager

Deciding who has ultimate responsibility for global brands is the first step toward going global and ensuring buy-in among country teams. To fight local bias and exploit cross-country synergies, a company must assign managerial responsibility for its brands. Depending on the company's makeup, responsibility for global brand leadership can follow one of four possible configurations: business management team, brand champion, global brand manager, and global brand team. The first two are led by senior executives; the latter two by middle managers.

Another way that companies can communicate information about their brands is by sharing research. Ford operates very differently from country to country in Europe, but its businesses share research methods and findings. Ford UK, for example, which is very skilled at doing direct mail and research on segmentation, makes its technology and research methods available to other countries. That's especially important for businesses in small markets that are short on budget and staff.

Supporting Global Brand Planning

Two years ago, the newly appointed global brand manager of a prominent packaged-goods marketer organized a brand strategy review. He found that all the country brand managers used their own vocabularies and strategy templates and had their own strategies. The resulting mess had undoubtedly contributed to inferior marketing and weakened brands. Another packaged-goods company tried to avoid that problem by developing a global planning system. Brand managers weren't given incentives or trained

properly to use the system, however, and the result was inconsistent, half-hearted efforts at planning.

Companies that practice global brand management use a planning process that is consistent across markets and products—a brand presentation looks and sounds the same whether it's delivered in Singapore, Spain, or Sweden, and whether it's for PCs or printers. It shares the same well-defined vocabulary, strategic analysis inputs (such as competitor positions and strategies), brand strategy model, and outputs (such as brand-building programs).

There is no one accepted process model, but all models have two starting points: it must be clear which person or group is responsible for the brand and the brand strategy, and a process template must exist. The completed template should specify such aspects of a strategy as the target segment, the brand identity or vision, brand equity goals and measures, and brand-building programs that will be used within and outside the company. Although various process models can work, observations of effective programs suggest five guidelines.

First, the process should include an analysis of customers, competitors, and the brand. Analysis of customers must go beyond quantitative market research data; managers need to understand the brand associations that resonate with people. Analysis of competitors is necessary to differentiate the brand and to ensure that its communication program—which may include sponsorship, promotion, and advertising—doesn't simply copy what other companies are doing. And an audit of the brand itself involves an examination of its heritage, image, strengths, and problems, as well as the company's vision for it. The brand needs to reflect that vision to avoid making empty promises.

Second, the process should avoid a fixation on product attributes. A narrow focus on attributes leads to short-lived, easily copied advantages and to shallow customer relationships. Most strong brands go beyond functional benefits; despite what customers might say, a brand can also deliver emotional benefits and help people express themselves. A litmus test of whether a company really understands its brands is whether it incorporates the following elements into the brand strategy: brand personality (how the brand would be described if it were a person), user imagery (how the brand's typical user is perceived), intangibles that are associated with the company (its perceived innovativeness or reputation for quality, for example), and symbols associated with the brand, such as Virgin's Branson, the Coke bottle, or the Harley eagle. A simple three-word phrase or a brief list of product attributes cannot adequately represent a strong brand.

Third, the process must include programs to communicate the brand's identity (what the brand should stand for) to employees and company partners. Without clarity and enthusiasm internally about the associations the brand aspires to develop, brand building has no chance. A brand manual often plays a key role. Unilever has a detailed manual on its most global brand, Lipton Tea, that puts the answer to any question about its brand identity (What does the brand stand for? What are the timeless elements of the brand? What brand-building programs are off target?) at the fingertips of all employees. Other companies use workshops (Nestlé), newsletters (Hewlett-Packard), books (Volvo), and videos (the Limited) to communicate brand identity. To engage people in this process, Mobil asked employees to nominate recent programs or actions that best reflected the core elements of the Mobil brand—leadership, partnership, and trust. The employees with the best nominations were honored guests at a car race sponsored by the company.

Fourth, the process must include brand equity measurement and goals. Without measurement, brand building is often just talk; yet surprisingly few companies have systems that track brand equity. Pepsi is an exception. In the mid-1990s, Pepsi introduced a system based on what it calls a "marketplace P&L." The P&L measures brand equity by tracking the results of blind taste tests, the extent of a product's distribution, and the results of customer opinion surveys about the brand. In the beginning, country managers were strongly encouraged—but not required—to use the system. But the value of the marketplace P&L soon become clear, as country managers compared results at meetings and used the shared information to improve their brand-building efforts. In 1998, CEO Roger Enrico made the system mandatory—a dramatic indication of its value given Pepsi's decentralized culture and the home office's general reluctance to impose companywide rules.

Finally, the process must include a mechanism that ties global brand strategies to country brand strategies. Sony and Mobil, among others, use a top-down approach. They begin with a global brand strategy; country strategies follow from it. A country brand strategy might augment the global strategy by adding elements to modify the brand's identity. For example, if the manager of a Mobil fuel brand in Brazil wants to emphasize that the brand gives an honest gallon (because other brands of fuel in Brazil are not considered reliable in their measurements), he would add "honest measures" to the country brand identity. For example, although the term "leadership" may mean "technology leadership" in most countries, the strategist may change it to mean "market leadership" in his or her market. In the top-down approach, the country brand team has the burden of justifying any departures from the global brand strategy.

In the bottom-up approach, the global brand strategy is built from the country brand strategies. Country strategies are grouped by similarities. A grouping might, for example, be made on the basis of market maturity (underdeveloped, emerging, or developed) or competitive context (whether the brand is a leader or a challenger). While the brand strategy for these groupings will differ, a global brand strategy should also be able to identify common elements. Over time, the number of distinct strategies will usually fall as experiences and best practices are shared. As the number shrinks, the company can capture synergies. Mercedes, for example, uses one advertising agency to create a menu of five campaigns. Brand managers in different countries can then pick the most suitable campaign for their market.

Assigning Responsibility

Local managers often believe that their situation is unique—and therefore, that insights and best practices from other countries can't be applied to their markets. Their belief is based in part on justifiable confidence in their knowledge of the country, the competitive milieu, and the consumers. Any suggestion that such confidence is misplaced can feel threatening. Moreover, people are comfortable with strategies that have already proven effective. The local brand managers may fear that they will be coerced or enticed into following a strategy that doesn't measure up to their current efforts.

Most companies today have a decentralized culture and structure. They find it difficult, therefore, to persuade country teams to quickly and voluntarily accept and implement a global best practice. To ensure that local teams overcome such reluctance, an individual or group must be in charge of the global brand. Our research suggests that responsibility for global brand leadership can follow four possible configurations: business management team, brand champion, global brand manager, and global brand team. The first two are led by senior executives; the latter two by middle managers.

Business Management Team. This approach is most suitable when the company's top managers are marketing or branding people who regard brands as the key asset to their business. P&G fits that description. Each of its 11 product categories is run by a global category team. The teams consist of the four managers who have line responsibility for R&D, manufacturing, and marketing for the category within their region. Each team is chaired by an executive vice president who also has a second line job. For example, the head of health and beauty aids in Europe also chairs the hair care global category team. The teams meet five or six times a year.

Because the teams are made up of top-level line executives, there are no organizational barriers to carrying out decisions. At the country level, P&G's brand and advertising managers implement the strategy. Thus local bias cannot get in the way of the company's global brand leadership.

The 11 teams strive to create global brands without weakening brand strength locally. They define the identity and position of brands in their categories throughout the world. They encourage local markets to test and adopt brand-building programs that have been successful elsewhere. And they decide which brands will get new product advances. For example, Elastesse, the chemical compound that helps people eliminate "helmet head," was first added to the company's Pantene product line rather than one of its three sister brands.

Brand Champion. This is a senior executive, possibly the CEO, who serves as the brand's primary advocate and nurturer. The approach is particularly well suited to companies whose top executives have a passion and talent for brand strategy. Companies like Sony, Gap, Beiersdorf (Nivea), and Nestlé meet that description. Nestlé has a brand champion for each of its 12 corporate strategic brands. As is true for the leaders of P&G's business management teams, each brand champion at Nestlé has a second assignment. Thus the vice president for nutrition is the brand champion for Carnation, and the vice president for instant coffee is the brand champion for Taster's Choice (known as Nescafé outside the United States). At Nestlé, brand leadership is not just talk. The additional work that the brand champion takes on has resulted in a change in the company's performance-evaluation and compensation policies.

Most global brand managers have little authority and must create a strategy without the ability to mandate.

A brand champion approves all brand-stretching decisions (to put the Carnation label on a white milk chocolate bar, for example) and monitors the presentation of the brand worldwide. He or she must be familiar with local contexts and managers, identify insights and best practices, and propagate them through sometimes forceful suggestions. In some companies, such as Sony, the brand champion owns the country brand identities and positions and takes responsibility for ensuring that the country teams implement the brand strategy. A brand champion has credibility and respect not only because of organizational power but also because of a depth of experience, knowledge, and insight. A suggestion from a brand champion gets careful consideration.

P&G plans to evolve over the next decade toward a brand champion approach. It believes that it can achieve greater cooperation and create more global brands by concentrating authority and responsibility in the hands of high-level brand champions. At the moment, P&G regards only a handful of its 83 major brands as global.

Global Brand Manager. In many companies, particularly in the high-tech and service industries, top management lacks a branding or even marketing background. The branding expertise rests just below the top line managers. Such companies are often decentralized and have a powerful regional and country line-management system. Effective global brand managers are necessary in these cases to combat local bias and spur unified efforts across countries.

Some local brand managers have sign-off authority for certain marketing programs, but most have little authority. They must attempt to create a global brand strategy without the ability to mandate. There are five keys to success in these situations:

- Companies must have believers at the top; otherwise global brand managers will be preoccupied with con-

vincing the executive suite that brands are worth supporting. If there are no believers, a brand manager can try to create them. The global brand manager for MasterCard did just that by convincing the organization to form a "miniboard" of six board members and nominating one to be its chair. That person became the brand's voice during board meetings.
- A global brand manager needs to either create a planning process or manage an existing one. To make the process effective, all country managers should use the same vocabulary, template, and planning cycle. This is the first step toward fighting local bias.
- A global brand manager should become a key part of the development, management, and operation of an internal brand communication system. By traveling to learn about customers, country managers, problems, and best practices, he or she will be able to maximize the opportunities for cooperation.
- In order to deal with savvy country brand specialists, global brand managers must have global experience, product background, energy, credibility, and people skills. Companies need a system to select, train, mentor, and reward prospects who can fill the role. At Haagen-Dazs, the global brand manager is also the brand manager for the United States, the lead market for its ice cream. The latter position gives the manager credibility because of the resources and knowledge base that come with it.
- Companies can signal the importance of the role through the title they give the manager. At IBM, global brand managers are called brand stewards, a title that reflects the goal of building and protecting brand equity. At Smirnoff, the global brand manager is given the title of president of the Pierre Smirnoff Company, suggesting how much the company values his position.

Global Brand Team. A global brand manager, acting alone, can be perceived as an outsider—just another corporate staff person contributing to overhead, creating forms, and calling meetings. Sometimes adding people to the mix—in the form of a global brand team—can solve this problem. With a team working on the issue, it becomes easier to convince country brand managers of the value of global brand management.

Global brand teams typically consist of brand representatives from different parts of the world, from different stages of brand development, and from different competitive contexts. Functional areas such as advertising, market research, sponsorship, and promotions may also be represented. The keys to success with these teams are similar to those for the global brand manager.

One problem with a global brand team (unless it is lead by a global brand manager) is that no one person ultimately owns the brand globally. Thus no one is responsible for implementing global branding decisions. In addition, team members may be diverted from their task by the pressures of their primary jobs. And the team may lack the authority and focus needed to make sure that their recommendations are actually implemented at the country level. Mobil solves that problem in part by creating "action teams" made up of people from several countries to oversee the implementation.

Some aspects of the brand's management will be firm, but others will be adaptable or discretionary.

Some companies partition the global brand manager or team across business units or segments. For example, Mobil has separate global brand teams for the passenger car lubricant business, the commercial lubricants business, and the fuel business because the brand is fundamentally different in each. A global brand council then coordinates those segments by reconciling the different identities and looking for ways to create brand synergy.

And consider how DuPont handles its Lycra brand. The 35-year-old synthetic is known worldwide for the flexibility and comfort it lends to clothing; its identity is embodied in the global tagline "Nothing moves like Lycra." The problem for Lycra is that is has a variety of applications—it can be used, for example, in swimsuits, in running shorts, and in women's fashions. Each application requires its own brand positioning. DuPont solves the problem by delegating responsibility for each application to managers in a country where that application is strongest. Thus the Brazilian brand manager for Lycra is also the global lead for swimsuit fabric because Brazil is a hotbed for swimsuit design. Similarly, the French brand manager takes the lead for Lycra used in fashion. The idea is to use the expertise that is dispersed throughout the world. The global brand manager for Lycra ensures that those in charge of different applications are together on overall strategy; he or she also pulls together their ideas in order to exploit synergies.

When local management is relatively autonomous, it may be necessary to give the global brand manager or team a significant degree of authority. Doing so can also reduce the chances that the manager or team will get smothered by organizational or competitive pressures; in addition, it can signal the company's commitment to brand building.

The team or manager may have authority over its visual representation and brand graphics, for example. In that case, the group or the individual would have to approve any departures from the specified color, typeface, and layout logo. Or a global brand team may have authority over the look and feel of a product. The IBM ThinkPad is black and rectangular; it has a red tracking ball and a multicolored IBM logo set at 35 degrees in the lower right corner. The global brand team must approve any deviations from that look. In another example, the global brand manager at Smirnoff has sign-off authority on the selection of advertising agencies and themes.

While companies are spelling out the authority of the global brand manager or team, they must also make clear what authority resides with the country team. Some aspects of the brand's management will be firm—the definition of what the brand stands for, say—but others will be adaptable or discretionary, such as the advertising presentation or the use of product promotions. The job of the person or group responsible for the brand is to make sure that everyone knows and follows the guidelines.

Delivering Brilliance

Global brand leadership, especially in these days of media clutter, requires real brilliance in brand-building efforts—simply doing a good job isn't enough. The dilemma is how to balance the need to leverage global strengths with the need to recognize local differences. Our research indicates that those who aspire to brilliant execution should do the following:

First, consider what brand-building paths to follow—advertising, sponsorship, increasing retail presence, promotions. The path you choose may turn out to be more important than the way you follow through with it. Experience shows that if the path starts with advertising, as it usually does, other sometimes more innovative and more effective brand-building approaches get the short end of the stick. Second, put pressure on the agency to have the best and most motivated people working on the brand, even if that means creating some agency-client tension. Third, develop options: the more chances at brilliance, the higher the probability that it will be reached. Fourth, measure the results.

P&G finds exceptional ideas by encouraging the country teams to develop breakthrough brand-building programs. Particularly if a brand is struggling, country brand teams are empowered to find a winning formula on their own. Once a winner is found, the organization tests it in other countries and implements it as fast as possible.

For example, when P&G obtained Pantene Pro-V in 1985, it was a brand with a small but loyal following. The company's efforts to expand the product's following in the United States and France did not increase the product's popularity. In 1990, however, brand strategists struck gold in Taiwan. They found that the image of models with shiny healthy hair resonated with Taiwan's consumers. The tagline for the ads was "Hair so healthy it shines." People recognized that they couldn't look just like the models but inside they said, "I've got to have that hair." Within six months, the brand was the leader in Taiwan. The concept and supporting advertising tested well in other markets and was subsequently rolled out in 70 countries.

Another way to stimulate brilliant brand building is to use more than one advertising agency. It's true that a single agency can coordinate a powerful, unified campaign; using only one agency, however, means putting all your creative eggs in one basket. On the other hand, using multiple agencies can lead to inconsistency and strategic anarchy.

In Europe, Audi gets the best of both approaches by following a middle course. It has five agencies from different countries compete to be the lead agency that will create the brand's campaign. The four agencies that lose out are nonetheless retained to implement the winning campaign in their countries. Because the agencies are still involved with Audi, they are available for another round of creative competition in the future. A variant on this approach would be to use several offices from the same agency. That may not lead to as much variation in creative ideas, but it still provides more options than having just one group within one agency.

Adapting global programs to the local level can often improve the effectiveness of a campaign. Take Smirnoff's "pure thrill" vodka campaign. All of its global advertising shows distorted images becoming clear when viewed through the Smirnoff bottle, but the specific scenes change from one country to another in order to appeal to consumers with different assumptions about what is thrilling. In Rio de Janeiro, the ad shows the city's statue of Christ with a soccer ball, and in Hollywood, the "w" in the hillside sign is created with the legs of two people. The IBM global slogan "Solutions for a Small Planet" became "small world" in Argentina where "planet" lacked the desired conceptual thrust.

And yet managers won't be able to tell how well they're building brands unless they develop a global brand measurement system. The system must go beyond financial measures—useful as they are—and measure brand equity in terms of customer awareness, customer loyalty, the brand's personality, and the brand associations that resonate with the public. When these measures of the brand are available, a company has the basis to create programs that will build a strong brand in all markets and to avoid programs that could destroy the brand.

All multinational companies should actively engage in global brand management. Any company that tries to get by with unconnected and directionless local brand strategies will inevitably find mediocrity as its reward. In such cases, an exceptionally talented manager will, on occasion, create a pocket of success. But that success will be isolated and random—hardly a recipe that will produce strong brands around the world.

David A. Aaker *is the E. T. Grether Professor of Marketing Strategy at the University of California at Berkeley's Haas School of Business and is a partner in Prophet Brand Strategy, a consulting firm based in San Francisco and New York.* **Erich Joachimsthaler** *is a visiting professor at the University of Virginia's Darden Graduate School of Business in Charlottesville and is the chairman of Prophet Brand Strategy.*

The Nation as Brand

Many marketers fail to exploit the national identity of their brands.

By Simon Anholt

Few things in marketing are harder to define than the personality of a brand, and seldom is this task more complex than when the brand is sold in many different markets. What is it, exactly, about the Coke brand that makes consumers around the world prefer to be associated with it than with a dozen nearly identical products in different cans?

A brand is a complex mixture of attributes: Its visible face is its packaging and visual identity, its voice is its advertising…but its actual personality is something that really exists only in the mind of the consumer.

One attribute particularly important to international brands is the influence that the brand's country of origin—or the country that people *believe* it comes from—has on the consumer's perception of the brand. The fact that Coke and Levi's and Nike and Pepsi are known to come from America is a fundamental part of their success, and the reason why their advertising messages have always stressed their sheer Americanness.

In a similar way, car brands are often strongly linked in the consumer's mind to their country of origin—it's hard to think of BMW or Mercedes except in the context of their being German; a Rover or a Jaguar is linked with Britishness (despite the fact that both brands are now under overseas ownership); and Ferrari is a brand that is Italian before it's anything else at all. Provenance is such a powerful element of a brand's equity that it's common for a company to imply a false provenance if it creates better, more natural associations than the true country of origin. For example, Brooklyn, Italy's leading brand of chewing gum, is manufactured near Milan by a company called Perfetti and, in its long history, has never been anywhere near the United States.

In fact, a brand's native country behaves exactly like the parent company of any product: At best, it can act as an umbrella of quality that reassures consumers that they're buying from a trusted source; at worst, an inappropriate or negative image can make it extremely difficult to export anything from that country unless its provenance is disguised.

Just like corporate brands, country brands evoke certain values, qualifications, and emotional triggers in consumers' minds about the likely values of any product that comes from that country. In the United Kingdom, consumers are happy to buy banking services from Sainsbury's—a grocery chain—because there is a healthy and attractive match between the values, qualifications, and emotional triggers they already associate with the Sainsbury's corporate brand, and the attributes that they demand from people who handle their money. Likewise, we're happy to buy outdoor clothing from Australia because the country that produced Crocodile Dundee is surely well qualified to protect us from weather and wild animals, and there's a good emotional match with the perceived Australian qualities of humorous, rough-and-ready, unselfconscious masculinity.

Look around, and there are many powerful parent brands that haven't yet explored the rich potential of unexpected yet compelling brand extensions: Boeing suitcases? Greyhound sunglasses? Swatch skis? NATO computers? It's a game almost as amusing to play as the converse—trying to mismatch parent brands and brand extensions as horrendously as possible: Boeing toilet paper? Greyhound air freshener? Swatch cough syrup? NATO pizza? (This is more than a game—it's an exercise I often use to help companies get their own heads around what their brand is, what it could be, and what it definitely *shouldn't* be.)

In exactly the same way, when you try to match provenance with product, there are some pairings that clearly make brand sense, others that just don't. People might well purchase Indian accountancy software or a stylish Lithuanian raincoat, and although I'm tempted to say that they probably *wouldn't* buy Peruvian modems or Dutch perfume, attitudes can and do change awfully quickly. A decade ago, who would have believed that we'd be happily consuming Japanese beer, Malaysian cars, and Danish mozzarella?

A Nation's New Reputation

These changes in purchasing habits often come about because nations can enhance their own brand values, just as manufacturers can enhance the brand equity of their commercial brands. Japan is perhaps the most striking example of a country that has succeeded in completely altering its value as a provenance brand in a short space of time. Thirty years ago, "Made in Japan" was a decidedly negative concept; most Western consumers based their perception of "brand Japan" on their experience of shoddy products flooding the marketplace. The products were cheap, certainly, but basically worthless. In many respects, the perception of Japan was much as China's is today.

Yet Japan has now become enviably synonymous with advanced technology, manufacturing quality, competitive pricing, even style and status. Japan, indeed, passes the best branding test of all: whether consumers are prepared to pay more money for functionally identical products, simply because of where they come from. In the 1950s and '60s, most Europeans and Americans would opt for Japanese products only because they were significantly *cheaper* than a Western alternative; now, in certain valuable market segments, such as consumer electronics, musical instruments, and motor vehicles, Western consumers will consistently pay *more* for products manufactured by previously unknown brands, purely because they are perceived to be Japanese. And this kind of worldwide consumer preference is of almost incalculable value to the country's economy as a whole; no wonder so many nations are working hard on their branding strategies.

Korea, too, has undergone a similar and even more rapid transformation in its brand image, thanks to the efforts of such corporations as Hyundai, Daewoo, Samsung, and LG, and perhaps the Japanese example unconsciously aided consumers in their acceptance of the brand.

Needless to say, country brands can decline as well as prosper, and the familiar, depressing marketing tenet holds as true for countries as it does for companies: It can take decades of excellent products before consumers start to equate a company with quality, but one single bad product to damage this perception (anyone remember the Yugo?).

Having said this, the most robust brands are invariably the biggest, most complex, and oldest ones, and their overall image tends to suffer relatively little as a result of occasional slip-ups. Consumers appear to need, and want to believe in, the basic validity of powerful brands, and will forgive them their mistakes more readily than they will with newer, simpler, or more superficial brands. And because a country's brand is usually highly complex and highly robust, and built up over centuries, it is relatively hard to alter or damage it except through major political, economic, or social upheaval. Like a supertanker, a country's brand image takes miles to pick up speed, but equally, it takes miles to slow down again, change direction, or stop.

Some countries, of course, are "launch brands," and don't have centuries of history, tradition, and foreign interaction upon which to build their reputations. For a country like Slovenia to enhance its image abroad is a very different matter than for Scotland or China. Slovenia needs to be *launched*—consumers around the world first must be taught where it is, what it makes, what it has to offer, and what it stands for, and this in itself represents a powerful opportunity: the chance to build a modern country brand, untainted by centuries of possibly negative associations.

A country like Scotland, on the other hand, which people around the world feel they already know, has a high profile, ready appeal, robust equities, and powerful associations. But to update or modify these qualities—and reposition Scotland as a country with commercial, economic, and technological relevance in the modern world—is correspondingly harder. In other words, this is a supertanker that has been gathering speed for centuries, so steering it is proportionally slower and harder.

Many other countries could capitalize on the success of their high-profile brands: for example, Finland and Nokia. If Finland intends to make itself into a valuable nation-brand, the country must capitalize quickly on the significance of Nokia's origin. Through a combination of high product quality, speed to market, excellent marketing (including placement in films such as *The Matrix*), and distribution, Nokia has transformed itself from a moderately successful domestic producer of rubber boots into one of the world's most successful high-tech brands. In doing this, it has also managed to create an entirely new set of associations of "brand Finland" in many consumers' minds—no longer just a quaint fairyland perched on the fringe of Europe, this is a country that can *do* technology, can *do* marketing, and can become world-beating.

And there's a good deal of that mysterious, associative consumer logic that makes this shift believable. Who knows—perhaps it's something to do with the fact that cold-climate countries are believed to be precise and efficient, and therefore good locations to design and manufacture high-tech products. If other Finnish companies—and Finland itself—don't move quickly to build on and leverage this climate of global consumer acceptance, they are missing a great opportunity. Sadly, Nokia itself seems at pains to diminish its own origins in the way it markets its products, perhaps in an effort to appear "global," which means that this valuable pro-Finnish opportunity may be going to waste.

The Upside of Stereotypes

When you look in detail at the issue of provenance, it becomes clear why certain countries behave like brands. Just like commercial brands, "country brands" are well understood by consumers around the world, have long-established identities, and can work just as effectively as an indicator of product quality, a definer of image and target market, as the manufacturer's name on the package.

I have already mentioned Coke, Levi's, Nike, and Pepsi, and the importance of their American origins to their brand values, and there's little doubt that the United States is the world's most powerful country brand. This may well be connected with the fact that Brand USA has the world's best advertising agency, Hollywood, which has been busily pumping out two-hour commercials for Brand USA for nearly a century, and which consumers around the world have enthusiastically paid to watch.

Brand USA also has a dynamic sales-promotion agency called NASA, which periodically sends a rocket into space (primarily, it often seems, to demonstrate the superiority of American technology). American brands can simply hitch themselves to this powerful national brand. . ., and a cultural and commercial trail is instantly blazed for them around the world.

Only a few other countries have clear, consistent, and universally understood brand images, and most of them are European: for example, England (heritage and class), France (quality living and chic), Italy (style and sexiness), Germany (quality and reliability), Switzerland (methodical precision and trustworthiness), Sweden (cleanliness and efficiency), Japan (miniaturization and advanced functionality).

As might be expected, all of these countries produce successful international brands, which are in turn strongly associated with the brand qualities of their provenance. In fact, it's hard to find any international brands that *don't* come from strongly branded countries: Brand-neutral countries such as Belgium, Portugal, Austria, Chile, or Canada have produced remarkably few international market leaders.

There are, however, several strongly branded countries that produce no international brands of their own. Brazil is a fine example of this phenomenon, which is surprising because the brand personality of Brazil is a strong and highly consistent one. No matter who you ask, no matter where, the same list of associations come out—samba, football, carnival, music, dancing, happiness, ecology, sex, beaches, and adventure—a list that could form the brand print of almost any successful youth product on the market today.

Of course, the average Brazilian may find these clichés depressing and even insulting, but they are undeniably an excellent platform on which to build a believable global brand. One of the more important tasks of advertising and marketing is to weave these commonplaces of provenance into something more creative, more substantial, more fair, more true.

The fact that there may be negative associations—pollution, overpopulation, poverty, drugs, crime—within Brazil's brand print isn't necessarily a problem. Strong brands tend to be rich and complex, successfully combining many different character traits within their personality. The United States' brand equity is at least half negative, but this doesn't appear to spoil it in any way. For younger consumers in particular, the suggestion of risk is irresistible—remember, these are consumers who want to challenge and to be challenged.

Many "emerging" markets in the past have exported their products around the world in the form of unprocessed or partly processed commodities, but almost none have ever managed to produce a successful international brand. The real profit margins have been enjoyed by the companies in developed nations that have finished, packaged, branded, and retailed these goods to the end user.

Such an arrangement works well to keep Third World countries firmly in the Third World, and First World countries in the First. This problem is made only more serious by the fact that the emerging markets are, by and large, able to continue exporting in quantities large enough to sustain their fragile economies only by depleting their natural resources and allowing the exploitation of their workforce.

Brands, however, unlike commodities, are made of air, and are thus infinitely sustainable, so long as the investment in marketing is maintained, which makes them the ultimate ecological

export. In the long term, they can also contribute to a positive perception of the country, which in turn favors tourism and inward investment. Young Asian consumers, for example, might well be tempted to visit Brazil if that was where their favorite brands came from, just as Disney and Coke and Nike are part of the reason why they want to visit the United States now.

It's not just Brazil that could benefit from exporting brands rather than produce. Of course, few emerging countries have Brazil's natural advantages: a strong nation-brand, an increasingly vigorous economy, a government that actively encourages export, long experience in building successful domestic brands, and one of the world's most active and creative advertising industries. Even so, it doesn't take much imagination to see how certain other nations—perhaps Russia, China, India, and some African countries—could quickly develop the potential to become strong "nation brands."

Looking Beyond Brand USA

For much of this century, global brands have been the exclusive province of European and American producers. But much has changed during this time: Consumers in many parts of the world are becoming wealthier, better informed, and able to exercise more power over manufacturers than ever before. As the basic requirements of product quality and affordability are catered to and choice becomes the norm, consumers become, by degrees, more and more sensitive to brand values: how the product is presented, how it speaks to the consumer, how it addresses her needs.

As consumers begin to look for a more sophisticated combination of *import-style quality* and *domestic-style relevance* in their imported brands, we may well begin to see a consumer backlash against the insufficiently sensitive marketing techniques traditionally practiced by some foreign brand-owners. The simplicity and robustness of an approach like "buy this, it's American" won't work anymore. Sensitivity to culture could well become one of the defining characteristics of the new century's successful global brands. In the past, the brands that shouted loudest were the ones that grew fastest; in the 21st century, the ones that *listen first* could be the ones that last longest.

It may also turn out that Brazilian and other Third World brands have an innate advantage over American and European brands when it comes to making friends among consumers in the world's growth markets—the Far East, Eastern Europe, Latin America, Central Asia, and South Asia—because of their humbler provenance. Unlike the old European powers, these countries don't need to undo the damage done to their brand images by centuries of military and political colonization: They start with a clean slate, with basically benign commercial colonization. Brazil and other emerging nations enjoy the privilege of being "colleague countries," and may well find that their provenance is not merely an important characteristic of their brand personality but, rather, a fundamental preliminary to consumer acceptance.

For rich nations looking for innovative and effective ways to help developing countries become self-sufficient rather than aid-dependent, this approach is the perfect combination of capital investment and intellectual support: venture capital for building export businesses, and professional expertise for helping those businesses to build global brands.

Launching global brands requires flair, confidence, and courage as well as money (although, thanks to the way that the Internet has put global viral marketing within the reach of everybody with a brain and a computer, the level of investment in media need no longer be as colossal as it once was). It requires objectivity to an unusual degree—the ability to see yourself as others see you, and to accept that this is, at least in commercial terms, more important than the way you see yourself. It requires government support. It requires reduced trade barriers. It requires competent and internationally minded marketing people and a strong advertising resource.

It also requires a basic readiness on the part of the target consumer to believe that the country of origin possesses the necessary skills and resources to manufacture a "world-class" product. Many would claim that this factor is the biggest single obstacle standing in the way of poorer countries producing global brands. Interestingly, however, it's a barrier that appears to be diminishing, and this is partly through the experience of seeing countries like Japan and Korea develop, in an amazingly short time, from negative-equity nation brands to almost "compulsory-source" countries for certain products.

Wealth Redistribution Through Branding

But there's a more subtle reason for this change in attitudes, for which we must thank some of the world's biggest brands. For decades, companies such as Nike, IBM, Disney, Mattel, and Sony have been unwittingly promoting their supplier nations as sub-brands, simply by putting little stickers on their products saying "Made in Malaysia," "Made in Vietnam," "Made in Thailand," and so forth. This low-pressure trickle campaign has effectively communicated to hundreds of millions of consumers the simple fact that most of the world's best products are now manufactured in the Third World, thus neatly paving the way for manufacturers in those countries to start developing their own brands.

Simplistic, maybe, but undeniably attractive: Simply add the right branding expertise to a country living on sweatshop labor and break-even trading, and you have the beginning of a fast-growth manufacturing economy instead of a submerging service state.

There is much simple justice in this, and a simple formula is irresistible:

If a company in a rich country sells brands to rich consumers in the same or other rich countries, nothing really happens—money simply circulates within a more or less closed system, and there's little to criticize on moral grounds.

If a company in a rich country sells brands to poor consumers in the same or other rich countries, there is a risk of exploitation and a further widening of the wealth gap.

If a company in a rich country sells brands to consumers in a poor country, the risk of exploitation is far higher, partly because the cultural vulnerability of the consumers is greater: They haven't yet been "inoculated" against brands by repeated exposure to sophisticated marketing techniques.

But if a company in a poor country sells brands to consumers in a rich country, the overall balance begins to be redressed, and justice begins to be done.

Global brands as the ultimate distributor of wealth? It's an intriguing thought. After all, marketing did much to increase the unequal distribution of wealth during the last century, so why shouldn't marketing be used to reverse the trend—and balance things out a little better during the next?

SIMON ANHOLT is chairman and founder of World Writers, a London-based international brand strategy and advertising consultancy. He is author of *Another One Bites the Grass: Making Sense of International Advertising* (Wiley).

From *Across the Board*, November/December 2000, pp. 22-27. © 2000 by The Conference Board Inc. Reprinted with permission.

Industry/Company Guide

This guide was prepared to provide an easy index to the many industries and companies discussed in detail in the selections included in *Annual Editions: Marketing 02/03*. It should prove useful when researching specific interests.

INDUSTRIES

Industry/Company Guide

COMPANIES AND DIVISIONS

Glossary

This glossary of marketing terms is included to provide you with a convenient and ready reference as you encounter general terms in your study of marketing that are unfamiliar or require a review. It is not intended to be comprehensive, but taken together with the many definitions included in the articles themselves, it should prove to be quite useful.

acceptable price range
The range of prices that buyers are willing to pay for a product; prices that are above the range may be judged unfair, while prices below the range may generate concerns about quality.

adaptive selling
A salesperson's adjustment of his or her behavior between and during sales calls, to respond appropriately to issues that are important to the customer.

advertising
Marketing communication elements designed to stimulate sales through the use of mass media displays, direct individual appeals, public displays, give-aways, and the like.

advertorial
A special advertising section in magazines that includes some editorial (nonadvertising) content.

Americans with Disabilities Act (ADA)
Passed in 1990, this U.S. law prohibits discrimination against consumers with disabilities.

automatic number identification
A telephone system that identifies incoming phone numbers at the beginning of the call, without the caller's knowledge.

bait and switch
Advertising a product at an attractively low price to get customers into the store, but making the product unavailable so that the customers must trade up to a more expensive version.

bar coding
A computer-coded bar pattern that identifies a product. *See also* universal product code.

barter
The practice of exchanging goods and services without the use of money.

benefit segmentation
Organizing the market according to the attributes or benefits consumers need or desire, such as quality, service, or unique features.

brand
A name, term, sign, design, symbol, or combination used to differentiate the products of one company from those of its competition.

brand image
The quality and reliability of a product as perceived by consumers on the basis of its brand reputation or familiarity.

brand name
The element of a brand that can be vocalized.

break-even analysis
The calculation of the number of units that must be sold at a certain price to cover costs (break even); revenues earned past the break-even point contribute to profits.

bundling
Marketing two or more products in a single package at one price.

business analysis
The stage of new product development where initial marketing plans are prepared (including tentative marketing strategy and estimates of sales, costs, and profitability).

business strategic plan
A plan for how each business unit in a corporation intends to compete in the marketplace, based upon the vision, objectives, and growth strategies of the corporate strategic plan.

capital products
Expensive items that are used in business operations but do not become part of any finished product (such as office buildings, copy machines).

cash-and-carry wholesaler
A limited-function wholesaler that does not extend credit for or deliver the products it sells.

caveat emptor
A Latin term that means "let the buyer beware." A principle of law meaning that the purchase of a product is at the buyer's risk with regard to its quality, usefulness, and the like. The laws do, however, provide certain minimum protection against fraud and other schemes.

channel of distribution
See marketing channel.

Child Protection Act
U.S. law passed in 1990 to regulate advertising on children's TV programs.

Child Safety Act
Passed in 1966, this U.S. law prohibits the marketing of dangerous products to children.

Clayton Act
Anticompetitive activities are prohibited by this 1914 U.S. law.

co-branding
When two brand names appear on the same product (such as a credit card with a school's name).

comparative advertising
Advertising that compares one brand against a competitive brand on a least one product attribute.

competitive pricing strategies
Pricing strategies that are based on a organization's position in relation to its competition.

consignment
An arrangement in which a seller of goods does not take title to the goods until they are sold. The seller thus has the option of returning them to the supplier or principal if unable to execute the sale.

consolidated metropolitan statistical area (CMSA)
Based on census data, the largest designation of geographic areas. *See also* primary metropolitan statistical area.

consumer behavior
The way in which buyers, individually or collectively, react to marketplace stimuli.

Consumer Credit Protection Act
A 1968 U.S. law that requires full disclosure of the financial charges of loans.

consumer decision process
This four-step process includes recognizing a need or problem, searching for information, evaluating alternative products or brands, and purchasing a product.

Consumer Product Safety Commission (CPSC)
A U.S. government agency that protects consumers from unsafe products.

consumerism
A social movement in which consumers demand better information about the service, prices, dependability, and quality of the products they buy.

convenience products
Consumer goods that are purchased at frequent intervals with little regard for price. Such goods are relatively standard in nature and consumers tend to select the most convenient source when shopping for them.

cooperative advertising
Advertising of a product by a retailer, dealer, distributor, or the like, with part of the advertising cost paid by the product's manufacturer.

corporate strategic plan
A plan that addresses what a company is and wants to become, and then guides strategic planning at all organizational levels.

countersegmentation
A concept that combines market segments to appeal to a broad range of consumers, assuming that there will be an increasing consumer willingness to accept fewer product and service choices for lower prices.

customer loyalty concept
To focus beyond customer satisfaction toward customer retention as a way to generate sales and profit growth.

demand curve
A relationship that shows how many units a market will purchase at a given price in a given period of time.

demographic environment
The study of human population densities, distributions, and movements that relate to buying behavior.

derived demand
The demand for business-to-business products that is dependent upon a demand for other products in the market.

differentiated strategy
Using innovation and points of difference in product offerings, advanced technology, superior service, or higher quality in wide areas of market segments.

direct mail promotion
Marketing goods to consumers by mailing unsolicited promotional material to them.

direct marketing
The sale of products to carefully targeted consumers who interact with various advertising media without salesperson contact.

discount
A reduction from list price that is given to a buyer as a reward for a favorable activity to the seller.

discretionary income
The money that remains after taxes and necessities have been paid for.

disposable income
That portion of income that remains after payment of taxes to use for food, clothing, and shelter.

dual distribution
The selling of products to two or more competing distribution networks, or the selling of two brands of nearly identical products through competing distribution networks.

dumping
The act of selling a product in a foreign country at a price lower than its domestic price.

durable goods
Products that continue in service for an appreciable length of time.

economy
The income, expenditures, and resources that affect business and household costs.

electronic data interchange (EDI)
A computerized system that links two different firms to allow transmittal of documents; a quick-response inventory control system.

entry strategy
An approach used to begin marketing products internationally.

environmental scanning
Obtaining information on relevant factors and trends outside a company and interpreting their potential impact on the company's markets and marketing activities.

European Union (EU)
The world's largest consumer market, consisting of 16 European nations: Austria, Belgium, Britain, Denmark, Finland, France, Germany, Greece, Italy, Ireland, Luxembourg, the Netherlands, Norway, Portugal, Spain, and Sweden.

exclusive distribution
Marketing a product or service in only one retail outlet in a specific geographic marketplace.

exporting
Selling goods to international markets.

Fair Packaging and Labeling Act of 1966
This law requires manufacturers to state ingredients, volume, and manufacturer's name on a package.

family life cycle
The progress of a family through a number of distinct phases, each of which is associated with identifiable purchasing behaviors.

Federal Trade Commission (FTC)
The U.S. government agency that regulates business practices; established in 1914.

five C's of pricing
Five influences on pricing decisions: customers, costs, channels of distribution, competition, and compatibility.

FOB (free on board)
The point at which the seller stops paying transportation costs.

four I's of service
Four elements to services: intangibility, inconsistency, inseparability, and inventory.

four P's
See marketing mix.

franchise
The right to distribute a company's products or render services under its name, and to retain the resulting profit in exchange for a fee or percentage of sales.

freight absorption
Payment of transportation costs by the manufacturer or seller, often resulting in a uniform pricing structure.

functional groupings
Groupings in an organization in which a unit is subdivided according to different business activities, such as manufacturing, finance, and marketing.

General Agreement on Tariffs and Trade (GATT)
An international agreement that is intended to limit trade barriers and to promote world trade through reduced tariffs; represents over 80 percent of global trade.

geodemographics
A combination of geographic data and demographic characteristics; used to segment and target specific markets.

green marketing
The implementation of an ecological perspective in marketing; the promotion of a product as environmentally safe.

gross domestic product (GDP)
The total monetary value of all goods and services produced within a country during one year.

growth stage
The second stage of a product life cycle that is characterized by a rapid increase in sales and profits.

hierarchy of effects
The stages a prospective buyer goes through when purchasing a product, including awareness, interest, evaluation, trial, and adoption.

idea generation
An initial stage of the new product development process; requires creativity and innovation to generate ideas for potential new products.

implied warranties
Warranties that assign responsibility for a product's deficiencies to a manufacturer, even though the product was sold by a retailer.

imports
Purchased goods or services that are manufactured or produced in some other country.

integrated marketing communications
A strategic integration of marketing communications programs that coordinate all promotional activities—advertising, personal selling, sales promotion, and public relations.

internal reference prices
The comparison price standards that consumers remember and use to judge the fairness of prices.

introduction stage
The first product life cycle stage; when a new product is launched into the marketplace.

ISO 9000
International Standards Organization's standards for registration and certification of manufacturer's quality management and quality assurance systems.

joint venture
An arrangement in which two or more organizations market products internationally.

just-in-time (JIT) inventory control system
An inventory supply system that operates with very low inventories and fast, on-time delivery.

Lanham Trademark Act
A 1946 U.S. law that was passed to protect trademarks and brand names.

late majority
The fourth group to adopt a new product; representing about 34 percent of a market.

Glossary

lifestyle research
Research on a person's pattern of living, as displayed in activities, interests, and opinions.

limit pricing
This competitive pricing strategy involves setting prices low to discourage new competition.

limited-coverage warranty
The manufacturer's statement regarding the limits of coverage and noncoverage for any product deficiencies.

logistics management
The planning, implementing, and moving of raw materials and products from the point of origin to the point of consumption.

loss-leader pricing
The pricing of a product below its customary price in order to attract attention to it.

Magnuson-Moss Act
Passed in 1975, this U.S. law regulates warranties.

management by exception
Used by a marketing manager to identify results that deviate from plans, diagnose their cause, make appropriate new plans, and implement new actions.

manufacturers' agent
A merchant wholesaler that sells related but noncompeting product lines for a number of manufacturers; also called manufacturers' representatives.

market
The potential buyers for a company's product or service; or to sell a product or service to actual buyers. The place where goods and services are exchanged.

market penetration strategy
The goal of achieving corporate growth objectives with existing products within existing markets by persuading current customers to purchase more of the product or by capturing new customers.

marketing channel
Organizations and people that are involved in the process of making a product or service available for use by consumers or industrial users.

marketing communications planning
A seven-step process that includes marketing plan review; situation analysis; communications process analysis; budget development; program development integration and implementation of a plan; and monitoring, evaluating, and controlling the marketing communications program.

marketing concept
The idea that a company should seek to satisfy the needs of consumers while also trying to achieve the organization's goals.

marketing mix
The elements of marketing: product, brand, package, price, channels of distribution, advertising and promotion, personal selling, and the like.

marketing research
The process of identifying a marketing problem and opportunity, collecting and analyzing information systematically, and recommending actions to improve an organization's marketing activities.

marketing research process
A six-step sequence that includes problem definition, determination of research design, determination of data collection methods, development of data collection forms, sample design, and analysis and interpretation.

mission statement
A part of the strategic planning process that expresses the company's basic values and specifies the operation boundaries within marketing, business units, and other areas.

motivation research
A group of techniques developed by behavioral scientists that are used by marketing researchers to discover factors influencing marketing behavior.

nonprice competition
Competition between brands based on factors other than price, such as quality, service, or product features.

nondurable goods
Products that do not last or continue in service for any appreciable length of time.

North American Free Trade Agreement (NAFTA)
A trade agreement among the United States, Canada, and Mexico that essentially removes the vast majority of trade barriers between the countries.

North American Industry Classification System (NAICS)
A system used to classify organizations on the basis of major activity or the major good or service provided by the three NAFTA countries—Canada, Mexico, and the United States; replaced the Standard Industrial Classification (SIC) system in 1997.

observational data
Market research data obtained by watching, either mechanically or in person, how people actually behave.

odd-even pricing
Setting prices at just below an even number, such as $1.99 instead of $2.

opinion leaders
Individuals who influence consumer behavior based on their interest in or expertise with particular products.

organizational goals
The specific objectives used by a business or nonprofit unit to achieve and measure its performance.

outbound telemarketing
Using the telephone rather than personal visits to contact customers.

outsourcing
A company's decision to purchase products and services from other firms rather than using in-house employees.

parallel development
In new product development, an approach that involves the development of the product and production process simultaneously.

penetration pricing
Pricing a product low to discourage competition.

personal selling process
The six stages of sales activities that occur before and after the sale itself: prospecting, preapproach, approach, presentation, close, and follow-up.

point-of-purchase display
A sales promotion display located in high-traffic areas in retail stores.

posttesting
Tests that are conducted to determine if an advertisement has accomplished its intended purpose.

predatory pricing
The practice of selling products at low prices to drive competition from the market and then raising prices once a monopoly has been established.

prestige pricing
Maintaining high prices to create an image of product quality and appeal to buyers who associate premium prices with high quality.

pretesting
Evaluating consumer reactions to proposed advertisements through the use of focus groups and direct questions.

price elasticity of demand
An economic concept that attempts to measure the sensitivity of demand for any product to changes in its price.

price fixing
The illegal attempt by one or several companies to maintain the prices of their products above those that would result from open competition.

price promotion mix
The basic product price plus additional components such as sales prices, temporary discounts, coupons, favorable payment and credit terms.

price skimming
Setting prices high initially to appeal to consumers who are not price-sensitive and then lowering prices to appeal to the next market segments.

primary metropolitan statistical area (PMSA)
Major urban area, often located within a CMSA, that has at least one million inhabitants.

PRIZM
A potential rating index by ZIP code markets that divides every U.S. neighborhood into one of 40 distinct cluster types that reveal consumer data.

product
An idea, good, service, or any combination that is an element of exchange to satisfy a consumer.

product differentiation
The ability or tendency of manufacturers, marketers, or consumers to distinguish between seemingly similar products.

product expansion strategy
A plan to market new products to the same customer base.

product life cycle (PLC)
A product's advancement through the introduction, growth, maturity, and decline stages.

product line pricing
Setting the prices for all product line items.

product marketing plans
Business units' plans to focus on specific target markets and marketing mixes for each product, which include both strategic and execution decisions.

product mix
The composite of products offered for sale by a firm or a business unit.

promotional mix
Combining one or more of the promotional elements that a firm uses to communicate with consumers.

proprietary secondary data
The data that is provided by commercial marketing research firms to other firms.

psychographic research
Measurable characteristics of given market segments in respect to life-styles, interests, opinions, needs, values, attitudes, personality traits, and the like.

publicity
Nonpersonal presentation of a product, service, or business unit.

pull strategy
A marketing strategy whose main thrust is to strongly influence the final consumer, so that the demand for a product "pulls" it through the various channels of distribution.

push strategy
A marketing strategy whose main thrust is to provide sufficient economic incentives to members of the channels of distribution, so as to "push" the product through to the consumer.

qualitative data
The responses obtained from in-depth interviews, focus groups, and observation studies.

quality function deployment (QFD)
The data collected from structured response formats that can be easily analyzed and projected to larger populations.

quotas
In international marketing, they are restrictions placed on the amount of a product that is allowed to leave or enter a country; the total outcomes used to assess sales representatives' performance and effectiveness.

regional marketing
A form of geographical division that develops marketing plans that reflect differences in taste preferences, perceived needs, or interests in other areas.

relationship marketing
The development, maintenance, and enhancement of long-term, profitable customer relationships.

repositioning
The development of new marketing programs that will shift consumer beliefs and opinions about an existing brand.

resale price maintenance
Control by a supplier of the selling prices of his branded goods at subsequent stages of distribution, by means of contractual agreement under fair trade laws or other devices.

reservation price
The highest price a consumer will pay for a product; a form of internal reference price.

restraint of trade
In general, activities that interfere with competitive marketing. Restraint of trade usually refers to illegal activities.

retail strategy mix
Controllable variables that include location, products and services, pricing, and marketing communications.

return on investment (ROI)
A ratio of income before taxes to total operating assets associated with a product, such as inventory, plant, and equipment.

sales effectiveness evaluations
A test of advertising efficiency to determine if it resulted in increased sales.

sales forecast
An estimate of sales under controllable and uncontrollable conditions.

sales management
The planning, direction, and control of the personal selling activities of a business unit.

sales promotion
An element of the marketing communications mix that provides incentives or extra value to stimulate product interest.

samples
A small size of a product given to prospective purchasers to demonstrate a product's value or use and to encourage future purchase; some elements that are taken from the population or universe.

scanner data
Proprietary data that is derived from UPC bar codes.

scrambled merchandising
Offering several unrelated product lines within a single retail store.

selected controlled markets
Sites where market tests for a new product are conducted by an outside agency and retailers are paid to display that product; also referred to as forced distribution markets.

selective distribution
This involves selling a product in only some of the available outlets; commonly used when after-the-sale service is necessary, such as in the case of home appliances.

seller's market
A condition within any market in which the demand for an item is greater than its supply.

selling philosophy
An emphasis on an organization's selling function to the exclusion of other marketing activities.

selling strategy
A salesperson's overall plan of action, which is developed at three levels: sales territory, customer, and individual sales calls.

services
Nonphysical products that a company provides to consumers in exchange for money or something else of value.

share points
Percentage points of market share; often used as the common comparison basis to allocate marketing resources effectively.

Sherman Anti-Trust Act
Passed in 1890, this U.S. law prohibits contracts, combinations, or conspiracies in restraint of trade and actual monopolies or attempts to monopolize any part of trade or commerce.

shopping products
Consumer goods that are purchased only after comparisons are made concerning price, quality, style, suitability, and the like.

single-channel strategy
Marketing strategy using only one means to reach customers; providing one sales source for a product.

single-zone pricing
A pricing policy in which all buyers pay the same delivered product price, regardless of location; also known as uniform delivered pricing or postage stamp pricing.

slotting fees
High fees manufacturers pay to place a new product on a retailer's or wholesaler's shelf.

social responsibility
Reducing social costs, such as environmental damage, and increasing the positive impact of a marketing decision on society.

societal marketing concept
The use of marketing strategies to increase the acceptability of an idea (smoking causes cancer); cause (environmental protection); or practice (birth control) within a target market.

specialty products
Consumer goods, usually appealing only to a limited market, for which consumers will make a special purchasing effort. Such items include, for example, stereo components, fancy foods, and prestige brand clothes.

Standard Industrial Classification (SIC) system
Replaced by NAICS, this federal government numerical scheme categorized businesses.

standardized marketing
Enforcing similar product, price, distribution, and communications programs in all international markets.

stimulus-response presentation
A selling format that assumes that a customer will buy if given the appropriate stimulus by a salesperson.

strategic business unit (SBU)
A decentralized profit center of a company that operates as a separate, independent business.

Glossary

strategic marketing process
Marketing activities in which a firm allocates its marketing mix resources to reach a target market.

strategy mix
A way for retailers to differentiate themselves from others through location, product, services, pricing, and marketing mixes.

subliminal perception
When a person hears or sees messages without being aware of them.

SWOT analysis
An acronym that describes a firm's appraisal of its internal strengths and weaknesses and its external opportunities and threats.

synergy
An increased customer value that is achieved through more efficient organizational function performances.

systems-designer strategy
A selling strategy that allows knowledgeable sales reps to determine solutions to a customer's problems or to anticipate opportunities to enhance a customer's business through new or modified business systems.

target market
A defined group of consumers or organizations toward which a firm directs its marketing program.

team selling
A sales strategy that assigns accounts to specialized sales teams according to a customers' purchase-information needs.

telemarketing
An interactive direct marketing approach that uses the telephone to develop relationships with customers.

test marketing
The process of testing a prototype of a new product to gain consumer reaction and to examine its commercial viability and marketing strategy.

TIGER (Topologically Integrated Geographic Encoding and Reference)
A minutely detailed U.S. Census Bureau computerized map of the U.S. that can be combined with a company's own database to analyze customer sales.

total quality management (TQM)
Programs that emphasize long-term relationships with selected suppliers instead of short-term transactions with many suppliers.

total revenue
The total of sales, or unit price, multiplied by the quantity of the product sold.

trade allowance
An amount a manufacturer contributes to a local dealer's or retailer's advertising expenses.

trade (functional) discounts
Price reductions that are granted to wholesalers or retailers that are based on future marketing functions that they will perform for a manufacturer.

trademark
The legal identification of a company's exclusive rights to use a brand name or trade name.

truck jobber
A small merchant wholesaler who delivers limited assortments of fast-moving or perishable items within a small geographic area.

two-way stretch strategy
Adding products at both the low and high end of a product line.

undifferentiated strategy
Using a single promotional mix to market a single product for the entire market; frequently used early in the life of a product.

uniform delivered price
The same average freight amount that is charged to all customers, no matter where they are located.

universal product code (UPC)
An assigned number to identify a product, which is represented by a series of bars of varying widths for optical scanning.

usage rate
The quantity consumed or patronage during a specific period, which can vary significantly among different customer groups.

utilitarian influence
To comply with the expectations of others to achieve rewards or avoid punishments.

value added
In retail strategy decisions, a dimension of the retail positioning matrix that refers to the service level and method of operation of the retailer.

vertical marketing systems
Centrally coordinated and professionally managed marketing channels that are designed to achieve channel economies and maximum marketing impact.

vertical price fixing
Requiring that sellers not sell products below a minimum retail price; sometimes called resale price maintenance.

weighted-point system
The method of establishing screening criteria, assigning them weights, and using them to evaluate new product lines.

wholesaler
One who makes quantity purchases from manufacturers (or other wholesalers) and sells in smaller quantities to retailers (or other wholesalers).

zone pricing
A form of geographical pricing whereby a seller divides its market into broad geographic zones and then sets a uniform delivered price for each zone.

Sources for the Glossary
Marketing: Principles and Perspectives by William O. Bearden, Thomas N. Ingram, and Raymond W. LaForge (Irwin/McGraw-Hill, 1998);
Marketing by Eric N. Berkowitz (Irwin/McGraw-Hill, 1997); and the *Annual Editions* **staff.**

Index

Index

Test Your Knowledge Form

We encourage you to photocopy and use this page as a tool to assess how the articles in *Annual Editions* expand on the information in your textbook. By reflecting on the articles you will gain enhanced text information. You can also access this useful form on a product's book support Web site at *http://www.dushkin.com/online/*.

NAME: _____   DATE: _____

TITLE AND NUMBER OF ARTICLE: _____

BRIEFLY STATE THE MAIN IDEA OF THIS ARTICLE: _____

_____

LIST THREE IMPORTANT FACTS THAT THE AUTHOR USES TO SUPPORT THE MAIN IDEA:

_____

WHAT INFORMATION OR IDEAS DISCUSSED IN THIS ARTICLE ARE ALSO DISCUSSED IN YOUR TEXTBOOK OR OTHER READINGS THAT YOU HAVE DONE? LIST THE TEXTBOOK CHAPTERS AND PAGE NUMBERS:

_____

LIST ANY EXAMPLES OF BIAS OR FAULTY REASONING THAT YOU FOUND IN THE ARTICLE:

_____

LIST ANY NEW TERMS/CONCEPTS THAT WERE DISCUSSED IN THE ARTICLE, AND WRITE A SHORT DEFINITION:

We Want Your Advice

ANNUAL EDITIONS revisions depend on two major opinion sources: one is our Advisory Board, listed in the front of this volume, which works with us in scanning the thousands of articles published in the public press each year; the other is you—the person actually using the book. Please help us and the users of the next edition by completing the prepaid article rating form on this page and returning it to us. Thank you for your help!

ANNUAL EDITIONS: Marketing 03/04

ARTICLE RATING FORM

Here is an opportunity for you to have direct input into the next revision of this volume.
We would like you to rate each of the articles listed below, using the following scale:

1. **Excellent: should definitely be retained**
2. **Above average: should probably be retained**
3. **Below average: should probably be deleted**
4. **Poor: should definitely be deleted**

Your ratings will play a vital part in the next revision.
Please mail this prepaid form to us as soon as possible.
Thanks for your help!

RATING	ARTICLE	RATING	ARTICLE
	1. Future Markets		36. International Marketing Research: A Management Briefing
	2. High Performance Marketing		37. Extending the Reach of E-Business
	3. Marketing High Technology: Preparation, Targeting, Positioning, Execution		38. Continental Spendthrifts: Influential Euroteen Demo Has U.S. Marketers' Attention
	4. The Internet as Integrator: Fast Brand Building in Slow-Growth Markets		39. The Lure of Global Branding
	5. Marketing Myopia (With Retrospective Commentary)		40. The Nation as Brand
	6. Why Customer Satisfaction Starts With HR		
	7. Stairs of Loyalty		
	8. What Drives Customer Equity		
	9. A Primer on Quality Service: Quality Service Makes Happy Customers and Greater Profits		
	10. Why Service Stinks		
	11. Lighting the Way		
	12. Trust in the Marketplace		
	13. To Tell the Truth		
	14. Marketing Research		
	15. Product by Design		
	16. A Beginner's Guide to Demographics		
	17. Getting Inside Gen Y		
	18. The Multicultural Report		
	19. Asian-American Consumers as a Unique Market Segment: Fact or Fallacy?		
	20. Attention, Shoppers!		
	21. The Lure of Shopping		
	22. Defining Moments: Segmenting by Cohorts		
	23. The Very Model of a Modern Marketing Plan		
	24. Got Emotional Product Positioning?		
	25. Get to Market Faster		
	26. The Best Global Brands		
	27. Kamikaze Pricing		
	28. Pricing Practices That Endanger Profits		
	29. The Old Pillars of New Retailing		
	30. Designing a Trust-Based e-Business Strategy		
	31. 10 Top Stores Put to the Test		
	32. Choices, Choices		
	33. Tips for Distinguishing Your Ads From Bad Ads		
	34. 2001: Year of the Hard Sell		
	35. Segmenting Global Markets: Look Before You Leap		

(Continued on next page)

||||

BUSINESS REPLY MAIL
FIRST-CLASS MAIL PERMIT NO. 84 GUILFORD CT

POSTAGE WILL BE PAID BY ADDRESSEE

McGraw-Hill/Dushkin
530 Old Whitfield Street
Guilford, Ct 06437-9989

|||..||..|.|..|.||.|..||.|.|.|.|..|.||.|..|.|.|

- -

ABOUT YOU

Name _____ Date _____

Are you a teacher? ❏   A student? ❏
Your school's name _____

Department _____

Address _____ City _____ State ___ Zip ___

School telephone # _____

YOUR COMMENTS ARE IMPORTANT TO US!

Please fill in the following information:
For which course did you use this book?
_____

Did you use a text with this ANNUAL EDITION? ❏ yes ❏ no
What was the title of the text?
_____

What are your general reactions to the *Annual Editions* concept?
_____

Have you read any pertinent articles recently that you think should be included in the next edition? Explain.
_____

Are there any articles that you feel should be replaced in the next edition? Why?
_____

Are there any World Wide Web sites that you feel should be included in the next edition? Please annotate.
_____

May we contact you for editorial input? ❏ yes ❏ no
May we quote your comments? ❏ yes ❏ no